A Chorus of Praise for

Shining Brightly

Shining Brightly is a story of resilience and hope as we reach out through our families, our communities and around the world to form truly supportive friendships. That's why such a vast chorus of friends surrounds this book. From Howard's career as a Silicon Valley entrepreneur, to his conquering advanced cancer twice, to his compassionate outreach as a peacemaker, to his love of sports—this ultimately is not one man's story. *Shining Brightly* is a story shared by countless men and women—and may wind up changing your life as well. That's why this book opens with these dozens of impactful words of advanced praise, grouped into the major realms of Howard's life. Please immerse yourself in the next few pages in Howard's worldwide community— and picture for just a moment how you might join them in shining your light in our world.

Colleagues in Entrepreneurship

"The golden light of hope that Howard weaves throughout his stories of triumph and tragedy is a contagious gift, calling all of us to share our own gifts of hope!"

Jenny Mulks, Founder of Circle of Hope Cancer Support

"It is impossible to meet Howard Brown and not become a better version of yourself. His life story of resilience embodies the heart of a warrior, the soul of a dove and the wisdom of Solomon. He encourages us always to look for the calming warm light of a rising sun, so we are ready to face life anew with a welcoming smile and generous spirit."

Jon Rappaport, CEO, CYRIAS Technologies

"This is the story of a man who, in confronting death so boldly, now points others toward introspection and personal growth. This book is a must-read for those who seek wisdom, clarity and hope for the future."

Kayla Bradham, Sports Philanthropy Network and podcast *Legacy after the Locker Room*

"Howard Brown knows how to own a room! Whether one-on-one, or in front of a large gathering, Howard's approach to life is infectious. He's a captivating storyteller and audiences find his openness, compassion and selflessness truly inspirational."

Michael Weissman, CEO SYNQY Corporation

"Howard Brown is a great example of entrepreneurship at its best: extraordinary drive, out-of-the-box thinking and the ability to overcome challenges."

Leonard Green, author of *The Entrepreneur's Playbook*

"I grew up with Howie Brown and our life-long friendship is a true bond of brotherhood. *Shining Brightly* shows us the true meaning of integrity, loyalty and determination."

John Robert Hoyt, retired Commander U. S. Navy Seals

"Those of us who grew up with Howie have experienced his incredible journey through life's struggles to inspiring successes. This story teaches all of us who occasionally get knocked down how to get back up again with the help of our friends."

Robert Dlott, insurance agency executive

"People like Howard are rare in this world—a true champion with a heart of gold. Howard's journey illustrates ways in which all of us can live our best lives in service to a greater good."

Brent Cohen, co-founder of PlanItJewish and CircleBuilder

"*Shining Brightly* is a perfect title to encapsulate the way Howard Brown has lived his life. Following his story, we come to appreciate the values of caring and warmth that are embedded in every aspect of his life: family, faith, sports and business."

Roy Kessel, founder of Sports Philanthropy Network

"Howard Brown takes readers on a courageous and inspirational journey of a two-time cancer survivor who shares his experiences of selflessly providing a bright light of hope, unity and encouragement. As we turn the pages with Howard, we develop our own self-awareness and purpose."

Gregory Tufankjian, owner of Toyota of Braintree and Babson alum

"'When we shine brightly, we give others many forms of hope.' That's Howard's affirmation in this book. As someone who has known him for a dozen plus years, I can tell you he lives that day to day and this book is a guide to help you live that way too."

Terry Bean, business coach and author of *Be Connected*

"No matter what life throws at him, Howard Brown keeps getting up! His mission is to bring inspiration, meaning, and hope to those facing similar challenges, as well as to anyone who needs a lift."

Debra Eckerling, author of *Your Goal Guide*

"Howard Brown inspires us to reconsider our life purpose, even if we find ourselves facing challenges, loss or failure. We learn from Howard that we are not alone in experiencing dark moments. Yet, it is how we respond and maintain a sense of purpose and humanity that will bring us to a more meaningful and fulfilling place. Ultimately, *Shining Brightly* gives all of us hope."

Brett Rappaport, professor, entrepreneur and policy expert

"Howard's story is powerful and tenacious. As someone who's also overcome multiple challenges, I feel his strength and resilience through every word in *Shining Brightly*."

Tylar Paige, author, *F*ck You Watch This*

"In *Shining Brightly*, you'll come to admire Howard's courage, drive and fighting spirit—then, you'll want to carry that spirit forward."

Bob and Ginger Penfil, People and Products LLC

"*Shining Brightly* is a profound opportunity to learn about Howard's philosophy and experience as he illuminates the twists and turns of his life story. May it spark many readers to kindle their passion to live closer to their highest hopes, deepest dreams and best self."

Scott Vineberg, president SDV Financial

"Husband, father, son, brother, friend, entrepreneur, community leader, hero and survivor are some of the words people have used to describe Howard Brown. I have known him both as a co-worker and dear friend. For more than a quarter of a century, our fantasy football league has become an extension of our families and, now, *Shining Brightly* invites everyone to come along with us on this heartwarming and uplifting journey."

Henry G. Medina, Quantum Fantasy Football League

"*Shining Brightly* is a call to action for all of us to make a difference where we can. Howard shows us how hope can help ordinary people unlock extraordinary potential in themselves and in others."

Luis Fernando Parra, Quantum Fantasy Football League

"Howard's strength and resilience are a constant reminder to me about how precious life is, and that close friends and family are essential to our happiness. Howard, you are an inspiration to many!"

Lee Paries, Quantum Fantasy Football League

"In *Shining Brightly*, Howard Brown takes readers on an up-close-and-personal look into his incredible life. Be prepared to be inspired!"

Bob Powell, automotive marketing

"Howard Brown is a true leader in business, the community and the basketball court. For over 30 years the core of our friendship has been based on mentorship. Each Friday without fail, we text "Good Shabbos" to each other. *Shining Brightly* is the best path forward in our world today!"

Bradley Gibbons, real estate executive

"Howard Brown's inspiring attitude, fearless courage and defiant resilience make *Shining Brightly* a triumphant experience for readers."

Larry Nusbaum, CEO/COO Globein

"*Shining Brightly* is a roadmap to dreaming big and dealing with life's difficulties head on! This memoir is an inspirational guide to anyone dealing with hardships in their lives."

David Infante, 3 Gorilla Films

"*Shining Brightly* is a page turner of valuable life lessons about family, friendships, business, community, health and hope."

Cristian Valencia, CEO Dide Chemicals

"No matter what challenges lay ahead, we can always maintain an inspiring attitude and a benevolent spirit. In his memoir, Howard encourages all of us to live that way. His passion and vision speak to that ever-positive entrepreneurial genius in him. Personally, my favorite story in the book is about Bubby Bertha, whose spirit and endurance will stay with me forever and I hope will inspire every reader to make an impact on the community they live in and the world at large."

Uma Sharma, founder and CSO–MMS Holdings Inc.

"This is such an extraordinary story about resilience, giving back and uncovering one's true-life purpose! *Shining Brightly* provides a real-life opportunity to see the positive impact of having someone to accompany us and guide us in our journeys, even in the bleakest moments of our lives. Golda Meir said it best: 'Make the most of yourself by fanning the tiny, inner sparks of possibility into the flames of achievement.'"
Stephen Shaya, Managing Director of Akkad Holdings

Interfaith Peacemaking

"Together we can shape history.' That's a core belief that animates longtime interfaith bridge-builder par excellence, Howard Brown. The global challenges are so profound that we need all hands-on deck. *Shining Brightly*, shows how one person, despite facing life-threatening challenges, can help to heal our troubled world by reaching out to other communities at home and abroad. That makes this book such timely and valuable reading."
David Harris, CEO of the American Jewish Committee

"At this very dark time in a world filled with hate and uncertainty, Howard Brown's book can fan the fire of love within hearts to see the possibility of creating relational equity and crossing divides that many think are impossible to cross. May everyone who reads this book be inspired to reach out across a divide, make a new friend and shine their bright light in the world."
Brenda Rosenberg, author of *Reuniting the Children of Abraham*

"As a Muslim neighbor, I know Howard as a dedicated interfaith partner, uniting communities, seeking common ground, building relationships—a talent most needed in our divided world."
Victor Begg, author of *Our Muslim Neighbors*

"While *Shining Brightly* reflects Howard's Jewish identity, heritage and values, I was struck by how it also sounds so very Islamic in the ideals that we as cousins and children of Abraham hold so dear and in common."
Saeed A. Khan, Near East & Asian Studies and Global Studies, Wayne State University

"Howard Brown embodies all our hopes for the world: life above death, health above illness, stick-to-itiveness above giving up, triumph above failure. Read this book to understand how to face adversity straight on, to rediscover your dreams and visions for who you are as an individual and how important *you* are to our world."

Rabbi Asher Lopatin, Executive Director, JCRC/AJC Detroit

"Howard Brown is one of the most passionate and committed people I know. He lives and carries out his mission to unite all people and communities. In *Shining Brightly*, you will be inspired by how Howard has overcome sickness and struggle to become a symbol of peace and promise for so many."

The Rev. Stancy F. Adams, Chair, Interfaith Leadership Council of Metropolitan Detroit

"Howard Brown proves to us, by example, that each one of us is here to serve a purpose, and that we are more than capable of changing the world for the better. Sharing his story with great humility, Howard teaches us that—in a world that can be dark and lonely at times—we must always choose kindness."

Aisha M. Farooqi, attorney at law

"*Shining Brightly* is a reflection of a man of steel, a family man, a partner, an entrepreneur, an author, a peacemaker, a communicator, a bridge builder, a survivor and—above all—an international personality. Howard is an inspiration to me and to others in the faith-based community."

Sam Yono, Chaldean Federation International

"*Shining Brightly* is Howard's testament to the transformative power of mentorship. In 1993, he became a Big at Jewish Big Brothers Big Sisters of Los Angeles (JBBBSLA) to Ian and truly made a difference in his life. The staff at JBBBSLA are proud to have matched these two incredible people and to have supported their growth—and are so happy to learn in this book that the scholarship provided by JBBBSLA helped Ian afford college and pursue his dreams. Howard exemplifies the efforts our mentors make to transform the lives of youth, and how in some special cases they go above and beyond and become family for life."

Cari Uslan, CEO of Jewish Big Brothers Big Sisters of Los Angeles

"Whether getting pragmatic business advice, finding someone who can productively facilitate difficult community conversations—or gaining inspiration from his extraordinary resiliency—Howard Brown has been one of my 'go to' guys for two decades. I was blessed to learn important lessons in both business and life directly from Howard. Now, through *Shining Brightly*, everyone has the opportunity to learn these lessons from a truly remarkable guy."
Scott Kaufman, past CEO of the Jewish Community Federation of Metropolitan Detroit

"*Shining Brightly* is beautifully conceived and written in Howard Brown's unique voice. My longtime interfaith-activist partner's story will assuredly touch many lives and, I suspect, save more than a few. Howard is a blessing."
Bryant M. Frank, Co-Chair Muslim Jewish Advisory Council Detroit

"This warm, thoughtful and honest book is wonderfully inspiring. It illustrates how to take adversity, turn it around and create deep, meaningful and authentic friendships. Howard has become an important and salient mentor to me. As his co-chair of the Diplomatic Committee of the JCRC/AJC, he has taught me the importance of partnerships, relationships and reaching out to build bridges to peace."
Carol Ogusky, Diplomatic Committee and Board of Directors, JCRC-AJC Detroit

"Howard's philosophy of embracing life is so thoroughly embodied in this book that the 18th and final chapter is all about sharing hope. In Judaism, the number 18 is a symbol of *Chai* or life. As you finish this story, may you join us in proclaiming: *L'chaim! To life!*"
Jerry Naftaly, former Mayor of Oak Park, Michigan, author of *Images of America: Oak Park* and *Northland Mall* and *The Hill that Grew*

Resiliency and Cancer

"As a mentor in our American Association for Cancer Research Scientist-Survivor Program, Howard motivates everyone to build mutually beneficial relationships that educate, inspire and ultimately heal. When faced with two diagnoses of advanced cancer, he turned to his life experience and love for basketball to 'know cancer,' build a strong team and play to win. Defeating these formidable cancers shaped Howard into the incredible student, teacher, entrepreneur, survivor and advocate that he is today. *Shining Brightly* offers a compelling landscape of possibilities for cancer patients, survivors and indeed anyone who wants to become their best self!"

Anna D. Barker, Chief Strategy Officer Ellison Institute for Transformative Medicine of USC, Distinguished Visiting Fellow, Arizona State University, Co-Founder, AACR Scientist-Survivor Program

"Sharing stories of survival, no matter how long that time may last, is vital to the continuing conversation of quality of life and cancer care. Every journey offers a unique perspective and Howard Brown's memoir *Shining Brightly* is no exception. His journey emphatically highlights what can happen when you embark on saving yourself and end up shining a light for so many others."

Suzanne Stone, Chief Strategic Solutions & Programs Officer at Livestrong

"Howard Brown inspires us to embrace the life-sustaining power of community in *Shining Brightly*. Through their stories, we meet the people who shaped and even saved Howard's life through two fierce battles with cancer. Along the way, we're reminded of what's good in the world and the precious, delicate nature of life— wisdom Howard embraces every day as a passionate ally in our mission to end colorectal cancer."

Michael Sapienza, CEO, Colorectal Cancer Alliance

"*Shining Brightly* is a reflection of the positivity that Howard Brown lives every day. His ability to form lasting relationships is forged from his rich culture as well as his reflection on life as he has faced death. In the colorectal cancer world, Howard has become a source of strength and humor when cancer patients need it most. *Shining Brightly* is a fantastic resource for anyone facing the worst of times to be able to find that shining light."

Chris Evans, President of Colon Cancer Coalition

"My dear friend and fellow stage IV colorectal cancer patient, survivor and advocate Howard Brown is one bad ass that cancer does not want to mess with. In *Shining Brightly*, he eloquently and appropriately writes about the unbreakable bond created from cancer whispering and mentoring between cancer patients and the gratitude for our superhero care partners and families. *#KFG HBstrong and get busy living!*"

Trevor Maxwell, founder of Man Up to Cancer

"Howard Brown's against-all-odds story not only inspires but challenges us to live a more meaningful life defined by hope as a 'currency' we can each give and receive freely. Mixing humor and humility with an indomitable spirit, Howard finds the threads of hope that connect us all."

Susan Wysoki, Interim Executive Director PALTOWN Development Foundation and Colontown.org and author of *Winks from Heaven*

"Love, grit, family, friends, the right docs at the right time and the value of *never* giving up—that's what you'll find in this guidebook to facing cancer and thinking about how your own 'village' just might help to save your life. *Shining Brightly* offers hope for others facing long odds and dark days."

Nancy Seybold, COO, PALTOWN Development Foundation and Colontown.org

"I've had the pleasure of working alongside Howard on colorectal cancer patient advocacy. His empathy coupled with the will to fight for his life and others is beyond inspiring. Every patient, caregiver and advocate should read his story."

Trevor Barlow, Chair of the Board of Directors, PALTOWN Development Foundation and Colontown.org

"Wow, this book blows me away! Howard demonstrates how the power of friendships and family support can help ease the hardships in a person's life, particularly when that person has been diagnosed with a life-threatening condition, not once, but twice. Howard, through his resiliency, determination and positivity epitomizes how it is possible to still shine brightly when it feels like all hope is lost."

Dave Herman, vice president of Cybersecurity Sales

Finding Your Happy Place (Basketball)

"In *Shining Brightly*, Howard Brown shares a little secret he has learned over the past two decades on the basketball court: Men from different cultures play basketball as a means of exercise, competition, trash talk and brotherhood. He calls basketball his happy place and it is mine too!"
Danny Kallabat, attorney at law and real estate developer

"After meeting and playing basketball with Howard Brown for over 17 years, we have bonded like brothers. Basketball is our passion, happy place and a team sport. In *Shining Brightly*, readers will discover that battling cancer, raising a family and serving the community is a team sport too."
Bryant Kallabat, storage management solutions

"On the basketball court, Howard Brown is a crafty point guard with great court vision and deep knowledge of the finer points of the game. Once diagnosed with stage IV colorectal cancer, he kept playing hoops while dealing with chemotherapy treatments, multiple surgeries and God-awful side effects galore. He maintained a warrior spirit and provided inspiration to us all. We are in awe of his inner strength, mental toughness and sheer will to stay positive in the face of death. I highly recommend this memoir as a playbook for living a life of hope and determination."
Alan Bakst, medical device sales director

"Howard embodies two of the most important pillars in my life: loyal friendship and basketball. Howard's story is the stuff movies are made of— inspirational and uplifting as he faces and overcomes great challenges."
Daniel H. Serlin, attorney at law

"Even though basketball is how we bonded, and his mantra of 'keep your head up' is a common phrase in the game we love, HB embodies that every day. He has kept his head up in situations most wouldn't. It is that enduring spirit and positivity that has taught me that keeping your head up goes far beyond any basketball court."
Dan Butler, founder and president, Rapid Metals

Babson College Leadership

Shining Brightly

Howard Brown

To learn more about this book and Howard Brown, and to get a free discussion guide for this book, please visit:

ShiningBrightly.com

Cover design and illustration by Rick Nease
www.RickNeaseArt.com

Published by Read the Spirit, an imprint of
Front Edge Publishing
42807 Ford Road, No. 234
Canton, MI, 48187

Front Edge Publishing books are available for discount bulk purchases for events, corporate use and small groups. Special editions, including books with corporate logos, personalized covers and customized interiors are available for purchase. For more information, contact Front Edge Publishing at info@FrontEdgePublishing.com.

To Lisa, my *bashert*, and Emily, our miracle girl—

Our family is a powerful circle of love.

Together we shine!

Contents

Foreword

By Dr. Robert J. Wicks

From the opening story in *Shining Brightly* there are teachings that are both simple and difficult. Filled with tradition and insight, Howard Brown shares stories not only about the persons he describes but, upon reflection, about ourselves and our stories of life. He speaks about the koans (puzzles that have no right or wrong answers) all of us face, the dangers we must confront, and the ultimate decisions we must make each day—sometimes without knowing it!

The lessons in this book stand out even more because the author is not a mental health professional, professor or in ministry. Instead, he is an "educator of life" in the wisdom tradition of mentorship. To accomplish his goals, he communicates through the lives of people that might have lived next door to us as a volunteer fireman, truck driver or as exotic as a war correspondent. In his vivid and colorful description of them, Brown regales us with stories that make us reflect on the relationships in our own lives and even the ongoing developing relationship we have with ourselves.

In this book, we learn anew about the "American dream" in ways that reflect the character of young and seasoned persons alike who live humbly and share wisdom that allows others to flourish as well. They are persons who enjoy a challenge, love the freedom of independence while simultaneously respecting the import of interdependency. Such persons see themselves as a part of nature and are sensitive to the dangers when they are—even in their minds—apart from it. Moreover, as adults, the "street sages" in this book who walked with Howard Brown, and now journey with us if we let them, model, rather than simply speak about, ways we can impact the young who are the future of America and the world.

In *Shining Brightly*, Brown's stories and guidance also help us to meet suffering and uncertainty in new ways. In the pages and chapters that follow, his own story of confronting death is one we now refer to as an example of "post-traumatic growth" (PTG). This occurs when someone facing serious stress or trauma actually deepens as a result of it in ways that would not have been possible had the trauma or stress not happened in the first place. It is very similar to what for ages was known as "the spirituality of suffering" in which the person did not seek the undesirable, play it down, or romanticize it, but was also open to where such frightening events might take them. In other words, they did not see darkness as the final word but possibly the first step in new meaning-making and personal depth.

This new sense of perspective on life, as you will read further on, indicates that it is not the amount of darkness in the world or even in yourself that ultimately matters. It is how you stand in this darkness that turns out to be crucial going forward. As you will also sense in the words of Howard Brown and others, humility—which is not very popular today—is a key element in dealing with vulnerability and fostering resilience.

With a healthy attitude, the author also notes that we shouldn't be surprised by failure or get discouraged by it because of our ego, but instead to expect it. This is not a defeatist stance but a realistic one because statistically the more you are involved in life, the more you will miss the mark at times. Instead, we are called to energetically march on with respect, compassion, integrity, perseverance, a sense of intrigue and hope.

A contemporary of Jesus, Rabbi Tarfon once said, "The day is short, the work is great, the laborers are sluggish, the wages are high, and the Master of the house is insistent. It is not your duty to finish the work, but you are not free to neglect it." Ultimately for me, that was one of the messages I took from this book.

Brown, who casts himself like one of his role models, Roger Babson, is truly an "angelic troublemaker" in this work. He seeks to have us face our lives with complete clarity and kindness. Much good can be gained from reading and reflecting or even meditating over its contents. However, in the end, *Shining Brightly* is more like an unstructured projective device such as the ink blot (Rorschach) projective personality test. What you make of it and take from it will say more about you than the challenging themes and enchanting stories it contains.

And so, in the following journey you are about to take, I wish you well. How you respond will determine which fork in the road you take.

Dr. Robert J. Wicks received his doctorate in psychology from Hahnemann Medical College and Hospital and is Professor Emeritus, Loyola University Maryland. Dr. Wicks has lectured on the importance of resilience, self-care, the prevention of secondary stress, and maintaining a healthy perspective in 20 different countries around the world as well as at the Mayo Clinic, Harvard Divinity School and on Capitol Hill to members of Congress. He has written and edited dozens of books, including *Bounce: Living the Resilient Life* and *Riding the Dragon: 10 Lessons for Inner Strength in Challenging Times*.

Welcome!

Have you ever stopped to think about your life? I mean, have you ever set aside time to reflect on the meaning and purpose of your life?

I have.

I decided to take stock after years as a Silicon Valley entrepreneur, a mentor to college students, an interfaith peace advocate—and a cancer whisperer to other patients after having survived two long-shot bouts with cancer myself. After fully expecting to die more than once in my life, I wondered: Why am I still standing? Who helped me? And then: What can I share to help inspire people to build their own resilience?

As you will learn in the true stories in this book, one key to resilience is not trying to tackle life on your own. We are always at our best when we draw other people around us and, right there, you've got a central theme of this book.

That leads to the questions: How do we draw people around us? How do we make and keep friends? How do we build a community? How can each of us contribute to our families, our friends and to the larger world?

Answering those questions will give you hope and will lead you to greater strength, love and joy in your life. Taking those questions to heart will help your light shine brighter in this often very dark world.

I set out on my journey in an unusual way that you will discover in these pages—and may want to try yourself. Over a two-year period, I sought out people who had played a significant role in my life—from camp counselors and basketball coaches I knew as a kid to family and friends to business and community leaders to some of the world's top faith and health professionals. Because my quest unfolded during the COVID pandemic, I met these more than 100 men and women via Zoom.

And here's the biggest surprise: Everyone loved the experience. While they were doing me a favor—and I am thankful for everyone who shared stories with me—the truth is: Most of them enjoyed the experience as much as I did.

That's why I am confident you will enjoy this adventure, too, and you may decide by the end of the book to set out on such a quest yourself. No matter how you choose to reflect on your life's purpose, I hope this book fans your inner flame so you can shine ever more brightly.

Our matriarch Bubby Bertha lived more than a century. One photo was taken shortly after she had reached her goal of becoming an American; the other photo was taken much later in life as most of us living today recall her. Cheryl and I were 4 years old as we grinned for the photographer at a local department store, where Mom took us for family photos like millions of other American moms. The ceramic bank is my daughter Emily's first tzedakah box, which our family began filling at her baby-naming ceremony.

I

A Shining Circle

Living to 101, Bubby Bertha linked me to my family's deepest roots. Even as a child, I was in awe of this tough little woman who was born in an impoverished Eastern European shtetl yet managed to reach the safety and opportunities of America where she could build a better life for her descendants. Everyone in our family knew her story and respected her hard-earned wisdom. She enjoyed that authority and took every opportunity to teach us something.

The most indelible lesson she taught my twin sister Cheryl and me came during a stroll along a sidewalk in what, as a small boy, I knew as the old town of *Wuh-ster*. We were accompanying her on one of her weekly errands to the butcher and the baker about a mile from her apartment.

Suddenly, something glinted in the distance along the pavement ahead of us. Sunlight glanced off a silvery circle. My first thought was: If I don't move fast enough, Cheryl will get there first. So, I raced the next few steps and stooped to peer at the find.

A quarter! This could buy a lot of candy! I picked it up and held it out toward Cheryl.

"Finders keepers," I exclaimed, confirming my ownership.

Then, I looked up into Bubby Bertha's face and I knew something was seriously wrong with my assumption.

"No," she said firmly. "It's not yours. Found money is God's money. It goes to *tzedakah*."

I stared at the quarter, which looked like any other quarter I had ever seen. "Tze-what?" I stammered. "Does God have money?"

"Found money goes to tzedakah," Bubby repeated. "Tzedakah is Hebrew for charity. Since this money was never yours to begin with, you have a chance—you have an obligation—to help someone in need."

To this day, whenever anyone in our family finds a coin on the ground, we put it into a tzedakah box.

Sprinkled through all the adventures in this book—some of them ordinary, heartwarming family stories and some of them so remarkable you will be tempted to call them miraculous—there are truths like this one Bubby Bertha was trying to explain that morning on the sidewalk in Worcester, Massachusetts. There are more to come, but here are four of these truths as we set out on our journey together in these pages:

+ Each of us has our own special light.

+ We shine more brightly when we share our light with others.

+ True resiliency—the kind that is strong enough to overcome trauma at seemingly impossible odds—rests on letting in the light of others.

+ As our light circles the world, we illuminate and celebrate our diversity.

I'm sharing these truths right away so that perhaps you'll turn down the corner of this page and flip back to it from time to time. This is your book as much as it is mine, after all, and I wrote it with the intention that you will mark it up and return to its pages occasionally for inspiration. Plus, as you read through these chapters, you'll find lots of ideas for fun and inspiring things you can do to shine your light in the world.

Although these truths may sound simple, each of the four represents my own hard-earned wisdom from my encounters with terrible challenges that, at this point, I won't fully detail. Let me just say: I pray you won't experience all that I've experienced! My passion for these truths began in childhood, then later was seared into my heart when I came prematurely to the encounter we all will face someday.

I met death.

In fact, I met death twice. Against overwhelming odds both times, I lived to tell this story—which is why I won't waste time telling you anything but the most essential truths in these pages. Meeting death shines a clarifying spotlight on one's life. In actually confronting death, all the superfluous stuff that usually fills our days is burned away. What becomes clear as we grapple tooth and nail with death is a glimpse of the true purpose of the life we've been given in this world.

What is the purpose of a good life? First, a disclaimer: In answering this question, I am not pretending to be one of the world's great sages. What I can do is the same thing you can do. I can tell you my story—with all of its laughter, warm embraces, crazy brainstorms, daring leaps of faith and cliffhangers. By the end, you will recognize how much our stories are connected. You may discover that all of us are part of a much bigger story—or, we might say, a much larger circle.

So, what *is* the purpose of a good life? What is the message you'll find shining through all of the stories in this book? It's a question I was forced to answer when I met death each time. Wrestling with death month after month was so bone-wearying that I had to answer this core question each morning just to climb out of bed: Against all odds, why should I go on living? Millions of cancer patients like me know this haunting question all too well. Some days, it feels easier to just lay back, surrender and give up.

When I faced that question the first time, I was surprised by my own answer. I realized how completely my confrontation with death was stripping away all of the inconsequential noise in my life. Why should I live? One easy answer to that question that I could have voiced is a cry of defiance mixed with regret: "Because there's so much more I want *to get!*" But, no, I never said that. I never got lost in that trap, because that answer really is a first step toward letting cancer separate us from the people surrounding us—narrowing our focus to all that the disease may be taking away from us as individuals.

My honest answer always was: "Because there's so much more I want *to give.*" On my worst day—and there were hundreds of worst days—that was always my answer.

Why should I live?

Because there is so much more I can give.

By joining me on this true-life adventure—from the height of the Silicon Valley software bubble and the heady hopes of global peacemaking to the depths of my two battles with cancer—I hope that I can inspire your own natural impulse to give back. As you read, you will meet my family, lifelong buddies, quirky collaborators and courageous companions. In writing this story for you, I spent a couple of years going back through my entire life, interviewing in depth everyone from my earliest childhood pals through the friends who dared to launch international companies and peace initiatives with me. It was a humbling and often deeply emotional experience as we met mostly via video streaming, shared memories and collectively shaped the stories in this

book for you. Everyone was happy to help. No one held back. We laughed.
We cried.

Why did we do all of this for you? Because this much is true in every single
life: We all will meet death at some point. We all must face that question:
What is the purpose of a good life?

My answer may not be precisely your answer—but I do invite you to join
me in these real-life adventures and then see how close our answers may be by
the end. All I can do is tell you my story as openly as I possibly can—recreated
in all its details through this year of conversations with dozens of friends, family members, colleagues and caregivers. That year of painstakingly preparing
this book for you strengthened my resolve: Giving is the true purpose of a
good life. As counter intuitive as it may seem, giving is one crucial key to individual resiliency.

In my life, I was fortunate as a little boy to encounter a powerhouse of
resiliency. Bubby Bertha had that capacity baked into her bones! She was
an immigrant just like matriarchs and patriarchs in nearly every family living these days in North America. Perhaps you know the stories of your own
ancestors' decisions to find a new life on this continent or, in some cases, of
your ancestors' enslavement or compulsion in their journey to this land. Or
perhaps your ancestors were refugees and found themselves storm-tossed
onto these shores with only the clothes on their backs. Whatever your origin
story as an American family may be, there are lessons in resilience we all share
from our common experiences as newcomers.

Bubby Bertha died in 1993, but she left us an oral history of her own
relentless struggle for new life. Whenever I reread her story, I'm overwhelmed
with the image of the shtetl where she was born. Unfamiliar with the concept?
Perhaps you can close your eyes and remember scenes of village life in *Fiddler
on the Roof*.

Here is Bubby Bertha's story:

> I was born in 1892 in a small town in Russia in a region with
> borders that kept changing over many years. At different times,
> our town was claimed by Lithuania, Latvia and Russia—
> even though we weren't much of a catch. Our village was far
> away from the big cities and had a population of just 2,000.
> Our town had one butcher shop and two tiny grocery stores.
> When I was a little girl, our three-room house with its dirt
> floor was home to six of us. Like other families in our town,
> we managed without electricity, running water or steam heat.

For heat, we had a wood stove. In the winter, we chopped a hole in the ice on the lake big enough to dip our bucket.

Living there was a hardship for the Jewish people, but we always shared what gifts we had. When I was 10 years old, my grandmother came to live with us. She was blind, but she was well educated and had memorized the Jewish Bible, word for word. She taught us, as children, to crochet and knit and sew. Our respect for her knew no bounds, because one of her gifts was a traditional knowledge of home remedies. We were in awe of the way neighbors from across our village would come to our home, asking my grandmother to care for them. She always tried her best.

All of us lived in terror of the cruel czar and the atrocities committed by his men. Everyone in our village knew stories about this cruel ruler even though none of us had ever seen him. We were terrified of his power, hoping that none of the czar's men would ever come for us. When my brother Edward turned 16, we knew that these fearsome horsemen would come for him eventually. Then, he would be forced into the czar's army like a slave and we would never see him again. That's why my mother wrote to her two uncles living in America, asking them to send a ticket for Edward. We were thrilled when we finally received a response—along with a ticket—and soon Edward was on his way to safety. We prayed he would survive the journey. Then, for a long time we had no idea what had happened to him. We did what we always did— we just went on scratching out a life by tending our gardens, milking our cow and raising a few chickens. Then, two years later, we heard from Edward. He was alive and sent us some ABC books to help us study English in the hope that, one day, we too could come to the United States. Sadly, my father died before we had any chance to make that journey. My mother became the head of the household, trying to keep us all alive while we hoped for something better.

Four years after those ABC books arrived and two years after my father died, in 1910, Edward had saved enough money to send us tickets to America. We sold our little house and prepared for the journey. So that we would not be a burden in our new homeland, we had to prove that we were not illiterate, and we had to be examined by a doctor to receive a health certificate. The steamship lines that sailed from Bremen, Hamburg and Antwerp in those years were very strict about this, because they faced big fines from the U.S. government for every unacceptable immigrant who reached the American ports and had to be shipped back to Europe. That medical exam is what separated us. As we reached Germany and were ready to board our ship, the others—my mother and my sister and brother—were all approved for travel. But the doctor found that I had trachoma, an infection of the eyes that millions of people around the world have to this day. If left untreated, it leads to blindness. One person can infect others, especially on a crowded ship. That's why I couldn't get on the trans-Atlantic steamship with my mother. But fortunately, my family had friends who had lived in Germany, and they told us about a rooming house in a small German town where I could stay on my own. I was able to get medical treatment in that town and wound up living for eight months, supporting myself as a dressmaker. My grandmother had taught me well. I adapted. I even learned enough German to get around in that community.

Finally, my doctor cleared me to travel, and Edward generously sent me another ticket, this time departing from Antwerp, Belgium. So, I was back on the road again! And, once again. a medical examination turned up evidence of the damage to my eyes. I argued that I was cured, but trachoma leaves its marks on the surfaces of the eye for a long time. Once more, I was barred from getting on board. I had to survive alone in a foreign land while my eyes continued to heal. I asked around and finally found a spot to stay. I even found a clinic where I could get weekly appointments for treatment, which wound up lasting for one whole year! Fortunately, I knew how to make dresses, a skill always in demand—and I also found work as a nanny for a merchant family. My mother had taught me well about caring for children. I adapted. I even added Flemish to the growing number of tongues I could speak.

Not everyone was able to cope as well as I could, you know. Antwerp was one of three big international ports for migrants trying to leave Europe. These were huge gateway cities to the whole world. So, there always were hundreds of people who got that far but were barred from getting on board because of one condition or another. Many of them were so poor and had so few skills that they could do nothing more than hunker down at the Antwerp immigration center. Belgian government authorities were very concerned about this. They wanted all of these stranded men and women and children to go back home—but most of them had no way to do that, even if they wanted to go back. It was an impossible, life-and-death situation for so many families! That's when I saw first-hand how Jewish philanthropies cared for these poor people who were sick and hungry and homeless, so far from anyone they knew. I don't know how these families would have survived without that help from the charities. Jewish volunteers helped them find medical services and places to sleep and eat as they tried to wait through whatever illness had prevented them from using their tickets. The larger Jewish community looked after them—and everyone hoped and prayed against all odds that they could continue their journey.

Right away, I got to know some of the other women stranded there from all over Eastern Europe. I met a Romanian woman with two children who had just booked her passage to Montreal, Canada, to be reunited with her husband. Before she left on her steamship, she convinced me to travel to Canada first because we realized that the medical restrictions were not as strict along that route. From there, I could travel into the U.S. When I finally got on board my ship to Montreal, I was terrified by the two weeks on stormy seas—waves crashing around us as tall as a three-story house! Then, I felt such relief when I got to Montreal and that Romanian woman welcomed me with open arms. I stayed with her until I could book a train to my family in Boston.

Even after reuniting with relatives in Boston, we still had to figure out how to survive. We learned that an uncle owned a coat factory, which meant that my brother Irving, my sister Lilly and I could find work in his factory. Running a sewing machine every day, we earned $7 a week, and at night we attended classes to learn good English.

We lived in the west end of Boston until I met my future husband, Louis. We were married in the parlor of a cousin's house. My husband was a carpenter and was asked to build a house in Worcester, which is why we settled there in 1921. He worked hard on building homes, at first, and then commercial buildings like car dealerships. For a time, we had a big home; we could afford a grand piano.

None of us saw the Great Depression coming and Louis was way overextended when it hit. Everything crashed. Builders all across the country were ruined. He lost everything. We lost our big home. But, this time, we decided not to travel any farther. Worcester was our home and we stayed. We found a smaller place to live. We always adapted.

"We always adapted." I know those words by heart. What I didn't know—and, to this day, I still don't know—is the entire meaning of that phrase in Bubby Bertha's life. No one ever talked in detail about the more traumatic turns in her life. For example, at some point and for some reason, she decided she was finished with Louis and made him move out. I mean, that was that! Louis was gone. She never divorced him. She just decided to run her own household and raise her children without him. The fact that all she could afford was the top floor of one of Worcester's old triple-deckers—which meant climbing steep flights of stairs with groceries or children in arms—never slowed her down.

Even very late in her life, when she looked so small and frail to all of us, she refused to slow down. My mother Nancy tells our favorite story about Bertha in her 90s.

On a very rainy day, Bubby Bertha decided she needed a quart of milk. The sabbath was coming and, on the sabbath, she stopped doing everything, except walking to the synagogue of course. So, she wasn't going to be stopped by the rain coming down in sheets. She walked downstairs and over to the bus stop—and rode the bus to shop at a particular store she liked. As she was walking along the street toward the store, her oldest son was driving by and happened to see her.

He pulled over. "Mom it's pouring! Hop in!" She got in, but instead of taking her the rest of the way to the store, he took her back to her apartment. She didn't argue with him. She walked upstairs, looked out the window until his car drove away, then went back down to the bus stop and rode toward her store, again.

This time, her daughter happened to be driving along that same street. Again, it was: "Mom, it's pouring! Hop in!" She did. And, once more, she was driven back to her apartment.

I know about this because that's when I got a telephone call.

"Nancy, can you go get me a quart of milk?"

I couldn't believe it. I mean, we lived a half hour away. A quart of milk?

"I really need it," she said. "But every time I try to go get it, someone makes me go back home."

What could I do? I got in the car. She got her milk.

Throughout her entire century of living, Bubby Bertha quietly but firmly stuck to the Jewish traditions she knew from that little village where she was born, traditions that today we call Orthodox in America. Over the years, a stark contrast developed between the life in her apartment and life when she would visit the homes of her descendants. For example, my father Marshall was a busy man working several jobs to support our family, including extra shifts every weekend. In making that commitment as a father, he certainly shared the work ethic of our ancestors: no nonsense, stoic, hard-assed discipline about working very long hours to make a better life for the family. Mom was just trying to keep her head above water raising twins while Dad was on the road a lot. Dad simply had no patience for all the complex Hebrew language and customs of the Orthodox world—and Mom was happy to adapt as well. In fact, that's the story of millions of American Jewish families who became Reform Jews in the 20th century. My family joined a nearby Reform temple.

We were curious about this obvious contrast as kids. Bubby Bertha never wavered. When she visited our house, Mom had to make sure she had packages of new paper plates and new plastic coffee cups handy for her—because our everyday dishes weren't kept kosher. That would have involved, among other things, a rigorous separation of dishes used for meat from those used for dairy. The majority of American Jewish families did not maintain that custom. It was far easier for us to have packages of Dixie cups and disposable plates handy for Bubby Bertha's occasional appearances. We all adapted.

To her credit, she never scolded. What she did was remind, encourage and entice us with her unswerving adherence to tradition.

"I can still remember her visiting with us," Mom recalls. "In the afternoon, she was so eager to see you twins that she'd sit by the window waiting for the school bus. Then, when you came in, she'd make sure you went and washed your hands—and said the Jewish prayer after handwashing."

There are several traditional Jewish handwashing prayers and Bubby Bertha tried her best to teach us at least one of them. In my interfaith work, people of other faiths are often surprised to learn that this idea of prayerful washing stretches back many centuries through nearly all of the world's faiths. Ablutions are required every day in Islam, of course, but they're also a part of other religions—and handwashing prayers are even practiced to this day in some ancient branches of Christianity. My sister and I still can recall our handwashing prayers, so Bubby Bertha's plan worked somewhat. But truth be told—it's a fond memory, not a daily practice.

Bubby's most effective strategy was enticement with food. My sister, Cheryl, says, "I still remember her giving us cookies and milk—and only after the handwashing prayers. She made good cookies, but she wasn't as famous for her cookies as she was for her latkes."

Everyone who ever tried one of her crusty potato pancakes holds them up as the gold standard of latkes. My mom says that was partly because of the sheer quantity she produced. She would make them anytime throughout the year. "We all know that latkes usually are for Hanukkah, but she was so good at it—she would make them at other times," Mom recalls. "Her place often smelled like the hot Wesson oil she used. She was proud of those latkes; happy to make them. I remember calling up once because your dad wanted some. I asked her: Would she make us some? Of course, she would! And they came wrapped in paper and tied with a string—old school. You know, a package of Bubby Bertha's latkes was kept in our freezer for years—*for years*—after she died just as a reminder of the love she put into those latkes."

"We'll never forget those," Cheryl says, "even though I'm sure they were terrible for us. I can remember eating so many my stomach would hurt from all that grease. We'll always remember her latkes just like we'll always remember her prayers. And the stories of her village, too! We couldn't forget her telling us about the terror she felt from the Russian pogroms and how much everyone in her village all feared and hated the czar. She saw the czar's men come through at least once on horseback and take boys for the army. Sometimes they would come through just as a warning—a show of their power over the people. Her family lived every day in fear that her brothers would be taken. The czar's men could ride through, again, any day. We grew up knowing about all those fears.

"In fact, that's one reason found money went to others," Cheryl says. "So many people around the world are in danger and need help. We took what she said about found money so seriously that—even if we found money when we were nowhere near her—we would tell Mom, who would get word to Bubby Bertha because we knew she'd be so proud of us. It was never much money, you know—just coins. I remember Mom once finding a $20 bill. But, large or small, we all knew where that money went."

Bubby Bertha taught us well.

On that first day I found a quarter as a little kid, standing at her side, I honestly did not know what to do. At first, I held that shiny new quarter out to her, assuming she would take it.

She shook her head. "No, I'll show you what we do."

When we got back to her triple-decker, we climbed all the stairs to her little place: just one bedroom with a kitchenette, bathroom and sitting room. As we took off our coats, she directed my gaze to a little tin canister that stands in most Jewish homes: a tzedakah box. The Hebrew word often is translated as "charity," but the larger meaning of tzedakah includes "doing right" and "justice." Jews consider giving tzedakah a moral obligation and a way of promoting social justice.

I picked up her box, which was surprisingly heavy in my little hand because it already was more than half full.

"Found money is for tzedakah," Bubby Bertha said. "Put it in." Then, she watched approvingly as I dropped my quarter into the slot with a telltale clink and set the can back in its place on a table near her favorite chair. She nodded. "We always give back."

At that time, I had little idea of why she was so committed to this teaching. It was only as an adult that I understood much more about history and could fully appreciate her entire life story. When all those pieces fell into place, I realized: Why am I the person I am today? Because for more than a century, my own family kept giving back. If Bubby Bertha's brother had been abducted into the czar's army, he would have become cannon fodder a few years later in the first World War. Against long odds, he was saved by a couple of uncles half a world away who remembered that they should give back and generously sent the steamship ticket that saved his life. Even though the family didn't know whether Edward was even alive for a very long time—while he was struggling to scratch out a life in a tough new homeland—he still remembered to save and give back. He sent what he could afford. First, he sent the package of English primers. Later, when he could save what must have been an astronomical amount of money—he sent trans-Atlantic tickets. Because he gave back, Bubby Bertha had a chance at a long life. Just a few decades later, those shtetls were cleared by the Nazis. Once Bertha reached Antwerp, she saw first-hand how local Jewish families gave back to the immigrants crowding in around them. She met the Romanian woman who survived because these Jewish neighbors helped her. Then, that Romanian woman gave back when Bubby Bertha finally made her voyage to Montreal. The Romanian family took her into their home until she could arrange her next passage to Massachusetts. Once in Boston, an uncle gave back and provided jobs for the newcomers. My mother was alive because of Bertha's amazing journey—and, ultimately, I am here today because countless people through several generations remembered to give back.

Today, after years as a volunteer and lay leader in various Jewish nonprofits, I understand firsthand how a network of religious charities circles the globe to help needy men, women and children. Those charities exist, in part, because millions of children were taught from childhood to give back, even as little as a few coins in a tin can. And, of course, our own ancient Jewish sacred obligation to give generously carried over as a central tenet in Christianity and into one of the pillars of Islam. Now, Christians and Muslims have their own terms to describe this traditional value of giving and their own philanthropic networks around the world.

That's the big picture. As kids, all we knew were Bubby Bertha's simple words: "Found money is God's money. Found money goes to tzedakah." Like most Jewish kids, we learned a lot about tzedakah boxes. In the ancient world, a tzedakah box was affixed to the wall of the temple in Jerusalem and money was collected to support communal life. When Romans destroyed the temple and Jews were scattered around the world, boxes became a common fixture in synagogues. Then, in the 1700s, the custom expanded to encourage small boxes in everyone's home to support causes near and far away. From the simplest of lessons, then, family traditions grew. In most families, kids accumulate multiple boxes or banks. In our home, we were taught to set aside some money to give back in a tzedakah box—and some money to save for our future in another bank. These containers blossomed in a huge array of shapes and sizes. Search "tzedakah boxes" online and you'll find countless designs—from interpretations by fine artists, to simple metal cans for various nonprofits, all the way to do-it-yourself PDFs to print and assemble paper boxes.

"The main one I remember in my room was shaped like Smokey the Bear," I told Cheryl as we reminisced. "You had some girly design, didn't you?"

"Hey, I liked my rainbow bank!" she protested. "It was ceramic with red, orange, yellow, green, blue and purple stripes."

I told my friend Rabbi Josh Bennett about my plan to tell these family stories as a starting point for this book. He grinned and nodded.

"It's so appropriate that you're going to start your story with tzedakah boxes," he said. "I'm moved by that because this really is part and parcel of the values we are taught by Jewish tradition."

He paused for a moment and, when he resumed, the emotion was obvious in his voice. "I've known you for years, Howard, and I can tell you: This is the core, the basis, of your life Howard—giving back. I love this story about your Bubby Bertha's life and her lessons. Let me suggest you add a passage that often is read at funerals to sum up the meaning of life. It's from Psalm 24 and begins: 'The earth is the Lord's, and the fullness thereof; the world, and they that dwell therein. For he founded it upon the seas and established it upon the floods.' It reminds us that God has given us so much in life. But the passage also reminds us that all this stuff we think we own is really not ours to keep. We just have it for a time. We are caretakers in this life. We are caretakers of the Torah and caretakers of the stories of those who came before us until the moment of our own death. We are caretakers of everything that comes our way in life, especially the relationships that come our way.

"That's what I mean, Howard, when I say your story of a little boy finding a quarter—then learning from your bubby that it's not yours to keep—that's deeply rooted in our Jewish tradition and extends into the way we treat the world throughout our entire lives. We know we are living on borrowed time. We must give back while we can.

"The root of the Hebrew word tzedakah is *tzedek* and has to do with righteousness, even holiness. There's a Jewish mystical tradition of people who embody this so fully that they are called *tzadiks* or *tzadikim* in plural. Often, stories say these tzadikim are traveling rabbis. The stories remind us that we should all behave in our lives as though everyone we meet might be a tzadik."

Christians share a similar sacred story in which Jesus tells his followers to give back. In fact, Jesus pointedly tells his followers that their greatest challenge in life is to welcome the hungry, thirsty and homeless strangers they meet with hospitality—because "just as you did it to one of the least of these who are members of my family, you did it to me."

This is a universal story. When I run workshops for nonprofit volunteers and community leaders, I tell people my own tzedakah story. Then, I invite them to design their own tzedakah box decorated with their hopes for the world. Sometimes, I simply ask people to draw a box on a piece of paper, representing one side of a box, and focus on how they would decorate it. People get very enthusiastic and sometimes draw multiple images. As I was working on this book, one of the most enthusiastic suggestions from early readers was that I provide a printable paper template for a simple, small box. It is a powerful, hopeful and tangible reminder to set a box in your home.

In fact, as Rabbi Bennett suggests, you could think of this entire book as a kind of tzedakah box. With each of the stories in these pages, I am dropping another coin—another valuable insight—into the bank of stories we can share with each other. At the end of each story, I'm even going to nudge you a little bit—to act on what I hope you'll be feeling.

Right now, if you wish, you can visit my website and download the free tzedakah box PDF. Print a copy, cut it out, add a little tape and, within several minutes, you'll have a little reminder in your home to keep giving back. It's fun. It's easy. You don't even have to call it by its Hebrew name if that's a tough word for you to pronounce. You could call it your Shining Brightly box. You can set aside some of your coins in it and, even more importantly with each coin dropped through the slot, some of your intentions to give back, to help others, to reach out.

Who knows when you'll face the question: Why should I live?

You'll have a ready answer: Because there is so much more I can give.

Shining Brightly

If you want to fully enjoy the stories in this book, take a moment right now to connect with me at ShiningBrightly.com. At my website you will find lots of helpful and inspiring resources, including more information about tzedakah boxes.

I am the son of a bootman, Marshall Brown, the entrepreneur who was my first mentor. My father sold shoes and boots all his life, declining salaries in favor of straight sales commissions—the mark of a true entrepreneur in his heyday. My family was eager to achieve the American dream. My grandfather Papa Leo, posing proudly in his best overcoat, returned injured from his service in World War II to work as a truck driver. I was 5 as I pushed my own truck around the kindergarten floor. My parents made a classic suburban home for my twin sister and me, where we established lifelong friendships throughout the neighborhood.

Birth of an Entrepreneur

Each month, I check in with students I am mentoring and following at Babson College, my alma mater and the nation's go-to school for preparing young entrepreneurs. Don't take my word for it. Babson owns that niche. For three decades, Babson's entrepreneurship program has rated No. 1 in that category of the *US News & World Report* college rankings. Among the thousands of entrepreneurs who attended Babson across the past century are co-founders of companies such as Gerber, Zumba, Spanx, Home Depot and Ring, all known for their game-changing concepts. No one dreamed of canning and selling strained baby food until Daniel Gerber convinced his father to produce that new line of foods at the family's canning plant in Michigan in the 1920s. Babson alum Alberto Perlman took a tip from his Colombian American mother who loved working out to Latin music; he partnered with Alberto Perez to launch the Zumba craze. Babson grad Arthur Blank partnered with Bernard Marcus to revolutionize the home improvement business with their Home Depot. Jamie Siminoff's Ring was bought by Amazon and now dominates the video-doorbell home security market.

Certainly, innovative thinking is one of two qualities that define successful Babson graduates. The second is a recognition that our true vocation is making the world a better place. That's why Arthur Blank inspires me. In 2019, his foundation gave the largest one-time gift in Babson history: $50 million, which included funding for scholarships each year to pay the way for students who show promise as entrepreneurs but could never afford to attend Babson.

Jimmy Carter sums up Blank's credo in the Foreword to Blank's 2020 memoir, *Good Company*. Carter writes that his own evangelical Christian sense of mission parallels Blank's Jewish commitment to service. "In a world often fixated on quantification of things, Arthur effortlessly integrated that which cannot be counted into his life and work. Arthur knows what all servant leaders know: Our communities are the bedrock of our country."

Roger Babson must be beaming down on his ever-growing legacy. When he started the Babson Institute with his first 27 students in 1919, he asked them each to make a pledge: "We are embarking on a business career as a means to render service to humanity." Since that founding, his school has educated government officials, military leaders, corporate CEOs and even some top athletes.

Since Babson was so foundational in my own life, one way I give back these days is to encourage young men and women who are drawn to this high-stakes vocation. I served on the board of the Babson Alumni Association from 2006–2020 and was president from 2014–18. Until the pandemic struck, I enjoyed scheduling in-person conversations with prospective Babson students and graduates over coffee in various cities as we all were moving around the country. That wasn't just my idea. That's what the leading mentors among Babson's alumni have taught me: We are called to more than individual success; we are called to form supportive relationships.

Real relationships. For example, I'm forever thankful to Babson alum Robert Weissman for his kindness through the years. He was a pioneer in cable television in the 1970s, then was an innovator in computer time-sharing and wound up as Chairman and CEO of Dun & Bradstreet for 17 years. His lifetime philanthropy to Babson, including multiple scholarships for needy students, has passed the $100 million mark. His generosity is amazing, but that's not the only reason he shines so brightly in my mind. My thankfulness to him has to do with the deep sincerity of his care for others.

The second time I was fighting for my life against stage IV cancer, Bob spotted me across the room during a ribbon-cutting ceremony honoring him and his wife, Jan. One of their larger gifts built The Weissman Foundry, a new building with space for students to work on projects, use prototyping resources, attend conferences, and enjoy a kitchen and study space.

Any time Bob is out in public like that, he is inundated with people who want his attention, you know, "for just a moment." It's easy to understand why. When he speaks, his words just might be gold. So, as Bob crosses a room like that, the world stops. But, this time, he kindly but quickly waved away several outstretched hands and, instead, he reached out for my hand and pulled me into a quiet corner.

I was surprised that he wanted time with me. Then, when we were alone, he looked into my eyes, "What I want to know is: How ya doing? How ya really doing, Howard?"

I was overwhelmed by his attention. I managed to say, "I'm fighting, man." At that point, I honestly didn't know if I was going to beat cancer again. I was flat-out honest with him. I was fighting for my life.

He wasn't posing an idle question. He wanted to encourage me. He truly cared. And he closed our time alone with a sincere invitation: "Come on down to my home when you can. We'll have an iced tea on the lanai."

I never had time to go while in treatment and surgeries—but I also never forgot his caring pep talk.

I do the same thing. To avoid COVID-19, of course, we all hunkered down and moved many of our conversations online. Now, I have daily online conversations with people all over the world. As I was finishing this book, I connected by Zoom to San Francisco with recent graduate Anneliese Glaubitz, who surprised me that day with news of how well she is doing in California. She's the first student from Michigan who I had mentored all the way from high school application through graduation. Then, when the pandemic hit, I was especially concerned for her, because her business is event design and planning—a sector that took a huge hit from COVID. When she graduated from Babson in 2019, event design had seemed like a dream job for a professional in the arts. Back in high school, Anneliese had been a promising ballet dancer, photographer and ice skater. She wanted to pursue a career in the arts. Anneliese told me, "I knew that whatever I hoped to do in the arts, I'd better have a solid business education. Arts professionals need to understand the business side if they hope to succeed."

Smart! In fact, Anneliese is blessed with so many talents that the launch of her career after Babson was smooth and sure—more so than I initially guessed.

"You're actually a lot tougher than I gave you credit for," I told her after she won her dream job at a San Francisco-based event-design company. As we caught up via Zoom, I felt the need to apologize. When I had talked with her back in 2019, before she began applying for jobs, I thought she was making a mistake by setting her sights on moving to San Francisco. Limiting herself geographically made me anxious and I told her so. "The San Francisco area's a tough market—and so expensive. I know. I've worked and lived there," I told her over coffee at a café on Babson's campus in her senior year. "I mean,

Anneliese, it's *sooo* expensive. My wife Lisa and I were shocked at the prices we had to pay out there and it's even more expensive today."

"I want California. I want San Francisco," she said confidently as if that ended the conversation. I looked down at my coffee cup and idly tapped the rim as I formulated another argument to deter her from this exclusive commitment to one of America's most competitive and over-priced cities. I was thinking of starting my next comment with: "You've got to be flexible—"

But she knew what I was thinking and cut me off with a shrug and three simple words: "I want California."

With that, I took the cue. I stopped pushing. She knew what she wanted—and she got it. Soon, after she landed the job she wanted out there, I found her smiling face popping up among the handful of principal professionals featured on the event-planning firm's website. In my initial check-in calls with her, I could tell she was very happy. She told me she was "all in" on event planning as a way to move deeper into the arts world, working with clients and venues and artists, including top musicians.

That's also what made me so anxious for her after COVID hit. She was out there trying to promote high-end event planning in the middle of a global pandemic.

When our Zoom screen lit up and our faces appeared in that call toward the end of 2020, the first words out of my mouth posed the same anxious question Bob Weissman had asked to me: "So, how ya doing? How ya really doing, Anneliese?"

On my computer screen, I could see her standing just inside the big front window of a home that looked out over a picture-postcard slice of Victorian architecture stacked up, one pastel façade after another, along her street. I said, "Gorgeous place! Looks like you're happy. But tell me: Has event planning evaporated? Are you still finding work?"

"Sure," she said as confident as always. "You know what Babson teaches: There's always work—if you've got the right skills. And I'm always adding value to my skill set so I'm ready for whatever is coming. When everything moved online with COVID, we all scrambled for a while along with our clients, and all the venues and the artists we book for events. We all had to pivot and rethink our business in an instant. But I adapted. That's what we do, right? That's why I say the potential of my business degree is endless. I'm doing things now that I never took a class in at Babson—and yet what I learned at Babson prepared me to do all of this now. The most important lesson is: Always learn new things. So, here's the latest: I just decided to learn OBS (Open Broadcaster Software) for streaming video and now I'm the resident OBS expert on our team. Since most of the events we're doing now are online, we all pool our skills to work with clients. So, one skill I have is OBS. If anyone in our team needs help editing and adding video to an event, I'm the go-to OBS person," she said.

I laughed. "Wow. That's another thing we share. You know, when I was starting in southern California, I was on the ground floor of Avid, which totally shook up the film and video world with the first digital editing systems that replaced the old cut-and-splice equipment for movies and TV stations. We rocked the world. I mean, I was riding the cutting edge in the early 1990s. I was flying around the country for Avid, selling these game-changing systems for the first time to TV newsrooms. They couldn't believe what Avid could do—after years of all that cumbersome videotape they needed to produce, carry around and edit for the evening TV news. Suddenly, they had all this power and flexibility and speed. Those were big sales, too. To fully equip a TV station—all the hardware, software and training—some of those Avid sales could total a couple million dollars—and those are 'dollars' from decades ago."

She smiled and said, "OBS is free. The value is in knowing how to use it well."

"Free." I chuckled again.

"Yes, open source, you know. I was able to just download it and then train myself and now I'm the go-to OBS person on our team."

"Free," I repeated. I can still remember the big celebration when we landed our first multi-million-dollar Avid sale. So much money. We enjoyed a huge blowout that evening. And, four decades later? Anneliese was quietly celebrating with me her milestone of mastering—in her spare time and free of charge—a video software that's 10 times as powerful.

"That's wonderful," I told her. That's also a foundational truth in sales. Markets always are shaken by innovation. Nothing stays the same for very long.

I learned that lesson from my father as a little boy.

Marshall Brown is the quintessential American entrepreneur: a traveling salesman working strictly on commission. My father built his career on quality products, persistence and integrity—but the core of his success lay in the relationships he fostered and carefully tended over many decades. That was a lesson he learned from his parents and the close-knit Lithuanian-Catholic-Jewish-American neighborhood where they raised him in Worcester, Massachusetts.

All of my ancestors on both my mother's and my father's side of the family came to this country in the tidal waves of immigration that flowed from northern, southern and eastern Europe from the mid-1800s up through the first decades of the 1900s. Jewish families were among the millions of other immigrants from across Europe during that period. As that worldwide migration continued, the waves of migrants emerged from farther and farther east in Europe and the Middle East. In an innovation that would connect with my own interfaith work later in my life, the original Henry Ford became the first big American industrialist to encourage hundreds of Syrian men to come work in the booming auto industry in southeast Michigan—which is why the first mosque built in the United States was in Highland Park, a Detroit enclave. That mosque was within walking distance of Ford's factory, where Syrian Muslims worked side by side with Protestants, Catholics and Jews from across Europe. Ford even hired African American workers arriving from the American South. Yes, he was an infamous antisemite, but Ford wanted a diverse workforce. In part, he hoped it would discourage the growth of unions—and, of course, he was dead wrong about that. Relations between ethnic and racial groups were not always ideal. There were horrendous clashes across the 20th century, including in Detroit—but a strong union movement sprang up in the Detroit-area auto factories. Despite his own personal biases, Ford had stumbled upon a real and enduring truth: The strongest work forces are diverse work forces. The migrants from Europe and the American South he hired for his factories were all here to work hard and provide for their families. They shared a common ground, even if they could not always see it at the time.

There were so many immigrants passing through Ellis Island and pouring into factories across the U.S. that my family has been unable to track down the specific details of my great-grandfather's arrival from the Baltic region of Eastern Europe. We think his family name originally was something like Bronovsky or Bradofsky from the few strands of oral history passed down to us—but the agents at Ellis Island erased his original Lithuanian name and slapped a common new name on his paperwork: Charles Brown. He was a tailor and immediately found work in the textile and clothing industry in Boston, where he was often in contact with toxic chemicals that contributed to his untimely death. The most important thing Charles did in his new life as an American was to move his family about an hour west of downtown Boston. Before the birth of Charles' son—my grandfather, who we knew as Papa Leo—Charles had resettled the family in a little slice of Eden he had found in Worcester. It was a neighborhood centering on Vernon Hill Park that locals called simply "the Hill" or "the Park." It was one of those ideal American communities where Christians and Jews got along famously. That was because their ethnicity trumped their religious differences. Everyone spoke Lithuanian. By the time World War II rolled around, the local families' patriotism and their eagerness to defeat Hitler and Mussolini trumped everything else.

How do we know this isn't just a rosy family memory with more nostalgia than accuracy? Because a venerable journalist stumbled across this neighborhood many years after World War II. That's the era when Papa Leo went off to serve with the frontline American troops liberating Italy and my father Marshall was born not long after he left. The journalist was Louis Marano, the son of an immigrant family himself and a U.S. Navy veteran who earned a doctorate in anthropology and worked for decades as a reporter, based on the East Coast. Many decades after the war, Marano stumbled across stories about the vibrant Vernon Hill neighborhood. He eventually wrote a United Press International (UPI) feature story that circled the world, describing the warm relationships maintained between Park GIs serving overseas and their families back home during World War II.

The more Marano dug into the story, the more he fell in love with this blue-collar neighborhood, which he described for UPI as "conjuring up images of Norman Rockwell paintings and Frank Capra movies. During the Depression, the boys played ball in Vernon Hill Park. As teenagers and young men, they hung around Oscar Leavitt's soda fountain and flirted with the nursing students who flocked there on their breaks from nearby St. Vincent's Hospital."

What's remarkable about that soda fountain is that Papa Leo and other Jewish guys hung out there along with the Catholics and Protestants in the neighborhood. Before World War II, Papa Leo married my Nana Rose, so we assume he didn't continue to flirt with the girls at the soda fountain after that. But Papa Leo was a true extrovert who was part of that crowd. He also was one of the guys from the Park who Marano described for UPI as maintaining a kind of hyper-local news service—direct from the front lines back to the old neighborhood. There were more than two dozen regular Park correspondents, servicemen scattered all around the world during World War II. In their letters home, they had to avoid military censors that prevented them for sharing any sensitive news about their units—but they could send home heartfelt best wishes and little anecdotes that would amuse and inspire the folks back home. The hub of this impromptu news operation was the soda fountain where families would drop off the guys' military addresses. The men in service would send handwritten letters to the soda fountain for a little newspaper called *The Vernon Hill Spiel*, the German-Yiddish term for "a talk." The editor, Don Gribbons, was a volunteer firefighter and worked at a real local newspaper. Like a Frank Capra movie, everyone pitched in for a few years! Don would type up stencils for the *Spiel* at the firehouse, then carry them to his local newspaper offices and run them off on a borrowed mimeograph machine. Then, some copies were left at the soda fountain for families of the servicemen; some were mailed around the world. Soon, every two weeks, Don and his friends were sending out 850 copies. What filled all those pages of Gribbons' hand-crafted, indie newspaper? His stories came from nearly 1,500 letters that were mailed to him by local guys from wherever they were serving on the planet.

Papa Leo was a regular correspondent to his buddies back home. To this day, we cherish his handwritten V-Mail letters to the *Spiel*. "It feels swell to read about the old gang from the Park," he began one letter from the front lines in Italy. All he managed to get past the censors about his location was this: "I'm here somewhere in Italy and the scenery here is very beautiful, but I would rather be back in the Park any day. My wife tells me that you have put up a beautiful plaque with all the names inscribed at the Park. I sure am proud to know mine is on it and hope that real soon I get to see it myself."

Only many years after the war did my family learn the details of that brutal campaign to recapture Italy all the way from Sicily northward through the boot across one horrendous German line after another. More than 300,000 Americans were wounded and more than 60,000 died in bloody, entrenched battles for places like Anzio, Moro River and Monte Cassino. Papa Leo was one of the casualties, wounded in his leg. Somehow, he even managed to turn that story into ray of sunshine. As he described it for the *Spiel*, he lay there bleeding with a makeshift bandage, hoping that an ambulance would take him to a field hospital. As one came rumbling along, he was stunned to discover a buddy from the old neighborhood driving toward him. In his *Spiel* story, he wrote, "I met none other than Sgt. Tanona driving the ambulance that I rode in! He almost jumped out of his uniform when I told him I was from Vernon Hill. Had a nice chat as I rode to the hospital, talking about all the boys from the Park."

The wound was serious enough to require hospitalization, but it wasn't dire enough to send him home. The Army needed every soldier the doctors could patch up sufficiently to keep doing something for the war effort. Papa Leo couldn't march anymore but he soon was driving trucks—a profession he continued when he eventually got home. I was always wide-eyed when he told his war stories. Always on the move, he wound up in Milan and witnessed the crowd stringing up the battered corpses of Benito Mussolini and his mistress. What a horrific scene! During the war, he was not able to get that story past the U.S. Army censors to the *Spiel*. But, around that time, he was able to report a much sunnier story about meeting yet another hometown resident near the battlefield. This time, the story concerned a woman named Shirley Albert, who was part of "a USO stage show that's over here touring the foxholes. It sure felt good to talk to someone from Worcester—and a gal at that!"

When the war in Europe finally was over, he reported for the *Spiel* about all the guys who went from "living in foxholes to moving into hotels" as they waited for available transports back home. Many feared they would be shipped to the Pacific, where war was still raging, he reported. In his final columns for the *Spiel*, his fondest wishes remained for the health and safety of "the boys from the hill."

Real relationships. And, when the gregarious Papa Leo did get a transport home from Europe, his wounded leg still had not regained its full agility. It never would, but he kept moving anyway and because of his experience driving in Italy he found a job as a truck driver. He lived long enough to see me win my own war with stage IV cancer. I will never forget the day he came to the hospital where I received the treatment that eventually knocked out that first cancer. Papa Leo and Nana Rose had come to visit me that day—but he also began walking along my entire hallway in the hospital shaking the hand of every nurse and doctor in sight, thanking them sincerely for saving his grandson. His compassionate eye was always on the other men and women in the community around him.

What mattered? Papa Leo knew: caring relationships. That's also the core value my father embodied every day on the road, toting his big cases packed with the lines of shoes and boots he was selling to retailers.

"I've been working since I was 14," my father says. "After the war my father went back to work as a driver, but we really needed more money—so much so that I remember him taking me down to this Italian neighborhood when I was just 14. He got me a job lifting 50-pound bags of cement off trucks. I could do that for a while—but, I mean, you had to be a horse to keep doing that! So, instead, he got me a job as a stock boy in a shoe store and that's how I first got into shoes."

That early start at juggling various jobs on top of his schoolwork was training for the life my father would lead. He always took on as much work as was humanly possible. He managed to complete high school and college, the first in his family to go so far. As he began his own career, just like me years later, my father was eager to move farther westward—striking out for St. Louis to work for Brown Shoes, which was founded in the 1870s by another traveling salesman who was no relation to our family. That's why my twin sister and I were born in St. Louis. But my father chafed at Brown. His supervisors wouldn't unleash him as a salesman for a big enough region to fully support his new family. And there was one more problem.

"I ran into this problem a couple of times through the years," my father says. "When we did move back to Framingham, not too far from Worcester, my new shoe company was talking about giving me a region selling men's shoes way out around Kansas City or even down in Mississippi. The problem was my accent, you know? You can just imagine! I'd drive up to some shoe store in a small town in Mississippi and try to talk with the owner. Between his Southern accent and my Boston accent, we'd never understand each other."

I grew up with that accent myself but shed it many years ago as I packed up and left for California. But, hey, to be honest? It still comes out when I visit family. I'm talking about the famous Boston accent mainly known for its "No R" swagger. A classic line from the guys on public radio's *Cah Talk* was, "Go *pahk* the *cah* in *Hahvud Yahd*." But it's so much more than that. The accent is just the leading edge of a whole world we all know and love. Where I come from, things aren't just good, they're "wicked." You don't make a U-turn, you "bang a uey." If you're going out with the guys for the evening, you might just pick up some grindahs for suppah. We love our local institutions like Dunks and our teams: Sox, Celts and the B's. Of course, everybody where I grew up knows football rules all the other sports—so, of course we're talking about the Pats.

While my father initially felt that heavy accent constrained him to sales in New England—the truth is that he eventually branched out to land some big national accounts as well. Over time, the accent became more of a badge of honor than a handicap. That's notable because, to this day, one of the most common expressions of bias in America is a knee-jerk assumption about the way other people will speak. Doubt that? Just ask my African and Asian and Arab American friends. Eastern European immigrants and Jews? Yeah, we often face the same unspoken bias. However, for as long as I can remember—and as long as my father can remember—our family didn't "sound like" Eastern Europeans or Lithuanians or Jews, or whatever those accents were supposed to be in popular assumptions. Those stereotypes didn't apply. As far back as Papa Leo and his letters home to the *Spiel*, we all were just Americans like everybody else. To this day, some of my family still calls the Boston area home—and, yeah, we'll drop some R's sometimes when we get to telling stories. But, if we collectively sound like anything, we sound like the Walberg brothers, as all-American as can be.

We were living the American dream like the descendants of millions of World War II veterans. The house in Framingham that my father stretched his budget to buy for us looks like thousands of typical suburban homes. Just like Papa Leo made lifelong pals in his diverse neighborhood, I grew up just assuming I was making lifelong buddies with the white, Black, Catholic, Jewish and Protestant kids my age who lived a bike ride away from our house. I assumed it; and I did it. We kept our bonds strong and those friends came back to help save my life many years later—true story later in this book. Why did so many of them come around as I was growing up? Truth be told, I had a home field advantage. After my father stretched his budget even further to install an in-ground pool in the back yard, my friends' first choice of a gathering spot was usually our place. Our front porch, in Boston slang, became the neighborhood *parlah*. We were the local hangout home. All my friends were welcome. Our driveway often was a forest of bikes, so much so that my father sometimes had trouble getting in and out of the garage. That's where he parked the big Lincoln town car he drove on the road; that's also where he built his stockroom. He filled one entire wall of the garage with sturdy wooden shelves from floor to ceiling to hold hundreds of sample boots and shoes. Not pairs. Samples never came in pairs. All rights.

"I'm the guy who always gets rights," my father would say in amusement. "Why? I don't know! Maybe there's another salesman out there who always gets the lefts. But me? I lug rights around with me on the road."

My friends and I grew up with that wall of rights as a fixture in our lives as we scrambled all over the house and yard and pool. We always knew my father as "a shoe salesman," but the truth is that he worked multiple jobs. At one point, three jobs: selling shoes full time across the New England region Monday through Friday, plus selling retail on weekends at a local shoe store— and, on top of that, he added night shifts at the enormous Continental Bakery where Hostess cupcakes and Twinkies were made.

"Ahhh," my father now says in disgust. "That was probably a mistake. That was a young man's game, and I was a young man, you know? So, I tried it for a while. I was trying to get by on maybe four hours of sleep a night and that's no way to live for long. I knew that. But we had two kids and the mortgage and, you know, you do what you've got to do. And, fortunately, it didn't last too long. One night I was put in charge of one of the huge ovens they used at Continental and the truth is: I didn't watch the temperature right. I made a mistake and burned up more than 1,000 cupcakes. About a month after that, they let me go."

We love to laugh about the night Dad burned the cupcakes, because we all know cupcakes weren't his specialty. His talent to this day is sales, pure and simple. How many salesmen work all their lives purely on commission? Not many. That's old school. But my father pounded out a career like that, never taking a base salary.

"At first, Papa Leo worried about me," my father admits today. "I guess he was right to worry. At first, I wasn't making a lot of commission and there I was buying a house and getting in debt over my head, but I wanted what all American families wanted—and I made it happen, too."

Dad left an indelible impression on me about the nature of sales—and of living a good life.

"What's the first selling point?" he asks to this day. "It's me." He pauses and then he adds, "Me and the person I'm going to see. We build a relationship and it's because of that relationship that I can even get through the door in the first place and show them my samples. Then, it's the quality of the products and the ways we can work with people to make it affordable for them."

Occasionally tagging along with him, I heard a lot of those exchanges.

As soon as the door opened, we would hear a hearty, "*MASH*-al! *MASH*-al!" Soon followed by: "How're the twins? Oh, there's your son! He's getting big!"

My father would smoothly open his cases. He knew just how to handle them, stacking them against each other to produce the best display. As he worked, he described all the latest details that could close another sale. He also taught me another truth of the entrepreneurial life: For every success, there are a lot more failures. There are booms and there are busts. A lot of things we try to launch simply don't go anywhere—and a lot of the winning and losing is beyond our control.

"You remember the John Travolta movie *Urban Cowboy* back in 1980?" my father explains. "Remember all those Western bars. Mechanical bulls. Country music. Line dancing. We've still got some of that with us, today, but I'll tell you: Everybody in this country who was selling Western boots made a lot of money in those few years after *Urban Cowboy*. A lot of money. And then, line dancing? In the early '90s, that took off all over the country and millions of people—millions—wanted the right cowboy hat and boots. Those booms had nothing to do with the salesmen carrying boots—they just happened to us and they were a windfall. But then? Then there are years where people are going for other trends. I remember going to see a good friend of mine, a guy who I'd done a lot of business with over the years, and the first thing he says to me, before I can even open my cases, is, 'Marshall, this season, you know the money I'd use to buy your lines? This time, that money's going to buy these hot new brands of sneakers. I'm all in for the Nikes this season. I can't keep them in stock. I just can't help you this time.'

"Was there anything for me to do about that? No. He was a good business-man. He was being honest. I just didn't carry those lines. That year, I was out with him. And that's the way it is. Up and down. Up and down. But, you know, I went back to him later, when he was buying again. He was a good friend, even when he wasn't buying."

What my father couldn't abide was incivility. I'll never forget that lesson, either. One day in the summer, when I wasn't at school or at camp, he let me tag along on an extended road trip through upstate New York. Just the two of us on the road—and I loved it! In the middle of the trip, he had to make a particularly long detour to a tack shop way out in the country. We had to drive a couple of hours each way and the final stretch out there in horse country was along these muddy roads. The Lincoln was going to need a major wash after that. I can still see the rail fences and smell the manure. Finally, we got to the door of the tack shop—Dad toting his cases and me tagging along—and the woman who runs the tack shop holds up her hand toward us.

"Stop," she said. "I just don't have time today."

My father tried to say something and she cut him off with a curt, "Just leave your catalog on the counter. Thank you!" And she turned away. Just like that.

We walked silently back to the mud-encrusted Lincoln. Dad silently stowed his cases in the back. He was nodding his head like he was hashing over what he might have said. When we were buckled up and he slid the car into gear, he said to me simply, "Find the page for this place."

Everything was paper back then and I flipped to his page for the tack shop. "Take the pencil and write across that page NDG."

I had no idea what that meant, but I dutifully wrote the big block letters. Finally, as we bumped back along those muddy ruts, I asked, "What's it mean?"

He waited another moment, perhaps weighing his answer. "It means No Damned Good. That woman didn't think anything of wasting all my time and hours on the road. It wasn't even that valuable a sale, but I schlepped all the way up here at her request." He paused a moment more. "That's just not the way you treat people."

I looked into his face and he looked over, meeting my eyes. He simply repeated his words, "That's just not the way you treat people."

No, it's not. What's remarkable, though, is that even when he hit a day like that, I still loved what my father did for a living. Yes, there were bumps in the road, but I loved seeing his flexibility and initiative and this big network of friends he had all over the country. It was natural for me to fall into his footsteps. Of course, I didn't want to sell shoes. I wanted to sell technology. The exact line of products was not the issue—it was the way of life. The undergirding values I saw in his life—and the other lives who shone their light on me.

I've already told you about Bubby Bertha's shining light. What I haven't told you is the astonishing similarity of Bubby Bertha's oft-repeated lessons and those espoused by Roger Babson—wisdom that instantly made me feel at home at Babson College. The two of them could not have been more different. She was a poor Eastern European Jewish immigrant. He liked to boast that his wealthy evangelical Christian family stretched back 10 generations along the Atlantic coast of Massachusetts. They lived most of their adult lives just 30 miles from each other, west of Boston, although their social circles never so much as touched. But the values they both drew from their religious and cultural traditions? They taught the same basic truths.

Bubby Bertha taught that all of us are caretakers of God's world and building relationships to give back to others is what truly matters. What we think we own really isn't ours to begin with, she taught. "Found money is God's money" was just one of her slogans that distilled those truths into practical daily living. And that's precisely what Roger Babson loved to do. During his long life from 1875 to 1967, he wrote a whole shelf full of books.

In one of them, he wrote, "It is fundamental law, Whatsoever we sow that shall we also reap. Those who serve will be served. ... Those who boost will be boosted. ... We are forgiven as we forgive. If we are friends, we will make friends."

And in a line that could have come straight from Bubby Bertha's lips, Babson wrote, "We are paid in the coin that we give."

Had they ever met and had a chance to talk, Bubby Bertha would have liked this guy. Just like her, Babson had a passion for boiling his wisdom down into the simplest phrases he could devise, which he talked about frequently in public and even displayed on signs he set up around that region of Massachusetts. One of his favorites was just three words: "Prosperity follows service." He saw the world's greatest potential as a network of trusted, selfless friends who would boost each other and give even more than they received.

Roger Babson taught that it doesn't take much to shine a life-changing ray of hope into another person's life. Remember my story about Anneliese Glaubitz at the beginning of this chapter? Remember how I feared for her stubborn commitment to living in one of the nation's most expensive and competitive communities *before* she even had a lead on a job out there? I told you she's a success, which is true. But how did she land that job? How did she make her immediate dream come true?

The answer is: She had the talents and a solid skillset for the job. She won that job on her own merits. But how did she even know that job existed?

"It's true that I had my plans made before I even had a line on a job," she says. "Right after graduation, I just moved out there. But, as we all know, community is so important, especially in the entrepreneurial mindset. And I'm always looking beyond what I'm doing right now—thinking of what I could be doing in the future. Someday I'd like to help organize a nonprofit to help children, especially those who are challenged with mental health issues or eating disorders. But that's down the road someday. How did I find the company I'm working with right now? I met the owner through someone at Babson College. I kept in touch with my freshman year accounting professor, Michael Fetters, and he told me that, if I got out here to California and was looking for a job, he would introduce me. He did that. He knew the owner of my company. And I was lucky they were hiring when we were introduced and I had the right skillset."

A little ray of coast-to-coast sunlight from a friend illuminated Annaliese's next steps along her path.

Shining Brightly

Think about the key people in your life that made a positive impact on your life.

Say thanks. That's a powerful ray of sunshine.

Want more ideas? Visit my website, ShiningBrightly.com, and you will find "10 Ways to Say Thank You," fresh ideas for expressing gratitude and renewing friendships.

Although my memories of summer camp are as big and bright as a Technicolor movie, I have very few snapshots from Camp Milbrook. One shows me in my happy place, shooting hoops. The other shows our "DUKE" cabin, with counselor Marcus seated in the lower right corner and me waving as I stood to his right. By the late 1980s, I was training at another kind of camp, NCR's famous Sugar Camp, this time with a different kind of uniform: white shirts, ties and pens in our pockets. In 2019, Emily (previous page, at top) and I crested the volcanic Gros Piton on St. Lucia, a World Heritage Site. I'm wearing yet another kind of uniform: one of my trademark HB Strong shirts that I designed to capture the mental toughness it takes to conquer cancer.

3

Choosing Our Mentors

Some of the most important relationships in our lives are with mentors.

Recently, I set out on a daylong hike up an especially steep mountain in the tropics with my college-age daughter Emily. That's when I discovered she already knows what it means to serve as a mentor. The hike started with a stern warning from my daughter—not something I expected to hear. And, to be honest, not something I wanted.

"You don't have to make this climb," she said bluntly. "I can do it alone. You can go back and spend the day on the beach. Remember that I do this kind of thing all the time, and I definitely want to make this climb. But I could go on alone. You could stop before we get too far into this."

"No! No!" I protested, laughing. "Piece of cake. Don't worry about me. This is nothing."

"It's not nothing," she said, shaking her head. "I gotta be honest with you, Dad: When you talk like that, it annoys me. I'm trying to help you—to warn you. I know what I'm doing here. This is going to be hard. This is going to hit you. This is going to hurt you. Your muscles are going to ache for days."

"I know, I get it. You're worried about me. I'm an amateur," I said—and I still thought I was joking with her. "I get it: You're the professional tripper, now."

I didn't quit. We kept hiking and, to avoid more warnings, I got her talking about all the work she had to complete to become a certified leader of multi-day trips for children into some of northern Michigan's wildest regions. As a child, she had been a summer camper at Michigan's Camp Tamarack for many years, then she made the transition to counseling and eventually was qualified to serve as a leader supervising wilderness immersion experiences: a tripper. The previous summer, she had served as a tripper on five of these outings with kids.

"I had to learn a lot," she recalled. "I'm lifeguard certified. I'm wilderness first-aid certified. I've learned about assessing medical issues in the wild, using epi pens, even suturing wounds. I've learned to purify water, set up a camp, cook. And we practice leave-no-trace camping, so I'm in charge of making sure we clean and clear any sites where we've stopped. We don't even leave toilet paper behind. And, when we hike, I've always got the heaviest pack on my back. You know, I'm going out with 12-year-old kids and they can't carry everything we need on their backs. So I'm packing like 75 pounds or so—including all the pots and pans and extra food. And then, on top of all that, what I'm really in charge of is making sure these kids have a meaningful experience in the woods. This job is not just about taking them out and bringing them back again. We want these kids to build positive memories they'll hold onto and share with others. We're constantly teaching them as we go—not only stuff like how to start a fire, purify water, clean a campsite and all that—but about how to find deeper meaning in their lives."

"Reminds me of when I went to camp," I said. "At camp, you really do learn a lot about life—and today? An even bigger issue as you lead your groups is teaching about environmental sustainability. I love how you embrace that and teach it to your campers."

"A lot of what I do as a tripper involves seizing every opportunity to help the kids think about their lives and the world in new ways," Emily said. "Like, when the trails are wide enough, we hike with two people side by side. I tell the counselors who are on the trip with me to think of questions they can ask the kids as we walk like that—questions to get them thinking, get them talking. Like, one question I ask is, 'If today was the last day of your life, what legacy would you leave behind?'"

Even as she said this, that life-and-death question surprised me. I thought: Now, that's a question asked by a young woman who has suffered through her own years of wondering if someone she loves—meaning me—might suddenly die of cancer. Based on her experience, Emily assumed that was a natural question to ask kids. It didn't occur to her that was a mature-beyond-her-years issue.

We kept hiking along that Caribbean mountain trail, and Emily kept describing her experiences as a tripper: "You know, there is a lot on your shoulders as a tripper and I don't just mean the weight of your pack. Trip after trip, you're ultimately responsible for everything. Sure, you've got other counselors along on the trip to help you, but ultimately the responsibility is all on your shoulders. You're the one who deals with the rangers, paying for the permits, choosing campsites, making sure the water's safe and there's enough food. You don't want anyone to get sick or hurt, or worse. Everyone depends on you."

I finally spoke up. "You really ask 12-year-old kids questions like: If today was your last day—?"

"Yeah, of course," she continued. "They want to talk about that."

"They talk about something so deep?"

"Oh, yeah. They talk. And you want these kids to come back with memories and insights that they'll think about for a long time after that. They want to talk about stuff like that, which is why we ask those questions," she said. "One of the most meaningful experiences I had last summer was up on North Manitou Island off the northwest coast of Michigan. Our group was miles away from anyone else, climbing up toward this high bluff that overlooks Lake Michigan. We planned to camp on the bluff and watch the sun set right in front of us. But, that afternoon before sunset, we all went down into the lake. We were out in the water together and I said, 'Now, I want everyone to hold hands.' And they made this big circle so they could link hands. I said, 'Now, we're each going to think about something in our lives that we wish we could leave behind—something we wish was gone, or something that just doesn't serve us in a good way any longer, something that holds us back, something negative. OK? So, just focus on that thing you wish was gone from your life. Channel that feeling. And, when I count down, we're all going to hold hands, then we're going to go down underwater together—and we're going to let all those negative things wash away from us as the waves roll over our heads. Ready?' And I led them through it. We all went down. Those Lake Michigan waves swept all around us and over us. And, when we came back up again, I mean: wow. Some of those kids were crying. Even afterward as they talked to me about that experience, they were crying about it in a good way. That meant a lot to them. It was a memory I know some of them will hold onto for a long time.

"One girl was really moved by that. I wound up giving her one of my bracelets as a reminder and she wears it to this day. Those connections meant a lot to them. Some of the kids started following me on Instagram and texting me. I realized that, even at 12 years old, these kids can attach themselves to you, if you care about them and help them to get in touch with their own lives. It's an important role with a lot of responsibility. Back at the dining hall at camp, for instance, they would run up to me and hug me and want me to come over to share something with their friends from their cabin. You know, they'd say something like, 'It's the birthday for a girl in my cabin, so come have cake with us. Please? Please?' And you begin to appreciate how serious these relationships have become, because it means so much to them. You're forever a part of their lives."

She went on. But my own memories had jumped back more than 40 years to when I was that kid looking up in awe to my own camp counselors. As Emily kept talking, I was shaking my head and grinning. "This sounds so familiar. *Sooo* familiar," I said softly.

I never became a tripper myself, but I was an avid summer camper for seven years starting when I was just 8 years old—back in the era when Bill Murray and Ivan Reitman were making the quintessential summer camp movie, *Meatballs*. Murray's decision to play the charismatic camp counselor, whose name was Tripper, was his first appearance in a movie after leaving *Saturday Night Live*. Now, we know that risk paid off and paved the way for all those later hits from *Stripes* to *Ghostbusters*. But back when they were producing *Meatballs*, Paramount wasn't so sure how well Murray would play in this summer camp comedy. They wanted to ensure its success. So, as the producers were rolling out their marketing campaign in the summer of 1979, our entire summer camp was bused to a special East Coast promotional screening of the movie to help build a word-of-mouth buzz in our part of the country. This was old-school marketing decades before the internet and social media. We were thrilled! We loved seeing what amounted to our own stories played out on that big screen. Then, a lot of the antics in *Meatballs* sprang to life back at our camp. Until that movie, nobody at our Camp Milbrook had thought of pranking a counselor by putting his bed up in the branches of a tree. It was such a hilarious stunt that everybody soon was scheming ways to pull off that feat at our camp.

A lot of what had been purely fiction in *Meatballs* soon was hot on the trail of becoming fact at our beloved Milbrook. What made the movie such a huge hit with us was that the truth of our experience already was there on screen. Just like Murray's Tripper was a kind of angelic troublemaker in the movie—leading his merry band of counselors and campers through all kinds of adventures—I was determined to become an angelic troublemaker myself. But, let me also be clear about one thing: While Murray wound up as a hero and in some ways a model for a lot of us, he wasn't our mentor. He was just a character in a movie.

Mentors play real hands-on roles in our lives. By the time I saw that movie at the big preview screening, I already had chosen my own mentors at Milbrook, two guys who I regarded as rock stars. In fact, these guys actually played rock stars in one of our favorite annual evening programs at camp, an air-guitar, lip-sync rock concert complete with special event T-shirts the counselors made for us to make those special occasions complete.

Let me set the stage: Most of the kids who lived in my neighborhood did not go to camp all summer like my sister, Cheryl, and I did. On the East Coast, at least, Jewish families were more likely to send their kids to summer camp. Now that I've spent years in leadership in Jewish communities across the country, I understand the data about this. What experiences are most likely to build a sense of Jewish identity in future generations? We know that outcome is more likely if there is some Jewish school experience in childhood, a Jewish camping experience, and later a trip to Israel. Those three things are formative. Although my parents weren't very religiously observant, they were determined to maintain this particular summertime custom. So, they looked for affordable sleepaway programs we would enjoy. For my part, I didn't have a clue about strategies for building formative experiences. I was just a kid who loved camp. My first summer, when I was only 8, my parents tested the idea with a four-week option, then I begged them to let me stay at Camp Clark on Cape Cod for an additional two weeks. They agreed. Clearly, I was hooked. By age 12, the summer of the *Meatballs* preview, I was dreaming about June, every year. When school let out, each year, I knew I had a week or so to pack up my trunk for camp. I would spend eight weeks at the main camp—then my parents let me add on a ninth week with a special focus on basketball. Milbrook wasn't a Jewish camp, although its owner Norman Frank was Jewish. In fact, a personal Jewish connection got me into the camp in the first place, because Norman's daughter Carolyn attended Hebrew school with me, and middle school buddy Scott Ober went and recommended it to me. Because we had that connection, before my parents formally enrolled me at Camp Milbrook, Dad drove me over to Norman's house to talk about the camp. By coincidence, that's when I first met my Milbrook mentors Marcus Brown and Al Lyons. They just happened to be leaving Norman's house when we arrived. I was impressed at the first sight of these guys. I can't even remember what Dad and Norman talked about, but, that summer, I went to Milbrook and I came to idolize Marcus and Al.

Marcus, the only African American counselor at the camp, was in charge of my cabin. Al was in charge of another cabin and had various specialties around the camp, including teaching our soccer sessions. At Milbrook, we always were learning something, mainly about sports. Day would start at 7:15 a.m. with an old recording of reveille blasting from every speaker in camp. We'd line up, raise the flag, go have breakfast. Every camper had work assignments that rotated. Sometimes, for example, we served as waiters or cleaned up trash, swept and so on. Then, the main part of the day was divided into five periods for activities. One period might be with Al up at the soccer field, or over at the archery range or down at the waterfront. There were activities every hour of the day, except for an afternoon rest period. The littler kids went to sleep at night an hour or two before the older kids, which is when we had the best chance to interact with the counselors. Your overall experience really did depend on the inventiveness of the counselors; and Marcus and Al were two of the best. When it rained, for instance, Marcus didn't let us sit around the cabin and get into mischief. He would set up a makeshift, indoor tennis tournament for us and, despite the rain, we still had fun all day long. But my respect for these guys was based on more than fun and games. These guys talked to us about deep stuff—just like Emily does with her campers today.

My experiences with those guys led me to the natural assumption, years later, that I should look for mentors when I started working for NCR. I was attracted to NCR because the company's reputation for innovation stretched back more than a century. The initials originally stood for National Cash Register back in the 1880s when those machines were revolutionizing the country. By the time I was hired for a paid internship as a Babson student in the 1980s, NCR already was on the cutting edge of helping companies to replace their old mechanical systems with powerful new digital services. This was an ideal opportunity for me, because I always knew that I wanted to go into sales like Dad, but not shoes or other retail merchandise. I wanted to sell technology. That was the future. In fact, I was so eager to get in the door at NCR that I gave up playing on Babson's basketball team to take my first paid internship—and that was a serious sacrifice for me because I love basketball. Initially, the company assigned me to the hospitality division as a sales installation representative who would train the staff at bars and restaurants to switch from pen-and-paper to digital systems. For a college student, this was a great job that also paid my mileage and expenses and sent me all over six New England states and occasionally to other parts of the U.S. Our transformations ranged from tiny mon-and-pop joints all the way up to major national chains. Here I was, this kid in a suit and tie, landing in the middle of some café or bar or restaurant or hotel with new equipment, new software and my specialized knowledge about how to use it all. While I was on the installation, I was the guy in charge of making sure things went smoothly. Everyone from the owners and managers to the bartenders, cooks and servers looked to me to help them turn their business around in just a couple of weeks. It was challenging, but also tons of fun. Among other things, I ate better than any other student I knew. Every night, the manager would pack up a doggie bag for me as a way of showing thanks and appreciation.

By the time I graduated from Babson, I had been carefully watching the NCR staff long enough to know that I didn't want to work full time in hospitality. The hours were way too long, running into the wee hours of the morning. The company's other top salespeople were over in the bank data services division. These guys were selling and servicing important accounts to bring banks and credit unions into the digital age—or at least the first wave of digital outsourced services. Truth be told, at that point, we still were transitioning from punch cards to modems that would seem like snails today. Nevertheless, the data services division of NCR seemed to be making the future happen, making their clients more automated, profitable and making a lot of money for NCR—and themselves—in the process. That's where I wanted to work.

Just like I realized Marcus and Al were rock stars, I could see that same light shining from potential mentors when I moved into that data services division. NCR culture was founded on that idea that the best employees were carefully trained at the company's Dayton, Ohio, headquarters—then we were put out into the field with seasoned veterans looking over our shoulders. In short, NCR encouraged mentoring relationships.

To double check my memories, I looked up my first mentor: Michael Brennan, who supervised my work when I started full time at NCR in January 1988. I found Mike online and invited him to talk on Zoom. When Mike's face first appeared on my screen, I jumped at the chance to sincerely express my thanks. "Mike, I hope you know how much you influenced me," I began. "You took me under your wing when I barely knew what I was doing. I worked as hard as I did partly because I did not want to let you down."

"Well, you added a lot to our team," he said. "You were this hard-charging young guy and you had good ideas about the challenges we all were facing at that time. And you did what we told you to do."

"Yeah," I laughed. "That was my job at first: Work hard, soak it up and do what I was told."

"There was a lot to learn—for all of us," Mike said. "NCR had always been known for their machines, these physical devices we'd deliver. The big change in the 1980s was we were learning how to sell intangibles, what we called 'data center services' at the time, which was the best we could do back then without today's internet and cloud services. We were selling services that we would push out to these banks over modems from one of our computer centers. We were meeting with bank executives and trying to sell them something that was hard to explain—and for some of them could sound pretty boring if we did try to explain it. So, we usually would try to reach a point when we could physically host them at our data center. Once we got them on our home court and they could walk around and see real equipment, we could close the sale. We'd give them detailed presentations, demonstrations and a tour and show off our rows of mainframes, spinning tape drives and blinking lights."

"Oh, yeah, the dog-and-pony show at the data center," I said. "I remember that very well. You knew you were close to a sale if you could get them to the data center."

"Yeah, each of us had a little different way of making those sales, but we all brought people in for those dog-and-pony shows. The bankers loved to see those tape drives spin and those lights blink," Mike said. "As salespeople, I remember we used to talk a lot among ourselves about this challenge. Only the best salespeople can sell something intangible like this kind of new technology. The truth is, most of the executives who were making these decisions didn't understand and didn't care about how that technology actually worked on the back side. So, how could we make those sales? We'd have to really get into their shoes, walk around with them and understand the issues they faced everyday with their employees and clients at the bank. You had to find the functions in the system that would make their lives better—and make their clients' lives better, too. We had to figure out what parts of our new technology really would improve their workday. If we could do that—and Howard, you learned along with us how to do that—then we weren't pushing something on them that they didn't understand. We weren't *selling* them. We were making their lives a little easier in ways they could actually see while using the computer screen in front of them. And that's truly the mark of a great salesperson. Your customers don't feel you're selling them something; they know you're helping them. Big difference."

"I saw how you did that, and I wanted to be just like you," I said. "I got to know you and I admired what you had: a great job, a great family. You seemed to have such a perfectly balanced life."

Mike held up his hand, cutting me off. "Well, you are right about how we really were a little family at NCR, at that time. But what you just said is very important and it isn't always true, if we're honest. The truth is: We never are completely in balance and that's one of the biggest things we all have to keep learning and watching in our lives."

I nodded my head. "I learned that firsthand, soon enough."

"That's right," he said. "When you got sick, you know—" His voice trailed off as he pondered what he wanted to say, then he began again. "I don't know if we, as a team, worked you too hard. I wonder—" Then, he stopped once more.

When he spoke again, his voice was slower. "Let me just say this because I think it's very important if you're telling these stories in your book to help readers. I've thought a lot about this question of balance. It's so important. In life, we've got to start by admitting this: We're all imperfect. Yes, we can agree on what truly should be important in our lives: things like our family, our religion, our friends, our work. But too many times when we're working on high-stakes projects, the demands of work can get way out of balance. Then, if we're going to survive, we've got to realize what's happening in the first place. We've got to recognize something is wrong. That's really the hardest part. Then, we've got to draw ourselves back and rebalance what we're doing with our lives. It's not easy."

"No, it's not," I said.

Then, he said, "You know, looking back more than 30 years later, it really was a golden time. We had a lot of fun. We made a lot of sales. We learned a lot together."

I thought about my talk with Mike for a long time. The truth is that mentoring relationships work both ways. Mentors and mentees leave indelible marks on each other. Then, that made me want to dig back even further into my history with mentors. Could I find Marcus and Al from my Milbrook days more than 40 years ago? Would they remember me? Had our time together at camp made any lasting difference in their lives? With social media, finding them wasn't hard. I was anxious at first because I only went to Camp Milbrook for three summers. I was pleasantly surprised when they both immediately agreed to come on Zoom with me to reminisce about Camp Milbrook.

"You guys were the coolest cats!" I told them when they came up on my computer screen. "When I was a kid, I really looked up to you guys. But I wonder: I was just one kid. Do you remember me? Do you even remember much about Camp Milbrook?"

"Are you kidding?" Marcus said, laughing heartily. "Do I remember those days? Well—yeah! I have to be careful who I say this to now, but Milbrook was the happiest time of my life. That's where I decided to devote my whole life to working with kids and, now, I've just retired as a school principal. I care so much about this that I even wrote a whole illustrated book for kids full of funny stories about things like how to deal with bullies. Everything in the book is based on real stories I've experienced with kids all these years, including at Camp Milbrook. Because I'm a retired principal, my book is set in a fictional elementary school that I've called Milbrook School. Same name! So, in a way, I've never left Milbrook behind. Since I finished the book, I've even led school programs for teachers and kids using those stories to entertain them, first, and then to teach them some important truths. And, you know what? They get it. These are universal stories, and the kids recognize them right away."

Al chimed in next. "Camp Milbrook was just as big a turning point for me as it was for Marcus. It helped me to finally come out of my shell," he said. "You see, I grew up with two older brothers who were the best athletes in town. I was just an average athlete in terms of my natural abilities, so I learned to work a hundred times harder to compensate. And, even after all that work, I was never going to be better than my brothers. Then, at Camp Milbrook, I was finally out from under the shadow of my brothers."

"How'd you guys wind up at Milbrook?" I asked and their stories quickly connected back to Norman Frank. Just like me, they had personal connections with the Frank family.

"You're probably wondering specifically how I wound up as the only Black counselor," Marcus said. "It's because my father worked for Honeywell back in the '60s and he was assigned to work in Boston on a temporary assignment. Just like today, big companies like Honeywell would put their employees up in hotels for temporary assignments, but this was the '60s and there were still racial barriers. Black employees and their families were placed with other Black families for these temporary assignments. So, they matched us with a family where one of the boys already had been going to Milbrook as a camper. The mom we were staying with worked for Norm Frank. So, I got an invitation through that family. We had moved on by the time summer rolled around, but I flew back to go to Milbrook as a camper. I was in the oldest cabin at that time. I was 15 and I made friends right away with this kid who was nearly 15. That was Al. This was a whole new world to me. I'd never been to a camp with that level of sheer camaraderie. There wasn't a lot of negative stuff we had to deal with at Milbrook. It seemed like all you had to worry about was how much fun you were going to have the next day. So, I just kept going back as long as I could, every summer. I followed the typical steps in camping. I became a counselor-in-training. The truth is, I wasn't the greatest counselor when I first started. I wasn't mentally prepared for it. But by the time I was finishing high school and then I was in college—by then, I was more mature and I was pretty good at it. I understood that my focus was on the kids and making sure they were learning something while they were having a great time."

"Tell him about *Meatballs*," Al said to Marcus.

Marcus looked at me with a sheepish grin. "OK, well, I have to explain this, first. Back in the day, Al and I used to joke that we managed to get through the other 10 months of each year just so we could be back at camp for those two months every summer. Other counselors were going to Milbrook just to make some money for school—or maybe just to kill time in the summer months. For Al and me, Milbrook was our purpose in life."

"So, tell him about *Meatballs,*" Al said.

"Well, every year on what would have been the first day of camp, I take out my copy of *Meatballs* and I watch it again. I've been doing this long enough that I still have an old VHS tape of the movie. Late June rolls around and my family's probably sick of it at this point, but they know: Dad's got to watch *Meatballs* again."

Al also had a family connection to Norm Frank. "The experience was great because we really could see what was possible in our own lives. Pretty quickly, Marcus was known as the best basketball player at camp and I was the big soccer guy. Of course, I had the advantage that not as many people were playing soccer at that level back then. It was fun to be the big men on campus. But you know what really made this such a huge part of our lives?"

"The friendships we made," Marcus said.

"The friendships," Al said. "In fact, we helped to change the camp rules so that these friendships would deepen. When we first got there, Norm had this rule that no counselor could have the same kids in their cabin two years in a row. He did that because he thought it was a way to guard against the turnover in counselors. If a counselor moved on, Norm thought their regular kids wouldn't want to come back again. We convinced Norm to change that rule."

"There still were some counselors who would show up for one summer and never come back, but we worked hard to encourage people to keep coming back," Marcus said. "This may surprise you, but we're still in touch with people we knew back then."

"Oh, the magic of Facebook!" I said. Then, we talked about the Camp Milbrook Facebook page, which is the gathering place for alumni now that the camp no longer operates. We love seeing posts from former counselors and some of Marcus' and Al's friends: Steve Nussbaum, Darrow Fontera, Donnie Veneto. Plus, Kate Brannum, Paolo Massara, Bill Brannum, Kathleen Tsouprake-De Hart, Stacey Bergman-Thal, Harlan Coben—and former campers: Todd Guber, Jimmy Guber, Rise Fanger, Miriam Sittenfeld, Betty Sittenfeld, Russ Goldman, Keith Blechner, Scott Ober, Jay Silver, Carolyn Frank-Brombacher, Wendy Weinstein Karp, Jill Litman-Weiner and so many more.

"Not a week goes by that I don't talk to someone from those days," Al said. "In fact—a lot like Marcus was just describing about his life—there are lessons I learned at Milbrook that are a part of my life to this day. Learning to be a counselor at Milbrook was all about learning how to help kids navigate a competitive sports environment—competing and persevering and accepting the losses and then keep going in a resilient way. And that's what I do for a living today. I own and run a gymnastic school with a special focus on resilience and balance in life. It's called Junior Gym in Van Nuys, California. What sets us apart is that we tell families from the start: We're not the win-at-any-cost people. There's a lot more in life and in sports than winning."

"That's a direct outcome of those years at Milbrook," Marcus said. "I really admire what Al has done there."

"Well, it goes back to the fact that I was never going to be the star athlete," Al said. "I was always the average player who worked my ass off because I loved sports, but the most important lessons you can learn in sports aren't what it feels like to win every time. The most important lessons are about how you feel when you're knocked on your butt over and over again by life—and you've got to find the strength and purpose to get up again."

As Al was talking, I could tell where he was heading—just like Mike Brennan had looped around in our conversation until he reached my cancer.

Just like Mike, Al's voice slowed and filled with emotion. "Howard, if you're telling these stories in the book, you've got to let people know that's part of the secret of your miracle strength against cancer. You knew that getting kicked in the butt is a part of life—whatever it is that hits you, we all get hit hard at some point in life. And the purpose of life is learning how to keep getting back up again. For a good life, we've got to learn resilience—and resilience begins with having the right kind of teachers and friends."

"Thank you guys," I told them. "I mean, I can't really thank you enough, but: Thank you."

"Well, we're still honored to be part of your life," Marcus said. "We mean what we're saying."

"Want some proof of that?" Al said. "I'm sending you a photo of the mission statement we have posted in big letters on the wall of our gym."

The photo came through: "Our mission is to teach children of all ages, through both the sport of gymnastics as well as a comprehensive fitness program, many valuable life skills including perseverance, resiliency and sportsmanship, to take with them as they grow into fitness-conscious, healthy, confident adults. ... It is in this very decision to focus on life lessons over a 'win-at-any-cost' mentality that we set ourselves apart from other gymnastics schools and training centers."

What I discovered in talking with Mike, Marcus and Al is that mentoring was as powerful for them as it was for me.

As I spent a year looking across my life in preparation for writing this book, my appreciation for mentors kept moving earlier and earlier into my childhood. I've always benefitted from great mentors and, when I'm working with groups in seminars or at conferences, I stress the importance of wisely choosing your mentors. To business professionals, I explain, "Babson teaches us as entrepreneurs to look for mentors. Life is a team sport." If I'm adapting a seminar for community service leaders, I'll say, "Combatting hate is a team sport. Fundraising is a team sport." And, all of that is true.

Until I spent this year delving deeply into my past, I typically would talk about those first mentors at NCR as my formative experience in life. But the truth is, we can serve as mentors in many ways. Marcus and Al were powerful mentors. In fact, stretching back even further in my life, Mom and Dad were mentors and, of course, that's a nearly universal truth we all share. For better or worse, parents form our personalities. How many of us, especially when we become parents ourselves, find words coming from our mouths that we once heard at home as kids. I was lucky enough to have wonderful role models in my family stretching all the way back to my grandparents and great-grandparents.

Whether your formative years were shaped by wonderful or problematic adults, almost everyone has some mentor—some guiding relationship in their life. Hopefully, you can remember and appreciate someone who shone a bright light at a time you needed that encouragement.

Perhaps you are in a mentoring relationship right now—and have not even thought about it in those terms. Especially if you have learned from a memorable mentor, at some point in your life, you can certainly go and do likewise. You can become a mentor to someone else.

Who were your mentors? Have you reached out to them, lately? You might be surprised at what's possible with social media today.

Who have you mentored?

Who could you mentor?

Shining Brightly

More than 14 million children and adults enjoy summer camps each year, ranging from day programs to overnight camping, according to the American Camp Association. All camps took a hit during the pandemic but camping remains a hugely popular part of family life nationwide. At camp, children grow, explore and learn about themselves and the people and world around them—and they have fun throughout the entire process. Now, thousands of camps also offer specialized programs that extend beyond sports into the arts, vocational and technical skills.

Consider these widely shared benefits of summer camp:

+ Develop skills and strengthen talents

+ Enjoy sports

+ Learn skills from swimming to sailing and arts and crafts

+ Gain independence

+ Disconnect from digital devices

+ Connect with nature

+ Build teamwork, leadership and communication skills

+ Have fun

Consider helping a child you know make it to camp next summer. They will enjoy many adventures while making new friends and lasting memories. And, someday, they may return to tell you: "Thanks!"

The NCR World Headquarters in Dayton, Ohio, once was a dream destination for young entrepreneurs. In 1989, I was so proud to have reached that landmark that I posed with my red Pontiac Grand Am, so my mother Nancy could get this snapshot for the family back home. We shared this proud moment just weeks before my first diagnosis of stage IV cancer. This once world-famous NCR landmark later closed, remained vacant for years and eventually was repurposed as a building for the University of Dayton.

4

I Met Death

I did not see death coming.

My life after Babson College seemed as sweet as the Sugar Camp training program at NCR that launched me into a promising career with top mentors like Mike Brennan. Yet, within a matter of months, I tumbled from a plum assignment on digital disaster planning for NCR Corporation's Data Services Division—to sitting across a table from my friend David Herman with a legal pad between us, trying earnestly to handwrite my will at age 23.

The irony was that my promotion at NCR was to take the lead in selling a cutting-edge product called "911." This was in 1989. So, it was long before September 11, 2001, and the domestic terrorist attack on the U.S. Launching 911 was a brilliant next step in digital migration for NCR's banking industry customers and I was in on the ground floor of rolling it out nationwide. Once companies committed to new digital systems, they needed to have a government mandated electronic disaster plan for what might happen to all of their buildings, people, assets and data if catastrophe struck. Pick up a phone and dial 911? That would bring police and firetrucks to the disaster site, but it wouldn't recover a company's most valuable digital assets. NCR was offering a solution to make that happen and I was assigned to crisscross the country selling those unique services. At least, they were unique at the time. This was more than a decade before anyone was talking about cloud backups. NCR's offering at the time was for banks to periodically fly and truck in backup tapes and microfiche and lock those materials in secure vaults. Bank executives wanted to book a space in the vaults so they could sleep at night and summon the tapes and only lose one days' worth of data and transaction history.

Because I already had shown initiative and successful sales numbers as a salesman with Mike Brennan's team, I was chosen to become the 911 guy. I loved it. My initial sales presentations to clients showed huge promise. When I stood up and explained to bank executives and boards of directors everything that could happen if disaster struck their bank, I could see them feeling the chills and getting ready to sign up for the program. I had a strong sales pitch. In business, everyone wants to be ready—*needs* to be ready—if that rare but fatal lightning bolt strikes, right?

Well, everyone but me.

Naturally, I was entirely consumed with all the possibilities NCR was laying out on the horizon for me. That laser focus started right after I finished Babson and ended my college internship with NCR in the Hospitality Services Division. Based on my record as an intern, I was able to land a full-time job with NCR Corporation's Bank Data Services Division. I was thrilled to be hired by District Manager Chuck Sterling, who assigned me to support the best and most successful senior account executives: Robert Elliott, Kent Kasica, Richard Talentino and Mike. After I started full time, NCR had me shadow Mike and the team for a couple of weeks, then I was sent to Sugar Camp near the corporate campus headquarters in Dayton, Ohio, for six months of advanced industry, product and presentation training. Today, that storied educational center—the world's first sales training program when NCR founder John H. Patterson established it in 1894—no longer exists. AT&T acquired NCR in 1991 and Sugar Camp closed down a decade later. That whole transition deeply saddened me, because the vision of NCR's founder was a lot like Roger Babson's view of our vocations. Both men understood that the key to success was investing in people. Patterson was way out ahead of his peers in deciding to provide an extensive base of training for his sales force. At a time when other business leaders thought it was a waste of money, Patterson started his in-house school in the 1890s. He could feel it in his bones that proper preparation would produce the best, most-resourceful generation of self-starters the country had ever seen. That was Babson's vision, too, when he started his college in 1919. Why was Patterson's school called Sugar Camp? At first, Patterson tried to hold his classes in a cramped cottage on his family farm in Dayton. Then, when his first graduates proved the value of such training, he greatly expanded the program along a hillside grove of maple trees where his family once made syrup. The first accommodations on that hillside were tents with wooden floors, but his vision was as grand as Babson's was out in Massachusetts. Patterson wasn't merely giving a brief orientation to business. This was NCR's University Under Canvas. By the 1930s, the tents gave way to wooden cabins. Some historians say that completing Sugar Camp in its heyday was the equivalent of earning an MBA. In the 1940s, this already prestigious center took on an even greater reputation for cutting-edge research and development when the U.S. Navy centered one of its top-secret teams developing new forms of coding at NCR with the participants living in the Sugar Camp cabins. To say that Sugar Camp was "storied" is an understatement. I was thrilled when I was sent there to start my career and I quickly made lifelong friends, including David Herman.

To help tell the story of what happened next, I enlisted Dave Herman, or "Herms", via Zoom. Like everyone else I contacted in my yearlong journey to research this book, he was happy to talk over both the good and the bad times we shared.

"Let's start with why we became friends almost immediately," he said. "What made us so close was that I realized you could keep a secret."

"I remember that," I said, laughing. "I kept the secret about your family. You were trying to make it through Sugar Camp incognito. Your father was Don Herman, executive vice president of NCR's Network Products Division right there in Dayton, but you didn't want anyone else in this training program to know about that inside connection. You wanted to do this entirely on your own."

"Hey, I did get the job on my own. I didn't get any special favors," he said. "Dad didn't even know I had applied—until after I got the job. Still, I didn't want the other guys in the training program to think I was some insider. I thought no one would know about my father, but somehow you figured out the family connection. That's how our story really begins: On our first day at Sugar Camp, Howard, you started kidding me in this cocky way. You said to me, 'Herms, I know you've got a secret, but I'm cool. I won't say a word. It's in my vault.'"

"Did I say that?" I asked. "In my vault?"

"Yeah, I'll never forget those words and, at first, that actually annoyed me. Then, I realized: Hey, this is a good guy. And to your credit, Howard, you kept that secret. I'm very serious about this. Here's what I tell people about you: 'One of the things I've always admired about Howard—one of the reasons I was drawn to him in the first place and that we've become such good friends— is that he had this cocky confidence that made you want to hang around with him. And, at the same time, he also had this real integrity in his friendships.' That's what I say. Everything that has happened in our lives since that first encounter on that first day really hangs on those two things. That's become the story of our friendship: Over the years, I've wound up doing a lot to help support you, Howard, in the tough times—and you have helped to support me in a lot of my own tribulations over the years, too. That's the essence of true friendship, supporting each other through whatever life throws at you."

"Well, at first, we had no idea of what was coming, did we? It was exciting to be at Sugar Camp but I was fresh out of college and you were transitioning to NCR from a banking role. As you learned about me, I was all about work hard and play hard!"

"Let's not underestimate it. A lot of important training and skill building happened, too," Dave said. "But, yeah, the truth was we were young and had nothing to worry about back then. Sugar Camp was just amazing, and it truly was a lot of fun, as well. It was a great place to make friends you'd keep through the years. We got quite close, then—and we kept in touch. I wound up based in Florida as part of the same banking services division of NCR as your team up in the Northeast. Then, when I heard the news that you'd become this big specialist selling the new 911 disaster recovery product across the country—I was thrilled for you. And that's why it was such a huge shock to see you at the airport the first time you flew down to Florida to make some 911 sales calls with me."

"I wasn't at my best when I flew down there," I admitted. "I was so unprepared for that first encounter with death that, to be honest, I downplayed the obvious signs that something was wrong to the point of—well, of flat-out lying about it to myself, to you and to everyone around me."

I was in complete shock and denial. This is the point in our story when I first was experiencing one of the hardest truths to learn about cancer: This disease can absolutely shatter your life in ways far beyond the physical impact. Today, when I describe this first life-and-death encounter to other cancer patients, caregivers and support groups, I use phrases like "a deer caught in the headlights" and "Humpty Dumpty shatters." They're all true.

In my case, cancer literally popped out of nowhere. As I've said, I was focused on the sweetness of life. I was thrilled to have been selected as lead sales executive for the nationwide rollout of 911, which included a relocation to the Dayton headquarters. I was ready to enjoy this next chapter in my life after college. For example, until that point, I had driven big old clunky hand-me-down cars that I got from relatives. Now I wanted a youthful car, a single guy's car, nothing fancy but something nice. So, Dad and I went to the Pontiac dealership in Framingham, Massachusetts, and I spotted this beautiful magenta-red Grand Am with a gray interior and mag wheels. That's the car

I wanted; that was how I was thinking about my future at that point. When it was time to move to Dayton, I shipped some of my clothes ahead of me, then I filled the Grand Am with everything else and headed out on a two-day drive with a one-night stop at a motel in Pittsburgh. No smartphones back then. I had a leather briefcase beside me in the passenger seat and was blaring Aerosmith, Queen and Guns N' Roses on cassette tapes as I drove.

Somewhere on the Pennsylvania Turnpike, I noticed this annoying little bump on my left cheek. I thought it was just a pimple or some other kind of skin irritation, but it bothered me. I remember thinking that I'd need to get a good look at that in the motel mirror, that night, and maybe put something on it. In an otherwise uneventful trip, that little spot was the only irritation. I managed to push it out of my mind. The next day, when I reached Dayton, I dove into the whirlwind headfirst. I began working extremely long hours, living out of a hotel room for the first couple of weeks. In advance, I had arranged for Mom to come out a couple of weeks after I arrived to help me lease an apartment and get my new place cleaned up and organized. I didn't have enough time to do all that myself and she was eager to visit.

"But I was not happy at all when I saw you!" Mom said as she described that meeting at the Dayton airport. "Here you were working extra-long days with this new job, and I felt you weren't taking care of yourself. You had this bump on your left cheek closer to your ear that I could tell right away that wasn't some bug bite or pimple. I actually had to struggle to hide my reaction to what I saw: This black-and-blue lump was growing on your cheek."

"But remember how it was. We didn't have any quick access to a doctor," I said. "We didn't know what this thing was, and I tried to convince you it wasn't something to worry about."

"No, when I first saw that lump at the airport, I knew we should start worrying, but that's not what I said to you at the time," Mom said. "I said, 'Do you have a doctor here?' And we didn't know any doctors in Dayton, so we just went ahead and took care of the business at hand. We got your apartment, cleaned up the place, set it up with fresh linens and all that we had planned to do. But I insisted that you come home right away to see a doctor, didn't I?"

"You did."

Within 30 days of my first noticing that small swollen patch on my cheek during the drive west, the lump had grown to the size of a marble, then a golf ball. I wore glasses in those days, and this thing was close enough to my left eye that my glasses didn't fit right. It was bad enough during Mom's visit to Dayton that she took me to the makeup counter at a local store where we bought some concealer to at least hide the deep purple color. People still noticed it, though, so I made jokes to colleagues about a bad bruise from a foul on the basketball court. I downplayed it and just kept working and selling those 911 contracts. I was an absolute workaholic, sometimes leaving the office at 11 p.m. for a trip to Gold's Gym for a quick workout before bed. Plus, I turned into an absolute road warrior for NCR, traveling anywhere we had good prospects. I racked up enough sales beating my quota that I earned a reward. It was a trip called the NCR Century Point Club to a fancy resort in Acapulco, Mexico—but I didn't wind up taking that, of course.

When I did fly home, it was because I also could schedule a major appointment with banking clients in Boston. I was more annoyed by all the fuss about the bump than anything else. I flew into Logan airport on a Friday night and the next morning Dad and I had planned to play some tennis and then have breakfast together. That's what I thought we were doing when he rolled the car out of the driveway that morning. Then, as he left our neighborhood, I didn't recognize the turns he was making.

"Where are we going?" I asked.

He said nothing, but we soon wound up at the emergency room of a local hospital.

Again, I was annoyed, but Dad was insistent, so I said, "OK, Dad, let's get this checked out." We went through the doors, checked in, and they took my vital signs. A doctor looked me over and told me that it probably wasn't anything to worry about. He gave me some erythromycin tablets—and Dad and I still were able to catch a late breakfast.

The sales call was an important opportunity to address an American Bankers Association luncheon in Boston and, on Monday, that presentation started very well. I was able to warn these bankers about new federal regulations threatening big fines if banks didn't have a disaster-recovery plan in place. This 911 product was a perfect answer to their immediate needs. Then, right in the middle of my talk, I started feeling sick. I kept going. When I finished I was mobbed by bank executives. Thank goodness my college roommate Greg Tufankjian came with me and helped hand out my business cards and sample 911 floppy disks.

I didn't get back to Framingham until around 4 p.m., when Mom and Dad immediately pushed me back into his car, and we headed once again to the local hospital. I'll never forget that second visit, when we saw a different doctor. This guy examined me, heard the story about my nausea from the pills—and grabbed my bottle of erythromycin out of my hand and threw it into a trash can. I could tell he was worried. He ordered a biopsy. Still, we couldn't leave. Then, we learned something wasn't right about that first biopsy, because he ordered a second one. I was clueless about what was happening, except that I knew I had sales calls lined up next in Pennsylvania and Florida and I did not want to cancel those meetings. For their part, the hospital staff reassigned my case from the ER staff to another physician (I learned later that physician was an oncologist) for follow-up and continued a series of tests spread out over more than a week. The whole time, my focus was on my travel schedule. I didn't fully realize that Mom and Dad were seething over the delays at the hospital. There was just no news for us, day after day. My parents were so worried that they stopped eating regularly.

To my relief, I was able to get out of that pressure cooker of waiting for answers and head back to work for a while. I made the trip to Philadelphia and then headed down to Florida. I knew Dave Herman would be waiting for me at the airport. He had set up sales calls in the Tampa area and this would be a great combination of work with a chance to visit his new home and spend time with him.

"I was looking forward to this, too," Dave recalled in our Zoom. "Our plan was to hit the first sales meetings right away, then head to my home and relax. But, when I saw you at the airport, I couldn't ignore that bump. It must have been pretty obvious to you that I was staring at it. I remember you said something like, 'Rough time on the court.' You insisted it was a basketball injury."

"I'm sorry," I told Dave. "I was lying. At the time, I was lying to everybody. The truth is that I didn't know what the hell it was. And, until I knew more, I didn't want anyone to worry about me. It could have been a rash. Who knew what it was?"

"I certainly knew it was something serious," Dave said. "Remember what happened after we went to our first sales calls, then came back home to change for the evening? You were in the guest room taking off your suit and tie and you called to me, 'Hey, Herms! Come in here!' And I'll never forget stepping into your room and seeing all those discolored patches on your skin under your shirt. You asked me, 'What do you think of these?'"

"I remember," I said. "And, what did you think?"

"Well, I had bought your explanation at the airport about the bump on your cheek coming from basketball. Plus, it was clear you didn't want me to worry, so I said something about it maybe being a rash. I shrugged and walked away. But I'll tell you: I worried! I went back into our bedroom and told my wife, 'Something's wrong with Howard and it's not good.' At that time, I didn't know your parents at all, and didn't have their phone number in Massachusetts, or I would have gotten on the phone and called them right then. That's how worried I was."

Other than the rising fears, we enjoyed our time together in Florida. All too soon, I flew back home again to my folks' house. They declared it was time for a show down with the local hospital staff. Mom and Dad were so worried, they had lost weight.

"I actually lost 10 pounds," Mom recalls. "I was so frustrated and angry! They wouldn't tell us anything."

That's true—until Dad and I drove over to the hospital. Finally, Dad and I sat down across from the physician who had been collecting my test results. He brought an oncologist with him to meet with us.

"He mumbled," Dad recalls. "I couldn't understand. You couldn't understand. Finally, I said, 'What are you saying to us?'"

The doctor's next words were, "We just don't know. You need to go see the experts at Dana-Farber in Boston. We're going to send the biopsy results over there. We've already called them and made an appointment for you. They can get you in right away."

So, first thing the next morning, my parents and I left Framingham for the Dana-Farber Cancer Institute in Boston. That's the day I started feeling overwhelmed. That's when my world really began to turn upside down. I should have seen it coming. After all, my case already had been reassigned to an oncologist at our local hospital. The three of us walked into the main Dana-Farber waiting room, each one of us staring at children with bald heads sitting beside their parents at the Jimmy Fund section of the clinic.

"I was wondering what was wrong with each one of those children," Mom recalls. "I was praying for them—and I was praying for us."

There was no immediate answer, just more tests, at first. So many tests! They gave me a full physical, ordered a complete blood panel, even took to a sample of my bone marrow. I don't remember all of those steps, but I do recall every single detail of the first 10 minutes when the three of us were invited into the office of Dr. George Canellos, the top man at Dana-Farber for developing combination chemotherapies. He was a world-renowned expert and served as editor-in-chief of the Journal of Clinical Oncology. He was the man who finally was going to answer our questions and standing right behind him was a younger man who would become a lifelong friend, Dr. Eric Rubin, a Harvard Fellow. Eric now has moved on to become senior vice president of clinical oncology at Merck. As I was researching this chapter, Eric agreed to a Zoom interview.

"What I'm trying to describe happened a lot of years ago, Eric, so I really need your input" I began. "And I know you're busy. Thanks for making time to talk."

"Certainly, I'm happy to talk with you about what happened. I do remember. After all, Howard, you're a very special case. There just aren't many from those days who've survived like you have," he said.

"What I remember of that meeting with Dr. Canellos was that he sat there at his desk with a pile of reports," I said. "He was this big, impressive senior expert at Dana-Farber. And I could see right away that you were much younger, closer to my age."

He nodded. "I remember."

I continued, "Then, Canellos said these words, 'Howard, you have a very serious form of cancer and it's already stage IV. It's very aggressive. It's very hard to knock this out at this stage, but you're a young man and I hope—' And then Canellos went into this cancer talk about the technical names and details and treatments we could try. I had a very aggressive, advanced form of non-Hodgkin T-cell lymphoma. But, Eric, as he spoke, I was mainly just staring up into your face. You looked at me, and I saw your expression, Eric. That's when I just lost it. I didn't cry. I just started to disassociate from what Canellos was saying. Next to me my mom was bawling—tears streaming down her face. I just went numb. I didn't even fully grasp the gravity of it all. I remember I even thought: Does this mean I can't go to New York for my next sales call? Why was I so worried about that? The whole thing was surreal. I don't remember much of anything else."

Eric kept nodding. "I'm sure your description is accurate, even the disorientation," he said. "Any cancer diagnosis is scary, and we were telling you and your parents that your particular type of cancer was not likely to be cured with standard chemotherapy. This was horrible news. Shocking. You may not have understood everything we were telling you—but that's understandable. We were trying to explain that you were about to go from this very athletic and very active professional life to a very difficult new life focused on all the intricacies of the treatments we were going to provide. For our part, we were trying to be honest that, even after all of the treatments, there wasn't a good chance that you'd survive."

We both paused in the Zoom conversation for a long moment.

Then, Eric said with emotion in his voice, "That's why I say it's so good to talk to you again, Howard. Anytime over the years that we've have a chance to see each other again is a good time, by definition. You're alive, Howard. Most of them—"

"Most of them in my shoes from that era are dead," I said, finishing his sentence.

He nodded.

Then, he said, "There was blood cancer throughout your body and it was affecting you physically. This was bad. This cancer typically is found in lymph nodes and you had reached the point of obvious bruising," he said. "Your local hospital wasn't able to provide the treatments we were offering at that time. You needed to be at Dana-Farber and, even then, we weren't likely to be successful. Your cancer was rapidly growing and we had to be very aggressive with chemotherapy to have any chance at all."

One week later, I started my first course of chemotherapy. It was rough. I mainly remember throwing up a lot and having trouble sleeping. Then, things only got worse when a second course began several weeks later.

"Howard, you lost weight and you were so uncomfortable that it really was breaking my heart," Mom said as she recalled my daily struggles. "But you know what really worried me? It's when you just stopped talking to us. You've always been this talkative, outgoing person and suddenly you weren't saying anything much. I could tell you were thinking and worrying all the time. I kept asking questions, but you didn't answer. That was the worst. You were becoming so deeply depressed that I just didn't know what to do. I didn't know what you needed."

I did. One night at 2 a.m., when I couldn't sleep from meds and steroids and my mind was thrashing through all of my fears for the hundredth time, I picked up the phone and called Dave in Florida.

"I'll never forget that night," Dave recalls. "It was 2 in the morning and you were on the phone raving and swearing. Your first words were, 'It's cancer, Herms! It's bad, Herms!' And then you just went off. You were shouting."

"Yeah, I was out of control. I finally just shouted, 'Herms, I'm going to fucking die! Get up here! Get up here, *please*! I need you.'"

"And I got on a plane. That's what our friendship meant. You called and I came. But I've got to tell you, Howard, I was in no way prepared for what happened."

"I know. I wanted you to help me write my will and you really didn't want to do that."

"I wasn't a lawyer. I had no business trying to write something like that."

"I know. I just needed to see you—needed to sit across that table in the park with no one else around and talk this over with you."

"You really were out of your mind with the fear of what was happening. I mean, you chose a park in the dead of winter to sit down and work on writing a will. Who does that? We were nuts. It was freezing."

"But we sat there at that picnic table and did our best and I'll never be able to thank you enough for doing that."

"A will? Why did you need one? You didn't really have anything, at that point. You had $10,000 in a bank account that you wanted to go to your twin sister CJ. And you had a baseball card collection you wanted to go to a young cousin. We were freezing to death and you were wanting to list everything from your baseball cards to your—I don't even remember it all."

"But you came. You sat with me. That was the thing I needed."

"And you just wouldn't *quit* that day. Here you were in the middle of chemo-therapy and, before your mom even allowed me to take you out of the house, I had to go through this whole detailed interview about all the hundred things I wasn't supposed to do with you. You weren't supposed to get cold or get tired or have a drink or—There was this whole long list of things you couldn't do. I think she was sure I was going to wind up killing you somehow, if I took you out of the house. When we got to the park, you were obviously weak, then we sat at that table for way too long. And then—then, when we finally stood up from that picnic table, do you remember what you said, Howard?"

I laughed. "Yeah. Yeah, I do. I said, 'Hey, Herms, I've got a ball in the car. Do you want to shoot some hoops? It may be the only time in your life that you'll beat me.'"

"Crazy! What was I supposed to do? You kept insisting and so we played! I mean, basketball is physical, and I was trying to play without making any contact with you. I didn't want to knock you over. Then, you charged me. You stumbled. I had to grab you to keep you from falling on the concrete. It was nuts!"

"Yeah, it was. But it was what I needed."

"And then, you wanted to go drinking!"

"And you took me. I'll never forget that."

"I don't know if that's a good or a bad thing. We had margaritas and you should not have been drinking during the chemo. Dude, this was a very, very bad idea."

"It was what I needed, Herms. I suffered for it, but that day was what I needed."

"I'm glad it was, because I faced the full fury of Nancy Brown at the front door when we finally got back home. And I mean I took her full-force, screaming fury! First of all, as we started for the door, it was obvious you were hammered. You were wobbling and sort of stumbled. I had to support you. You were so wobbly, your dad had to help you get inside."

"I remember. Mom screamed at you, 'You took my son drinking! I told you he couldn't drink!' I couldn't help you, Herms. I was just trying to make it to the bathroom to go throw up again and she was back there at the door just attacking you."

"I tried to explain, 'No, I didn't take him *drinking*. I took him to the park.' I was trying to explain. And that just made her madder. She roared, 'What? You took him to the park! In the winter! What were you thinking?' She literally pushed me back outside and ran after me across the lawn until I had to run over to a neighbor's yard just to get away from her."

"Well, Dad finally did come out and he saved you. He drove you back to the airport. And let's be honest about the whole story: My parents eventually came to love you, Herms. After I survived that day, they realized it was important for me to spend time with my close friends."

"They did. And, yeah, I love your parents, too. They're great people."

I'm writing this story with all of these troubling and disorienting details because I want readers to know what it feels like to face a cancer diagnosis. Yes, I know what many readers will say: Every person is different and every case is different. But most of us do share this truth. When the diagnosis hits you, the foundations of your life suddenly start crumbling beneath you. Most of us feel anger and fear and emotions we can't even begin to name. Some of us feel pain. I was spared that the first time. I never experienced pain as the cancer was growing inside me—or really any tell-tale sensation other than the uncomfortable emergence of the lump on my cheek. Although, the side effects from toxic chemotherapy and full body irradiation are very real. Twenty-six years later, my second encounter with death was different. So, yes, our cancer stories will differ in many details—except this one: When you first meet cancer, life as you know it suddenly changes you, your caregivers, family and friends.

If you are someone with cancer, or perhaps you are a longtime cancer survivor, I have learned that it is important for us to be open and honest about our stories—if we can. I say it that way, because I know that not everyone is comfortable being as transparent as I have decided to be about my life.

If you are a loved one of a cancer patient, I hope my stories are helping you to understand more about the disorientation—the life-shattering effects—that may have an even more traumatic legacy than the physical challenges of the cancer journey.

As you continue to the next chapter, which tells about the community that soon formed around me, think about sharing your own story with someone you know.

Shining Brightly

Shine brightly by example. Consider volunteering, making a gift or learning about some of the organizations that touched my life. Share what you learn with friends. You can find the heroes at Dana-Farber Cancer Institute in Boston, MA, at Dana-Farber.org.

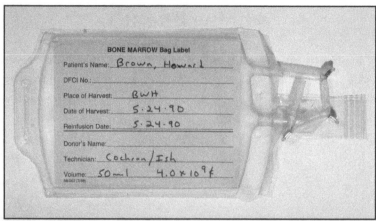

BONE MARROW Bag Label

Patient's Name: Brown, Howard

DFCI No.:

Place of Harvest: BWH

Date of Harvest: 5·24·90

Reinfusion Date: 5·24·90

Donor's Name:

Technician: Cochran/Ish

Volume: 50 ml   4.0 × 10⁹ f

Life took a desperate turn as I fought cancer with the help of my family and the Dana-Farber medical team. When Cheryl and I turned 24, we all thought this would be my last birthday. Against medical advice to avoid any chance of infection in a crowd, Cheryl and I celebrated our birthday at a bar with friends. Then, two months later, this small bone marrow collection bag was filled with cells from Cheryl's hip, a priceless gift that saved my life.

5

The Gifts of Life

In my first war with cancer, my mother rallied the troops. Even though she blew up when Dave Herman broke open the isolated regimen of our household on that winter's day, the truth is that Nancy Brown was a wise and loving caregiver. At first, she was furious with Dave, but she soon forgave him and learned that the surest way to recharge my spirits was to open our home to friends wanting to support me.

Like other successful generals, she even wrote and self-published her own 35-page memoir about how she led our family's campaign against non-Hodgkin lymphoma. She describes her growing realization about the importance of welcoming friends: "If small acts like having his friends come over to our house made Howard happy, then we made it happen. Howard has always had many friends and they all rallied around him. High school friends, college friends, work friends, neighbors and family all stopped by our house to cheer him up. They would reminisce about old times and plan for future good times they would share. We played Nintendo, board games, watched TV and read books together. We all kept his mind busy so he would not dwell on the discomforts of the treatments—and his uncertain future. Even the NCR staff pitched in encouraging Howard to do whatever he felt up to doing. At one point, he even went into the office for a few hours. Another time, Mike Brennan took him to his own home gym for light exercise. Although Howard was so weak, he loved exercise because it helped him feel that he had some control over his body."

That was one part of the story. Here's the other part: Decades before the world discovered COVID-19 isolation measures, I lived through a similarly extreme regimen to protect my severely compromised immune system. Yes, Mom welcomed visitors, but she also insisted anyone who came near me wear a face mask and gloves. There were lots of side effects to the chemo and radiation. I lost my sense of taste and developed dangerous fevers, coughs and infections. Long before the rest of the world, we were veterans of social distancing. Then, I lost my hair as well. Mom wanted me to wear a wig and even bought one for me, but that's not my style. I've always been open about my life and the only adaptation I made to the hair loss was regularly wearing a baseball cap. The weaker I got, the more my parents were terrified. In her memoir, Mom wrote: "Day after day, we watched doctors put poison into Howard's body to kill the cancer cells and day after day we wondered if this was the treatment that would work."

There were days when I thought death was just around the corner, because I had no energy left at all. Occasionally, I managed to summon enough strength to take a walk or stop by the NCR office. At one point, I felt strong enough to fly with Dad back to Dayton to close up my apartment and move my furniture into storage. However, even as we made that trip, I had to force myself to stand up and keep pace with Dad. Throughout that whole trip, he and I rarely talked. Walking was hard enough for me; I just didn't have any energy left to carry on a conversation. Through it all, NCR was very supportive and put me on medical leave, but it eventually became clear that they needed someone else to take over the 911 sales campaign. So, a few weeks later, Dad went back to Ohio—alone this time—to clear out stuff we had left in storage on our first trip, and he drove my jam-packed Pontiac Grand Am back home. We all assumed that, for the foreseeable future, my whole life depended on simply hunkering down at our family home and fighting cancer with every ounce of my fading energy.

Despite our strongest resolve, cancer had its own surprises waiting as 1989 turned to 1990. For a while, there were signs that I was improving. Then, one morning that January, I suddenly woke up back at square one! I discovered new rash-like patches on my body. Then, the dreadful purple lumps reemerged. Dr. Rubin was throwing everything he could at the cancer, short of killing me—and he almost did that. Day after day we were going back and forth to Dana-Farber. One day, with no warning, my blood count was so low and my fever was so high, Dr. Rubin checked me into a hospital room for 10 days of around-the-clock care to save my life from the nearly lethal effects of the chemo. Those were dark days. While I was in the hospital, Dad had to help me crawl out of the bed so I could try to stand and walk across the floor.

That's when the medical team decided to try a bone marrow transplant. Dana-Farber's Dr. Robert Soiffer still is one of the nation's leading experts in treating leukemia and lymphoma with cellular therapies and transplantation. He became a major part of my medical team when a bone marrow transplant seemed to be the only chance to stop this cancer. The procedure still was relatively new. The first successful bone marrow transplant to cure lymphoma was at the University of Minnesota in 1975. However, by the time I talked to Dr. Soiffer for this book, more than 30 million people had registered as potential bone marrow donors at hospitals around the world and U.S. hospitals were successfully completing more than 9,000 transplants each year.

"We've come a long way since 1990 when you had your bone marrow transplant, Howard," Dr. Soiffer said when I reached him by Zoom. "I wouldn't say the procedure was in its infancy at that time, but it certainly was still in its adolescence as a procedure. We knew that it was highly risky. For example, the average age range of persons who received this kind of transplant when you received yours was the 20s or maybe early 30s, but no older than that. Now, all these years later, bone marrow and stem cell transplants are available to people in their late 70s."

"How did the Dana-Farber team decide I was right for this?" I asked.

"We all discussed it and then we made sure you and your family understood the risks," he said. "The key factors were: Your lymphoma was very aggressive and nothing else had worked at that point; your youth was a major factor in your favor; you had a very positive attitude and that was important; and you had a strong support system—we could tell that from your parents. So, we concluded that a bone marrow transplant should be the next step."

"And remember, I also had a twin sister," I said.

"Yes, but before we tested Cheryl that wasn't a factor we could count on. She isn't an identical twin, so her likelihood of being a match was the same as any sibling, about 1 in 4. Looking at it that way, the odds were against her being a match. You were very fortunate that she turned out to be such a good match. Actually, you were fortunate in many ways. By the time we did the transplant, you had become one of a select number of people who went forward with a transplant at that time. Today, this is much different, of course. But, at that time, you became part of a very limited fraternity of people. And the fact that you're still with us, talking to me today and writing this book—"

"I know," I said. "I'm a rare survivor."

He nodded. "There aren't a lot of persons from that time—"

"—who survived this long. I know," I said. "That's why I've devoted so much of my life to advocating for other families fighting cancer and for the lifelong issues survivors face. I'm a rarity, so talking with me gives people hope. When I went in for that bone marrow transplant with your team I was staring death in the face. I will never forget our reaction when we heard that Cheryl was a 100% match. You had warned us that she probably would not be a match. So, a 100% match? We were thrilled! We felt we had just won the lottery! That news was the first ray of sunlight we'd seen during that whole dark winter."

"Let's talk about that darkness you're describing," Soiffer said. "A patient's journey begins with the diagnosis. Then, we all focus on treatments and, in your case, we started with chemotherapy and, along the way, there were some signs that it might have worked. Then—*bang!*—you had that relapse. Along the way, you had multiple relapses. When that happens to any patient, it feels like the floor has fallen out from beneath you. When a treatment fails as dramatically as it did with you, suddenly it feels like there's no clear path to recovery. So, your case definitely had become very dicey before we got to the point of a transplant. Naturally, there was a lot of fear. As we are caring for people, it's important to understand that, beyond the treatments, there is this whole struggle going on within them and within their families. Things can get very dark."

I was nodding to him across the Zoom connection as he spoke. "And those fears—and that darkness—that doesn't just go away," I said. "We can celebrate the rays of sunlight but we also need to know that it's going to be a long haul. These fears are real, and they keep coming back in waves."

"Right," he said. "When we presented this idea of a bone marrow transplant to you, as a patient you had faith in us that we were offering this lifesaving therapy. Howard, you just said it a moment ago, 'It felt like we won the lottery.' But even as we are trying to encourage our patients, we also are trying to be honest about two very difficult truths: First, there's no guarantee it's going to work. The disease may not go away at all, or it might seem to stop and then come right back again. Second, even if it works, there are always side effects, potentially two buckets of side effects: symptomatic side effects like vomiting and diarrhea and, if that's not bad enough, there can be more life-threatening side effects such as graft vs. host disease or a complete rejection of the bone marrow transplant. Then, you remain at risk for quite a while and have to live a very restricted life as your new immune system builds back up with masks and gloves and limited contact for weeks. Given your personality, probably the worst of that was sitting in the hospital alone for a month, just looking out the window and hoping you would get to head back out into the world again. It's a bit like our protocols for COVID patients today and the issues they can face with prolonged isolation. You were running a long gauntlet with this disease, and like every other patient who goes through these treatments, you were constantly feeling squeezed between the risks—all the painful things you were going through to try to fight this disease—and your hopes and fears about the rest of your life. That's a lot of pressure and, Howard, you and your family experienced the full force of that."

"We sure did," I said.

"I'm glad you're writing your book because you can really speak to this experience for other persons facing these challenges. We need them to know that, in addition to all the treatments, the patient's attitude and energy—and the supportive energy of people around them—these factors all are very important to survival."

"That's what we're trying to tell readers in many ways throughout this book," I said. "And you are right, Dr. Soiffer. We need them to understand this is never easy. There were so many awful days in my own journey, and I did get very, very weak—very, very low. For a while, I thought I was going to die. Some days became an endless blur; some days had horrible surprises. I'll never forget that first day when you guys took a bone marrow sample from my pelvis bone. Oh! Even with the local anesthetic you gave me, that hurt so bad! I started crying like a baby. I mean, I'm Jewish and I was screaming for Jesus to come help me! People at the other end of the building must have thought someone was being murdered in there."

"Even with preparation it can hurt. We are basically going into your bone and pulling the marrow out. If that sounds painful—yes, it can be painful."

"And my family weren't the only ones feeling the stress. You and Eric and your staff—you all deserve medals for patience from the pressure Nancy and Marshall Brown laid on you guys. I remember one day Dad literally backing Eric up against the wall and reading him the riot act. He kept demanding more answers—answers that Eric didn't have. Dad can be a very forceful presence. I felt sorry for Eric, but I just didn't have the strength to intercede. You guys put up with a lot with the Brown family."

"Howard, you used a word a moment ago that I want to return to: horrible. You talked about how horrible some days were. That's true. Part of fighting cancer sometimes involves going through horrible things, but that's not the whole story. Howard, you came along at the right time in your life, and the right time for our team at Dana-Farber, with the right factors lined up around you so that we were able to try the bone marrow transplant. You had this very supportive family. And your sister scored a perfect match. You had many wonderful things happening to you, too. I'd say your long struggle really was a mix of horrible and wonderful."

"Horrible and wonderful," I said, mulling over his words. "I like that phrase. I tell people that I do believe in miracles. I mean, I've experienced too many miraculous turns in my life not to believe in miracles. But telling my story and saying that it was a miracle isn't very helpful to people. I know, because every day now, I'm in touch with people around the world who are struggling with cancer. It's one of the ways I give back. When I was in need, so many people helped me to get through this that, now, I'm giving back by serving as a cancer whisperer to other people. I know what they need to hear and part of that is encouragement, we all need encouragement to get through each day, but it's also honesty. That's why I've devoted this year to working on this book, because acknowledging the horrible might be just as helpful as painting an optimistic, wonderful picture."

"I agree. We have to be encouraging and we have to be honest," he said.

"The truth is that I've known hundreds of men, women and kids who have gone through a long struggle with cancer, and then it doesn't wind up with the outcome they want," I said. "When you open yourself up to care about people on this journey, the truth is that some of them are going to die. That's why, if I just say to people that my experience was miraculous, it's not helpful in itself. Yes, I do give people hope because my survival is truly rare. I beat the odds. But there's more than just saying: Hey, you can beat the odds, too. It's important to encourage people to realize that, even in the middle of all the horrible stuff they're going through, there can be some pretty wonderful stuff as well."

"That makes sense," Dr. Soiffer said. "People need to know about both the horrible and the wonderful. In your case, there were risks at every step. One of the big ones was when we started that regimen of different chemotherapy drugs along with twice daily full body radiation that we gave you right before the transplant. That's the conditioning we did to suppress your own immune system so your body would not immediately reject the donor cells you would be receiving. But the risk is that, if your sister's replacement bone marrow didn't start working, then we had already killed off your own bone marrow. If her cells didn't start working, you would never survive that. Of course, this was on all of our minds."

"Very high stakes," I said. "That's why I've hung onto a little souvenir of that day." I held up a small plastic bag with a Dana-Farber label on it and moved it near my camera so Dr. Soiffer could see it on his screen. "Recognize this?"

"Is that a bag we used for your sister's bone marrow?"

"It is. And I remember how long and hard you had to work to fill this little bag. I keep it just to remind me of the gift of life Cheryl gave me that day. There's no way to ever thank someone for a gift like that, but I'm forever grateful and thankful to her for everything she went through for me."

"We brought your sister Cheryl into the operating room. We put her under anesthesia, so she could withstand the procedure. We were hand drilling into her hipbones. Once we had placed the trocar in a hole, we used a syringe to pull fluid from it, a couple of pulls from each hole we made. We had to keep repeating that through a whole series of pulls. It took an hour plus to do all of that. Then, it took us more than four hours to process the bone marrow. We took it through a procedure that made it less likely that your body would reject the cells."

"I remember that day," I said.

But like a lot of cancer patients, the truth is: No, I don't remember all the details, because like most survivors I have consciously tried to put cancer in my rearview mirror. When I do want to relive that life-and-death day in detail, I turn to my mom's paperback memoir. She put the story in terms far closer to the raw emotions of that day than my conversations with the doctors over Zoom decades later can convey.

Her four-word summary: "We prayed a lot."

Experience this story, for just a moment, from my parents' perspective, as she recorded it:

> We arrived at Dana-Farber on May 17, 1990, and were taken up to the 12th floor to a room where Howard would spend weeks in isolation. Howard's entire immune system was about to be wiped out. It was critical that he not get an infection, so even Cheryl could only look through a small window on the door. Only Marshall and I were allowed in Howard's room after putting on a hospital gown, washing our hands to make sure they were extremely clean, then pulling on gloves and a facemask. Howard's life depended on this. Howard was frightened. Doctors had warned us that this might not work. Both my children were about to undergo medical procedures. We prayed a lot.

> On May 19, I arrived at the hospital so early that I sat and watched Howard sleep as they had started the chemotherapy again, which would continue for two more days. Marshall and

I were all but living at Dana-Farber. I would spend the days; Marshall would stay all night. We never left Howard alone through this whole horrendous ordeal. We did not eat much. The stress was almost unbearable.

Then, on May 21, I arrived very early again because Howard was preparing for radiation. The nurses helped him into clean pajamas, robe, slippers and a mask to cover his mouth and nose. They lifted him onto a gurney and covered his body from neck to toes with a long sheet and then placed another cloth over his head to avoid contamination as they moved him through the hospital. All I could see were Howard's eyes and I knew how scared he was. I was too. A nurse, a hospital guard, Howard and I traveled by ambulance to Brigham and Women's Hospital, a Harvard teaching hospital that was on the same street as Dana-Farber. As we went with Howard's gurney on this journey, along corridors and into an elevator, the nurse kept asking people ahead of us to turn their backs, so no one would breathe toward Howard. That process went on day after day. He received full-body radiation twice a day until the transplant. By that time, he seemed to be constantly needing to vomit.

Finally, May 24 arrived. After six months of treatments that had not killed the cancer cells, the transplant day arrived. We took it as a good sign that the sun shone brightly on us. Cheryl had to be at Brigham and Women's Hospital early for pre-operative tests. By 8 a.m., she went under anesthesia so the doctors could repeatedly insert the large needle into Cheryl's hipbone. I was waiting near Cheryl while Marshall stayed near Howard. As Cheryl's procedure went on and on, I sat in the waiting room feeling pain rising in my own lower back as if they were drilling all those holes in me. When Dr. Soiffer came out of surgery, he said that Cheryl was fine. I could not stop crying.

"Is her bone marrow good?" I asked.

"Best I've ever seen," he said.

I rushed over and hugged him as I thanked him. "You're holding the lives of both of my children in your hands."

"We're taking very good care of them."

I was eager to share the good news with Marshall and Howard. I knew the hallway along which they would pass, so I ran through the hospital to a window through which they could see me and held up both of my thumbs. Marshall grinned.

Then, we waited. We prayed. Marshall and I switched places so he would wait for Cheryl and I would be near Howard. When I got to Howard's room, he was so weak that he asked me to lie down with him. I took him in my arms. He asked me to tell him a story, which told me how scared he was. We used to do this before bedtime. So, I lay there with my son at his weakest, telling him all the happy stories I could remember from his childhood.

That was the longest day of my life. Finally, at 5:30 p.m., after they had processed Cheryl's bone marrow for Howard, the little plastic bag arrived that looked like it was filled with soft purple bubblegum—Cheryl's bone marrow. It only took a short while for that little IV bag to flow into Howard's body, yet that little bit of life from Cheryl could save Howard. We called Cheryl in her hospital room so Howard could tell her that her bone marrow was flowing into his body.

"I love you," he told her. "Thank you for saving my life."

Marshall and I were crying. We looked around and the nurses were crying with us.

Howard stayed in the hospital for six weeks, three weeks of it in strict isolation. Now that the bone marrow was in his body, he still had a 50 percent chance of rejecting it. His long isolation started with sweats, chills, headaches, nausea and jitters.

Some days, Howard told us, "This all feels like a blur."

After the first 21 days, the doctors opened the door of solitary confinement. His first visitor other than Marshall and me was Cheryl. Then, his grandparents came to see him. Papa Leo thanked every person he met in the hospital for saving his grandson. Love, joy, happiness and prayer surrounded Howard every day. And soon he was exercising again. At first, he made laps in the hospital with his IV stand. Then, we moved a stationary bike into his hospital room and he quickly worked his way up to 5 miles per ride. His determination grew with each passing day.

On June 20, 1990, Howard walked out of Dana-Farber and we drove him home where a huge sign was waiting near the front door: "Welcome Home Howard."

Cheryl greeted us at the front door.

Thirty years later, I wanted to hear Cheryl's perspective.

I asked her, "Why did you decide to go through all of that?"

She told me it was a silly question. "Of course, I would do it. There was no question. We grew up as twins and we always had each other's back. We always had different interests and friends, partly because you were a boy and I was a girl—but there was no question. You needed me and I could help. It's the core value we learned as we were growing up: always be positive—and always be kind and giving to help others. Today, I try to pass that onto my kids."

Not too many years after the bone marrow transplant, Cheryl wrote a letter to Oprah Winfrey in response to a Mother's Day request for memories of great mothers. In that letter, Cheryl used nearly the same words she uses today. She wrote:

> Growing up, my parents stressed how important a positive attitude was. My mother is an upbeat, vibrant woman. Her positive attitude is contagious. That became especially meaningful when my twin brother was diagnosed with cancer. At the age of 24, my brother was not only losing his hair and losing weight from the chemotherapy and radiation treatment—but was at risk of losing his life.
>
> My mother dedicated all her time, energy and efforts to care not only for my brother, but also for all the other patients at Dana-Farber. She walked through that hospital day after day with a smile on her face, even though my brother's cancer

had left my family feeling helpless. Instead of dwelling on the fears, my mother channeled her energy into positive activities to help others. When she heard that a blood drive would help, she contacted friends, acquaintances, relatives, neighbors and co-workers until 400 people showed up to give blood! When she heard that cancer patients and their families enjoyed having a piece of candy—but there really wasn't a budget for that at Dana-Farber and their stock was running low—she wrote letters to candy companies for donations until they were flooded with sweets. When she realized how much time patients spent at Dana-Farber with little to do during their treatments, she wrote to video companies to get equipment and tapes of movies.

When a bone marrow transplant finally was needed to save my brother's life, I gave my bone marrow. I honestly believe that along with the medical technology, my brother's positive attitude played a key role in his ability to survive. And that is one of the attributes that my brother and I learned from my mother.

I wanted to know from Dr. Soiffer, "What cured me?"

"The bone marrow transplant is the accepted curative element," he said.

"One reason I'm asking is that, after the transplant, I was put on a whole course of interleukin-2 to grow my 'natural killer T cells', which I remember you told me was a new type of early immuno-therapy treatment you were just studying. Was it that drug? Or the transplant? Or both?"

"At the time, Dana-Farber was doing research on the way interleukin-2 (very early on immunotherapy back then) could help in cases like yours. At high levels, it would cause problems for patients, but we believed that it could be used safely and effectively at low doses. With you and other patients we showed that it could help with positive outcomes, but this was 30 years ago. Research has moved in many other directions with this and other treatments. The best way to describe your curative process is to point to the bone marrow transplant."

Dr. Soiffer paused for a moment and then continued, "But I don't think your emphasis should be on words like 'cure' or 'triumph.' Your story really illustrates persistence both in science and in your own life. In one way, your story is a testament to the way we are constantly trying to improve the science.

That's our focus. We can never expect to rack up one home run after another. We keep working through the innings, we keep learning and innovating and eventually we hope to win the game. And, Howard, your story also is a testament to the character and persistence of you and your family. You refused to lose."

Not only did we refuse to lose, but we all have committed ourselves to telling these stories to help other families. That's why Mom sat down and wrote her short memoir and paid to have copies printed. That's why Cheryl sent her letter to Oprah. That's why I'm writing this book right now.

Just as Dr. Soiffer said, we couldn't possibly know what lay ahead of us, when I walked out of Dana-Farber 30 years ago. Mom optimistically titled her memoir, *The Nightmare's Over—I Can Finally See the Light at the End of the Tunnel*. She didn't know what was on the horizon. Dr. Rubin and Dr. Soiffer couldn't predict the effects of the massive chemo and radiation I received to save my life. As much as my family wanted to put cancer in the rearview mirror, the truth is—we couldn't and we didn't. And that's a truth every family that has been touched by cancer will understand.

One way we can help others in their struggles with cancer is by registering as a potential bone marrow donor. As I finish this book, Dr. Soiffer is the current chairman of that international nonprofit's board of directors. He's professor of medicine at Harvard and has published more than 250 articles in peer-reviewed journals throughout his career. The Be the Match Registry is the world's largest of its kind, listing more than 22 million individuals who could help patients with a variety of disorders from cancer to blood or immune system disorders.

Finally, I don't want anyone to read these chapters about my treatments 30 years ago and assume that's how things are done today in our health care systems. For example, becoming a part of the Be the Match registry today is simple. It involves a cheek swab to collect DNA, just as you would to participate in a genealogy database. And, while it's true that when I had a bone marrow sample taken, I experienced searing pain that made me holler—don't let fear of pain paralyze you. Health care systems today offer a wide range of options, including complete anesthesia to allay patients' fears. Drug regimens have changed. The age ranges of patients have vastly expanded. The odds of survival now are far more positive—especially if more and more people agree to help.

"Like you, Howard, I've always been committed to giving back," Dr. Soiffer said. "That's why I give time to Be the Match. This isn't some sort of fancy biotech company. It's an international network of people who are willing to give of their time and of their bodies to help someone else. Many times, they're giving to strangers and are selflessly paying it forward. Why do they give to someone they don't even know? Because it's part of the social contract that if I'm there today to help someone in need, then someone else will be out there in the future if my family needs help. And really, Howard, that seems to be a central message of your book."

Shining Brightly

A simple swab of your mouth could wind up saving a life. Please consider registering as a donor. Learn more at these websites:

- **Be The Match** — BeTheMatch.org
- **Gift of Life** — GiftOfLife.org

I was part of a Dana-Farber Cancer Institute support group as I was recovering from my first stage IV cancer. I was moved by the experiences we all shared, including the need to remember what we like about life and ourselves. I designed pocket mirrors that have a small reminder printed across the top: "I LIKE ME!" When I gave them to members of my group, one woman told me. "It's a great way to remember that, while I'm going through hell right now—I do like myself. My life has value. I want to survive. I will survive."

6

I Like Me!

What happens after such a crisis? Anyone who has survived advanced cancer will tell you: Life changes forever—and not always in sunny ways.

"After this kind of unimaginable crisis, life really is so messed up that the stress and worry inside our heads can spin out of control." That's my daughter Emily speaking to me as I was working on this book, describing her own hard-earned wisdom that she hopes we can share with readers in these pages. However, here's the irony: With those words, Emily wasn't talking about the trauma of cancer. She was describing the trauma of the COVID-19 pandemic on college students like herself and her friends. In study after study, researchers have found that loneliness, anxiety and depression all soared among college-age men and women during the pandemic. Even at her age, Emily already is a wise woman whose wisdom relates to many forms of life-threatening trauma.

"No one really knows all the stuff that's going on inside our heads as this thing stretches on and on," Emily said about young adults going through the pandemic. "So, let me try to describe this."

Here is what she said:

> To survive, we have to find new ways of living. I've realized I have to focus on ways to be strong, not only to survive this pandemic myself but also to help others. Fortunately, my family has always been supportive of me and has given me lots

of resources. For example, I've seen both of my parents—no matter whatever else is going on in the world—find ways to give to charity, give their time and speak out for people who are in need, especially those who don't have a voice. My family has always done that. They've shown me: Even if my cup is nearly empty, I'm still going to find a way to make someone else's day better by adding a little goodness to their cup. That can help to break the cycle of worrying—by getting actively involved in helping others. It's not healthy to sit alone worrying about what has happened to us—or what might happen in the future. Think about it: Worrying about something you fear puts you through that bad thing twice.

This is not easy. I can tell you that because I'm someone who feels others' pain intensely. In my own life, I know what it feels like to go through trauma, to feel really deep fear and to freak out. So, I have worried. I have felt immense anger. I have seen and felt injustices that are so infuriating that they can mess with your sense of reality. I know that, when this happens, we have to intentionally open our eyes in new ways, to see new possibilities and new landscapes out there. We must actively and directly address our pain, even if it's difficult. That is the only way to change our lives so we can feel more joy. There's this line in the movie *The Shawshank Redemption*: You can get busy living, or you can get busy dying.

Sometimes, it's impossible to be the strong one, because sometimes we get hit with so much unbelievable stuff that it knocks us down. But the question we must keep asking is: Can we somehow find meaning and purpose in our lives? In a world of highs and lows, can we find a balance? The answers to these questions begin with opening your heart and your mind to rediscover the possibilities of life. You've got to come to a point where you can remember what you like about your life—what you want to see in the future—and then take a small step toward making it happen.

In that heartfelt message about her life in 2020–22, coping with the global pandemic, Emily explained more eloquently than I could about my family's turbulent legacy after that first war with cancer 30 years ago. In the midst of crisis, and even after the immediate danger has passed, we often need help with our emotional well-being.

Thirty years ago, that's also what the team at Dana-Farber advised me to do as signs of my cancer seemed to disappear. I had survived such a life-and-death struggle that I needed to talk to others who could understand my jumble of lingering side effects, emotions and anxieties. So, I followed my doctors' recommendation in the fall of 1990 to enroll in Stepping Stones, a transitional support group for cancer survivors that met with Dana-Farber social workers and counselors. That program was essentially a time for cancer survivors to vent to each other. It has since been replaced by newer support programs at Dana-Farber.

What fascinates me is that Mom and I had very different reactions to Stepping Stones. The program split up caregivers and cancer patients, then they also would bring us back together, so Mom's experience was largely separate from mine. She was thrilled with her portion of the program. She assumed I was, too. Her memoir says, "Howard thought it was wonderful as they all discussed feelings, families and even possible relapses. It pleased me that he was attending this group. These people understood exactly what Howard went through and continued to go through. They all had a connection. As much time as I spent with Howard, I did not have cancer, nor had I gone through treatments. It was also a sounding board for him that was not his family. This is a wonderful organization that helped Howard cope with the stages of recovery."

Well, that's sort of true. During and after a struggle with cancer, we all benefit from talking with people who have been through this before us. That's why I devote a significant part of my life, to this day, to cancer support networks. However, I did not really like the Stepping Stones approach to having patients share. In our sessions, the group leader allowed far too much time for what Dr. Robert J. Wicks calls "depressive experiences." Of course, back in 1990, I had never heard of Wicks and did not have the awareness I have today about the needs of cancer patients. My main reaction to the men and women who sat around me in that Stepping Stones circle was: These people don't like their lives. I realized that they were coming to the group to vent about how much they hated their lives—that's how it was designed. I stuck with the process, but the stories in each session were so unrelentingly negative that it didn't help me much. I was finding far more support from my own friends outside that program.

My instinct was that I needed to put more of my focus on what Wicks describes in his books as "self-care." I needed to get active, to return to the basketball court, to have fun with friends, to get back to work with NCR. I needed to "get busy living." Of course, I had a horrific series of side effects for a long time after my bone marrow transplant, so I had to take things slowly. Among the many steps that helped to restore my self-esteem was a visit to a plastic surgeon who helped to surgically restore the normal look of my left cheek where that first purple tumor had appeared.

Like many leading cancer advocates today, I learned the hard way about grappling with stage IV cancer—twice in my life. As I recovered, I used whatever had worked for me to help others. It was not until I began researching this book that I discovered Dr. Wicks' 2009 book for Oxford University Press, *Bounce: Living the Resilient Life*. I flipped open the cover and the dedication page spoke to me like a letter I might have written myself. Here is how Wicks puts it on that first page: "Resilience is more than a function of who we are and what we know—as important as both of these factors are. It is also dependent upon those who comprise our personal circle of friends. In our interpersonal network, it is crucial to have people who believe in us and what we are doing for others—people who consistently stand behind us and provide the resources that allow us to develop and share with others our personal gifts and professional talent."

I chuckled and actually said aloud: "He's writing about me. This is my story."

As I read further, I knew that I had to reach out to Wicks. When I did, he graciously agreed to talk with me over Zoom.

After I had introduced my story to him, he gave me some practical advice. "The best suggestion I can give you is being clear that resiliency is not simply about bouncing back from stress but comes as the result of going deeper as a person into our own lives and reaching out to other people as well. There is a tendency to romanticize some of these stories as a kind of heroic individual journey, but we have to be completely honest in the way we write about this. And, if we are honest, we realize that we simply cannot make it through this process alone. Then, the other suggestion I want to make is: Begin with the positive stories from your life. You're a real character, Howard. You've had quite a number of remarkable things happen in your life. Emphasizing the positive side of your experiences is what will attract readers to spend time with you and learn from what you have to tell them."

"Positive," I repeated his word. "Positive. I hear that word loud and clear, because it rings so true for me. One of the things I have found in going to war with stage IV cancer twice in my life is that you have to work to push away all the negative stuff around you. You have to look for the positive. In your book, you talk about that over and over again." In fact, *Bounce* is all about self-awareness, self-care, compassion, positive psychology and even creating your own resiliency profile. Wicks devotes his final pages to a long list of other books he recommends on resiliency and positive psychology.

As we talked, I described my honest reaction to the Stepping Stones program in 1990. "I just felt so much negativity in that room. And I really felt for these people in the group with me. So much of our time was devoted to the problems we all were facing—and anyone who survives cancer has lots of problems, we all know that. But it's like people in the group had reached a point where their problems were overwhelming them. They weren't happy with their lives."

In response, Wicks talked more about how positive psychology is changing assumptions about such programs, which is also a central theme in *Bounce*. I was in Stepping Stones in 1990 and today's positive psychology movement really didn't start until Dr. Martin Seligman moved it to the center of national conversations among his colleagues nearly a decade later. In 1998, Seligman became president of the American Psychological Association and challenged his colleagues to explore positive psychology as their collective theme during his term. He went on to help establish the Positive Psychology Center at the University of Pennsylvania and today works globally with the United Nations on researching sources of positivity in cultures around the world.

Wicks said, "We have to remember that for most of the history of mental health treatment, we focused on the diagnoses and disorders and problems, what you're describing as the negativity, Howard. That was the focus of our work as therapists: identifying and dealing with disorders. But that's changing, and Martin Seligman was a big part of that. He launched this movement that focuses more on a person's strengths and what we can do to encourage resilience through those strengths."

"That makes sense to me," I told him. I had never heard Seligman's name until I read about him in *Bounce*. It's only in recent years that health care systems and medical schools have reached out to advocates like me—and other people who have actually survived cancer—to appear regularly in panels discussing how we can work together. Most cancer survivors have had to chart their own post-treatment survivorship journeys with little sense that there is a community working together on these challenges. Sometimes in our journeys, we find each other and the help we need. Sometimes we don't. That's what motivates me now to work with these national networks to build awareness of all the help that is out there, today.

"And that's one reason I have to thank you for *Bounce*, which I'm now recommending to others," I told Wicks. "That book really does describe my life, too. It could be my story. You write about the importance of self-care and you give readers these long lists of things they can do, like exercising, spending time with friends even if it's on the phone, Facetime or Zoom now, digging into projects that seem exciting. You're describing my path, what gives me my mental toughness, what makes me resilient."

"But we need to be clear about this," he cautioned. "When we're talking about positive psychology, this isn't some kind of cosmetic. It does not deny the valleys. The truth is we will find ourselves in the darkness. We have to accept that is a part of life—and you know this, Howard. But our vulnerability can become a portal to appreciating life in new ways. Would we wish what happened to us on anyone else? Would you wish stage IV cancer on anyone? No. But, remember that the question is not: Can we avoid the darkness? No. The question is: How do we stand in that darkness when it comes? No one wants people to go through these traumas, but if we do experience them, this becomes an opportunity to go deeper as a person—and to explore what is possible now in your life because you've gone through this trauma. And it gives us an opportunity to reach out to others in new ways."

"Yes, I know all about that," I said. "And that's why I'm on this Zoom connection with you right now. That's why I'm asking so many people, this year, including my own daughter, to share what wisdom we've learned about the journey through trauma and beyond."

"So, let me leave you with this," Wicks said. "The next step to think about is: As we stand in that darkness, if we are open to seeing our loss and trauma and helplessness honestly, the result will be to experience the virtue of humility. And, today, that's not a virtue that people appreciate. You know this: Everyone wants to portray themselves as successful. Our culture today is all about projecting a successful image in the world and diminishing any shortcomings. That's why celebrities hire public relations teams. No one seems to care about humility. But I want to tell you, Howard: Humility is a very powerful psychological and spiritual virtue. That's because, when we combine humility with the knowledge we can gain through our humility, then we get real wisdom. And when you take that very wisdom and combine that with compassion, then you are able to give the world selfless love. And that truly is the most wondrous outcome of all."

"That's our hope, isn't it?" I said.

"It is."

But how do we help people through this journey?

That starts, as Wicks points out, by understanding the darkness that can surround us in the midst of a life-and-death struggle with trauma. That darkness is unpredictable. Sometimes, it waits to fully manifest itself until after the danger seems to have passed. People around us feel we have moved on from our trauma, although many of us have not. People assume we are just fine. No one is looking. When darkness comes, no one seems to understand the depth of our despair. As I was writing this chapter, a woman I had befriended in an online cancer support group posted a stream-of-consciousness narrative about her efforts to do what Wicks describes: to stand and survive in that darkness. She is Carrie English-Elliott, who was diagnosed with stage IV colorectal cancer and, throughout her treatment, we frequently messaged or talked on the phone. Eventually, she beat those long odds and had reached the point of No Evidence of Disease at this time (NED). Despite that apparent success, here is what she wrote about her experience of post-cancer darkness.

> I'm sure many of you can relate to this. Often, cancer can leave a warrior feeling broken. They may smile and laugh when you're around them, tell jokes and seem normal, but something not often talked about is the mental distress of cancer and the way cancer can mentally take a toll on you for a long time. I have been at the lowest point ever in my life during my cancer journey. I have been through extremely terrible chemotherapy treatments that I would never wish on anyone. The way chemotherapy makes you feel is so hard to describe to others. When you are physically unable to pull yourself out of bed to do a simple task, such as go use the restroom, that is an all-time low! When you can literally smell the poison being pumped into your body and all you want to do is smell normal again, that is an all-time low! When you know that all of your friends and family are having the time of their lives and you're sitting there fighting for yours, that is an all-time low! When surgeries leave scars on your body that remind you every single day as you look in the mirror of your cancer, that is an all-time low! And one of the biggest struggles cancer patients deal with is when we find ourselves constantly thinking: When is this cancer going to come back? And that is the ultimate all-time low!

Even when we kick cancer's ass physically, mentally we are struggling, trying to pick up the pieces of our life that fell apart, trying to mentally prepare ourselves for a bad scan, trying to mentally prepare ourselves to hear the doctor say, "Your cancer is back." Luckily, some of us go into remission for a very long time and don't have to hear those words. Then, there are those who don't get to remission and hear those words far too soon.

Yes, there is a physical battle with cancer, but the mental aspect of cancer isn't talked about enough. So, next time you are talking to your friend or your loved one who seems to have survived cancer, don't just assume they are OK. Ask them how they're *really* doing. Mentally, they may not be OK. PTSD becomes a new diagnosis for a lot of us, and that journey is just beginning when the physical signs of cancer seem to be ending. We can't jump back to our pre-cancer days and reclaim all that was taken from us. That pre-cancer world will never be our reality again. We can only cherish the best pre-cancer memories, continue to smile at the goodness around us now and fight like hell that we will continue to survive.

My aim is to shed light on how we can overcome any challenge, not just cancer. That's why I asked my daughter Emily to share from her broader vision of the challenges we all may face in life. And there is one more story that Emily asked me to share in this chapter.

"Encouraging people to focus on the positive is important," Emily said, "but positivity alone won't save anyone who is in a deep crisis; taking action and getting help will. Depression is very real and can lead to suicidal thoughts, if someone reaches that point. I think you should add hotline numbers for people reading this chapter in case they feel helpless."

I agreed right away, of course, then I asked her, "As you say that, are you thinking about the girl you met when we went to St. Lucia and climbed that mountain with our guide Cameron Vaudroque and Wendy and Joby Orlowsky from Chicago?"

"Yeah," she said. While staying at our hotel, Emily had met and befriended a mother and her daughter who also were vacationing on the island.

"Tell the story," I said.

We met this girl and her mom when we shared a shuttle ride at Jade Mountain. I was 18 at the time and the girl was 16. The girl was nice and we got to talking, then we connected on Snapchat. She told me that, because of her family connections, she traveled a lot and had all these adventures in different parts of the world. We wound up spending the next day together at our resort and we went snorkeling together. We found this beautiful shell on the beach with two halves—and we each took half to remind us of that day.

We talked about our hopes and found that we had a lot of interests in common. She wanted to play volleyball in college, and she was interested in my experiences at the University of Michigan. We connected so well that we continued talking—on and off—after we went home. She really wanted to come visit me in the fall at UofM to see what it was like on campus. I was all for that because she was this bright light of a person who I enjoyed being around. It would have been great if she had come to UofM.

As we stayed in touch, I realized that she was trying to become an Instagram influencer. So, she would share all these photos of herself looking pretty—in all these different places. She did all these amazing things and saw all these wonderful sights. Her life looked so great. But on the inside? Only afterward did I realize that was such a big front. Only afterward did I realize she felt completely broken.

One day in the fall, which is when we had talked about her coming up to visit me, I was just checking my phone—and suddenly I saw this photo of her with the words, "Rest in Peace." I went: What!?! Oh my God! I couldn't believe what I was seeing. It took me days to process all of this. I learned she had killed herself. How could she have done that?

As time went on, her story got bigger and bigger and bigger online. She got more than 50,000 likes and positive comments from people all around the world. Thousands and thousands of people were out there surrounding her. But she didn't see that while she was alive. Somehow, she reached a point where she couldn't go on. When something like that happens, you naturally think: What if—? What if I had known?

As a result, I started texting and calling all my friends, telling them how much they mean to me and saying, "I love you. Let me know if you're ever struggling." I told them her story. I told them I didn't want to see that happen ever again. If you're struggling—we'll talk.

I only had that one wonderful day on the beach with her—but she's become a part of my life. I won't forget her story. That's all we can do after something like this: Promise we will not forget and try to make sure it doesn't happen to others.

As Emily fell silent, there was a long pause.

"I knew almost nothing about this," I said. "I had no idea of the depth of your connection with her and what happened to her. I didn't know."

"That's how it is," Emily said. "We often don't know anything about what's going on when a suicide happens. We can't see what's happening on the inside. But sometimes the darkness can just become too dark for someone. Sometimes people don't think they can find the strength to go on. That's why I'm glad you'll at least put the suicide hotline numbers in this chapter. They might help someone. Please put them in."

So, I am.

The Centers for Disease Control (CDC) provides a COVID-19-specific series of resources under the headline, Coping with Stress, at: www.cdc.gov/mentalhealth/stress-coping/cope-with-stress/index.html That page provides links to dozens of resources, including eight national hotlines. First and foremost, the CDC recommends that anyone in immediate crisis simply pick up a phone and dial 911 to get help immediately. If you're in crisis—don't wait.

The CDC's second recommendation for anyone in crisis with suicidal thoughts—or anyone who knows someone in such a crisis—is the National Suicide Prevention Lifeline. You can reach that service at suicidepreventionlifeline.org or by calling 1-800-273-TALK (8255) for English (or 1-888-628-9454 for Spanish) or you can text the word "HELLO" to 741741.

Finally, for help with a wide range of mental health issues including depression, professionals recommend contacting the Substance Abuse and Mental Health Services Administration (SAMHSA). This is a free 24/7 service that is part of the U.S. Department of Health and Human Services and provides referrals for mental health assistance to individuals and families in English and Spanish. You can reach SAMHSA's services at www.samhsa.gov/find-treatment, which also links to the suicide-prevention hotline listed above. Or call the national SAMHSA mental health helpline at 1-800-662-HELP (4357).

More than three decades ago, back in 1990, when I participated in Dana-Farber's Stepping Stones, a lot of the current resources and approaches to these issues simply weren't available. Like millions of other cancer survivors, I was figuring it out as I took each step each day.

Like Wicks and Emily, though, I did understand that the real key to survival is how we each choose to stand in the darkness. As Stepping Stones came to a close, my own response to the group naturally connected with my creativity as an innovator. I got this idea that—to this day—makes people smile and gives them a tangible reminder of the value of our individual lives. In my mind's eye, I envisioned a little gift that I could give to each of my friends in the Stepping Stones program—a reminder of that central truth. I sketched it. I ordered enough for everyone connected with the program.

I won't ever forget that last Stepping Stones session I attended. "I have a little gift for everyone," I said.

Then, I began passing out small mirrors—compact mirrors that someone might carry with them in a bag or pocket. Each one had a soft plastic cover that was a reminder of our circle with the words: "Dana-Farber Cancer Institute Stepping Stones." Pulling out the little mirror reveals the words: "I LIKE ME!" The words appear right above your face as you look into the mirror.

I told the group, "It may sound simple to say, 'I like me!' But that's also so easy to forget when you go through a time of real despair. That's when we have to search within ourselves for something we like—something within us that we can grab onto and can use as a springboard to survive all the emotional, physical and spiritual crises we're facing."

People were blown away. There were lots of hugs and tears that day.

One woman came up to thank me and smiled as she looked into her mirror. "So simple, yes! But it's a great way to remember that, while I'm going through hell right now—I do like myself. My life has value. I want to survive. I will survive."

There is so much emotion, even after 30 years, as I remember that day in that circle. The truth is that we were a circle of men and women who had struggled with stage IV cancer—and nearly everyone in that circle eventually saw cancer return with a vengeance. Even me. Most of those people in that circle? They're now, as we say in Judaism, "of blessed memory." I may be the only one left who remembers our circle of faces and stories.

Like Emily, I realize that I only had a short time with each of them. I am so glad that I made the effort to remind them of how much each one meant in the world—even if it was just through that little affirmation on those mirrors. Each one became a part of my story forever. And, like Emily, this chapter is my way of saying: We will not forget.

Shining Brightly

For the launch of this book, I ordered more of those little mirrors. If you would like one, visit the book's website at ShiningBrightly.com.

And, please consider volunteering, giving to or learning about these or similar organizations that touched my life:

- The **Leukemia & Lymphoma Society**® (**LLS**) is a global leader in the fight against cancer. The LLS mission: Cure leukemia, lymphoma, Hodgkin's disease and myeloma, and improve the quality of life of patients and their families. LLS.org

- **MyLymphomaTeam** is a free social network that makes it easy for you to get the emotional support you need from others like you, and gain practical advice and insights on managing treatment or therapies for lymphoma. MyLymphomaTeam.com

After beating cancer and discovering we were *bashert*, Lisa and I wanted our family and friends to share in our dream come true with all the Hollywood romance of a wedding at Shutters on the Beach in Santa Monica, California. In the summer of 1994, our chuppah, the Jewish wedding canopy, overlooked the sunlit Pacific. In one picture, we snuck in a kiss in front of our Ketubah.

7

Love of My Life

After my first encounter with death, I decided to move as far from my New England hometown as I possibly could and remain working for NCR. Like Anneliese Glaubitz as she approached her graduation from Babson in 2019, I dreamed of sunny California in 1991. I wanted the warm beaches. I wanted the competitive aura of a major market like Los Angeles. And, most importantly, I wanted the whole continent's distance from that overwhelming, suffocating, debilitating world of cancer recovery. I was developing a new mental toughness and refused to let myself sink back into that cocoon of helplessness and dependency that had surrounded me during so much of my battle with lymphoma. I was determined to put cancer in my rearview mirror.

The irony is that the farther I moved from home, the more I took hold of my roots.

In the closing pages of her memoir, Mom describes my journey to the West Coast as "Howard's new adventure far from home"—like a sunset scene at the end of a Hallmark movie. She writes:

> On May 20, 1991, Howard moved to sunny southern California where he rented an apartment one block from the Pacific Ocean in Marina Del Rey. His new position for NCR was in Los Angeles. Soon, he was back to his old self again. He met many new friends and spent time with them playing basketball and enjoying the sunshine. He spent much time

volunteering. Howard felt lucky to be alive and gave back as much as he could to those less fortunate. The next few years were good. Howard became more interested in the Jewish community. In one of their get-togethers for young adults, he met the lovely and charming Lisa, and they fell in love. In May 1994 Marshall and I gave Howard and Lisa an engagement party. From Dana-Farber, we invited Dr. Eric Rubin and his wife Kim. At the party, Howard honored Dr. Rubin by talking about his dedication and all the care the doctors and nurses had given to save his life. As Howard spoke, our guests cried. We realized that Dr. Rubin had become more than just Howard's doctor. They had become friends. On July 24, 1994, Howard and Lisa married in a traditional Jewish ceremony outdoors in California. Family and friends traveled from across the country to celebrate Howard's and Lisa's new life together.

There it is in 200 words: the perfect final scene for a screenplay. As Mom told the story, I was the hero who beat a death sentence and rode off into the western sunset—where I found the love of my life, renewed ties to the Jewish community and continued to celebrate friendships that remain the pillars of my life today.

That's all true. But there is much more to this part of my life story that might inspire your own quest to shine brightly in the world. One of the main themes of this book is that life is best when we don't try to go it alone. That's true of cancer, business, sports and civic causes. It certainly was true when I headed to the West Coast.

In writing this chapter of the book, I already had Mom's version of the story from her memoir to share with you. To get Dad's version of my big move to the Pacific, I invited him on to Zoom.

"Help me tell the rest of the story. I didn't just ride off into the sunset alone," I told Dad. "You reached out."

He shrugged matter-of-factly. "Of course, I did. I had to reach out to help you, as a good father, you know. My boy was moving thousands of miles away, bald and skinny and not fully on his feet yet. It was just natural for me to think: My boy's still not 100% yet! He needs support. He needs some good friends. And, you know what I mean: some good friends with connections back home."

That's true, too.

"So, tell the story, Dad," I said. "Who'd you call?"

"You didn't know anybody out there when you first got to LA, so I thought: Howard should get to know a good Jewish kid. I remembered that Morty and Sydell and Wolfie had a boy out there, too. I'd known them for years. Decades! They were a family who started with one shoe store up in Manchester, New Hampshire, and then they opened more stores around New England. I'd go see them regularly because I supplied boots for their stores. We'd talk. Morty and Sydell were husband and wife, you know, and Wolfie was the uncle— Morty's uncle. So, whenever we saw each other, we'd talk about our families and that's how I heard their boy—Morty and Sydell's son, Jay—had moved to California to pursue his dream of becoming a screen writer in Hollywood. We all worried as parents. So, we reached out together, and we connected you guys," Dad said.

He continued, "Then, the other family I reached out to was Al and Deedy Schiro, out of Bangor, Maine. Al and Deedy had opened stores across Maine. Just like I heard from Morty and Sydell and Wolfie—I heard that Al and Deedy's kid who likes to play basketball had moved out there, too. And I'm thinking: My Howard plays basketball. And I heard Al's boy, Craig, got connected into the Jewish community young adults program, you know, which was another plus. So—"

"So, you played matchmaker," I said, "and amazingly enough both of those 'boys'—Morty and Sydell's son Jay Rosen and Al and Deedy's son Craig Shiro—became my lifelong friends. You knew what you were doing, Dad!" I am still in touch and friends with them today over 30 years later.

"There you go," Dad said. "Three thousand miles isn't so far when you know people. You can still keep it all in the family, you know."

"Right," I said, laughing. "Wherever we are headed in the world, our question is: Hey, isn't there a someone we know here? And, when we remember a connection, we pick up the phone and connect with that person. It's not good to try to do it all on your own. So, we reach out. And that's what I'm trying to tell people in this book I'm writing. We all need to reach out. Life is better if we're connected and together."

"Yeah, of course," Dad said. "After all, it's the simple truth: Life's bedrock is the relationships we build, nurture and sustain."

Just as Dad and his friends had hoped, Jay Rosen became the first real friend I made in Los Angeles. We became so close over the years that there were times when Jay and I would talk several times a day. All these years later, we still feel as close as we always were, even though we talk more like once a month these days. Of course, all this family matchmaking among friends could have backfired. When they began pushing Jay and me to connect, Jay could have felt unduly pressured. He could have resented having to reach out to this sick-looking new guy from out East. Instead, like me, Jay trusted the suggestion and was a generous host. He worked in the film industry. At that time, he was working on productions at Twentieth Century Fox. My new job at NCR landed me for the first few weeks at temporary housing in Century City—so Jay and I lived and worked close to each other.

"I remember you coming to town," Jay said when I reached him to talk about those connections. "The first thing we did was invite you out to dinner, didn't we?"

"Yeah, it was the three of us: you and your girlfriend at that time and me. Because you were in the movie industry, you knew some really fun places to go. You took me to this restaurant where I was sitting just a table away from Jodie Foster. But I didn't recognize her—and you never told me, Jay! You never said a word while we were eating. Only later did I hear that I'd been that close to a big star."

Jay laughed. "Yeah, I remember that. I wasn't going to say anything. You don't do that. But we still had fun that first night, didn't we? And Howard, you and I certainly hit it off in so many ways. Our parents knew what they were doing."

"Yeah, you were kind to me, Jay. I certainly wasn't at my best, at first. I was just 136 pounds and bald and you helped me to get my life together again. You were my first friend out there," I said.

I called Craig Shiro, too, to ask him about this transcontinental family networking.

"Well sure it made sense for our parents to reach out," Craig said. "I grew up in a family retail shoe business and your father was a rep of a boot company. When Marshall would pay them a visit, they'd sit in the office and talk. You know—"

Then Craig rattled off the conversation the two fathers must have had as my father walked in the door of his father's office.

> "Maaaash! Maaashall Brown! So good to see you! So, how's it going since you were here last?"
>
> "Oh, you know, I worry for my son. He's just moved to California—to LA."

"Yeah? You know what? My son just moved to California, too! I worry, too."

"Where? ... LA? ... Really?"

"Yeah, what's your son like to do?"

"Well, my son likes to play basketball and drink beer and the usual things, you know."

"Yeah, my son loves to play basketball and drink beer."

I was laughing as Craig finished. "That's probably how it went," I said.

"I'm sure that's exactly how it went," Craig said, "and next thing we knew our phone numbers were being passed back and forth long distance. Dad called and told me: 'Listen, now! Write this number down! Call Howard!' This was before everyone had the internet or email or smart phones. No texting. If we wanted to talk, we picked up a telephone and called long distance. We wrote down phone numbers on paper and called them later. If the person wasn't in, we left messages for each other on our answering machines. We made the connection happen old school—and our fathers were right: A great friendship was born."

"Remember the crazy coincidence?" I asked Craig. "We lived so close that we actually had been playing basketball at the same local court—but at different times."

"Right, right," Craig said. "From the start, sports were a big part of our friendship."

"But, hey, we need to make it clear: This wasn't just a hobby," I insisted. "Basketball and all the other sports—golf and flag football and all the rest—they were my happy place where I could feel my body rebuilding. I was still in bad shape when I moved out there and I had to consciously put on some muscle. Basketball was a lifeline. When I landed in LA, I needed to attack life with new vigor."

"Basketball certainly was easy for us," Craig said. "We lived right near each other. The Dolphin school court was right there. We could play basketball after work. Sometimes we golfed. As time went on, for a while, we actually shared an apartment in Marina del Rey."

"We played flag football, too, with Jay. I wasn't any good at that, but I loved all of it. I could feel myself coming back and rebuilding from cancer."

"Oh, you want to talk football?!" Craig chuckled. "You were all about football, Howard. You were obsessed with it. You were the one who hooked me on fantasy football, which we play to this day. Back then, we called it 'rotisserie football' and we had to do our research for the fantasy football leagues by going out and buying magazines and newspapers. It took so much work! But Howard, you hooked me because you impressed me with how much you knew. You seemed to know everything about every player, which made the whole thing a lot more fun for me. Even though I was a fan of football, I was a novice to that whole idea of making up these fantasy teams."

"Yes," I said. "It started in August of 1992 in the breakroom of NCR's LA office in Century City. We called it the Quantum Football League."

"I remember. You had to help me make my picks for the first year. Then, I was off and running—and it's a big part of my life to this day, 30 years later."

We still make an annual pilgrimage to Las Vegas to draft our teams each year with a champion's steak dinner and huge Heisman-like trophy with the winning team's name on it.

"Oh, yeah," I said. "The names! I am the BeanEaters and I was a founding owner from NCR. You're the HiBanchies, after I invited you in year 3." Then, together, we listed the rest:

Henry Medina (founding owner / NCR), the Huge and Global Hitters
Lee Paries (NCR / Teradata), Whoop Ass Express
Fernando Parra (founding owner / NCR), Parrasites
Brian and Jenn Singer, Cavaliers
Todd Renner (NCR), Shake Weights
Chris White (NCR), Ski Demons
Ron Nickens, Slug Nation
Sonny Gulati, Cow Gas
Jeff Davidson, Air Attack
Jeff and Tony Crivello, Brotherly Love

We have had a bunch of other owners pass through during our three decades of league history. Fantasy Football is another way to keep long distance friendships connected, trash talk and have friendly competition that bonds us all.

"It wasn't just basketball, golf and fantasy football on the side," I said. "We also followed our favorite pro teams from back home. When New England teams like the Patriots, Red Sox, Bruins or Celtics came anywhere close to our part of the country to play—remember what we would do, Craig? We'd fill a car or hop a plane with everybody who wanted to go to the games. We'd drive for hours sometimes. We took road trips to Arizona, San Diego, San Francisco and Denver."

Guy stuff, pure and simple.

How did I recover from my death sentence with cancer? Sure, the chemicals and pills and treatments and radiation—all the medical procedures were life savers. But the truth of cancer survival is that there's a very long tail of recovery that extends for years after you leave the doctors' care. We each have to figure out a way to jump back into life again, if we ever hope to regain our equilibrium and joy in living. So, I rebuilt my physical and emotional strength with lots of guy stuff. Good sports; good food; good drinks—all stirred and marinated in an occasional late-night revelry or a road trip. This wasn't amusement. I was fighting to restore my life again after nearly dying. Through the long cycle of cancer treatments, I had driven my body right to the fragile edge of what I could survive.

"Attack life with vigor." That became my mantra. Along the way, my circle of friends grew as we all let off steam after our high-powered day jobs. If my friends made a suggestion, they knew I'd be game. Then, one day, after my hair grew back and I was feeling more like my old self, Craig slipped in a non-sports suggestion.

"There's this young leadership group sponsored by the local Jewish community," Craig said.

"I'm not looking to join a temple," I said, trying to politely shut this down right away. "My family has never been that observant. I'm not really—"

Craig cut me off. "No, that's not what I mean," he said. "There are lots of programs going on all the time, sponsored by the LA Jewish Federation, and this one is called the Young Leadership Development Group. It's a good thing. Just once a month. Plus, you'll meet a really good bunch of people there."

For Christians, this conversation may sound odd. The most common first step of getting involved in a Christian community is attending and then joining a church. Later on, at the pinnacle of my career in developing a global religious network, I became an expert in visiting congregations to help Christian leaders strengthen their churches through online networks. I became an expert at how churches function and grow, so I know also that Jewish communities are organized differently. Like Christians, millions of Jews do formally join congregations, but our community life is not built on the same expectations as churches. For example, many Jews in America don't regularly attend daily or weekly services. Our big crowds show up for major holidays and life events. While it is also true that millions of self-identified Christians rarely attend services, the difference is that, when Jewish families attend only a few times a year, that is not, in itself, considered a litmus test of their Jewish identity. There are many other ways that Jews join together to express and celebrate our core values of community building. For example, ever since the American colonial era, Jews in America have organized to help the needy. In 1895, the first of what we now call a community-wide "Jewish Federation" was founded in Boston. These nonprofit federations quickly became pillars in our communities and came to support a wide range of charitable causes as well as programs to promote the ongoing vitality of Jewish families.

Craig Schiro's casual invitation was for me to take one small step with him into one local Jewish group in Los Angeles. My initial hesitancy was natural. I already had a lot of commitments in my life. There's no question that my Jewish identity was a core part of my life, but I didn't need to prove that by joining a group. What amazes me, now, is that my first response to Craig soon changed and evolved until eventually I was making major commitments of my time and talents to helping people around the world through Jewish organizations.

How did I get there? Very small steps. My life took a dramatic turn because our parents had reached out to each other when we all moved to California, then Jay and Craig became good friends, we enjoyed hanging out together and finally Craig suggested a new way we could have fun together. I had no idea what doorways Craig was opening for me. Craig didn't know what would happen either.

This was unknown territory and that's why I wasn't eager to do this. We were having enough fun in other ways. In fact, and I will never forget this part of our conversations—as I continued to be skeptical about going to this federation program—Craig kept adding to his pitch. "C'mon Howard. You'll enjoy the programs. It's just 7 to 10 p.m. once a month—and they always bring in great speakers."

Still skeptical.

Then, he paused and added the kicker, "Plus, it's a great way to meet some incredible Jewish women." Yes, to be honest, that was the hook that closed the deal. It was a great place to meet women. And, obviously, Craig was right again. He was right about a lot of things, as it turned out.

First, Craig was correct about the amazing people the Los Angeles Federation attracted for these gatherings—top professionals who were so smart and kind and funny that, right away, I wanted to be a part of their circle. We were in our 20s, 30s and 40s, what we used to call "youngish." Most of us were driven. To be honest, a lot of us were flat-out workaholics. So, asking us to show up just once a month on a Thursday evening was smart. It was an invitation that most of us could squeeze into our jam-packed schedules.

Also, the moment we first walked through the door, I could see that there were, just as Craig had promised, many great women in this group. That pleased me but didn't surprise me. What actually surprised me on the first night was that the speakers really were fascinating. They talked about interesting global issues and then everyone was divided into small circles to talk over what we had just heard. Then, we were invited to consider opportunities for community service. I remember hearing that the Federation needed volunteer fundraisers to make calls on behalf of its charitable agencies. Making calls like this was not only my professional specialty as a salesman—but, more than that, raising money for the needy felt like I was connecting a heavy-duty extension cord that lit up all those memories about tzedakah boxes from my childhood. Sure, I could help!

Very quickly, just like Craig had been hooked into trying fantasy football "just once," I was hooked on serving the Jewish community. But wait. Does that sound inappropriate? Comparing Jewish volunteerism and fantasy football? The point I'm making is that, just like Craig, I had agreed to try something I barely understood. I hadn't done anything significant in any Jewish community since my bar mitzvah a decade earlier. I did not understand, at the time I started going to these young leaders' programs, just how deeply my commitment to the worldwide Jewish community would extend over the years. At first, this was just fun. I was good at it. The new people I was meeting were fascinating.

Then, I met Lisa.

This next story may sound like I'm returning to Mom's Hallmark movie script, but I have to be absolutely honest in telling you: Meeting Lisa felt like two great waves converging on the shoreline. Of course, waves on the shore is a Hallmark metaphor. Lisa and I tell the story, to this day, with a different term. Our meeting was *bashert*. That's Yiddish for "soulmate." It means more than love. Bashert conveys "destiny"—both in personal fulfillment and in the destiny of the world itself. Bashert is more than personal passion. Great Jewish sages reserve the word for two people who manage to find each other in the world as the completion of a timeless and divine match.

Bashert—love as eternal destiny. A powerful idea, right?

Imagine my surprise! Here I am swapping invitations with my friend Craig. He's accepted my invitation to try fantasy football and I'm trying his suggestion to check out this regional organization for young Jewish professionals. Our socializing was all just casual fun and games until—bam! There was Lisa.

And along with her came this fateful reconnection to my lifelong calling to give back to the world in some way. I was grappling with titanic spiritual concepts like bashert and *tikkun olam*, repairing the world.

To begin with, like another movie metaphor, Lisa was a stranger whom I saw across a crowded room on an enchanted evening. She was beautiful. I began to fall in love from a distance. But I was soon to learn that there was so much more to bashert than simple attraction. To begin with, we unknowingly had shared a whole series of Hallmark moments—converging milestones in our lives. For example, on May 24, 1990, Lisa was on an airplane moving to Los Angeles to start her new life on the West Coast—the same day that I was in the hospital receiving my bone marrow transplant that gave me a new chance at life. Then, three years later, we both joined the Jewish Federation's Leadership Development Group, neither expecting we'd meet our life partner as a result.

I invited Lisa to help me tell this part of the story. I began by saying, "Lisa, when I first spotted you at one of those leadership gatherings, I said to myself, 'I have to meet her.'"

"That's sweet," Lisa said. "I wish I could say the same, but there were hundreds of people around us at those events. I didn't notice you until you stood up at the Friday night service at the leadership retreat at the Brandeis-Bardin Institute."

I continued the story: "So, here's the setting: Brandeis-Bardin is this huge facility in Simi Valley, thousands of acres that also have been used by TV and film producers as a location, because it's so visually striking. The place is a magical hybrid of Judaism and California landscapes with touches of Hollywood. A lot of the property was donated to the nonprofit by the *Gunsmoke* TV star James Arness from land that once was his ranch. One of the roads within the center is named after him. Then, the architecture of the main hall, called the House of the Book, resembles a gigantic, unfolding Torah scroll, like something out of Star Trek. In fact, scenes from a couple of Star Trek movies were shot there. And in 1993, as Lisa and I were getting to know each other, kids across the country began to recognize the House of the Book as the Command Center for the Power Rangers. That sci-fi production team filmed there, too. So, Lisa and I were attending this weekend retreat in this amazing Jewish center—a place that's pure Hollywood, too—with a couple of hundred other young professionals."

"Quite a setting!" Lisa said. "But what I remember most vividly from that weekend starts with the Friday evening service at the retreat. In the service, it came time for the mourners' *kaddish*, and you stood up. You said the name of your grandfather who had passed away recently. It moved me that you did that for him."

As Lisa said this, I was surprised at the emotions those memories of Papa Mike and Bubby Lil triggered in me. "Papa Mike," my grandfather on my mother's side, was the lovable, cigar-chomping guy who enjoyed golf and games like cribbage and rummy cube and took my sister and me on vacation every year with our cousins.

"I'll never forget you standing up for your grandfather," Lisa said. "It touched me. But, we didn't actually talk at all that night. Once again, there were so many other people around us. The evening moved quickly. We never connected."

"It was very early the next morning that we talked, by accident really," I said. "We both had the idea of taking a very early walk to the House of the Book that Saturday morning before breakfast and that morning's Shabbat service. And, when I saw you walking along the same path, I think I said something memorable like: 'Good morning!'"

"Yeah, a great opening line," Lisa said.

We laughed, then she said, "Well, I guess I wasn't much more eloquent. I remember saying something equally memorable like: 'Hello.' I wanted to say more. A while later that day, as we were leaving breakfast, I finally said, 'I liked that suit you wore last night.' I guess I was trying to tell you that I had noticed you."

"Flattery gets you everywhere," I said. We laughed again. Our lines were hardly worthy of a Hollywood script—but it was that simple series of encounters at the retreat that started our lives together.

"When we finally got to the service that morning, we found the theme was all about new beginnings," Lisa said. "You came and sat near me and that's when I started to feel drawn to you, Howard. All day, after that, I would look for you and that evening, after the formal program, someone suggested we form a massage train with everybody sitting in a long row that wove across the stage and up some spiral stairs backstage. At first, I walked to the back, but then I saw that you were in the very front of the train. You didn't have a back to rub."

"You didn't let that happen, though," I said. "You got up the courage to come sit in front of me and ask, 'Is this seat taken?' Of course, I was happy to give you a back rub."

"Afterward, we took a walk, each of us still wearing our puzzle-piece-shaped name tags," Lisa said. "We ended up talking until 2:30 a.m. What really impressed me about you, Howard, was your positive attitude, your sense of confidence and, as I got to know you more, your good heart, kindness and generosity. That night, we were beginning to see that we may have been the missing piece in each other's lives."

As we began getting to know each other, Lisa amazed me with her experiences and her hopes that paralleled my own values and aspirations. We quickly realized that we shared a lifelong commitment to community service. The truth was that I had been so busy building my career and battling cancer that I had few charitable accomplishments to my name. We were in our 20s, but Lisa already had worked eight years in Washington, D.C. as part of the U.S. Congressional staff enacting legislation to protect children by enhancing child-welfare and juvenile-justice systems and funding community-based children's mental health treatment. She also was an accomplished activist for the needs of aging and disabled Americans and had worked on public policies to combat domestic violence. In her spare time, she volunteered with a national crisis hotline (like the ones Emily had me mention in an earlier chapter). Her list of accomplishments was far longer than mine. She had worked in homeless shelters and led community service for a newly formed chapter of the National Council of Jewish Women. When she moved to California in 1990 to work at the Los Angeles County Department of Children and Family Services, she was continuing to strengthen the national safety net for vulnerable young people. In her new role, she shaped the county's position on state and federal child welfare legislation and developed innovative programs for abused and at-risk youth to put these policies into practice. In fact, if I had to sum Lisa up in three words, they would be "compassion in action."

As I began dating her, I caught glimpses of her light as she talked excitedly about all these efforts. I learned that her sense of justice and her desire to help others was an intrinsic part of her life.

"Ever since I can remember, I wanted to do something to make the world a better place," Lisa said as we talked about those early years of our marriage. "I got that from Dad." Robert Naftaly, a CPA by profession, served in the Jewish community in many ways, including as the national treasurer for the Anti-Defamation League, the nonprofit that monitors and combats all forms of hatred. Among his many roles as Lisa was growing up, he was president of the Jewish Federation of Metropolitan Detroit and president of the Jewish Fund, which provides health and social-welfare grants in the Detroit area. He started Project Chesed to provide free dental and health care for the neediest families.

"One of my earliest memories of my father is seeing him walk around our synagogue as its president, schmoozing with the congregants," Lisa said. "I could tell how much people loved and respected him. I wanted to be like him. As I learned more about Judaism, I realized that we are chosen to be a light unto nations—to set a good example—and that we are called to repair the world's brokenness. That's why I responded so warmly when I saw that you were starting down that same path, Howard."

"We met at the right time," I said.

Our lives seemed to complement each other. While both of us had proven talents at persuasively addressing large groups, Lisa's work as a communicator was strongest through her writing, while mine was more as a public speaker. Lisa had researched and written speeches, press releases and policy statements that were delivered on the floor of the U.S. Congress. She had addressed national conferences on behalf of at-risk children and families. I admired her communication skills, since I was polishing my own talents in those days. She was stronger at writing than I was. I was more comfortable on my feet as I spoke with groups, weaving together stories and adapting my message as I saw the audience respond. That's why I created this book you are reading through two years of Zoom interviews and digital collaborations with scores of other people. That's why this book reads like I'm sitting down and casually telling you about my life.

"I was in awe of you, Lisa," I said as we talked about our courtship. "I couldn't believe how much you already had done to help children and families. I was impressed at how you expressed to people so clearly why these things were important. Your words flowed from your heart. You've always been a writer on a mission."

In 2021, while I was drafting this book—Lisa wrote a key chapter in another book. It is a guidebook, written by a dozen co-authors, to help the millions of unpaid American caregivers and their families. The title is *Now What? A Guide to the Gifts and Challenges of Aging.* Lisa was invited to be one of the co-authors because she has been working on this issue since the 1980s when the term "caregiver" was just emerging in the national conversation. In fact, she was one of the people who helped to place the need for respite care on the national agenda. Today, the issue is as urgent as daily headlines. In the midst of a pandemic, families nationwide depend on our nation's more than 50 million caregivers.

That's what I mean when I say we were bashert. With all my heart, I was falling in love with a beautiful woman whose vocation in life ultimately would enlarge my own commitment to repairing the world. Our union was destined. Without understanding that deeper level of what was unfolding between us, the actual details of how we met and fell in love may seem a little goofy in the way true-love stories can sound to others.

Let me give you a good example of how Lisa connects those passions through her writing and sometimes her public speaking. While researching this book, I recently found the text of a short, inspirational talk (a *d'var torah*) she gave to the San Francisco Women's Alliance Board, when she was its vice president of community outreach. But first, for non-Jewish readers, let me explain the central metaphor she uses from the Amidah.

Our friend Rabbi Joseph Krakoff helped me with the context. "Lisa starts her talk with a reference to a prayer that's familiar to any Jewish person, the Amidah," the rabbi said. "The word means 'standing.' And we all know that the Amidah is a way of showing that, as we approach God, we realize we are standing on the shoulders of our matriarchs and patriarchs. We are entering God's inner chamber and speaking to God about our hopes for peace and our need for help. Then, this prayer also has a traditional choreography to it. Eventually, we reach the part of the prayer where we say *Kadosh, Kadosh, Kadosh.* That's the 'Holy, Holy, Holy' passage from Isaiah 6. And as we say those words, we stand up on our tiptoes to signify that, although we can never actually reach God, we are extending ourselves toward God. When Lisa opens her talk with this prayer, this image, this experience is connecting with something that everyone listening to her would know."

Here's what Lisa wrote to inspire that gathering:

Kadosh, Kadosh, Kadosh!

Ever since I was a young girl, this part of the Amidah has always resonated with me—and not just because I wanted to be taller! In rising up on my tiptoes, I not only felt physically closer to God, but in some small way my spirit rose. Over the years, I've come to see it as both a reverent act and a physical expression of our spiritual yearning to be closer to God, to be a better person, to be holy: Kadosh.

If only we could become holy by standing on our tiptoes!

Luckily, the Torah offers us instructions on how to become more holy. This past Shabbat, we read the *parsha Kedoshim* which means "holy." It opens with God commanding Moses to tell the Children of Israel, "You shall be holy, for I the Lord your God am holy." God then proceeds to decree 51 *mitzvot,* good deeds, including some of the biggies like keeping the Sabbath and giving to the poor. Some of the commandments are more ritualistic in nature such as keeping kosher and not mixing certain materials; others are more ethical in nature like respecting one's parents and elders, giving tzedakah, not gossiping or committing adultery, and dealing honestly and fairly with others.

For some, Judaism is seen as primarily a set of rituals or behaviors that must be performed—or not performed. For others, Judaism is seen as a form of social action, the expression of ethical ideals. This week's *parsha* teaches us that Judaism—and the way to attain holiness—is through a combination of ritual observances and ethical behavior. That is because each one—ritual and ethics—informs and enriches the other. Ritual needs ethics to root it in the human condition; to make it more than just rote behaviors. Similarly, ethics need rituals to give substance to lofty ideals and rituals help to create community through shared values, standards and customs.

Instead of Kadosh, Kadosh, Kadosh, we might say: "Ritual, Ethics, Community."

But what does this have to do with our work as lay leaders?

We attain holiness when we give to those in need in our area and around the world.

We attain holiness when we enable those in repressed lands to observe the rituals of our culture or to emigrate to a freer society.

We attain holiness when we help build community, add a bit of Yiddishkeit to our events, or nurture the leadership and generosity of others.

And even when politics frustrate us or things seem mundane or overwhelming, we attain holiness by remembering what really matters—why we do what we do. As leaders in our community, we must do more than rise up on our tiptoes. We must take giant steps and help pave the way for others to learn, to grow, to give and to do. In so doing, we elevate not only ourselves, but our entire Jewish community.

Kadosh, Kadosh, Kadosh!

Do you see why I fell in love with Lisa? Why we are bashert? Quite unexpectedly, through the coaxing of my friend Craig, I found myself going to a program where I wound up meeting this beautiful woman. Then, Lisa and I kept running into each other—including a bit of LA movie-magic, complete with Hallmark moments. Then, the real revelation in our relationship was this bedrock foundation we shared from the deepest roots of Judaism and our families. Our hopes for our life together intertwined with our hopes for the world.

Not many months later, I found myself taking a very traditional step with Lisa's father. I asked for his permission. Because it was LA in the '90s, I called him long distance from my car phone. He was very supportive.

Then there were more Hallmark touches, of course. The night I proposed was December 31, 1993. We had reserved a room at the Channel Road Inn, a century-old southern California landmark near the beach in Santa Monica. Then, we booked a table for an elaborate New Year's Eve party at another century-old landmark, Four Oaks in Bel Air. A month earlier, The *LA Times* had raved about Four Oaks, calling it "Romance under the Trees."

"With all this preparation, of course I knew something was coming," Lisa said in helping to retell the story. "All through dinner, Howard, you said so many beautiful things."

"You gave me such joy. I tried my best to find the right words."

"You did. You did," Lisa said. "So, I was ready for you to ask me, you know, the big question—all evening long. Then—nothing. Hours went by."

"Well, I had a plan."

"I actually gave up on you asking. It was getting close to midnight and I was restless. I finally made a visit to the ladies' room."

"And that's when I jumped into action. I asked the whole restaurant crowd to be part of this. The room already was electric with New Year's Eve coming—then everyone got even more excited. My heart was absolutely pounding. When you know something like this is so right for you, you just burst with the emotion."

"So, I came back from the ladies' room not expecting anything—when suddenly the lights dimmed. Howard got down on one knee and said—"

"You are the love of my life. Would you do me the honor of marrying me and being my bride?"

"Yes! Yes! That's what I said, but it was hard to hear because everyone was cheering. We were hugging and kissing. And, a minute later, we all did the countdown to 1994!"

"Champagne toasts!"

"Mazel tov everywhere!"

Of course, then we had to top that with the location for our wedding on July 24, 1994. We booked Shutters on the Beach with the *chuppah* (Jewish wedding canopy) and all the seats arranged outdoors overlooking the ocean. At that point, Shutters was this gorgeous new hotel on the Pacific, and all the LA media were raving about it. Once again, the word "magical" popped up in those reports—and Shutters quickly was becoming a destination for celebrities. We were only the third wedding they held. Best of all for our families, the place was built with touches of "Cape Cod design" and "New England architecture" so my folks from out East felt right at home.

"It was one more step along the fairy tale," Lisa said, "but we also put a lot of thought into the traditions we followed that day, all the rituals were so carefully prepared."

The rabbi guiding us through those rituals, Rabbi Steven Leder, was the assistant rabbi at our Wilshire Boulevard Temple at that time but—like so many other people in our circle in Los Angeles at that time—he had his eyes on national media. He went on to write a series of popular books, appear on network talk shows and collaborate with Aaron Sorkin on one of the most memorable episodes of *The West Wing* about the morality of capital punishment. That's because Steven also was Aaron's rabbi and performed his wedding, too.

Our cantor was Meier Finkelstein, one of the most popular cantors and composers of new Jewish music. In addition to hundreds of pieces for Jewish worship, he also composed and arranged for TV series, including *Dallas*, and the movies. He collaborated with Stephen Spielberg on the musical soundtrack for the series *Survivors of the Holocaust*. To this day, Lisa and I love to hear his magical tenor voice.

"Our wedding really was Hollywood meets Jewish tradition," I said. "I got caught up in it all myself, I have to admit. We produced a wedding video that was like something you'd see on TV with these jaw-dropping shots we filmed of this storybook wedding along the Pacific shoreline. But, despite all that fun stuff going on all around us, we took very seriously the commitments we were making and the traditions we were following."

"In fact, we see the commitments we made that day—every day quite literally," Lisa said. "Our rabbi told us: One day doesn't make you married. That takes a lifetime. And this certainly has been true for us. Like most married couples, we need reminders all the time."

Lisa was referring to our wedding rings and our *Ketubah*.

"In Hebrew, we say *Ani l'dodi v'dodi li*, which means 'I am my beloved's and my beloved is mine' from the Song of Songs," Lisa said. "I recited those words under the wedding canopy as have Jewish brides for centuries before me. Howard and I loved those words so much we had them inscribed on our wedding rings—and they appear prominently in our Ketubah."

Millions of Jewish couples around the world have a Ketubah in some form. Joey Krakoff, our rabbi friend, explained, "The Hebrew word means 'written.' It's the traditional marriage contract in Judaism, written in Aramaic or Hebrew and sometimes other languages as well. And, often now, couples will commission an artist so that the Ketubah can be framed and hung on the wall. By coincidence, Lisa and Howard's was created by the same artist who created the one my wife and I have hanging in our house. Surrounding the text, it's got these beautiful images of Israel and lots of traditional symbols like the pomegranate are interwoven around the text. They chose to have their Ketubah lettered in Hebrew and English. The actual text is based on the covenants men and women have made with each other down through many centuries and then it often is adapted in some ways by the couples."

"In our case," Lisa said, "I did write a slightly modernized, more egalitarian version of the traditional words that then were used as our vows during the ceremony. Just before the ceremony, we signed the Ketubah in the presence of the rabbi, our parents and wedding party as part of the *bedeken*, or veiling ceremony, during which the couple reaffirms that each willingly chose the other to marry and the groom lowers the bride's veil. The Ketubah is displayed at the wedding and hangs in our bedroom as a constant reminder of our sacred obligations and intentions."

In English, Lisa declared in the Ketubah: "Affirming our people's covenant with God may we be consecrated to each other by this ring. I vow to love, cherish, honor and respect you, to nourish and sustain you as Jewish women have done for their husbands throughout the ages."

And I declared: "Affirming our people's covenant with God may we be consecrated to each other by this ring. I vow to love, cherish, honor and respect you, to nourish and sustain you as Jewish men have done for their wives throughout the ages."

Together, we promised: "Let our lives be intertwined forever. Let our hearts be united in love. Let our home be rich with wisdom and reverence. Limitless is my love for you and my devotion without end. I take you to be mine in love and tenderness. I take you to be mine in faithfulness. May our hearts beat as one. May our life together be illuminated by our people's heritage. May our home be built on Torah and lovingkindness. May my love for you continue to grow."

Our Ketubah closes with these words, "This covenant has been signed and sealed according to the laws and traditions that began with Abraham and Sarah and continued through Moses and the People of Israel."

If you are married, can you recall the vows you spoke on the day of your wedding?

Imagine our humbling reminder of those words on the wall in our bedroom, a reminder each morning and every night. It certainly is true—just as Mom told our story in her 200 words—we began with a Hallmark romance and we were united in a Hollywood fairy tale. But it also is true that, like most married couples, our covenant has been sorely tested. All too soon, Lisa discovered she had married an utter workaholic riding the crest of the Silicon Valley boom. And, of course, I would meet death yet again and suddenly Lisa would find herself testing all of those commitments "in sickness and in health" as my tireless caregiver.

Although it is lovely, our Ketubah is not merely a decoration. In our home, it is the roadmap that has carried us deeper and farther than we could have imagined along the Pacific Ocean shore that day we first voiced those words in the presence of our family and friends.

If you're not Jewish, this may be the first time you are reading about our custom of the Ketubah. Consider for a moment: If you were to make a lifelong pledge to someone you love—and then were to hang those words on the wall of your home as a reminder—what would you write?

Shining Brightly

Please consider volunteering, giving or learning about these or similar organizations that touched my life. There are many spiritual and religious organizations that need you!

+ **Jewish Federation of North America** — JewishFederations.org
+ **Islamic Society of North America (ISNA)** — ISNA.net
+ **National Council of Churches** — NationalCouncilOfChurches.us

One of the best decisions I made in my life was meeting Ian through Jewish Big Brothers in Los Angeles. We began in 1993 with sports and fun outings, then the relationship grew until Ian became like a real "little brother" to me. In 2018, I was honored to serve as best man at his wedding. Our relationship strengthened both of our lives in more ways than we could have imagined.

8

Expanding Our Family Circle

We all know someone with chronic family problems who sighs wearily and tells us: "Well, you can't choose your family!" Perhaps you've said that yourself.

But the truth is that our biological families are only the start of an ever-enlarging circle we draw throughout our lives. Throughout our lives together, Lisa and I have reached out our arms to warmly embrace those who need us.

That's why I was so pleased, during the pandemic, to discover an app for giving virtual hugs. Canadian entrepreneur Zamir Khan launched VidHug (now Momento.com) in 2018, mainly because his mom loved a video montage of best wishes he edited together for her birthday. Zamir thought other families might enjoy making and sharing such videos, if the process was simplified through an easily available app. Given his background in software development, this was easy to build and launch. However, few people had heard of the service Khan was offering until COVID prevented visits to our loved ones. Suddenly, VidHug was buzzing. Since much of my own entrepreneurial career has focused on media innovation, I was hooked the moment I spotted what Khan had created. VidHug lets you invite the whole extended family—including friends, neighbors, co-workers and anyone else in your long list of contacts—to post short video clips celebrating a loved one's milestone. As moderator, you organize the clips, wrap the whole thing in colorful graphics and a bit of fun music—then launch this once-in-a-lifetime gift of best wishes at the appropriate time.

The VidHug that I produced for my own mom's 75th birthday had 18 little video clips that absolutely delighted her—including one from our dog! After her Zoom party, I got a rave review in a phone call from Dad, who knows that I'm continually looking for new business ventures.

"Howard! Howard! That movie thing you made was amazing!" he shouted. "It should be your future! Remember when you helped to launch that TV thing Avid years ago? This hug idea is the next big thing for you! You gotta do this!"

"Dad! Wait!" I was laughing as I tried to interrupt him, but he was too excited to stop.

"I mean it, Howard!" he said, pouring on the sales pitch. "It could be your next career. You've got to do this for people, Howard. People love these videos. You can do this for the world."

"Dad! Wait a minute." I appreciated his encouragement and was smiling broadly as I told him over the phone line, "Dad, thanks for the kind words! But the problem is: Somebody's already done it. This guy up in Canada is behind VidHug. He put it online for the whole world. All I had to do was have videos uploaded, click a few buttons and then add some finishing touches to make and render their videos. Dad, I'm glad you loved what I put together, but the idea is taken—somebody's already built the platform."

"Ohhh," Dad said, deflated. He simply assumed that my VidHug for Mom was a complicated technical project I had cooked up, like some of the other platforms I developed with colleagues earlier in my career.

The simple takeaway is: People get really excited about these little videos. Mom's VidHug was such a hit that I decided to create one for my little brother, Ian, because he and his wife, Sara, were about to have their first baby in the spring of 2021. Lisa and I talked about this and decided a pandemic-safe baby shower for Ian and Sara could be built around mailing them our gifts in advance, then organizing a Zoom to have some fun together with family and friends—and finally creating a VidHug that we could play for everyone over Zoom as the centerpiece of the program.

However, as I began looking over Ian's and Sara's contacts, I was reminded— and reminded my wife, "Hey, Lisa, you know we've got a challenge here? We pretty much *are* Ian's family. Everybody else we could invite to the VidHug is from Sara's family and her circle of friends. So, we've got to step up on our end to balance out the video. When it comes to family, we're pretty much all Ian's got."

Now, if you've been reading this book carefully, you're wondering: When did a brother enter my story? In the opening chapters, my twin sister, Cheryl

(CJ), and I were the only siblings. And just to be clear: No, Mom didn't have anything to do with this brother, although she now loves Ian, too.

Lisa brought Ian into our lives in 1993 while we were dating. She did it through the force of her enthusiasm as we toured a regional Jewish fair, an event to encourage volunteerism with booths hosted by dozens of groups and agencies across southern California. We stopped and talked to people sitting at many different tables, but Lisa made a special pitch at the Jewish Big Brothers booth.

"You'd be a great Big Brother, Howard," she said and began to pile on the praise and encouragement. After all, her career was dedicated to helping families in at-risk communities. She knew all the data and the arguments. "C'mon, Howard, you'll love doing this and you'll make a big difference."

I held up my hand, surrendering. "Enough. And I thought I was the salesman."

She smiled. "You already know I'm right, don't you?"

As I have done so many times over the years, I admitted: "Yes, you're right."

Perhaps it was coincidence, but I believe destiny also was at work that day. I think Ian and I were fated to meet, and Lisa's pitch was just one step toward what was meant to be. Again, it was bashert. The fact is that 10-year-old Ian Ellis and 27-year-old Howard Brown entered the Los Angeles area Jewish Big Brothers program at the same time—and we met with the same social worker, Barbara Hament, a wise veteran with her own unfailing instinct for this kind of matchmaking.

While writing this section, I asked Ian to help me tell this story, prompting him with this: "To begin with, Ian, you'd had a tough life by the time we met, especially since your dad was pretty much out of the picture. You lived in an area where there were a lot of drugs. There were gangs. In a journal I kept that first year of our relationship, I wrote on the day Barbara matched us, 'Dad in rehab. Ian sees him infrequently.' I know that was hard for you."

Ian surprised me by saying, "Actually, I lucked out that Dad was an absentee. He was a nice guy when he was sober but actually getting to sobriety was a big lift for him. Because of my experiences with him, though, it wasn't surprising that I had a lot of serious daddy issues as a kid. My teachers called me 'precocious' and 'recalcitrant.' Basically, I was disruptive, so the school district asked Mom to take me to a child psychologist who was supposed to figure out what was wrong with me. But even that didn't work out as they planned, at first. Mom dropped me off for my appointment, but instead of actually doing the tests this psychologist wanted me to take, I managed to slip back outside and hid until Mom returned."

"But you eventually did spend time with the psychologist."

"I had no choice. We got to a breaking point with the school district, and they finally made me sit down with the child psychologist who started with an IQ test. That was easy. The test showed I was smart. Intelligence wasn't the issue. Then, he wanted me to talk about my feelings. That was hard, because I was just a 10-year-old boy and didn't have much idea what he wanted to hear. The psychologist concluded that I had attention deficit disorder, and today I quibble with that diagnosis. But, to his credit, the psychologist said, 'I think he'd benefit from having another solid adult role model he could relate to in his life. A lot of these issues will straighten out if we can find a positive role model.' Of course, I didn't understand those concepts at 10. But, today, I do believe this, Howard: I was headed for trouble back then. Given the neighborhood where I grew up and all the problems I was having, I wouldn't be where I am today, if you hadn't stepped into my life as that role model."

"I think it was meant to be for both of us," I said. On my end, Lisa was the one who pushed me to check out the program. What caused your mom, Susan, to take you there? I remember you lived near that Chabad house in Santa Monica, where you eventually did your bar mitzvah a few years later, but you and Susan weren't really active as Jews when I first met you."

"No, we weren't. For me, the connection with the program was made because my psychologist was a supporter of the Big Brother idea—but he didn't recommend the main Big Brothers group in Los Angeles. He pointed out that, because we were Jewish, we qualified for the Jewish Big Brothers, which he thought had a good track record. I remember him telling Mom: 'I've seen them do marvelous things.'

"That convinced Mom, who said, 'We'll give it a shot.' And that was that.

"Mom contacted the group and we met with the social worker Barbara Hament a couple of times before she connected us with you, Howard. And, man oh man! Looking back, I have to say: Barbara was extraordinary! She knew how to talk with Mom and then she met alone with me and we talked. I'm still surprised that she got me talking as much as she did. At 10, I didn't have any sense of introspection, but Barbara drew out of me enough that she finally was able to tell Mom, 'OK, I know who to recommend as a match. I want you to meet this guy who I think will be a perfect fit.' And, Howard, we both know that kind of match doesn't always happen."

"No, our kind of relationship is rare. In fact, I had heard lots of horror stories," I said. "To prepare the prospective Big Brothers for the program, we had to go through background checks. Then, we had to attend these workshops where their professionals taught us all the warning signs that something could be going wrong. They kind of went overboard with those scary stories, I think, just to make sure we took the do's and don'ts seriously. One of the big ones was that some moms could start to ask for money, or they might want to get romantically involved. I started to wonder what I'd signed up for when I heard some of those stories. But none of that was relevant in our case, was it?"

"No, not at all," Ian said. "First, Barbara met with all of us to try to explain what would happen."

"That was a meet-and-greet on October 11, 1993, so Barbara could see how we interacted, and it was a week before we had our first home visit and outing."

"I remember that first meeting with you and Barbara," Ian said. "I don't think I'd ever interacted with an adult your age, so I didn't quite understand how I was supposed to relate to you. Mom's only concern was figuring out what would be good for me, and she had a good sense that this would work. But she didn't have much specific advice to give me about this. My own first impression was simple: Yeah, this Howard guy seems nice. Let's try this."

"The truth is that, even with the training they gave us, I didn't really know what I was doing either," I said. "I do very clearly remember the first time I went to your place, which was a rent-controlled apartment near in Santa Monica. At first, when I stepped inside, I didn't see you in the room. It was just your mother, Susan, who brought me inside and eyeballed me up and down for a good minute or so. As she looked me over, I could tell she was one strong mother bear when it came to protecting you, Ian. She was this tough transplanted New Yorker, very skeptical about things, and I knew your dad was out of touch at that point. Of course, Susan's gone now, but whenever I think of her, I remember that cigarette clenched in her lips as she talked in her Brooklyn accent. I came to like your mother a lot, but she was a tough cookie. To their credit, Barbara and the Big Brothers staff kept us on a pretty short leash. We were required to check in regularly. It was a solid program. Your mom had made a good choice. Her whole purpose was laser focused on seeing that you had a better shot at life."

"She had to be tough," Ian said. "She'd had a very hard life. First, there were all the problems with Dad. Then, after a while, he was out of the picture. We lived in a poor section of Venice before all the gentrification you see today in that neighborhood. Mom had only a high school education and a little college. She got by doing sales for this company that produced training videos for first responders like firefighters. The problem was, there were only so many first responders in our area and they'd buy only so many training videos in any given year, so it was a very limited market."

"Susan painted, too. She was an artist and managed a gallery for a while."

"Yes, she worked hard at a lot of things, but we always were poor. Fortunately, Mom had lots of friends, which is what saved us from feeling the full effects of our poverty. I remember people bringing in food when we couldn't afford it. People would send us money from time to time. We were lucky." Ian continued, "Only now can I fully understand how hard she was struggling. I couldn't appreciate that when I was a kid. She kept working but could never make enough money. Then, she had to deal with me, this problem kid with a bunch of unresolved issues and no real introspection about how I should respond to all of our problems. That's basically how I would describe my situation."

"That's what I stepped into when I made that initial visit," I said. "First, I had to pass your mom's inspection. When you finally decided to step into the room with us, what I saw was this shy, scrawny little kid coming toward me very hesitantly. I held up my hand for a high-five and you tapped my hand. Then, you held out a Transformer toy that was your favorite at the moment. So, the first thing I did was ask you to show me how the Transformer folded and unfolded. Then, you wanted to show me your comic book collection, so we did that."

"You told me you collected sports cards. I was big into sports."

"So we were talking, which was a relief to me," I said. "The main plan for that first visit was a walk to a beach, maybe have some ice cream and come back home. Pretty simple."

"Before we left, I asked, 'Can I bring my chess set?'"

"I didn't expect that. Transformers, sports cards and comic books, sure. But chess? I asked, 'You play chess?'"

"I got out my set, which was this little board with magnetic pieces so we could carry it around easily and, if we were playing outside, the pieces wouldn't slide around when the wind blew."

"My first challenge was just getting you safely to the park. You were this hyper kid and you were kind of jumping as much as you were walking beside me. You wanted to go so fast that I wasn't even sure you'd stop for traffic at the corner. I held out my arm. You stopped. I thought: Whew! OK, that's one block. A dozen more to go. I was overly anxious about doing this right. Then, when we reached the park at the beach safely, we found a place to open the board and play. I thought I should say something wise, so I said, 'You know, you can learn a lot from chess.' I couldn't think of what else to say after that— then, I realized I didn't need to say anything. We took our first few moves, and I was quite impressed that you actually did know how to play the game. A few moves later, I was even more surprised. You zeroed in on my king. It was crazy. You beat me!"

"That sounds like how it went that day," Ian said. "One thing my mother enjoyed was a good board game. I grew up, first, playing the easy games with her: Candy Land and Chutes and Ladders. Then we moved up and played checkers, then chess."

"In that little journal I kept back then, I made a note on December 26 that year, "Shot some hoops, then chess and I finally beat him,'" I said laughing. "From the start, I was so proud of you. We had to regularly check in with the program, so I kept notes to remember things like I wrote down, 'very smart,' 'honest and open,' 'great kid.' You even gave me a couple of your report cards from middle school that I put in my journal. You'd had some trouble in school earlier, but that winter you got A's in math and humanities. Your schoolwork seemed to be taking care of itself. A lot of the time we spent together involved talking about family, comic books, music, movies and TV—and lots of sports."

"Of course, I always loved athletics."

"From the start, we played a bunch of basketball. You still play?"

"Today, I do more running or swimming or bicycling, but I played everything through high school: basketball, baseball, soccer, football."

"Plus, you've loved hiking all your life," I said. "That's one thing you share with Emily today. You're both big-time backpackers. For me, basketball's my happy place and I do enjoy some soccer. But for you and Emily? You two just love to strap on a pack and climb a mountain."

"I like that phrase you use, Howard: happy place," Ian said. "I run and swim and bike and hike not so much for keeping in shape but for the way they boost my mental health. I feel better when I do those things regularly. I guess those are my happy places."

"You enjoyed a lot more than sports," I said. "I remember quickly discovering that you were a big reader—I mean, more of a reader than I was. And by that I mean: You liked to read deep stuff. You went much deeper than I ever did in literature."

"True," Ian said. "By the time I got to high school, I took a class in existential literature. I loved Camus. I was a weird kid, I guess. I couldn't read enough books." He paused for a moment, then added, "Looking back, Howard, I appreciate the way you started off with superficial fun stuff like games and sports. We needed to start that way. Then, we went step by step and the relationship got deeper and deeper."

"That was intentional. Lisa and I both agreed we shouldn't push you or Susan. We should let the relationship grow naturally. I remember we asked you and Susan to come to our wedding in 1994, but you didn't come. That was OK. We understood. Later on, we did have some amazing experiences with her. When Emily was born, we asked you to come be with us at her baby-naming ceremony and you were there—you took part in the readings. Susan came to love being around Emily, too, almost like Emily was a granddaughter."

"It takes a while to build those kinds of relationships," Ian said. "I think the way you approached the Big Brothers program with me was perfect."

"That's the word Barbara Hament used: 'perfect,'" I said. "And, honestly, that's the reason I eventually decided we had to break the Big Brothers mold with you when Lisa and I moved up north. When we moved to Silicon Valley in 1997 that was outside the LA Big Brothers region. I knew I had to fight the system to keep our Big Brothers match going. The program had very strict rules against letting these relationships continue if someone moved out of the region. They felt it wasn't fair to the boy. Most adults could not sustain being long-distance Big Brothers. I understood the intention of the rule, but I wasn't going to let it keep us from being family."

"At that time, I didn't understand all you had to do, but I know you fought for me," Ian said. "From my perspective at that age, I was thinking more on this level: I've never had a brother. Now, I've got Howard. Howard is friggin' great! He's my brother. I don't want to lose him. That's what was going through my mind."

"The key to this—and the reason I think our relationship was meant to be—was the amazing support of Barbara from Day 1. She knew the rules. She knew no one had ever switched over to a long-distance relationship like we were proposing. But she understood that we were meant to be brothers. I learned later that Barbara actually put a note in our file at the agency offices that told the rest of the staff: 'Leave them alone. They're perfect.'"

"Yes, I know Barbara was key to this. That note she wrote for us, 'Leave them alone.' That's because she saw that we really were becoming family."

"Even with Barbara's help, it still took a lot of effort," I said. "I had to go in there like a high-powered cross between a lawyer and a salesman and make my case to the board of directors. They were not eager to let me break the rules. It helped that Lisa and I were very involved in the Jewish community and would continue to be as we moved to the Bay Area. They'd seen our track record and they trusted us. Finally, they agreed, and we set a goal of getting together at least once a month after our move. I would book a flight down to see you once a month—or I would book a flight for you to come see us and your mother would take you to LAX. Lisa and I would pick you up on our end usually before Friday dinner, then we'd have you back at our airport on Sunday afternoon, heading back to LAX and your mom. It took a lot of effort to make that happen, including on Susan's part, but we did it."

We both paused for a moment on our Zoom screen, thinking through those years. I was surprised by the emotion that swept over me.

"Having you as a brother became one of the most beautiful things in my entire life," I said. "Pretty quickly, I realized you were a *menschy* kid—a good, solid person. I'll never forget standing up with you at your bar mitzvah—such a proud moment even though we did your bar mitzvah in a bit of a crazy way. We held it at the Chabad house, because they were willing to do this for any Jewish family that wanted a bar mitzvah. This was a bit more like an assembly line. Normally, a kid prepares for months at a family synagogue or temple, studying the Torah portion, practicing it over and over before the bar mitzvah. These guys got right down to business. They handed us your Torah portion on the day you had to read it. To be honest, Ian, I was a little surprised that you were so eager to do this in the first place."

"One reason is: I got to invite friends from middle school. They served cookies and juice for us. I wore a suit. It was cool."

"When we got there, though, Susan wasn't happy about the arrangements, at all! These guys were Orthodox and made all the women and girls, including my mom and Lisa, sit behind a curtain called a *mahitzah*, which means separation. Susan wanted to be right there in the middle of the action. She was not happy having to peek through a curtain to see her son bar mitzvahed."

"It's unbelievable that we actually got through it all."

"I know!" I said. "There were so many quirky things that day. Remember how that rabbi nudged us and pulled us into a private room after the bar mitzvah? The other kids got their juice. For you, he whips out this bottle of vodka, pours shots for us and made us do this 'L'chaim!' toast before he would let us go back to the other kids."

"Amazing," Ian said. "Yeah, I was just 13. It was quite a day. But, looking back, I think of all these things as steps that broadened my horizons far beyond our little rent-controlled apartment. As our relationship deepened, my horizons kept expanding."

"You really were insistent about that," I said. "You were the driver behind a lot of things we did together. Remember when you asked me to take you to a rock concert? Your *first* rock concert?"

"Nine Inch Nails and David Bowie. I'll never forget that."

"What I'll never forget is all the promises I had to make to your mother so she was sure you'd be safe. If anything had happened to you, she would have killed me. I had to risk it. What could I do? You begged me repeatedly to go that concert. I was your big brother and I wanted to make this happen for you. It took a lot of effort on my part to convince your mom, but I did."

"I think those experiences were absolutely essential in my coming to understand the larger world," Ian said. "As a kid, I was only partially aware of all the rules and the possibilities of the Jewish Big Brothers program. It wasn't until I was part of the way through high school that I realized how important it was that we had kept the relationship going all those years without any interruption."

"I was aware of that from the start," I said. "The rules stated that, if we maintained our match from age 10 until you were 18, then you were eligible for serious scholarship money through the program. We're talking about big-time scholarships for multiple years of school. I was determined that you wouldn't lose out on that."

"That turned out to be very valuable."

"You did your four years at University of California, Santa Cruz, then you got a master's degree from Florida State University with the help of those scholarships. We maxed out that benefit. Then, you went on to University of California Hastings Law School to get a JD," I said. "We had become brothers. I was determined that you were going to have all those opportunities in your life. I remember helping you move into your first dorm room. Lisa and I met your girlfriends. We were at your high school and college graduations. We were involved in each other's lives in so many ways."

"More ways than I could have imagined," Ian said. "Through that program, I kept seeing new possibilities. Through my master's program, I had envisioned continuing through the whole Ph.D. track to become a professor of philosophy teaching at a university. But then, another way the Jewish Big Brothers program affected me is that they required these annual interviews as a part of the scholarship program. Each year, I'd have to meet and talk with someone else from the community. Well, when I was finishing my master's and was thinking about pausing before getting into the long haul of a doctoral program, my annual interview turned out to be with an attorney. That's when I began to think about law. One thing that attracted me was the realization that most doctoral students are poor and, even if I got my Ph.D., I'd still be struggling for years along the publish-or-perish track to earn a tenured teaching spot somewhere. Bottom line: There was a good likelihood I'd wind up poor again—and I'd had enough of poverty. The law began to seem pretty attractive. Eventually, I decided to switch careers. And Hastings Law offered me a good scholarship."

"OK, so let's fast forward in the story," I said, "You're a great student, and you've chosen law. You're way beyond my professional sphere by this time—but I do know one thing about law students: You need good internships. You need to make important first connections to build a successful career. And there, I could help you by reaching out—because I knew somebody."

"You're talking about Judge Helene White. She was on the Michigan Court of Appeals and eventually was appointed to the U.S. Court of Appeals for the Sixth Circuit. Now, that was an amazing connection," Ian said.

"That's what we do. We always enlarge the circle. By that time, Lisa and Emily and I were living in Michigan. I knew Helene. We served on the AJC Detroit board of directors together. Plus, I knew you were facing some challenges in making the right connections for that first internship."

"At that point, I actually was looking for what we call an externship, unpaid work while still in law school."

"I knew Helene had a couple of those slots, so I called her and asked, 'Would you do me the favor of including on your list of prospective candidates my little brother, Ian, who I think would be a great asset for you?' She was happy to do that, although all my request did was get your name on her list. You had to go through all the interviews and reach the finish line with your own qualifications. But I wasn't worried about that. You had the record and the personality. You just needed a connection to be considered."

"Then, when I was chosen for that summer of 2010, you and Lisa put me up."

"I'll never forget the day you showed up at our house looking like a lumberjack just stepping out of the woods! Remember that?"

"Well, I had a beard."

"You had a great big beard and hair out to here! And you had this old pack slung over your shoulder like you were just returning to civilization. You're getting ready to go work for this prestigious judge and Lisa said right away, 'We need to get you groomed!' I took you to my barber—even got you a shave. I drove you over to the Men's Warehouse and bought you three suits and ties and all the works. We did this whole elaborate makeover, including a new wardrobe and then it turned out—"

"It turned out I didn't need to wear suits, except for a few court appearances."

"Well, you would need the suits eventually, so I'm glad we got them. You're my brother—and, hey, that summer you acted like a brother. While you were staying with us, you ate us out of friggin' house and home and drove my car everywhere. Of course, all of that was fine with us. It just confirmed and deepened our relationships. Everything we had was yours. We also found time to go to a bunch of sporting events together. Emily loved having Uncle Ian around all that summer. That's how it should be in a family."

"It's great to see these relationships crossing generations," Ian said.

"Lisa and I are glad you've become a mentor in Emily's life—someone she feels comfortable talking to," I said. "When all of this started nearly three decades ago, I was hoping: Maybe I can shine a little light into this kid's life. As it turns out, today, I realize that light was shining both ways. And now, we're shining on to the next generation."

"Nearly three decades," Ian repeated. "Amazing."

"Our relationship is one of the most important things I've got in this world. I started out just trying to walk you safely to the beach so we could play a game of chess. Strange to think about this: I never had a brother while I was growing up, but now I've had a brother for the majority of my life."

"You stuck with me through high school and college and law school."

"You celebrated with us when we became parents. Then, you stuck with me through stage IV colon cancer."

"Now, you're celebrating with us as we become parents."

"We've loved every step of the journey, Ian. We were thrilled that you shared the first sonogram with us right away. We've been watching Sara's baby bump grow every week, happy to hear about every report from the doctor. This is all heightened because of this terrible pandemic. You have no idea how beautiful it is to watch a hopeful new life emerge in the midst of a global tragedy. It's been hard on all of us, especially on Emily, and there you are as a friend and mentor and hiking buddy to her. We've come a long way from Barbara guessing that we'd be a great match—to actually making it happen—to truly becoming the family we are today. You're right. It's pretty damned amazing."

With Ian, we have taken to heart the idea that we can, indeed, choose our families. He was born Ian Ellis, but—now that Susan and his father both are gone—he wants to intentionally focus on the new family that he and Sara are building. There were so many high hopes riding on that arrival that Lisa and Emily and I knew we had to pull out all the stops for this baby shower. The gift we shipped to their California home was a crib. Then, we all worked overtime to pack as many friends and relatives—admittedly, most of them from Sara's clan—as possible into the VidHug we produced.

Lisa and I kicked it off, literally hugging so we could squeeze ourselves into the video frame. Lisa called out, "Hi, Ian and Sara! We are so thrilled as you are embarking on this new journey called parenthood."

"Soon, you're going to be experiencing a whole new world of foods," I said. "Wait until you get a taste of squished peas and squash. And your lives are going to have a whole new soundtrack: Baby Beluga! You Are My Sunshine! And all the other baby hits."

"Our advice is: Start stocking up on sleep right now!" Lisa said. "We love you!"

Lisa created a more serious, heartfelt message of her own to Ian and Sara, realizing that Ian didn't have his mom or a big sister to offer advice.

Then, our daughter, Emily, created a third video from her apartment at the University of Michigan: "Huge congratulations on the baby! I'm so excited to have a new member of our family. I miss you. I love you. I'm so excited!"

Then, to further beef up Ian's arc within the VidHug family circle, we added a video of our dog, Cody. He refused to bark or even move for Ian and Sara—but, hey, my mother had loved seeing Cody in the mix. We were sure Ian and Sara would smile at Cody, too.

And they did.

Soon, we all welcomed a healthy baby boy, Noble Oren Ellis Van Loh, to our family.

Most families grow over the years through children and marriages. Most of us also have at least one close friend who is considered family—more than one if we are fortunate.

Consider being intentional about this. Thanks to Barbara's role at her agency, Lisa and Ian and Susan and I made that choice. In our family, that match three decades ago has made all the difference.

When is the last time you enlarged your family circle? Is there someone else you'd like to welcome or affirm as truly a part of your clan?

Shining Brightly

Please consider volunteering, giving or learning about these or similar organizations that touched my life. Many young boys and girl need you! It will change your life for the better like it changed mine—forever!

+ **Jewish Big Brothers and Big Sisters of Los Angeles** —
  JBBBSLA.org

+ **Big Brothers and Big Sisters of America** —
  BBBS.org

Movies and TV series now celebrate the explosion of entrepreneurial energy that emerged from Silicon Valley, tucked into the southern crescent of the San Francisco Bay Area. The small towns in that region suddenly became world famous. In addition to Redwood City, Silicon Valley included a half dozen other once-small towns such as Santa Clara, Palo Alto and Menlo Park. In the late 1990s, Silicon Valley raised-floor data centers were all the rage.

9

Silicon Valley

When I landed in Silicon Valley in 1997, people told me: "The math is crazy here. Two plus two equals 200."

As a top salesman for more than a decade, I was used to the roller-coaster ride of chasing big deals. I'd had my share of setbacks as well as breathtaking commission checks when great deals finally were signed. But moving into Silicon Valley was climbing to a whole new altitude. At the same time, I also was evolving from strictly sales to becoming a serial entrepreneur, a life whose ups and downs are less like a roller coaster and more like scaling the Himalayas.

Silicon Valley in the 1990s was as disorienting as *Alice in Wonderland* or *The Matrix*. With each passing quarter of the year, old assumptions were turned head over heels. I had come of age when aspiring salespeople, executives and entrepreneurs could develop their skills along comfortable on ramps like NCR's lavish training programs. There was no Sugar Camp with the implicit promise of a successful career. In Silicon Valley, it was learn fast, move fast and earn faster. Everything was new and speculative. There was no safety net. We were scrambling to find toe holds in startups operating out of borrowed garages, cramped cubicles, dusty attics—wherever we could pitch our tents. We were competing for seats at flimsy card tables where people were hunched over their plans to build the future. I was among thousands who were hooked on this adrenaline rush. I sweated toward my first big success in a claustrophobic basement startup that was overwhelmed with the odor of frying onions every day as the vents of the next-door Mexican restaurant turned on for the lunch and dinner rush.

When people first told me about Silicon Valley's crazy math, I laughed at the exaggeration. When I landed in the scrambler myself, I realized they weren't kidding. Within just a few years, Lisa and I were able to buy a beautiful, newly built home and increase our charitable giving significantly with our "found money." I earned big money via large commissions and stock options originally worth pennies working around the clock to build and sell a revolutionary product in the music industry that wound up failing not too long after it went public. We were ahead of our time in that basement, so our concept quickly fizzled. But in Silicon Valley? We still took money home. And, as surprising as it may seem, most of the investors weren't complaining. For the most part, they were clear-eyed venture capitalists pouring money into startups that sounded promising, hoping to strike gold on just a few of the many bets they were placing.

What about all that money? That's the first myth about the heyday of Silicon Valley that I need to bust. Many of us weren't in this for the money. Sure, we all hoped to strike it rich and make a better life for ourselves. Some of us made big money, often for an all-too-brief time. I know that I personally wanted to become a philanthropist and give back. But the money was not what drove us to work insane hours and to nearly abandon our families along the way. No, what drove us through each day was the heady dream of reinventing the way the world works—the way we all connect and move and interrelate—the way we do our work and the way we enjoy ourselves after work. We were the generation that firmly believed we could make the most fantastic tech dreams come true. And, if that sounds like the plot for a sci-fi movie, then so be it. The truth is that we could glimpse with aching clarity a better world we could build if we could just connect the planet more powerfully, completely, instantly.

Our heroes already were busting up the world's old connective infrastructure and then begging, borrowing and sometimes outright stealing every shiny new idea that sprang up in our collective pathway. An entire feature film, *The Pirates of Silicon Valley*, shows the daring way Steve Jobs swiped ideas from Bill Gates in the early days—and how they went on fighting tooth and nail like robber barons from the 19th century. Best-selling books and entire TV series have been produced about the relentless, sometimes predatory competition to build the next big thing.

The challenge in telling this story is conveying to people two decades into the 21st century what that enormous transformation felt like in the latter years of the last century. College students today can't remember a world without smartphones. From a 1990s perspective, it was pure science-fiction to imagine that kind of slim supercomputer we could hold in one hand. To understand the scramble that I am about to describe—for just a moment—try to think back perhaps in your own life or, if you're in your 20s, perhaps from what you've seen on TV about this distant past. Can you recall the first moment you held a smartphone and began to explore that little powerhouse? Can you remember other firsts? The first time you tapped an app in your palm to turn on the lights in your house? The first time you sat in an audience and Googled what a speaker was talking about up on stage—and in moments found out just as much information as that speaker was trying to convey? The first time tiny ear buds transported you into a whole new soundtrack for your life? The first time you asked Siri or Alexa to do something for you? The first time you Zoomed with a loved one on another continent?

All that stuff was about as real as George Lucas' *Star Wars* when I landed in Silicon Valley. We were still in the hardwired world of dial-up, slow-as-a-snail internet connections. Larry Page and Sergey Brin were just students at Michigan and Stanford. They didn't found Google until 1998. Media streaming was a fantasy. If you hoped to play a digital song in your home, you'd better expect to keep your landline locked onto the modem all night long—and even then the song's sound quality would be lousy. Widely available commercial broadband still was years away. Where was Wi-Fi? No one had even coined the term. Apple didn't start selling its revolutionary AirPort, a fledgling Wi-Fi component, until 1999. I am proud to say that I was among those hungry young entrepreneurs who wound up in the Valley because we could envision what should happen in the future—even though we all had to struggle, and many of us had to fail in this race. We were determined to build and then roll out all the vast infrastructure, the tiny gizmos and the endless oceans of software that could turn our sci-fi movie dreams into reality.

It was so exciting and all-consuming that I blew past any sense of balance in my life and ran face-first into a marital crisis with Lisa.

As usual, she summed it up with her own crystal clarity in a challenge that I ignored for a while, but that eventually stopped me short. More than once, she said, "If you think we're ever going to have a baby—then you've got to put more emphasis on family time. Period. For starters, we can't just have a baby the conventional way ... so there will be medical appointments for both of us. Then, if we are lucky enough to get pregnant and have a child, our baby (and I) will need you to be home more than a couple nights a week. Money is great, but a child needs love and attention."

She nailed it, of course. I had married an expert on family well-being. I wasn't surprised by what she said, but I was torn. I knew that I had to struggle to bring my life back into balance—but the narcotic of Silicon Valley was powerfully addictive.

How did I land there from my start at NCR Corporation? The truth is that NCR shoved me, more than once.

The first hard nudge was my realization that, despite all my success as an NCR salesman, my true vocation was as an entrepreneur. I sincerely appreciated the business training and foundational skills I learned and honed at NCR. But I was at my best on the cutting edge of new products in the 1980s and early 1990s, traveling thousands of miles to woo and then sign deals with giants like TRW and Hughes Aircraft. Then, in 1992, AT&T acquired NCR and almost overnight the sales force was tethered to layer upon layer of old-school management, and we were asked to shoulder big-company products, procedures and campaigns. I felt like my feet were Velcroed to the AT&T turf. I was getting so restless that, in June of 1993, I interviewed with a recruiter, which would be my first major steppingstone toward Silicon Valley: Avid Technology. That company was not a household name back then, but quickly became the standard for film, TV and postproduction editing and special effects. Avid looked like an exciting place to work, but I didn't make a move right away.

Then, the second shove came when AT&T announced an aggressive downsizing of the NCR staff they had acquired. Very attractive buyouts were dangled at the exits for anyone who would voluntarily take a hike without any fuss, including the youngest staffers. I was still in my mid-20s and they handed me a major check just to hit the road with no complaints.

I was itching to reach Silicon Valley, but Avid was located right next door to us in Burbank and was a very attractive team. I immediately liked Martin Vann, the West Coast director of sales. Avid, based in Tewksbury, Massachusetts, was building a major part of this new speed-of-light world of connections—disrupting Hollywood as fast as they could invent digital storytelling tools. Imagine the challenges we faced. Producers still were shooting movies and TV shows on film or videotape. That meant shooting, developing and editing on equipment like the Moviola, a mechanical dinosaur invented in the 1920s when films still were silent. After all, the producers and directors had to have some way of assembling all those miles of tape and film they were using. Today's powerful digital cameras had not yet been invented. So, the first thing the Avid team had to invent was a reliable method for moving the sounds and images from those reels of tape and film into the digital world.

In January 1994, I was hired as a salesman in the broadcast division, another area yet to be digitized. Avid was sparking worldwide headlines with Open Media Framework, a formatting system that made it much easier to transfer digital media. When I started at Avid, only three fairly obscure Hollywood movies had used Avid editing systems. By 1996, the producers of the Oscar-winning best picture, *The English Patient*, boasted of the new flexibility they found using Avid to finish their movie. Dozens of other Hollywood teams followed. And today? It's hard to find an Oscar-nominated movie that wasn't put together using some kind of Avid technology.

Now, don't worry, I'm only going to hit a few highlights in my own meteoric arc through those years in California. If I tried to explain every news-making advance at the companies where I worked—well, that would be another book.

So, here is the short version of the story. Before I finally made my move away from NCR, I was being courted by Bill Schultz, a headhunter who was helping to fill positions at Avid. Then, AT&T offered the buyout, and I was ready to jump. Even in the months between my first meeting with Avid staff, and my hiring in January 1994, things were moving so swiftly at Avid that their job offer changed. The evolving conversation with Avid's recruiters, over a number of phone calls and meetings, went like this:

"They actually don't need you in the movie side of the business," I was told months after my first interview.

Well, that was disappointing. There were lots of stories Avid staffers loved to tell—like the day Clint Eastwood and his cinematographer showed up for a demo. The cinematographer did all the talking that morning and, true to his reputation, Clint said almost nothing. When all the questions had been asked and answered, Clint finally nodded and said simply, "This is some cool shit you've got here."

Who wouldn't want to rub shoulders with Hollywood's elite? But Martin Vann told me they were launching a broadcast division because the interest in moving from analog to digital by broadcasters was expected to be explosive. It would be a big learning curve for me, but my experience on networking voice, data and video would be a big plus.

Martin's pitch to me went like this: "There's going to be huge growth in broadcast TV and cable, especially from local stations across the country. There are 1,500 commercial TV stations from Alaska to Florida—and, if we add cable and public access to that list, well, there's a ton of new business for us to pursue. We've been working on a plan to revolutionize local TV. Pretty soon, we'll be rolling out a whole series of products that should take off very quickly. So, right now, we're looking for a proven go-getter to attack the West Coast territory."

So, there would be no collaboration with Oscar winners in this new TV division, but this was an exciting pitch to be in on the ground floor in reinventing TV nationwide. I was hooked and wanted to know all the details.

The sales regions I was given were Arizona, Nevada, California, Oregon, Washington state, Alaska—and Hawaii, too. My excitement grew. I knew how major deals were made and then built upon to secure more business. A successful sales career depends on the company's follow through with a solid product and then word of mouth to other potential clients keeps the business growing. That meant a top salesperson never sold products like these without the support of a superb engineering and development staff who could turn our promises into reality. Avid already was expanding its rollout staff, but I could see there would be growing pains along the way. How could a salesperson motivate a young and sometimes overstressed staff of installers, trainers and service people to give his clients the highest priority? Well, it wouldn't hurt to hand your colleagues tickets to Hawaii as a part of these deals. I never had any problem promptly lining up great men and women to follow through on the deals I struck.

Very quickly, I racked up more frequent flier miles than I could ever hope to redeem. I was learning the broadcast television business at a breakneck pace. I would take chief engineers to lunch and ask them to teach me about the current technology in place to make a TV station run. Then I would show them a graphic of what the digital television station of the future would look like. The conversation, debate and discussions were robust! Many doubters told me we were pitching pie-in-the-sky. Others were more willing to believe the future was close and were eager to learn more, but all insisted that a digital signal going out over "their" airways must meet the highest technical specifications and quality.

As a newlywed husband, I was on the road 70% of my time with Avid, but I wasn't completely missing in action at home. I used my frequent flier miles to bring Lisa with me to Hawaii—well, at least once. She wanted to see Alaska, too, although that never worked out. I did bring her to Seattle, though, and a sales-award trip to the Bahamas that was a blast!

The sheer amount of time I had to spend away from home was partly due to my own enormous learning curve. I was the only one among the four regional sales executives who had no broadcast experience. Overnight, I had to learn a whole new industry. I knew that I could do it, and I did, but there were plenty of nights where I barely grabbed a few hours of sleep.

Every day held surprises. My colleagues would never let me forget the day I walked into KHNL in Honolulu wearing my usual dark suit, white shirt and tie.

"I'm here to see the station manager," I announced at the front desk.

The receptionist was skeptical. "Are you a lawyer?"

"A lawyer?" I said, chuckling. "No."

The receptionist just stared at my suit.

The station manager finally explained, "Nobody but the lawyers dress like that out here. In TV production, you'll scare my team in those clothes. We are much more laid back and relaxed in Hawaii."

An easy lesson learned. Business attire among Honolulu's TV crews was casual, loose-fitting clothes designed for comfort working both indoors and outdoors in the tropical climate. Easy to fix. I went out and bought a stock of Hawaiian shirts and khakis and never made that mistake again.

My goal in Honolulu—as it was in each market in my Western states—was to sell Avid broadcast and production products to all of the TV stations in town. Seeing was believing, so I would bring demo equipment to show and tell and then I would leave the equipment and encourage them to "try before you buy." They all followed the latest trade news and understood that the first product Avid offered was software so their production departments could make better local commercials faster and more flexibly than ever before. Ad production was the moneymaker at the heart of any TV station. Everyone in town knew that the first station to offer better ads, which could be rapidly reedited to adapt to a client's changing needs with special effects, would suddenly have a major advantage over the other broadcasters competing for that revenue.

My first step, then, was to establish relationships with KHNL and KITV, which became my reference stations. They were first for each of the new systems Avid was rolling out in those years. That also meant the station managers could bask in the spotlight of national headlines for these innovations. Reporters from media-trade magazines to *The New York Times* and *The Wall Street Journal* followed Avid's rapid-fire reinvention of TV and film. One example was a big state-of-the-industry report in *The Times* that described physically editing film and videotape as "old school" while the "new school" was computer editing on digital systems, pointedly naming Avid as the leading firm. Another *Times* story about these innovations featured Avid executives describing "the ability to compose effects frame by frame, to create multiple layers, images dissolving into new images. ... The technology encourages experiment." As a growing company, Avid couldn't buy advertisements as effective as that ongoing coverage in mainstream news media. As a regional sales exec, selling our products to all the stations in a regional TV market or big city was a matter of letting someone use it first, then referencing the success of that first station as I worked my way around town.

For three years, I crisscrossed the western states, grew my sales team to two dozen people with annual sales that skyrocketed in my division by the time I left for Silicon Valley.

With such a plum job, why would I jump again? Because I was recruited by a tiny startup that had not yet gone public. At Avid, I earned my salary, bonuses and stock, but the chance to take an explosive ride on a startup company that was still in its infancy was very enticing. Moving to that cramped, smelly basement in Redwood City to help build Liquid Audio meant that I was crossing over into the world of entrepreneurial risk and reward. The first employees in those startups received significant blocks of stock before the company went public. I arrived as vice president of sales, aka Employee No. 16.

The trade-off was that, instead of traveling 70% of the time, I was on the road for an absolutely exhausting 80% of the time during the less than a year I worked at Liquid Audio. Lisa did not even move with me right away. She stayed behind to wrap up her work in Los Angeles and sell our house. She didn't finally rejoin me until September that year—and I only worked for Liquid Audio through December. The balance in my life? Well, at that point, there wasn't any.

What I saw in Liquid Audio was all of Avid's potential in movies and TV, except that I had joined Avid eight years into its growth. With Liquid Audio, I was stepping into the starting blocks of the race to deliver digital music. Plus, this move finally made me a stakeholder in the now-legendary Silicon Valley, where Bill Hewlett and David Packard had once launched their global giant with just $500 and space in a rented garage.

I could see what was on the horizon: People wanted to choose their own music instantly and flexibly, which is the status quo in 2021. We don't even think about the ease of choosing songs with a few taps of an app—or a quick question to Siri or Alexa. But in 1997, no one had charted the course to that digital fantasyland of music. Music was heard on radio, cassette tapes and vinyl record albums but in my mind Liquid Audio had a good chance to become the Avid of music distribution. Now, I know that we were just way too early in that transformation—of cassette tapes to digital downloads of music—but, hey, that's historical hindsight from the 21st century.

Other than wafting smells of onions from the Mexican restaurant and occasional friction among the staff crammed into our office startup, I fell in love with Redwood City. Its charm in the '90s was that we were launching the world's future from what looked like an old-fashioned California village. I would park my car near the clock tower at the train station and walk to work. We loved the irony that our laid-back hamlet was a hive of growth. Behind the quaint facades, most of us were working 15-20 hours a day, every single day. We were up early, often starting with power breakfasts at joints like Buck's, a rustic place in nearby Woodside where you could walk among the booths and overhear people from all the famous companies talking about their next big deals.

Our goal at Liquid Audio in 1997 was convincing the music industry that they were destined to make money selling digital downloads of music directly to fans. We were early pioneers trying to prove that this fantasy could become reality. The problem was that music executives thought they had much more time before digital turbulence would sweep through their industry. I hit the global sales circuit for Liquid Audio two years before Napster turned the internet into a Wild West of stolen music, three years before Metallica sued Napster's founders for millions of lost revenue, and four years before Steve Jobs unveiled iTunes and the iPod in 2001 to try to control all that chaos. But in 1997? We could not see how early we were—but the Liquid Audio concept seemed rock solid. Like Apple's iTunes and all the other music-sharing services that eventually followed, we intended to form proper contractual relationships with artists and record labels to legally share revenue. In fact, we were so early that my entire year of sales development was not even focused on the end users, music fans. We had no product to launch at that point. I was circling the world selling the idea to the music professionals who we hoped would form a music ecosystem of the company's service. That is—if we could sway music honchos to give up their entrenched business practices for making, promoting and distributing music.

Just like I learned that I should wear Hawaiian shirts in Hawaii, the music industry's culture was another learning curve. To begin with, most artists and record labels had long-term contractual commitments for distribution that seemed to throw up iron-clad barriers to our concept. So, we started by looking for indie producers, new music and music that top stars had on the shelf but had never committed to a distribution deal.

On one big sales swing through Europe, for example, I attended an audio-video conference in Amsterdam, where I met with prospects from around the world, then I was scheduled to fly on to England for more meetings. That's when I learned I could speak directly with George Michael, one of the world's best-selling musicians. At the time, he was working at home in London on a

major retrospective collection of his solo hits. Our European managing director, Kevin Malone, was able to phone an aide at his studio and we chose a date.

"What time can we see him that day?" he asked.

"First thing in the morning."

"OK," he said.

I slept little in those days, so morning was perfect for me. After a short
night in our London flat, we slid out early the next morning on the tube to
his studio. It looked like lots of other studios I had seen that year with leather
chairs and couches, rock-and-roll posters on the wall and a pool table. Some
of his staff was there waiting for us, but Michael wasn't.

"Isn't George coming?" I asked.

"He'll be along," they said. "Let's head to the pub."

"To the pub?" I asked. It was 8 a.m. "They're open this early?" They were.
Soon, we each had pints of Guinness and we began throwing darts.

"When's George due?" I asked after we'd played a while and drained a few
rounds.

"He'll be along." We played another round. We tried to warm the staffers
to what we were offering, telling them all about Liquid Audio's grand plans. I
learned that, even though most of Michael's work was tied up in long-term
contracts, he did have some independent music that he had not yet committed
to any distributor. So, there was a possible deal here—if only Michael would
show up.

We played more darts. Drank more Guinness. His staff ordered lunch.
Then, we returned to the studio.

Finally, Michael walked through the front door. It was a chilly autumn
afternoon, and he was wearing a leather jacket. He sat down with us and
quickly confirmed that he was interested. At that point, he was nearly two
decades into a career that amounted to his own rollercoaster of popularity as
well as problems with record labels and the news media. He was not only a
great artist. He was a battle-scarred survivor like me. I liked him instantly. He
was a kind man who sincerely cared about reaching his fans with his music. I
was sad to learn of his death on Christmas 2016.

Those were the highs, occasional opportunities to sit down with top stars
and talk about the future of their work. This was a long way from my roots
in sales at NCR, where I was a suit selling to suits at bank conferences, trade
shows and board rooms. In my time at Liquid Audio, there were no typical
sales calls. Each was unique. From Avid onward, I developed a social and cultural flexibility that could change with each passing day, each city, each part of
the world and each professional sitting across from me.

Throughout that entire high-flying time with Liquid Audio, I had all the professional assets I could want. Like Avid, we started to draw headlines in the trade press and then in *The Wall Street Journal* and *The Times*. We were selling the future, even if we could not quite deliver it at that moment. The truth was that downloading a quality song on a dial-up modem in 1997 took far longer than most people wanted to keep their home phone lines tied to a modem.

By late that year, this fundamental disconnect was looming in my mind. The pressures at work and at home grew until I finally marched down into our basement offices and grabbed the CFO for what turned out to be a contentious private chat. Eventually, we worked out a severance deal that didn't fully satisfy either of us. However, I was able to hit the exit again with a buyout that included some very valuable stock options.

This time, I did not even have my next destination in mind. I was so weary that I could only focus on getting out of that basement. At home, our lives were out of whack. In desperation, Lisa and I celebrated my quitting by packing up for a long-overdue rest in Sedona, Arizona, late that December. I didn't have a clue what 1998 would bring, except that I had fully bought into Silicon Valley's vision. At that point in the Valley's dot-com bubble, people were entering and leaving—and entering and leaving—companies at a breakneck pace. No one cared, especially if you had the kinds of sales record I had stacked up. To have cycled through several companies in as many years was not a red flag on your resume—it was a red badge of courage.

I was already on headhunters' short lists of rising stars. Soon, I landed on the ground floor of another startup, CMGI's NaviSite based in Andover, Massachusetts, which today is part of Time Warner. I spent a couple of years helping NaviSite to organize its branding, marketing and sales for web-hosting data centers, the forerunners of today's cloud computing systems. Once again, I came in with a combination of salary, bonuses and the company had not yet gone public, so the stock I received was a valuable promise of the company's future. Meanwhile, I carefully watched that block of stock I held from Liquid Audio.

In 1998, still two years before iTunes and the iPod, Liquid Audio went public. At that point, the company had sealed deals with 250 record producers to use the basic software to compress their music in preparation for online sales. At that point, even Microsoft co-founder Paul Allen had risked some of his capital from Vulcan Ventures on the firm. The first day those shares hit the stock market, they more than doubled from their initial $15. Buried deep in wire stories about the IPO, though, was this brief warning: "The digital music distribution field is getting crowded." Nobody paid attention. By 2000, a year before Steve Jobs' big announcements involving music, Liquid Audio still looked golden. After all, it had signed a deal to distribute music through AOL, which business-news reporters still liked to describe as the future of the internet. Liquid Audio's staff grew until they filled three facilities around Redwood City. Then, four months after the debut of iTunes in 2001, Liquid Audio began to crumble and announced its first big wave of layoffs. Less than two years later, all that was left of Liquid Audio was a handful of court cases in which lawyers were fighting over who owed any money that remained.

I had sold my stock long before the crash, thankfully. We were able to purchase our newly built home where our daughter Emily—our miracle girl—would be born into the world.

How did Lisa and I reach that point?

She kept reminding me of how crazily I was rushing around the world pursuing—well, what exactly was I pursuing? When Lisa and I talked about this in the late '90s—in those brief hours when I was at home and we actually found a few moments to converse—I could never quite make a convincing case for what I was chasing. Money? Sure, but that wasn't really the goal. Both Lisa and I understood that. Was I chasing the future of global technology? Certainly. But how did "global technology" connect with my deepest values and vocation?

"I think it's actually pretty simple to describe what happened," Lisa said as I was working on this chapter. "You had become a workaholic. I was attracted to you from the start because of your drive, but we reached a point where I barely saw you some weeks. I knew you were wonderful in the Big Brothers program, because you somehow managed to keep up your monthly visits with Ian through all of that craziness. I believed you could become a great father someday. I also knew you had so many talents that you could contribute to the Jewish community—but honestly, I was the one who was really involved in those causes. That's because I had agreed to give up all my work in Los Angeles to join you up north. Then, you left me for long stretches, and I did not want to just sit around our house doing nothing. So, I jumped back into serving the community. And I waited for you to slow down. I waited and I hoped that you would realize something had to change."

"You didn't just wait," I pointed out. "I'll never forget that clipping I found one night when I finally came home for dinner after a long sales trip. There was this page from a magazine lying on my dinner plate. The headline was, *Families Thrive That Eat Dinner Together.*"

"Yeah, we talked that night," Lisa said.

"We finally talked. Or, I should say: I finally listened."

When I reached this point in describing my book to Dr. Robert J. Wicks, I could see him nodding on the Zoom screen even before I finished my story about the clipping from the magazine. Then, Wicks said, "Sometimes it takes a rude awakening to realize how far we've drifted from a balanced life. I can vouch for that myself—and I write about my own experiences with that quite honestly in my own books. We have to be honest about this, Howard, if there's any value in the story for our readers."

"You're right," I said to him. "Now, I can see so clearly how it all happened. When I finished with Cancer No. 1, I rushed to California and jumped into business with every ounce of energy I had in my body. When I finally got into startup companies, I worked a zillion hours a week because I simply loved it. I loved the rush. It was like running through a tsunami. If you fell down along the way, you managed to get back up on your feet even if you were bloodied and bruised, and you just kept running full force into the wind again."

In that era, I briefly kept a journal, of sorts. It amounted to very brief notations, sometimes just a few words each day. As exciting as the whole arc of the Avid-to-Silicon-Valley story may seem today, those hastily scribbled pages are peppered with the words "tired," "exhausted," "hectic." There's an entry where I only "slept 2 hrs last night" next to another day's entry "need to sleep, but when?"

Wicks said, "When you're caught up in a cycle like that, you can completely lose yourself—unless you are lucky enough to reach an *Aha!* moment. Howard, it sounds to me like your Lisa helped to engineer that *Aha!* moment for you. When you finish writing that chapter about Silicon Valley, I hope you will have conveyed to readers what an absolute adrenaline rush it was for you and everyone around you in those years. And there was, indeed, something great about that. You had a role in that whole transformation that is changing our world. But you also need to be honest about the imbalance—about the danger and really the darkness that also can come with that relentless race. And you need to remind readers that the hope, in such a situation, often involves someone who manages to grab our attention, to intervene, to give us that precious moment of—*Aha!*"

"That's how I'll tell the story," I said. "I'll tell it that way because it's true."

And now I have.

So with Dr. Wicks, I ask you to stop a moment and consider: How do you weigh the demands of your career with the love of your family? Have you managed to strike a balance—or do you sometimes find yourself falling so far off course that you strain the relationships at the core of your life? Have you ever had a loved one drop repeated reminders, as Lisa did?

Or perhaps you are reading this book and you are the person who needs to summon the courage to stage an intervention before a loved one's imbalance proves catastrophic. This is not an easy challenge, especially if your family's livelihood depends on long hours at work or perhaps juggling more than one job.

It's never easy, but if we don't at least try to help ourselves slow down, then we will never find a quiet moment to hear that soft: *Aha!*

Shining Brightly

Please consider learning about these milestones that touched my life. The Dot Com 1990s was a whirlwind roller coast ride. Check out these links below to understand why!

- **Silicon Valley** – Wikipedia.org/wiki_Silicon_Valley
- **Entrepreneur Magazine** – Entrepreneur.com/magazine
- **Computer History Museum** – ComputerHistory.org

Our miracle girl, Emily, became the light of our lives in so many ways. We made time for family outings. We enjoyed the shoreline at Carmel-by-the-Sea in Monterey. Lisa took Emily to a butterfly garden. When she was 8, Emily began playing soccer and was playing in national competitions by age 14. As she flew through the air to make a save in one game, a news photographer captured the moment. In July 2017, I posed with Emily and the trophy at the Under 16 US Youth Soccer National Championships in Frisco, Texas.

The Miracle Girl

I believe in miracles.

Our daughter Emily embodies two of them. The first miracle is that she is alive. The second is the way she began to weave our family's threads into a new tapestry as soon as she was born.

The miracle of Emily's birth swept away fears that had lingered for years in our families. When Lisa and I began dating, she was eager to tell her family about me—and did not expect to hear their warnings, in response. Some of those warnings were blunt: "Cancer can come back. You'd have to take care of him. You could wind up as a widow."

Just as troubling for Lisa was the next warning: "All those treatments they gave him could mean that he can't have children."

Thank God for Lisa's faith in me. She set aside her fears and stuck with me, although that didn't end the warnings. Her family's anxiety was obvious even the day we got married. As we look back at our wedding video, all these decades later, we can see little notes of caution pop up here and there. Our video captures all the traditional rituals, readings and vows—along with lots of asides from relatives along the way. During the first series of formal readings that day, our rabbi declared to the assembled family and friends, "With each bride and groom, we relive our past and we create our future. Be present—oh God—in the soul of this marriage."

Lisa had asked her beloved Grandma Grace to read the traditional invocation of Miriam, who was Moses' older sister and is credited with helping to deliver the Jews from slavery in Egypt. Looking down at her paper, Grace read the printed words: "May you be the mother of thousands of Miriams!"

Then she paused, looked at us, and added, "At least one will do."

We all chuckled. But Grandma Grace wasn't kidding. She didn't hold out much hope that we would have a child.

"I couldn't ignore the anxieties in the family," Lisa said as I discussed this chapter with her. "I actually adapted the language for our wedding ceremony to emphasize lots of little things that I thought were important, including having a child. Of course, I knew you would be a great dad and obviously I wanted you to live a long life, but I also wanted you to work on spending more family time with me. That was threatened when you spent so much time traveling—always on a plane going somewhere. So, you're right to say that I did try to set aside my fears. But the truth is that I still was anxious. I didn't know if we'd ever have a child."

"Eventually you staged your intervention with the magazine clipping," I said. "And I wanted to make those changes. One reason I was so eager to go full time with PlanIt Jewish in 2000 is that I could control my own schedule. With PlanItJewish, I finally was becoming a full-fledged entrepreneur starting my own company and building it from the initial concept. That meant I could spend much more time at home in the early stage of the company—more time with you, more time going to all the medical appointments with you. We made it work."

"There were lots of challenges. I had to overcome some of my own issues, too," Lisa said. "I'd had some serious back problems. For a while, there was a question about whether I should become pregnant and have a child—whether I'd face too many physical problems because of my back. The odds weren't in favor of getting pregnant."

"When you think about the long-shot odds of having Emily, that's why I'm planning to call this chapter 'The Miracle Girl,'" I said. "What do you think?"

"I agree," Lisa said. "So many miracles were involved, starting with the fact that your doctor had the idea to send you to that cryogenic center way back in 1989."

In fact, my cancer was so advanced in 1989 that my doctors did not expect me to live. My situation was so desperate that Dr. Eric Rubin at Dana-Farber wanted to start my treatments as soon as possible. There was no time to lose if we hoped to stop such aggressive cancer. Then, on the day I showed up at Dana-Farber for my first heavy-duty dosage of chemotherapy, a routine blood test before the treatment unexpectedly triggered a warning about my liver function.

Eric held the report out to us as if he needed that paper to prove his point. "The bottom line is: We can't start today," he said.

"No treatment?" Dad asked, looking at the paper even though the test results were cryptic. Dad sat like a great protective rock to one side of us, trying to be as supportive as he could—but I could tell he was shocked and was starting to get angry. "No treatment?" he huffed. "No treatment?"

"Not today," Eric repeated.

Mom wasn't even listening. She had lost it at "can't start today" and her head was down, cradled in both hands.

I hadn't slept the night before this. I was exhausted. Afraid. Shaken. Maybe this was it. Maybe no treatment was possible. Maybe my life was all over. Maybe—

My mind was running so fast I couldn't keep track of which fear to focus on next.

Eric could tell we were falling apart. "Not today, *but maybe tomorrow*," he said. "We can test again tomorrow and maybe the readings will look better."

I tried to be a rock like Dad, but even I was jolted by the fear in my voice when I asked Eric, "So, what do I do today?"

"Howard," Eric said my name slowly. Perhaps he was trying to calm me. Perhaps he was still deciding what to say next. "Howard, today, you'll take a field trip. I'm sending you over to a cryogenic center."

"Cryo-what? What is that?"

"It's a sperm bank."

"A sperm bank? Are you kidding? I don't understand. You've told me I only have months to live. Why bother with a sperm bank?"

Eric sighed and gripped my shoulder. "What else have you got to do today? Go on the field trip. It'll take your mind off all this."

So, I went and followed all the procedures that you may have seen in romantic comedies in which guys make such deposits: *Delivery Man, Back-up Plan, The Switch* and at least a dozen more.

"Remember Billy Crystal and Debra Winger in *Forget Paris?*" Lisa asked. Billy's character has trouble giving a sample at the sperm bank so he went home and filled his cup. Nervous about driving it back to the clinic in time, and stuck in traffic, he drives along the shoulder and gets stopped by a cop. Instead of winding up with a ticket, he winds up with a police escort to the clinic.

"We had our own run in with a sperm bank just months before we were married and before the movie came out," I said. "We were in Boston for the wedding of my Babson roommate Ed Sherr and Resa—and the whole family was curious about my fertility. So, we went to the cryogenic center—with my parents along for the ride."

"I was begging you not to make me go into that room with you, given that your parents were sitting just outside in the waiting room!" Lisa said. "But you made me come in with you. There were no intimidating nurses or sex tapes like in *Forget Paris* and everything had to be sterile. Still, it was so embarrassing. When we stepped back into the waiting room, I remember asking your mom, who smokes, 'Have you got a light?' I don't smoke but was just trying to lighten things up. Unfortunately, the test confirmed our worst fears about your fertility, but thank God you had taken that special field trip, so we had something to work with."

"We often joked around as we were going through this," I said. "Remember when we started the in vitro fertilization (IVF) process in 2000, we joked that since my sample had been on ice for so many years, we were going to defrost kid-cicles?"

"Kid-cicles," she said. "Yeah, I remember that. We heard Jay Leno joking on TV that there should be a movie called, *Honey, I Defrosted the Kids!*"

Infertility is heartbreaking and IVF is an arduous and expensive experience. Our jokes were just a way of adding some levity to a serious topic and to soften the blow if things didn't work out as we had hoped.

Now, the emotion we feel surrounding this living-breathing miracle that brought about Emily's life is more often gratitude and tears of joy than laughter. I have to admit, I've cried more about this miracle than anything else in my life. In 2019, three decades after Eric sent me from Dana-Farber to the sperm bank, I was asked to serve as a participant in an international conference about cancer-survival strategies. I flew in for the weekend event. At the conference, I saw Eric for the first time in years. He was there representing Merck as a keynote speaker. We made dinner plans. They got there first. As I crossed the room to our table, we grinned, then we hugged and we began to catch up on our lives. He was amazed at my survival of stage IV cancer—not just once, but twice by that time.

As dinner moved on, I said, "Eric, there's something I've got to ask you after all these years: Why did you have me go on that field trip to the cryogenic center? I mean, sitting there at Dana-Farber that day, we all knew that I probably was going to be dead soon. What was the point? I've wanted to ask you that question—because now, God blessed us with Emily."

I pulled out my phone and tapped until I brought up her photo. "This is Emily," I said. "Because of your instinct and direction, Eric, Lisa and I have Emily. I mean, the world has Emily because of a decision you made that first day of my treatment in October 1989—and you made that decision on the fly just because we got an unexpected blood test that stopped us in our tracks. Otherwise, I would have started the treatments without that field trip. What were the odds of it happening that way?"

We both looked at Emily, smiling back at us from the phone I held between us.

Then, I said, "Eric, I've got to tell you that I do believe in miracles. Just look at me—I'm alive—and look at her—she's here in this world, too. The miracles of surviving cancer twice—those are enough for any lifetime. But I got even more than that. I got the miracle of Emily coming into our lives."

People at other tables started to glance over at us—two guys and Eric's wife, Kim, just bawling our eyes out as we talked.

"Please, tell me, Eric," I said when I could speak again. "What prompted you to have me take that field trip? All these years, I've wanted to ask you that question."

He had to wait another moment. When he spoke, his voice was soft, "It was just good doctoring, I guess. We knew what these treatments would do—the serious side effects, I mean. It was a standard step so that later on in life—"

"Later on in life?" I said. "Honestly, in 1989, we didn't expect any 'later'."

For another minute, we just let the tears run down.

"You know," I said to him, "there are no words Lisa and I could find to properly express our thanks for giving me my life—since, by all the odds, I shouldn't even be here—and then giving us our daughter, too. There aren't words—"

He put his hand on my shoulder again, as he had that day in 1989.

"You've just told me the story, and that's enough," he said. "This is why we do what we do as doctors. And this is what you need to do as a survivor. Keep telling your story."

I nodded. I stood. I hugged him again.

That's honestly how the miracle of Emily unfolded—marked both by laughter and tears.

Here's more of our laughter: "Remember how surreal it was when we got to the point of implanting the embryos at the clinic?" Lisa said to me, "I never thought there would be so many people in the room when I conceived. We had two doctors and an anesthesiologist, plus nurses. I conceived in the middle of a crowd!"

And more of our tears: "Once the embryos were in place, Howard, you gave me a kiss through your green surgical mask," Lisa said. "Then, I was wheeled into another room where we said blessings over my tummy."

Within weeks, Lisa was writing in her pregnancy journal, already using the "M" word:

> Our baby is truly a miracle baby! We conceived through in vitro fertilization and got pregnant on the first try, which is a miracle in itself. It was hard for me to know that I was pregnant, because I had gone through so many changes with all the meds I had to take for the IVF process. I felt sick a lot of the time. When I went for my official pregnancy test, the blood tech said, "You sure are glowing!"
>
> "No, that's not it," I said. "I'm just feverish from the meds."
>
> No question: I was glowing. When I got the call from our IVF coordinator confirming the pregnancy, I was ecstatic! I was on a second phone with someone from the Federation about the program I was starting, called Club Fed. She almost knew before Howard did! I told her I'd call her back and called Howard. We screamed with elation and joy over the phone!
>
> Howard and I were so thrilled about being pregnant that we did not even bother with the 12-week waiting period that we had been advised to take before sharing the news. We called our families right away! Everyone was as thrilled as we were.
>
> I hope to be a loving, caring, patient mom. I want our child to feel happy and loved. Howard and I hope to set a good example for our child about being generous and compassionate. We will teach about tzedakah and tikkun olam, repairing the world. We hope to show, by example, the importance of treating each other with love, kindness and respect and giving to the greater community. We also will encourage our child to develop his or her unique gifts and talents and interests.
>
> Childhood should be a time of wonder and discovery. Every child should be loved and treated with kindness and respect. They should feel safe, have opportunities for growth and learning and friendships. They should know that they can come to us as parents whenever they need ears to listen, arms to hug or a proudly raised hand for a high five!

Two months after Emily's birth, we hosted her *Simchat Bat*, the Jewish ceremony for giving a baby girl her Hebrew name and welcoming her formally into the Jewish community. This was such a huge event in our two families—and among our circle of friends—that more than 50 people made their way to our California back yard that sunny afternoon about two months after Emily was born. Spread across the lawn, we had crisp, white-linen-covered tables with Jewish and secular baby-related items as centerpieces, set up for a banquet after the ceremony, the text of which Lisa put together using various sources and adding her own touches. This was still long before digital cameras, so we shot the ceremony on video cassettes.

"How good and pleasant it is when brothers and sisters dwell together," Rabbi Charles Briskin declared as the ceremony began. "Today we gather with Lisa and Howard to welcome their beautiful daughter into the Jewish community and to celebrate the miracle and resilience of life. As the baby is carried in by her great-grandmother Lillian Shapiro—who is here all the way from Boston—let us say together: 'Blessed is she who comes to us from God!'"

Together, Lisa and I turned to little Emily, cradled happily in her great-grandmother's arms. Again, we affirmed the "M" word, reading a prayer-poem Lisa had found:

Welcome to the world, little one.
Miracles are waiting:
Open your eyes.
You are our miracle;
You make us complete.
May you dance in sunshine.
May your dreams be sweet.

Emily's grandparents chimed in next. Robert and Anita Naftaly read: "God of all generations, we are grateful for new beginnings, for the bond of life that links one generation to another. We rejoice at this miraculous moment. We hope to be there for all of the milestones along her journey in life, big and small. May we all grow together as a family in health and in strength, in harmony and love."

Then, my parents, Marshall and Nancy, read: "A new life, a new child to love, the start of a new chapter in the chronicle of our family's life has begun with the arrival of our granddaughter. May she grow up in health and happiness, to become a blessing to her family, friends and community. And may we, her grandparents, be granted the joy of helping her develop to her fullest potential."

Then, right out of Lisa's baby journal, with a few new twists to the phrasing, Lisa had us read in unison: "We are grateful to God for the new life that has been entrusted to us. We strive to create a loving home for you, one in which you feel cherished and valued, not only for your achievements, but for the special person you are; a home in which you will feel safe and secure; a home in which you will know, deep in your heart, that we are always here for you, whether you need an ear to listen, a hug, a high five, someone to laugh and play with you—or just to change your diaper! We promise to provide you with ample opportunities to grow, learn and explore the world around you and to develop your own talents and interests. We strive to be the best parents that we can be: loving, compassionate, patient and firm, when needed—yet always kind. We hope you will love life, laugh often and that your days will be filled with lots of smiles."

Just before the rabbi unfolded a tallit, the traditional Jewish prayer shawl, for the blessing of Emily with her Hebrew name, Lisa added one more ritual to the ceremony. Customarily, a tree is planted in Israel to honor a new life—and that was arranged for Emily's birth, but that was half a world away from the circle in our yard that day. So, Lisa had brought out a planter filled with soil. She and I had chosen six special people to step to the front of our gathering, one by one, and read a passage about values we prize in our family. Then, the readers would place seed markers, labeled with these values, into the large pot. The markers were labeled:

+ Compassion, lovingkindness and generosity
+ Integrity
+ Friendship, respect and acceptance of others
+ Hard work, determination and ambition, coupled with balance
+ Curiosity
+ Positive outlook on life

Two decades later, if we still had those little seed markers, they could serve as a map of this book.

The first person to place a marker in the soil, Barbara Hart, was the head of the Jewish Community Center after-school program, where Lisa had worked. It was she who had given that final encouragement to Lisa to have children, saying wisely "as much as you love the children in your classroom, you will never love anyone as much as you will your own child." In her reading over the seed marker, she stressed the importance of tzedakah, compassion, lovin-gkindness and generosity. Five more friends followed her. We chose Ian as an embodiment of integrity. Lara Gelman, who had just had a baby herself, talked about friendship. My co-founder at PlanItJewish Steve Kaufman planted the marker for hard work. Lisa's beloved Aunt Janice Katz, who was a teacher, rep-resented curiosity. Because she could not make the trip, her passage was read by cousin Susan Katz. Then, the star of the show was Bubby Lil, my mother's mother, who we described as "one of the most positive people we know." Bubby Lil's final line was, "May you appreciate what you have, see the goodness in others, and find the sun in times of darkness."

In other words: May you shine brightly.

Then, the rabbi spread his arms to drape the tallit across our shoulders as we held Emily. He declared that, with this ritual, we were collectively "bringing our daughter into the covenant of Abraham and Sarah." The rabbi explained that most people would know our daughter henceforth by her English name, Emily Lauren Brown.

Lisa explained, "Emily Lauren is named first in loving memory of her great-great-grandfather Emil Kahan. The reason we picked his name is that all my life my father has been the biggest role model to me in exemplifying all the traits we have just planted here today, especially working in the Jewish community and practicing tzedakah. He got that from watching his grandfa-ther Emil Kahan. So, we honor my father's influence in our lives by naming this influence in his life, Emil—and naming our daughter Emily."

Then, Lisa brought out Emily's first tzedakah box, a white ceramic bank with a half dozen paintings of smiling children encircling the sides of the box. Lisa placed it on a table near us and immediately children in the crowd began rushing up to drop coins in the box. We all had a good chuckle at their eagerness.

Because everyone standing around us knew me as a relentless fundraiser, I was laughing as I said, "Hey, don't worry. Today is a non-solicitation event, by the way. No soliciting at my house!"

The crowd kept laughing with us.

When all the first coins had rained into the box, I explained Emily's second English name. "Emily's middle name is Lauren, which we chose in honor of my recently deceased grandfather Papa Leo, a true fighter, a World War II veteran who loved family and friends."

Finally, the rabbi wrapped the tallit more closely around Emily as we held her. With more traditional blessings, then, we officially gave her the Hebrew first name Eliana, which Lisa told the crowd, "means 'God answered our prayers'—and that's absolutely true. Howard and I each placed a wish for a child in the Western Wall in Jerusalem last summer and we were blessed to conceive a few months later, despite all odds."

Pointing to that tzedakah box, again, the rabbi said, "Remember that it is a mitzvah to give tzedakah at such times of joy, so please feel free to express your great joy by coming up and filling Emily's jar."

As we sang the final Hebrew blessing, the music was accented by the tinkling of even more coins as our guests filled that box.

And here's another funny thing: We always had so many tzedakah boxes around our home that, as I was working on this chapter, Emily told me, "The truth is that I can only remember the big brown one we had on the table in the living room that was almost too heavy to lift because there were so many coins in it."

"You don't remember the white one with the children holding hands around it? The one we gave you at your baby naming?"

She shook her head. "There were so many of them. But that doesn't really matter, does it? I may not remember the specific box, but I remember the point: We always give back. Our family has always given back. That's what we do."

"Yeah," I nodded. "That's the point."

Thank goodness for all the details captured on the video cassettes, because Ian did not remember the details either.

"No, I can't recall, except that I was there and planted one of the seeds," he said. "I think the important thing is that we've all seen these relationships cross generations now. As I've watched Emily grow over all these years, I've got to tell you, Howard: She really has become the perfect blend of you and Lisa. It's like she's woven you together."

Emily did that in so many ways over so many years that it would be impossible to capture all the details in the tapestry she has crafted, but the most vivid moments involve a whole series of artworks, scrapbooks, school projects and even poetry she has created over the past two decades.

One example is her love for her maternal great-grandmother, Grace Naftaly, who died in 2015 after having celebrated nearly every moment of her 101 years. It was easy to see why Emily would be drawn toward her. In high school in the 1920s, Grace was a student leader who made her school's swim team and was elected to student council. Later, she served the community in a host of ways. When Emily's Great-Uncle Jerry was elected the mayor of Oak Park, Michigan, Jerry made sure that Grace was named the community's honorary "First Mother." Plus, Grace loved sports as much as Emily. Even in her 90s, Grace avidly followed her Tigers, Lions and Pistons, plus her favorite golf pros. Although frail, she had her son drive her to one of Emily's soccer games and park the car at the side of the field so she could watch and cheer for Emily through the window.

Emily loved her dearly. Not long after Grandma Grace passed away, one of Emily's teachers assigned students a project on ethnic foods. Emily decided to research her Great-Grandma Grace's traditional Hungarian brisket, which everyone in the family insisted could never be duplicated. Grace had never shared her secret but was thrilled to write out the instructions on a sheet of the stationery she had made with a heading as Oak Park's First Mother. We all laughed when we saw the big, bold title Grace scrawled across the top of the page in all caps: SECRET RECIPE FOR BRISKET.

Emily spent a day with Lisa and her grandmother, Anita Naftaly, cooking and documenting every detail with notes and photos—all preserved for us now in a thick album. What was the secret? Well, first, it involved adding paprika to the usual blend of salt, pepper and garlic. Once again, Great-Grandma Grace used all caps to stress: HUNGARIAN PAPRIKA. Then, the roasting had to be low and slow in an oven no hotter than 325 degrees in a roasting pan tightly covered with foil. The brisket had to be checked and turned each hour, but the key was "I have no time limit." She could keep doing this for hours on end. For her project, Emily's brisket roasted for more than four hours. Emily was so thrilled with the whole experience that she even documented her Grandpa Bob Naftaly, Grace's son, sitting down to the brisket dinner and declaring it as good as the original.

As Emily has grown into adulthood, she has shown us over and over again how much her love of family has shaped her life. Another school assignment asked for an autobiographical poem based on poet George Ella Lyon's piece, *Where I'm From*. She illuminated the edges of this page with blue ocean waves, green grass and a soccer ball in one corner.

Where I'm From

I am from books
From computers and soccer cleats
I am from the shingled gray house on Franklin Park Drive
With a blue door and lush green grass outside
That felt so soft, it was like walking on silk.
I am from palm trees,
And the evergreens

Whose beauty is etched into my mind
And will forever stay a part of me.
I'm from Lisa and Howard,
I'm from the kind and the caring,
From "I love you" and "Haste makes waste."
I'm from tzedakah boxes and glistening menorahs and shiny mezuzahs.
I'm from Anita and Bob, Nancy and Marshall.
I'm from chicken soup and brisket from Great Grandma Grace.
I am from Massachusetts, Michigan and California.
I am from the beach in Maine.
And the spectacular family that awaits me there on the shore.

Does this chapter inspire you to explore your own family's miraculous traditions? Perhaps that recipe that only your grandma or grandpa could make? In what ways has God answered your prayers in the generations that surround you?

Take a moment and begin to list, just as Emily did, "Where I'm From." Don't worry about whether it's great poetry; it certainly will become a timeless scrapbook entry to save for future generations.

As you remember and write, you may rediscover some forgotten miracles, too.

Shining Brightly

Please consider learning about these or similar organizations that touched my life. Planting a tree in Israel upon the birth of a child or other milestone is a Jewish custom. In vitro fertilization gave us the miracle of our daughter, Emily. You can learn more about the process we went through in 2001.

+ **Jewish National Fund** – Usa.jnf.org/jnf-tree-planting-center/
+ **American Pregnancy Association** – Americanpregnancy.org/ getting-pregnant/infertility/in-vitro-fertilization/

My parents adopted a stretch of Maine shoreline at Ogonquit as a family home where outings have become sacred rituals, especially for the grandchildren. The customs include an annual photograph of the kids posing with their boogie boards. However, no single photo can capture the "connected memories and traditions," Emily recounted as we assembled this book. Lisa said, "Someday, maybe we can do something like this for our grandchildren. I'd like to continue the tradition."

11

Creating Our Own Traditions

Lisa and I knew we were doing something right when Emily finished her own rendition of the poem "Where I'm From" with these lines:

I am from the beach in Maine
And the family that awaits me there on that spectacular shore.

No one in our family actually lives in Maine and yet that state's Atlantic shoreline has become our collective home because of a generation-spanning tradition that my grandparents and parents have maintained for decades.

One of the most common truths about families comes from Leo Tolstoy: "All happy families are alike; each unhappy family is unhappy in its own way." Those words from one of his tragic novels have taken on a new life among researchers studying fields ranging from biology to entrepreneurial economics. These scholars call it The Anna Karenina Principle, a cautionary note that refers to the countless tiny details that can cause a project to fail. Tolstoy originally penned the line to explain the forces that doomed his characters. He was warning his readers that they should appreciate the fragile balance in a happy family because there are myriad ways our relationships can crumble.

That's a hard lesson we've learned in our family and it's why we are so devoted to shoring up all the "traditions" that contribute to our happiness. Since I'm Jewish, as I use that "T" word, I want to explain: Yes, I'm partly referring to the kinds of Jewish traditions that everyone knows about from

Tevye's bittersweet solo in *Fiddler on the Roof*. Many Jewish traditions define us as a family. One of Emily's first projects at school was a Passover Haggadah, the service families read at seder meals.

Nearly every day, somewhere in the world, our children show signs of the importance of our faith traditions and this warms hearts in Jewish, Christian and Muslim homes. Emily's creation of a Haggadah (a Passover prayer book) from a religion class at Hillel Day School has been used at many of our seders, including at my sister-in-law's interfaith home, as it covers all the key points of the service. We store it lovingly in a box of her childhood creations for posterity.

I grew up celebrating the Jewish holidays with the Browns on my father's side and the Shapiros on my mother's side. Both sets of grandparents lived in Worcester, Massachusetts, just 60 minutes from our family home in Framingham. It was easy to hop in the car and visit Papa Leo and Nana Rose, my father's parents, as well as their daughter, who we knew as Tante Carole, and Uncle Mark and their two kids: Adam and Hilary. My sister Cheryl and I were older than Adam and Hilary, so they looked up to us—a relationship all four of us really enjoyed. We all looked forward to cookouts, holiday celebrations and, in the summer, both families had pools. Whoever played host in the warm months, the kids could swim. We also grew up together marking Rosh Hashanah, the Jewish New Year, as well as Passover, Hannukah and other Jewish milestones. Of course, Hanukkah is a relatively minor holiday in Jewish tradition, but it has become very popular with American Jewish kids because of the gifts and the delicious food. Our gifts usually amounted to cash inside a Hanukkah card, which then gave us the fun of anticipating a future shopping trip.

In our family, however, it really was the food that represented the long-awaited sensory overload we craved each December! We would walk through Tante Carole's front door and smell freshly peeled potatoes in sizzling oil. As soon as we had pulled off our winter coats, we were eager to taste the first crispy-golden latkes, always served with heaps of sour cream and applesauce. In fact, Tante Carole was the keeper of all the distinctive recipes from Nana Rose. For example, any weekend visit began with her snacks, like chopped liver on crackers. My sister Cheryl hated that taste; I loved it and, to this day, enjoy chopped liver. While some snacks did not suit every kid's palate, all of us loved Tante Carole's dinners. Whenever we looked forward to a big meal at her house, we would dream about her secret recipes for beef brisket with gravy, sweet-and-tangy carrot tzimmes and from-scratch fudge brownies and blondies. When Cheryl and I went to camp each summer, Nana Rose made sure to ship a dozen brownies and blondies to each of us in the middle of our stay. They lasted all of one minute at camp. When the big distinctive box showed up each summer, counselors and other campers would swarm us and help us tear off the packing tape—grabbing the goodies so fast that Cheryl and I were lucky to snag one for ourselves.

As you are reading this, you might wonder: What was so secret about recipes like brisket that made each generation's dishes so distinctive? Isn't beef brisket just beef brisket? The answer is that as every matriarch—Nana Rose, Bubby Lil, Grandma Grace, Auntie Janice, Grandma Anita—eventually claimed her place as the head of a household in each generation, with distinctive touches to her home cooking: maybe a little extra garlic, or a cup of jelly, or more onion, or a different way of slow-roasting or cutting the finished brisket. These tiny details, which touched off appreciative "Ooohs!" and "Aaahs!" were the sources of immense pride among the home cooks in my family.

Why are these memories so reassuring? Because we know that our time together is fleeting. We've lost all of our grandparents on both sides. Tante Carole passed away in her early 60s—way too young and heartbreaking for all of us who loved her! We know that we must treasure the warm and loving and delicious moments to balance against all of life's inevitable tragedies. Even if you've never heard that Tolstoy line, any parent understands the truth of it: Our happiness is precious. We must celebrate whenever we can. Lisa and I understood that instinctively from our childhoods. We learned it through life-threatening struggles with cancer and other disappointments and tragedies in our circle of loved ones like the untimely death of Carole. Quite literally, when Lisa and I married and when Emily was born, we made vows before God to strengthen our family in any way we could. True to those pledges, and in the face of threats as dire as stage IV cancer, we have built a foundation of family commitments that nothing in the world can shake.

If that sounds daunting—think again! It's not a burden. It's a huge source of joy. For us, it's as simple and fun as making time each summer to romp through the surf along a strip of shoreline in Ogunquit, Maine.

The destination of our annual multigenerational pilgrimage migrated to Maine from an even older family tradition of visits with our grandparents Bubby Lil and Papa Mike Shapiro, my mother's parents. Papa Mike is the grandfather whose passing I honored one night during a young-adult program in Los Angeles and caught Lisa's attention with the obvious emotion I felt as I voiced his name.

Each year, Bubby Lil and Papa Mike Shapiro took their four grandchildren to upstate New York's Catskills, a region now nostalgically remembered as the

Borscht Belt. Because of antisemitic bias through much of the 20th century, Jews from across the East Coast chose to vacation in the Catskills' hundreds of welcoming hotels, resorts and camps. The 1920s through the 1970s were the Catskills' heyday, the era when nightly shows featured bands, dancing and especially standup comics like Jackie Mason, Mel Brooks, George Burns, Rodney Dangerfield, Phyllis Diller, Danny Kaye, Joan Rivers and Jonathan Winters.

As I began writing this section, my own childhood memories of our Catskills customs needed some dusting off. I got my twin sister Cheryl together with our first cousins Douglas Sufrin and Michelle Sufrin-Solomon to recall our childhood travel traditions with Bubby Lil and Papa Mike. Of course, the four of us met via Zoom this time, not in person.

"This is so cool! The four of us are back together again!" Doug said when all of us showed up on the Zoom screen. "We haven't been together in—well, in *forever*! And that feels weird to me, because we were inseparable through all those years we went to the Catskills together."

"Yeah, it's been way too long," I said. "When we all grew up and moved to different parts of the country, getting together got a lot harder. We all got busy with our careers. Then, there was my cancer in recent years. But you're definitely right Doug. Too many years have passed since we've been in the same place together. We've got to make that happen as soon as this pandemic is over."

"We should. It's too bad we let so much time pass," Doug said. "When we were growing up—for *years*—Bubby Lil and Papa Mike made sure we stayed together. We all loved going on those trips with them. How long did that tradition last? I was the youngest, so can someone help me with the timeline?"

"It started in the early 1970s and it went on for at least a dozen years until we were going away to college," Cheryl said.

"When I think back, it was crazy how close we got—four inseparable friends. We'd look forward to those trips all year long," Doug said. "Then, whenever we finally reached the hotel up in the Catskills—and Bubby and Papa turned us loose—we instantly became two crews. Howard, you and I were always one crew while Michelle and Cheryl were the other crew. I don't know about you guys, but I would dream about those trips for months."

"We all looked forward to it," I said. "We learned Bubby and Papa's rituals by heart."

"I can recite them," Michelle said. "The trip would start with Bubby and Papa driving to Framingham, first, and staying over Thursday night at your house. Then early Friday morning, they'd pack you two into their car with them and they'd drive up to Long Island, New York to get us. Then, the six of us would make the drive out to one of the big hotels, whichever one they had chosen that year."

Bubby and Papa loved the Catskill hotels. We stayed at several of them, but their favorites were Grossinger's and the Concord, names that now are legendary parts of Catskills lore.

Grossinger's was the inspiration for the fictional Kellerman's resort in *Dirty Dancing*. In its prime, the resort once boasted dozens of different sports, games, classes and entertaining programs—something for every guest's tastes. Grossinger's was spread out across more than 35 buildings and outdoor amenities. The main dining room seated 1,300 people, so two grandparents with four squirming children did not have to worry about disturbing that vast ocean of families. Before it finally closed in 1986, Grossinger's had tried to shift from its classic era of shows with stars like Sammy Davis Jr., Milton Berle and Jerry Lewis to booking pop singers like Eddie Fisher and even a few rock-era shows that capitalized on its proximity to Woodstock. In its waning years, Grossinger's even booked Abbie Hoffman for a week and offered tie-dyeing workshops. The main resort buildings finally were demolished in 2018.

The Concord didn't close until 1998 and was our destination in later years. It was the largest and most lavish of all the resorts with a dining room that held 3,000. Its headliners once included Tony Bennett and Barbra Streisand. In 1963, the Concord managed to have Dr. Martin Luther King Jr. make an appearance to receive an award for his work.

But could the four of us, today, recall any headliner we saw in a dozen years of visiting these resorts?

"Ahhh, I know there were big stars there, but—no," Cheryl said. "I've got no specific memory of that."

"I do remember there always was some kind of show at night: some singer, a comedian, a dancer," Michelle said. "But can I recall names? Ahhh, nope."

"That's weird, isn't it?" Cheryl said. "We know there were big shows, but who can recall them?"

"Most of the time, I don't think we stuck around late enough to see them," Doug said. "That really wasn't our thing when we went up there. Maybe we were too young to appreciate them. I remember what we dreamed about during the whole drive up to the Catskills: Fun and games. In the evenings, Bubby and Papa liked to play games. They loved that. They encouraged that. Do you remember Papa Mike's rolls of quarters, Howard?"

"Oh, yeah!" I said. "Papa Mike always packed rolls of quarters and the moment we climbed out of the car on the first day, he'd hand us each our own roll. We'd run to the big pinball arcade, and we'd play as many games as we could until we didn't have a single quarter between us."

"Correction," Michelle said. "You guys blew your quarters right away, then you'd beg us for our quarters, because we hadn't even opened our rolls yet. Cheryl and I never went to the arcade until later. Remember how much stuff there was to see, Cheryl? Remember all the shops they had? Cheryl and I always wanted to go look at all that stuff, first. We knew you two guys would blow your quarters right away. We kept ours to enjoy later."

"What do you remember about the meals?" Cheryl asked. "I remember we always went to dinner with Bubby and Papa in the big dining rooms."

"Oh, the dining rooms were massive—tables as far as you could see," Michelle said.

"I loved the food!" Doug said and soon we all were laughing in a knowing way.

"Let's be honest. We stuffed ourselves!" I said. "You could have as much as you wanted—and there were tons of fatty, sugary foods—stuff we never got at home. Late in the afternoon, before it got dark, there was always a cocktail hour, which is when they brought out stuff like thousands of mini egg rolls and pigs in a blanket—and tons of other finger foods."

"Yup, which we'd wolf down and be full for dinner," Doug said.

"Me too," I said. "I always managed to pack away a ton of that stuff."

"It was called the Borscht Belt, and I do remember Papa actually liked to have the borscht with his supper," Cheryl said. "And however much we'd eaten already, we always could have dessert."

"Do you remember the night you ate three desserts, Howard?" Doug asked. "I was in awe of you! I didn't know anybody could eat that much."

"We chose to spend that time together," Cheryl said. "What I remember most about those trips was the great feeling of freedom we had as kids up there. Suddenly, we were free to do anything we felt like doing, wherever we wanted around the place. Michelle, you and I always liked to hang out around the pool. Really all Bubby and Papa required of us was that we show up at mealtimes—and for games. And, of course, we wanted to do that."

"We loved the games," Michelle said.

"Oh, the games! I remember an epic shuffleboard tournament one year," Doug said.

"And there were pillow fights, too," Michelle said.

"We thought it was the greatest vacation kids could ever have," Doug said.

"What I remember about Papa was how kind he was, even when we sometimes got in trouble like after the big pillow fight," Cheryl said. "Another time

Michelle and I thought it would be great fun to steal stuff off the housekeepers' carts, taking things like those little soaps. Of course, we got caught and we got in a lot of trouble for that, but Papa wasn't mad at us. He was a teddy bear. Remember? Rather portly and jolly so you wanted to give him a big hug. He always had a big smile and a cigar in his mouth."

"He also loved sports," I said. "He loved to play golf and wanted to teach Doug and me how to play. I enjoy golf today mainly because I played it with Papa Mike and Doug as a kid in the Catskills. Plus, Papa Mike's the one who taught me to play cribbage, which I still love."

"What I remember most about Bubby Lil and Papa Mike is that they were perfectly matched, right down to their love of spending time with the family and playing those games. I can still close my eyes and see Bubby Lil playing canasta and mahjong," Cheryl said. "Those two—they loved each other so much. I'll never forget the way they would sit down next to each other at the end of an evening, and they'd automatically reach out and hold hands. What a love affair!"

"You know, we didn't appreciate it at the time, but they never had much money," Michelle said. "Yet they paid for that whole trip every year. Whatever they had, they'd save up and spend it on the family."

"That makes me sorrier that we haven't stayed together over the years like they wanted," Doug said. "We should have done better about that after they quit taking us on those trips."

"Bubby Lil did her best to remind us," Michelle said. "I can still hear her voice: 'You've got to stay together! You have to keep in touch! Family has to stick together!'"

"I still can hear her saying that, too," Cheryl said. "After the trips stopped, did she used to telephone you while you were at college, just to check in?"

"Yeah, she did," Michelle said. "She would call. She made a point of keeping in touch. She loved us so much."

She always sent handwritten letters to us and cards for every birthday and holiday.

She never missed one.

"And it meant so much to me when I was planning to marry Dave that Bubby Lil was the first one to accept him completely—totally," Cheryl said. "Because Dave isn't Jewish, I was worried what Bubby Lil would think. I mean, she took her Judaism so seriously that she was in the synagogue every Friday night. But, to her, family ultimately trumped everything. She could see how much Dave and I loved each other. She made both of us feel welcome right away. I'll never forget that kind of arms-wide-open love she showed us."

"I wonder how many kids had a tradition like ours with their grandparents?" Doug said.

Well, in fact, my own parents picked up that tradition, modified it to fit their circumstances and continue it to this day with their grandchildren: our daughter, Emily, and Cheryl and Dave's kids—Marly, Danielle and Luke. In their reinterpretation of the tradition, they decided not to limit it only to their grandchildren—so Lisa, Cheryl, Dave and I also are included every year.

To explore this second phase of the tradition, I asked my mother Nancy and my father Marshall why they were so eager to continue this kind of multigenerational family vacation.

"It wasn't a difficult choice. We saw how much you kids had enjoyed it," Mom said, "We knew that you loved that tradition of a trip with the grandparents—so, when we had our own grandkids, we just decided to keep it going."

"Emily grew up with the Maine tradition," Lisa said. "The first time we went up there, she was just a baby."

"Why Maine?" I asked.

"We'd heard that Maine was a nice place to go, but we had no idea when we started driving up there that Ogunquit would become such a very, very special place for us," my father said.

"There was more to our decision than that," Mom said. "Marshall's cousin Barry Bernstein owned part of a timeshare up there and he went every June for two weeks. Barry told us Maine was the place to go. He said, 'Come up here once and you'll fall in love with it.' And, boy, was he right. Given where we live, of course we had tried taking some family trips to Cape Cod—but that did not suit us. We had to drive through too many hours of traffic just to reach the place. Cape Cod involved too many cars, way too many people—way too much of everything for me. Sure, the ocean's a little cooler up in Maine, but it's not as crowded as Cape Cod. Sure, the Cape Cod beaches are longer, but that beach at Ogunquit goes on for 2 miles. That's plenty big enough for us. Plus, up in Ogunquit, there are all these little nooks to explore around town—stores and seafood places and ice cream shops and all kinds of fun."

"Best of all, from my perspective: Those spots up there around Ogunquit still are mostly independent, family-owned businesses," Dad said. "I'm a salesman all my life. I like supporting mom-and-pop local businesses. Once upon a time, they were the backbone of this country."

Dad paused, then added, "Of course, it's not exactly what you'd call a *Jewish* destination. For instance, you don't want to go to the Maine coast if you don't want to eat their lobster." We all nodded on the Zoom screen. Lobster, crab, shrimp and a number of other ocean delicacies aren't kosher, but my family is Reform—so that's not a problem for us.

"Yeah, I happen to love lobster," Mom said. "Lobster is absolutely a part of the annual tradition. I'm a lobster maven."

"I don't remember exactly which lobster place we chose in that very first year we went to Ogunquit. There are several family-owned lobster restaurants we love up there," Dad said. "And that's how this whole tradition developed. We went up there and tried things. We started this whole Ogunquit custom one step at a time, year by year. One thing I know for sure: From the beginning until today, we have always booked our rooms in the same family-run place, The Aspinquid Hotel. We always book two suites—one for your family, Howard, and one for Cheryl's family—and then a double room for Mom and me. Then, once we're settled in our rooms, it's a lot more comfortable, casual and easy than it ever was out on Cape Cod. Going to the ocean at Ogunquit beach is like going to a football game with your seats on the 50-yard line. We can walk out of the doors to our rooms and, in 500 feet, we're either on the beach or we're in the heart of the town."

"So that pretty much describes the Ogunquit tradition," Mom said. "We've got tons of photo albums about it, but that sums it up."

"Yeah, that's about it," Dad said.

What surprised and delighted us was Emily's reaction to their description. When she heard how they summed up the Maine tradition, she said: "No! No! No! That's not the whole tradition." Like Doug, Michelle, Cheryl and I recalling the Catskills, Emily and her cousins have evolved a much more detailed appreciation of the rituals my parents have laid out for them.

"The tradition doesn't even start in Ogunquit," Emily said. "It starts with a flight to Boston—and always in August. My birthday is in August, and I always looked forward to having my birthday with the family while we were on our trip. So, first, we all fly into Logan airport and take a commuter bus to Framingham. Bubby Nancy has lunch for us, a dip in Papa Marsh's swimming pool then the first stop is going with Papa and Bubby to Bob's, which is this giant superstore where you can find all kinds of shoes and lots of back-to-school clothes. Papa and Bubby always wanted to spoil us with new shoes and clothes at Bob's. I don't know why they loved Bob's so much, but that became an essential part of the tradition."

When I went back to talk with my parents about Emily's memories, Dad said, "I guess I forgot to mention that part, but of course we loved Bob's. It's a chain now, but it was family owned from the '50s. Started in Middletown, Connecticut. And of course, I wanted to get them shoes. I mean, who knows shoes like I know shoes? Bob's has thousands and at good prices. So, yeah, I can see how Emily says that the first part of the tradition was getting some shoes. I'm glad to hear she appreciates that."

"It wasn't just getting shoes," Emily said. "It was the whole experience of Papa fitting each of us for our new shoes. He'd get down on his knees and make us push our feet onto this big old-fashioned metal thing."

"It's called a Brannock," Dad shrugged. "It's just the device we use—you know, the big metal thing you use to measure feet. Nothing special about that."

"But it was," Emily said. "Papa was personally getting us ready for school and making sure our shoes fit. That's an important part of the whole experience."

Dad smiled wistfully at how much that all mattered to her over the years.

"And sometimes we'd have a chance to visit other family in the area," Emily said. "Remember, I'm an only child. I don't have brothers and sisters at home, so I love to have a chance to see the rest of the family. Then, Papa and Bubby would always make sure to choose foods we kids loved to eat. I still remember that our first supper was usually a trip to McDonald's where they'd let us order like—like French fries and dozens of chicken nuggets."

As Emily said this, I couldn't help but grin, remembering the mountains of stuff we wolfed down at Grossinger's and the Concord. We had our pigs in a blanket and mini egg rolls; they had their nuggets.

"We'd stay that first day in Framingham with the pool and the whole place just jammed full of people," Emily said. "Then, very early the next morning, we'd form our caravan. Dad and Papa always were in the first car with all the beach chairs and our ocean gear—all our Boogie Boards. That's always the way we went into the ocean—with our Boogie Boards. We've got all these annual photos of us lined up on the beach with our boards. So, Dad and Papa were always in the first car with all that gear. Sometimes, we'd let them go first and follow a few hours later."

"Yeah, she's right. We'd get up there first and make sure everything was set," my father said. "I forgot to mention that part."

"But there's even more to it!" Emily said. "The tradition is that Bubby and Papa always buy the same candies, snacks and drinks. Papa Marsh and my father always went first, Papa would make sure that those treats were already waiting for us in our rooms when we arrived. I don't know how they remembered them all every year, but Papa and Bubby made sure that those traditions were identical each time. Here's another example: We knew, like clockwork, that each night before we went to bed, Papa would go around and take each of our individual orders for his run with my dad to Dunkin' Donuts early the next morning."

"Well, yeah, she's right about my taking the orders," my father said. "I don't know if you'd call it a family tradition. I guess you could. Where we live, out here in the suburbs of Boston, you must go with Dunkin' Donuts. It's part of an international chain now, but people in our part of the country remember that it was founded right here by local people." In fact, blue-collar Boston natives of a certain age recall that it was William Rosenberg, the American-born son of Jewish-German immigrants who parlayed his eighth-grade education and street smarts to become one of the country's greatest food entrepreneurs. He noticed that workers in factories around Boston mainly preferred coffee and doughnuts during their daily breaks—so, in 1948, he founded the shop that would become Dunkin' Donuts. Instead of the limited handful of varieties offered in most local shops, Rosenberg boasted 52 varieties—hence the need for Dad to take careful notes on what everyone in our group wanted for breakfast in Ogunquit.

"There were so many choices, even donut holes called munchkins, bagels, croissants and muffins," Emily said. "And, then, from Papa's list everybody got what they wanted the next morning."

My father was nothing if not punctual about our Ogunquit schedule.

"And that's a very important thing to point out: We always knew when every single thing would happen," Emily said. "We knew when Papa would make the Dunkin' run. We also knew that, before we were even up in the morning, he'd be down at the ocean shore arranging our chairs for the day, claiming a prime spot for us before the beach filled up. For those few days up there in Maine every summer, I suddenly had a big family surrounding me and taking care of every detail to make sure the day would be fun. My cousins were like brothers and sisters. When I was young, I remember that I used to bug my aunt and uncle to let me sleep over in their rooms because I wanted to spend as much time as possible with my cousins. I didn't want to leave them even when it was time for bed."

"In spite of all the excitement, we usually slept pretty well up there," Emily said. "Then, we'd spend every day we could out there in the ocean—or at least as long as we could stand it. The water was cold, but we'd keep going all day long. Looking back, I think we were verging on hypothermia some days, but we didn't want to leave the water. Think about it: I was this kid who worried about lots of big questions from an early age. In Maine, we didn't have a care in the world except trying to catch the best wave with our Boogie Boards. How much did I live for those waves each year? I dreamed about it."

And, as she said that, I thought of my cousin Doug describing his dreams of the Catskills.

Emily continued. "I do remember one year there had been a terrible storm just before we got there, and the shoreline was closed on our first day. There were red flags up and nobody was allowed into the water. Then, the day after that, we got the best waves we'd ever had."

Emily chuckled as she said, "You know, when I went back to school, I have to admit that I told the other kids we rode waves 40 feet tall! I don't think I was lying exactly. That was—just a little bit enthusiastically exaggerated—but I think it shows how much I loved the waves."

"And the shells," my mother said, now remembering even more details of these annual rituals. "The kids always collected so many shells."

"More than shells," Emily said. "The whole time we were up there, we'd collect the best shells and unusual stones and colorful pieces of beach glass, too. We'd take them home and I loved the way just looking at those little collections would remind me of the great family time up in Maine, counting the months until we could go again."

Emily paused, then said, "Oh, there was so much more to it than we can even begin to tell in a single chapter of this book. There are so many connected memories and traditions from the smell of that place where we always stay— our rooms always had this musty ocean smell that I came to expect as a part of the whole experience—to the sand castles we'd build along the shore, walks along the Marginal Way to Perkins Cove, to the music we'd listen to especially as we got older, to the little trolley that ran around town, to the local candy shop where Papa would give us money to buy anything we wanted—to even the early bedtimes we had when we were young."

My father, Marshall, was the drill sergeant scheduling the earliest possible dinner times—just like my grandparents had done it in the Catskills—and ending the evening for the grandkids at a relatively early hour as well.

"Yes, that's all true," my mother said. "We tried to gear everything to make it the most enjoyable for our grandkids—and for our kids. I remember we always made a point of telling you—Howard and Lisa and Cheryl and Dave— to go enjoy yourselves somewhere at night when the kids finally got to bed. We'd set up a couple of beach chairs between the doors to your rooms and we'd babysit like a couple of bodyguards protecting the place."

Another reason they enforced an early dinner time was to optimize the chances that the grandkids, jazzed up by their long day at the beach, would behave at the dinner table.

"Most of the meals were for the kids—whatever they wanted," Mom said. "But part of the tradition—"

Emily used almost identical words, "But part of the tradition was one fancy lobster dinner. We always went one place, each year—"

"We always went one place, each year—" my mother said, "where we could get a full-scale lobster dinner. And I have to tell you: That wasn't always easy with four young kids."

I always remember the lobster dinners each year, but mostly I remember our favorite dinner places like Oarweeds, the Lobster Pound, Lords (now Hobbs Landing), Johnathan's, Barnacle Billy's, Clay Hill Farm and Arrows, to name a few.

"Yeah," Mom nodded. "We tried lots of different places over the years, but mostly we returned to the same ones."

Eventually, after multiple Zooms, phone calls and emails we had a family consensus about the basic outlines of our Catskills and Maine traditions. The loving debates about precise details continue, of course, as they would in any family when traditions are discussed. Exactly which foods, restaurants and activities were part of the annual rituals?

What surprised me as our discussions unfolded over several weeks were the memories from Lisa. After all, as I began working on this chapter, the focus was on what grandparents and parents plan for our children. As Lisa talked about the Maine traditions, I realized that this also was an essential part of her year, as well.

"Howard, your family was doing things like this for years before I met you and we got married, so this is something that I came to discover, I guess like Dave became a part of this when he married Cheryl," Lisa said. "And the main thing I need to say about this is: Maine became a special place, a happy place, for me as well. Howard, your mother embraced me like a daughter from the start and, when I first went up to Ogunquit, I found the ocean so calming and restorative. I love the whole experience up there—even watching the tides move in and out. When I started going up there, we lived on the West Coast. We had to fly across the country to take part in this and, rather than a stressful thing, I experienced it right away as a time when I could just relax."

"Well, so much of it was mapped out," I said.

Lisa laughed. "Your father is the ultimate creature of habit. Every year, it's the same order of things, the same places—right down to the Dunkin' Donuts orders we place at night, then he delivers to us the next morning. I found myself loving it. It was such a great opportunity for Emily to spend time with her cousins, so they could grow up feeling close to each other. Howard, you talk about how important it is to know your happy place—so you can rely on that when things are hard. Well, Maine definitely became one of my happy places where I felt worries lifted off my shoulders for a few days."

Lisa paused, then she added. "Who knows? Someday, maybe we can do something like this for our grandchildren. I'd like to continue the tradition."

This entire book is about appreciating and celebrating our shared strengths so that we form caring circles that can sustain us even when times aren't so happy. Leo Tolstoy's *Anna Karenina* was right about one thing: Happiness is fragile. We need to appreciate the countless tiny details that all mesh to create the loving, hope-filled relationships that make life worth living.

One of those sources of happiness is an appreciation of the children in our family circles. Many years ago, as she was reflecting on Emily's birth, Lisa wrote in her journal: "Being with children makes you live in the moment—and see things as if for the first time so we really can appreciate the smallest of wonders."

When she was 14, Emily wrote a Mother's Day letter to Lisa, thanking her for the many ways she had shaped her life, including annual traditions like Ogunquit. "Thank you for always being there for me and guiding my pathway in life," Emily wrote. "You are a symbol of strength and teach me every day how to lead. You have a heart of gold and, when I grow up, if I am even half as good a mother as you are, I'll be very proud."

Often, we don't stop to appreciate how family traditions strengthen our relationships. In fact, I thought I knew the Catskills and Ogunquit stories by heart—and was surprised to discover how much more there was to both stories. That is, until I asked the people involved to retell these stories with me.

Consider contacting some of your friends and loved ones and simply ask them to help you retell the stories of your own traditions.

You will be pleasantly surprised, too.

Shining Brightly

Do you have family traditions, foods and customs that you enjoy, love and carry on for years? Check out these links for Jewish foods. Sorry, but Nana Rose's brownie recipe is top secret. Please check out our family favorite road trips to the Catskills in upstate New York or Ogunquit beach on the coast of Maine on the Atlantic.

+ **Brisket** — TheMom100.com/recipe/jewish-brisket-for-the-holidays/
+ **Potato Latkes** — TheKitchn.com/how-to-make-latkes-at-home-251997
+ **The Catskills** — VisitTheCatskills.com
+ **Ogunquit, Maine** — VisitMaine.net/page/66/about-ogunquit

Religion is the largest social network in the world and my dream was to connect members of those communities online. My colleagues and I began within our own faith community, PlanItJewish. We grew until we reached toward an even larger global network in CircleBuilder, which included all Christian denominations. During those years, I spent a lot of time at trade shows and devoted a lot of creative energy to the design of our projects. To capture our central goal, we designed a photo of me standing in the central aisle of a church with a laptop as a unifying symbol.

12

A Circle as Big as the World

"Sunlight glanced off a silvery circle."

Do you remember that line on this book's first page? My life is defined by circles: family circles, community circles, religious circles, online circles. We all live on a huge, rotating sphere that circles the sun. In Judaism, the joy of moving in circles is called *Hakafot* or "going around." We dance in circles called the Hora at major life events like weddings and we often praise God in circles. On *Simchat* Torah—the holiday that celebrates the annual completion of Torah readings—everyone in the synagogue starts singing and dancing around the whole building, carrying the Torah scrolls in an exuberant circle formed by every man, woman and child in attendance. Circles are symbols of perfection, unity and reciprocity.

So, it was natural that I kept dreaming about enlarging circles to encourage healthier communities. For decades as a serial entrepreneur, I helped to forge the cutting edge of the internet—which now brings the world into the palms of our hands. Each one of us has become a touchpoint in our planetary circle.

Today, it's hard to remember when we didn't have that power of smartphones in our hands. Millions of young adults in their 20s never knew that earlier world. Nearly everyone now expects to join online groups and global networks. In 2021, more than 80% of Americans use YouTube and 69% use Facebook, according to the latest report on social media from Pew Research. Instagram is coming on strong among 40% of Americans, and Pinterest has risen to reach 31% of us. The list of other smaller social media options would fill pages! In fact, not too many years ago while I still was building our online communities, my team created a one-page graphic of available social media options. When we crammed all of those logos together on a single page, the type was so small that the names were barely legible—even when we projected that page on a large screen in public presentations. The point we were making was that each of us faces a bewildering number of invitations.

One of our slogans at that point was: "Stop social noise pollution."

But let me take you back even further in our online adventures to the year 2000, when my friend Steve Kaufman and I sat drinking coffee and dreaming about the future of social networks in a San Francisco café with Craigslist founder Craig Newmark. At that time, none of us had heard the term MySpace (which debuted in 2003), or YouTube (launched in 2005), or Facebook (a Boston-area college service started in 2003 that went national in 2006).

Then, consider this: On the day we met in that Bay Area café to discuss the future, every one of the guys who eventually would co-found Pinterest (2009) and Instagram (2010) were still teenagers!

As we brainstormed with Craig that day, the search engine that formed the backbone of the web was still Yahoo—whose stock hit an all-time high earlier that year. We knew that Google was a scrappy startup that had Yahoo in its sights, but Google's dominance was years away. There was no Gmail until 2004, no Google Calendar until 2006. The online community everyone was buzzing about coast to coast was Craig's innovative idea of strengthening communities by simply sharing lists. In fact, Craig's "list" started in 1995 as an email he distributed as a hobby to tell friends about fun things to do in the Bay Area. Craigslist became a web-based service in 1996—and did not really blossom across North America until 2000.

That's why our coffee-and-conversation that day was so auspicious.

Craig has always been a *mensch*, even before he became known around the world as a philanthropist. He has been humble and enjoys joshing about his own nerdiness. He embodies timeless Jewish values, especially hospitality and service, in his online efforts. That's true even though he describes himself as a secular Jew. Craig once joked with an interviewer that his personal rabbi was the late poet and songwriter Leonard Cohen. Steve and I managed to befriend Craig at a crucial moment in his life. Craig's email list of events had grown so rapidly that he reorganized it as a for-profit company in 1999—and then he stepped away from day-to-day leadership in 2000 to focus on discovering new ways to repair our broken world. *TIME* magazine called him one of the 100 people shaping our world. As Jews, we call that tikkun olam. As high as his star rose, Craig always had time for requests to help others. When I asked him to give an inspirational talk to young Jewish leaders in the San Francisco area, he was happy to do that. Later, he talked to a Babson alumni club I helped to organize in the Bay Area. He always made time to give back. In my mind, when I think of Craig, I think: mensch.

That day over coffee in 2000, we asked him to serve on the board of advisors for our new nonprofit PlanItJewish. At first glance, our online service seemed like a version of Craig's events lists—except focused on Jewish communities. We planned to start in the Bay Area just like he did. Then, as we talked, Craig realized we were launching something far more advanced. He was intrigued and agreed to join our board.

He peppered us with questions.

"So, this is specifically to connect Jews to strengthen the world, right? And to help meet new people? Help build relationships?" he asked.

"Yeah, we designed it to be really practical," Steve said. "For example: I'm single. San Francisco is enormous and the Jewish community is big, too, but it's very disconnected around here."

"There are 400,000 Jews in this area—and 600 Jewish organizations," I said. "That's the scope of what we're trying to serve."

"The geography is huge!" Steve continued. "And, just as Howard says, the number of events I could attend is overwhelming. So—as a single person—if I want to meet Jewish women, my question is: How do I know what's going on that might draw other Jewish people who I might want to meet? Where can I go to find a list of good stuff—events I might actually want to attend—and then sort out my list of options by type and topic and location?"

"I get it," Craig said. "This helps the individual—*and* it helps the hosts, too, right?"

"Exactly," I said. "This really represents a game changer for the leaders of these groups. Across this area, there are lots and lots of Jewish organizations with good people working every week to organize great events. But then, they're always worrying that they won't be able to get enough butts in the seats after all their hard work. From their perspective, PlanItJewish opens up a much larger audience of people who will see what they're planning."

Craig nodded.

I continued, "And, there's even more! For instance, here's a very important part of this: Afterward, the people who registered to attend these events get a survey asking them to evaluate the experience. This feedback, then, is collected and sent to the hosts. This is very valuable information that most of these groups have never received before."

"So the hosts, or the groups or agencies behind these events, can use that data to improve as they go," Craig said. As he kept asking questions, it was clear that Craig was especially fascinated by the tech side. One of his questions was, "So, when people decide to register for these events—what about tickets or payments?"

"That's a built-in part of the service," I said.

"OK, this is the nerdy side of me," he said. "But how are you going to build that? That's a big challenge with all the groups that may wind up selling tickets. What's the plan? What's the software?"

Then, we spent quite a while talking about the technical side of the system. This led to lots of other questions about expansion.

Craig said, "This makes a lot of sense to me. Just like you're hoping to do, I started locally right here and then grew. You guys already are well known in the Jewish community in the Bay Area, but how do you scale this? How do you reach communities that don't know you guys? That's the big challenge, isn't it?"

Steve and I explained that this was, indeed, our biggest challenge and that we had built this into our game plan. "Once people see how well it's working here, we'll take that data—we'll take that whole story—and we'll share it with other cities that want to improve participation in their events," I said. "We're going to meet with leaders in other big cities, one at a time. We're going to roll it out in various Jewish communities, one by one, and build nationwide awareness. We'll do lots of media on this. I'm sure we'll generate news coverage, too. Then, as the positive results become obvious in each new city, we expect that other cities will line up for a chance to be part of this."

"OK. OK. But how do you *monetize* that? You guys have nonprofit status. OK. I get that. But, you've still got to pay the bills. How does that happen?"

"We'll have rates scaled for each Jewish community to join the network," Steve said. "Bigger cities will pay more than smaller cities."

"I'm impressed. This is something good for the world, and something good for the Jews," Craig said—and he told us that he was eager to keep talking with us. Soon, our presentations to community leaders listed Craig among a dozen prominent members of our advisory board.

Craig was right. This was something good for the world, something good for the Jews—and for my family, because I was home for dinner with Lisa most nights. Of course, once again, I worked very long hours on the launch—but in that first phase I usually could add those extra hours from home after dinner.

As we got ready to launch, we listed three co-founders: Steve, myself, and early on, Martin Singer. Then, we added a vital team member: Julie Snyder.

She worked with us as an administrator, manager of web content and, on top of all that, she was a terrific designer and was responsible for so much of the material we developed both for PlanItJewish and for the CircleBuilder expansion we added by 2006. The final key player as PlanItJewish grew was Brent Cohen as chief operating officer, basically to serve as a second Howard Brown, rolling out the service to cities nationwide. Sometimes Brent and I split up the workload and the geography. Sometimes, we worked as a team on a particularly big challenge.

In 2000 alone, our team logged more than 100 breakfasts, coffees and lunches just like our crucial conversation with Craig. As entrepreneurs, we called that "socializing our idea." Our long list of encouraging conversation partners included the staff of JDate.com, the Jewish dating service that exploded internationally in the years just after 2000. In 2002, we partnered publicly with JDate.com as co-sponsors of the 22nd annual San Francisco Jewish Film Festival.

Once again, as I had seen at Avid and Liquid Audio, headlines about our innovations began to emerge, including one news story in 2002 about our connections with JDate.com. The story included this strong endorsement from our new friends: "JDate.com encourages its members to both attend and volunteer their services to support the San Francisco Jewish Film Festival," said Alon Carmel, president of MatchNet, parent company of JDate.com. "We joined with PlanItJewish.com because we support its mission to advance participation, membership and volunteerism in local Jewish communities."

In fact, my partner Steve Kaufman became an active user of both our service and JDate.com and eventually met his wife through their service. Steve's quest to find a Jewish wife actually wound up in a number of the news stories that popped up about us nationwide.

One extensive profile of us began:

> It started after a Jewish Federation meeting in San Francisco as a conversation between two Jewish guys—dot.com entrepreneur Howard Brown, whose wife was concerned about his workload, and Steve Kaufman, a single guy looking for a wife who could bug him about his workload. That conversation developed into PlanItJewish.com, an interactive web site that has revolutionized Jewish community calendars in a dozen cities in North America, so far.

And, they're just getting warmed up.

"PlanItJewish is an amazing way to inform, connect and build Jewish community," said Brown, PlanItJewish CEO. Visitors to the new web site can search, register and even pay online for local Jewish events and classes. "People can sync the information to their Palm Pilots and calendars and share events with their friends."

The site turns into a virtual "concierge service" by alerting registered individuals to upcoming events that match their interests. "Everything is linkable," said Brown, a technology entrepreneur. "Click on a month—and find an event you like. Click on the event and sign up for it."

Organizations like the service because they also can post volunteer opportunities and receive emailed feedback on all of their events, so they can plan more effectively for future events.

Did you catch that reference to Palm Pilots? To make a long, technical story short, our entire PlanItJewish team had to be agile to adapt to the many challenges of rolling out this service coast to coast, including: How would the interface look and operate on a host of emerging digital devices? We described ourselves as working on the "bleeding edge" of social media development, because each new major city that wanted to participate brought new problems we had to solve.

One huge challenge we discovered right away was simply figuring out how the hundreds—and eventually thousands upon thousands—of events would be entered into our system each week.

"Have you seen the amount of paper stacking up this week?" I said to Steve at one point after our launch. "We've got four interns trying to keep up with all that paper—the paper calendars, paper flyers, paper newsletters and press releases. We're receiving so much stuff for the listings that I can see already that this method isn't scalable even with an army of interns."

"You're right," he said. "We've got to put more emphasis on training the local leaders to enter their own events."

So, we invested in the development of printable manuals and digital training modules—and we hosted training events—and then we also had to invest in having even more software developed. We paid a team of coders to create a batch uploader for the groups' spreadsheets that would interface with our system. Soon, we discovered that only 10% of our partners in these cities were

using that software we had just provided for them. Of course, we went back
to the drawing board! We developed even more printable manuals and digital
training modules—and we hosted additional training events.

On and on the cycles went.

And so this story unfolded for several years through many cities. Each
new city also required a marketing campaign. Some were quite creative.
Pittsburgh's Jewish leadership produced a full-color postcard for a mass mailing that asked: "Don't know BUPKES about what's happening in our Jewish
Community?" Then, the card listed the PlanItJewish internet address to learn
more—plus, the card featured a color photo of a line of rainbow-hued computer cables plugged into wall sockets, each socket shaped like a star of David.
Very eye catching!

We launched the San Francisco Bay Area PlanItJewish in December 2001,
then spread to the Minneapolis and St. Paul area by late 2002, Baltimore
and Houston by 2004, then Pittsburgh, Cincinnati, St. Louis, plus Ottawa,
Canada, in 2005, followed by Denver and Kansas City in 2006 and Seattle
and Detroit in 2007. At our peak, we offered listings for more than 150,000
events each year; we served 30 metropolitan areas; and we had launched 50
other private label calendar sites for Jewish organizations that needed their
own event hubs.

Soon, my deal with Lisa to spend more time at home was being sorely
tested. Fortunately, I never required much sleep. Yet another news story about
our team began this way:

> At 8:30 p.m. every night, after a full day of work, Howard
> Brown and his wife Lisa put their 3-year-old daughter Emily
> to bed. Then, he goes to work. That's when Brown toils into
> the night working to help the Jewish community.
>
> Brown, the co-founder of www.PlanItJewish.com, has
> just received this year's San Francisco Jewish Community
> Federation's Lloyd W. Dinkelspiel Award for Young
> Leadership.
>
> "I've dedicated my life professionally to the Jewish community,
> using PlanItJewish to connect people," said Brown, who will
> be presented with the award at the JCF's annual meeting in
> San Francisco.

"It feels good, it's the right thing to do. Making the world a better place for the Jewish community as well as the overall community is very important to my wife and I," Brown said. Lisa Naftaly Brown also is active in the Jewish community, working alongside him many nights on their separate phone lines.

The Dinkelspiel isn't the first prize Brown has received for his volunteer efforts. He met Lisa back in the early 1990s, when both of them were involved in the young adult division of the Los Angeles Jewish federation. The Browns eventually moved to the Bay Area at the height of what Brown laughingly calls the "dot-com-a-go-go," riding out the tumultuous economic era with a couple of other companies before starting his own nonprofit PlanItJewish.com, which already has spread from the Bay area to Minnesota, Maryland and other regions of the U.S.

Even with the hectic schedule of a dot-com executive and a father, Brown has maintained a heavy involvement in Jewish leadership. He followed Lisa into the JCF's Young Adults Division, eventually working on its fund-raising campaign. He chaired a regional $4 million fund-raising drive as president of the South Peninsula Council—while at the same time serving on the United Jewish Community's national young leadership cabinet.

But the Jewish involvement he's most proud of is his 11 years as a Jewish Big Brother for Ian Ellis, who grew up with his own father out of the picture. "This is how relationships can grow if we choose to commit ourselves in a loving, compassionate way," Brown said. "Ian and I started out with a few home visits and, years later now, we're family. Period. Family. And we'll stay family for life."

What made those long hours bearable is that Lisa, Steve and I were dedicated to this work, having consciously made commitments to support and strengthen connections within the worldwide Jewish community. That news story about the Dinkelspiel Award lists some of the regional and national roles Lisa and I agreed to shoulder. But there was so much more beyond the scope of that news story! Looking back, I'm amazed at how much we all accomplished.

One major commitment we made was the Wexner Heritage Foundation Fellowship. Over a period of several different years, Steve, Lisa and I were chosen to participate in this prestigious fellowship for emerging Jewish leaders. Steve was first to go through the entire multi-year program; I was invited later; then Lisa was invited on her own merits as an influential leader. The program offered a deep dive into Judaism, requiring an extensive reading list of classic texts, history, theology, contemporary nonfiction about Judaism—and then lectures, seminars and scholarly retreats. It amounted to a master's-level immersion in Jewish history, ethics and spirituality designed for lay people who were committed to innovative forms of service. After each of us completed our formal participation, the Wexner Fellowship team then kept encouraging us in many ways. Among the dozen early PlanItJewish advisors was Rabbi Shoshana Boyd Gelfand, who was then the vice president of the Wexner Heritage Foundation. She's now working in the UK as director of JHub, a London-based nonprofit that offers space, resources, training and development for social change organizations to meet, work and learn.

This shared passion for tikkun olam (healing the world) super-charged all of us to work those crazy hours. Our entire PlanItJewish team understood that there was far more than financial success at stake. Christians often describe this deep passion for service as a "calling" or "vocation." When you feel that sense of mission, you begin to radiate a confidence that—well, that begins to shine through all of your work and interactions. Others see it and want to become part of the cause. Remember, in the era we were launching PlanItJewish, the most common news stories about organized religion focused on the anxieties religious leaders felt over declining participation. That was true across all faith groups, including Christianity, and it continues to this day. Our team radiated a confidence in the capability of participating faith groups to grow, if they reached out effectively and creatively. We were making an optimistic, countercultural claim. Our new service was sold partly on our message that online connections were the future of outreach—and partly on our high hopes for the future of Jewish life. Our bright lights kindled others.

Beyond our infectious confidence, we had accumulated plenty of data to back up our claims. Thousands of events were pouring into these calendars. Participation grew. One other clear sign of our effectiveness was the number of ideas for expansion that our new clients kept sending our way.

Ultimately, that experience led to the lightbulb idea behind CircleBuilder: If we're trying to repair the world, tikkun olam, then let's create a circle as big as the whole world. But, that clarity of our larger goal emerged only after several years of tireless work. To describe those heady days, I invited Brent Cohen, my partner in many of those cross-country travels, onto a Zoom conversation.

"I don't think I could keep up those hours today," Brent said. "Do you remember what it was like being on the road, working in some city either to sell the service or to train the volunteers?"

"I remember," I said. "I did some of those solo. We did some together. If you were with me on the trip, we wouldn't finally sit down for dinner until something like 10 p.m. Then, we might have a Scotch as we talked over how the day went and we planned for the next day. We'd talk until midnight or after that. Then, we'd try to get a little sleep so we could be back up early the next morning."

"People reading this story are going to want to know: Why did we do that?" Brent said. "And the answer is: Because we knew it was working, it was growing—and that was exciting. People were asking us all the time to expand. Remember all the crazy ideas we got? Remember people asking us to build PlanItKids?"

"Yes, that was a popular idea. And PlanItEnvironment. And PlanItNature. And PlanItPets. And PlanItRunning. And—I can't even remember all of the ideas that were sent to us. The list went on and on. With all that interest, we knew we were doing something right. But, as I look back, I'm so glad that we weren't distracted by all those other ideas, because the strongest idea—the really visionary idea that emerged—was CircleBuilder and that's where we chose to pour all the rest of our energy."

We both sighed deeply as we thought about that phrase: "the rest of our energy." We rarely had energy to spare!

I finally said, "Well, I should say: Whatever spare energy we could find we devoted to building this next big thing. I think, once that idea for CircleBuilder was clear to us—it was so compelling that we had to make it happen."

"Yeah, PlanItJewish was a great idea to build on what we saw developing out there. Then, CircleBuilder was the lightbulb idea," Brent said. "That was big. That was revolutionary."

"Edison at Menlo Park," I agreed. "I began to understand the power of that idea the moment I said: 'Religion is the largest and most underserved social network in the world.' And, of course, that sentence wound up in nearly everything we published about CircleBuilder over the years: brochures, fundraising flyers, handouts for conferences, on and on."

"So, back to the original question: Why did we work all those hours and log all those miles?" Brent said. "The deeper answer is: We knew that we were inventing the future that would be modern day community building—that's what drove us. When you asked me to come on board, I was fully aware of the risks and the rewards and the long hours in this kind of work. I was a veteran. In fact, I was available to join you in the first place because I had been running a tech company that imploded when the 2000 dot-com bubble burst. A lot of new companies didn't survive that big tech bust—and when my own company fell apart, that hurt. It was a gut punch. So, I was looking for something completely new and promising and—just like you and Steve and Lisa—I also had started to put a lot of my focus on helping the Jewish community."

"You had a very valuable skill set when you joined us," I said. "You added a lot to our team—even your earlier background in media strategy was important."

"Before I ever moved to Los Angeles, I had been a political media strategist in Washington, D.C.," Brent said, "so I understood the importance of computers and the internet and media overall in strengthening communities. Then, my desire to make a contribution to tikkun olam was becoming stronger all the time. As it worked out, connecting with you, Howard, was a perfect fit. And I think that's an important point to explain in your book. In this kind of work, relationships matter. The kind of solid relationship you and I had was absolutely essential in pursuing this kind of work. To put it simply: I liked you. I still like you. And, most importantly, I liked working with you day after day. We were driven by the same goals—and both of us were committed to the same values of respect and honesty and building a better world."

"We were a great match," I said. "In some ways, before we began working together, we had led parallel lives as entrepreneurs, which meant both of us fully understood what we were signing up for. We went into this eyes wide open."

Brent was nodding and added: "So, that's also how we found even more energy to throw into building CircleBuilder."

"We were sprinting," I said. "That's how this work got done: at a flat-out sprint. Everybody in that space was sprinting. We knew the benefits and the dangers, and we could see these big ideas we were trying to turn into reality. We could visualize them—just hanging out there ahead of us—waiting for us to build them."

"As you tell this story," Brent said, "remember to explain that it took a number of years of sustaining that kind of commitment to grow PlanItJewish—and only then could we even think of adding CircleBuilder. Yes, we were sprinting, but we also had to sustain that pace of work for a long, long time. As you tell this story, people need to understand the stamina this kind of work demands. CircleBuilder didn't pop into the world fully formed overnight. What we saw right away was the genius of that idea: There are way, way, way more churches around the world than there are synagogues. But it took years to map out what we could design for that global scale—and then try to build it—and try to draw people into it."

"And, along the way, we saw so many other services emerge. We knew they were breathing down our necks," I said. "Today, everybody assumes Google is this giant backbone of the internet. But that wasn't true when the Google team started. Those guys were incredibly lucky at several points in their development, which set them up finally to explode. But we all know the early history of Google. Those guys didn't start with the best software. They were sprinting like we were. Of course, they were really smart, and they learned from other smart people. They thought strategically, found some great angel investors—and they won out in the end. Just like what was happening at Google, we could see the potential in what we were building, too—even as we kept running across speedbumps in our expansion."

"There were a few of those," Brent said. "More than a few."

"Not everyone in every new city we developed showed up with a welcoming smile. Do you remember, Brent? There were always a few people who looked at us like dentists about to perform a root canal."

"A certain number of people in each city were anxious about moving from their paper flyers and newsletters to an online calendar—but we kept at it and won them over, one by one," Brent said. "Remember that our calendaring system was out there before Google Calendar, so this was not an easy path for a lot of old-school volunteers and staff to understand and follow."

"In the end, a few never did follow us," I said. "I'll never forget that one older woman who had been the volunteer in charge of calendars forever in her community—she was the *grande dame* who everyone knew had her fingers in everything—and she regarded us as these young upstarts who were trying to kick her into retirement. She was never happy with us."

Brent nodded. "But most people came around and really loved the results. And, to this day, I'm proud of the work we did. It was solid from the ground up," Brent said. "Think about this for just a moment: The PlanItJewish software platform was designed and launched and expanded in such a solid way that PlanItJewish lasted 16 years with only minor reengineering. So often these days, new platforms are launched as the software is just barely ready to go public. Then, people connect, there are bugs—or the fad runs its course in a flash—and that new software is out of date tomorrow. We had a 16-year run with PlanItJewish! That's a remarkable record for a software-based service."

By the time we were ready to launch CircleBuilder in June 2006, Lisa and I had already moved to Michigan. She grew up in Michigan, so this was a return to her home base, and my twin sister, Cheryl, her husband, David Gingras, and their kids Marly, Dani and Luke also had moved to the Metro Detroit area, which meant that Emily would have cousins living nearby as she grew up. Soon, she also was surrounded by Lisa's sister Beth Naftaly-Kirshner, cousins Zack and Benny and uncles Dr. Bruce Millman and Dr. Alan Millman. We settled into a home northwest of Detroit in July 2005. While we decided on this move for family reasons, I suddenly discovered that I had landed in the middle of one of the nation's longest standing and most diverse interfaith communities. We were surrounded by a vibrant Jewish community. Dating back to the 1920s, these Jewish leaders had built strong interfaith connections to one of the world's most famous centers of the Black church. Detroit was the hometown of some of the greatest Black preachers and church musicians the world has ever known. Plus, just a few miles from where we lived was one of the world's largest Arab-Muslim communities outside of the Middle East. We all were neighbors of an equally influential Arab-Christian community. The century-long story of interfaith relationships in southeast Michigan has filled many books. A United Nations-style diversity of other religious neighbor-hoods had been formed by families who had flocked to jobs in the Motor City over the past century. These connections also involved a host of smaller, yet globally influential groups. Some of the world's most prominent Armenian-Christian families were our neighbors.

What a perfect new home for our work! I was surrounded by religious titans who already understood the value of strengthening their congregations—and Michigan's business and civic leaders also understood the enormous energy within religious communities. Nearly every regional health care system, social service program and charitable nonprofit in Metro Detroit was connected in some way with the region's religious history. Thousands of faithful men and women had been trying to repair the world from the heart of the Motor City for more than a century—often overcoming horrific challenges like racism and bigotry along the way.

Right away, I was sharing breakfasts, coffees and lunches with potential allies in restaurants across Metro Detroit. Even better—this time, I was talking with potential investors who understood the value of networks like PlanItJewish—and who regarded our success with that launch as assurance of our capability to build even larger networks that could help strengthen the pillars of our religious communities. I will never forget the excitement of sit-ting across a table sipping coffee with the guy who was widely regarded as one of Michigan's top angel investors, Terry Cross. Every local entrepreneur knew Terry's biography, which included his agreeing to help with the second-round fundraising that was crucial for pushing the founders of Google toward their success. I was anxious to see how Terry would weigh our proposal. Then, I was astonished that he pulled out his checkbook right there at our first meeting.

"I never do this, but I think you're really onto something, so I want to help you get this going," he said, passing a big check across the table between our empty coffee cups. That decision by Terry that day—writing a check at our first breakfast—was even more valuable than his dollar amount.

"That's right," said Paul Kaplan, who soon became the second major angel investor in CircleBuilder. "I can't overestimate how influential Terry's buy-in was for me. When the potential in CircleBuilder proved to be that clear to a guy like Terry Cross, what investor wouldn't be interested to at least learn more? I certainly was curious."

When I reached Paul by Zoom to talk about that catalytic year as we got ready to launch CircleBuilder, he said, "I think as you tell this story, you should explain angel investing to your readers. Everyone thinks they know what that's all about, but there are a lot of myths about angel investing. For example, ultimately, CircleBuilder didn't succeed—yet we're still friends to this day. Yeah, I lost a lot of money in the end when CircleBuilder didn't work out. So, how is it possible? How can we still be friends after that? It's because angel investors understand that this is a high-risk and potentially high-reward process. We know going into these deals that many of them will never reach a big, successful exit for us financially. But this kind of investment really is the engine that helps entrepreneurs to build important new things. We might put money into maybe a dozen or more ideas before one of them pays off. And, for that reason, we tend to be very, very careful about where we put our money. Usually, these initial conversations go on for weeks or even months before a check is written. There's a lot of due diligence before we write checks. I think we met weekly for about six weeks before I wrote my first check, isn't that right Howard?"

"Yes, it was about two months," I said.

"So that story about Terry Cross writing a check after his first coffee with you still is surprising, no question," Paul said. "Terry's confidence influenced me enough to want to learn more. So, how did I make my decision to write my first check—and then a number of other checks after that? Well, ultimately, for me there were two important things and the first, and the most influential, was you personally, Howard."

"That's exactly how Terry Cross put it as he described his approach to angel investing," I said. "He told me, 'In a horse race, you can back the horse or the jockey—and I back jockeys.'"

"Right," Paul said. "The character and experience of the entrepreneur always is the most crucial factor for me. And then, second, I was influenced by the power of your idea: Religion is the world's largest and most underserved social network. That combination of a great entrepreneur with a great idea was very compelling."

Compelling, yes, but also an exponential leap from PlanItJewish.

Consider the scale of our ambitions. So far, we were successful in expanding across Jewish metropolitan areas, one major city at a time. That's because Jews tend to define themselves and their interests in larger circles than most Christians envision. Each host city we added to PlanItJewish had a form of collective Jewish federation with staffers, either paid employees or volunteers, who already were deeply committed to outreach. These federations could act on behalf of the entire Jewish community—and their staff members already were reaching out across their region to share news, promote upcoming events and recruit volunteers. That was a ready-made regional structure that did not exist in quite that form in the Christian world. Christians do have dioceses, synods, conferences and national ministries—but most Christians relate primarily to their local congregations. When we dug into that data, we found that our astonishing new goal was reaching 500,000 congregations across the U.S.—in addition to thousands more stand-alone groups and ministries. And the United States was only the first level of outreach. From the start, we envisioned worldwide options, so we planned to add multiple languages.

If that weren't overwhelming enough, the needs were different with congregations, compared to regional Jewish federations. Some of those needs were obvious. Every congregation wanted an attractive, publicly facing website—and that was the first basic service we offered through CircleBuilder. We could provide church leaders with a flexible new website built from professionally designed templates. That alone was a huge leap for many churches, since thousands of them still had almost no web presence in 2006. Then, second, every church wanted to share its public calendar—and that was our specialty, of course. But a website and a calendar were just the basics. The key to CircleBuilder was to provide a safe and secure place for members to talk with each other and their congregational leaders. That was not available to them as we launched CircleBuilder. In today's terms, we were offering each church a website, combined with a powerful calendar—and what would look like a private Facebook circle where communications could be shared with varying levels of privacy. We would offer these services with a sliding scale of annual fees, adding even more valuable services as a congregation decided to more fully commit to building these circles with us. This was an era when most congregations had not even begun to discuss secure online donations— and our premium service offered that, as well.

"This may not sound as revolutionary as it was at the time we launched," Brent said. "But that idea of private online communities where members and their leaders in each church could talk securely among themselves—that was revolutionary when we came up with this."

"It's why we were able to attract the initial investments," I said.

"And that's why we soon were in the middle of a neck-and-neck race—to use your jockey metaphor," Brent said. "I don't think any of us who worked on that launch will ever forget September 26, 2006. We had planned for CircleBuilder for at least a year before we launched in June that year. Then, on September 26, there was Zuckerberg's announcement."

"That definitely caught our attention—but remember that none of us could have predicted how quickly that announcement would catch on," I said. "That day—September 26, 2006—Mark Zuckerberg announced that his little Facebook service for students was open for business to anyone at least 13 years old with a valid email address."

"Here's what was so frustrating about that," Brent said. "It shouldn't have worked for them like it did! Facebook's mostly college student user base certainly wasn't happy about it. Suddenly, all of these students' parents could visit their Facebook pages and snoop on them. A lot of people were downright pissed that he threw the doors open like that! Zuckerberg was friggin' lucky with that move. You know, Howard, your readers need to remember that the list of social networks that launched and failed could fill an entire book on its own! Facebook shouldn't have exploded like it did. It could have vanished."

"But it didn't," I said. "And we pivoted, too. As they grew, we recognized that they were big-time competitors. We regarded them as a benchmark that actually could help us. The point we began to make was: 'We *aren't* Facebook. We're better for congregations.' That's why I hit the road to make all of those conference appearances with my trademark presentation called: 'Is Facebook the Right Book for Your Church?' That title was catchy. First of all, at these giant conferences, people had options of what sessions to attend and the title for my workshop always drew very well. And that title itself was smart on multiple levels. I didn't step out on stage railing against Facebook. People didn't want that kind of a hardcore sales pitch at these Christian conferences. Still, our answer was implicit in the question itself. Ask any church leader:

What's the most important book in your church? We all know the answer: the Bible. So, that title was a subtle way of reminding church leaders that their core religious values may not be the same as all these shiny new social media services that were popping up everywhere."

"We were a better choice for them," Brent said. "We had created an architecture for CircleBuilder that was perfectly suited to their needs."

"Yes, perfectly suited—and also a massive software development project," I said. PlanItJewish's architecture contained some elements we wanted to offer to our new clients—especially the powerful calendar, feedback on events and a commerce option for premium customers. But we needed an entirely new platform vastly bigger and more complex to serve the potential audience of CircleBuilder, including flexibility for languages from around the world.

"That's why you guys needed us angel investors," Paul said in our conversation about the launch. "That kind of new software needs a big infusion of money to make it happen. That's why, after I wrote my own first check, I also was glad to serve as personal reassurance for you guys as you were going for that crucial Automation Alley grant."

"You were great about that," I told Paul. "Those early steps all built on each other. First, Terry gave us his check. Then, you. Then, we tackled Automation Alley. I don't think you even had to say much in that one big meeting with the Automation Alley people. They understood the value of your showing up to support us through that whole process. That was the game changer for us—and it was so hard to convince them. Michigan had been heavily promoting itself as a place for entrepreneurs to thrive and build the future—but Automation Alley had never given an investment grant for software development until we made our case."

"That's right," Paul said. "And that really was the key to this—to build a platform that could expand like we all hoped it could."

"It was good for Michigan, because we put that Automation Alley money right back into the Michigan economy," I said. "We hired guys out of Grand Rapids to build the code." For many years, Grand Rapids in northwest Michigan was known as a national center of Christian publishing as well as the development of Christian-themed forms of new media. Among the many examples: The Grand Rapids area had been the home base of the giant evangelical publisher Zondervan, had launched the multimedia career of Rob Bell and had given birth to BibleGateway, one of the world's largest Bible study websites. In many ways, Grand Rapids had become the Silicon Valley of Christian media.

"We had solid people working on this," Paul said. "Everything looked promising."

Pretty soon, we could clearly see that Zuckerberg's daring new idea was not failing. Within a year, his online network was exploding. More than 100,000 companies now were present on Facebook as well as a huge number of individuals. Soon, Facebook encouraged developers to build Facebook-friendly software that would allow other online sites to interact with Facebook. By 2009, Facebook had added organization pages. We quickly made sure that our CircleBuilder websites, while privately controlled by the congregations, also could choose to share some of their information across Facebook and other emerging social media. Everyone had friends and family on Facebook, so we had to be a Facebook-friendly service.

The distinctive cornerstone of our pitch was summed up in a giant blue-and-white image of an iceberg that I would display on big screens as I gave my presentations. That giant chart was headlined: "CircleBuilder—Why Private Social Circles?" The top of this enormous blue image—the 10% of an iceberg that is visible above the ocean's surface—was labeled with the parts of church life that everyone wanted to share far and wide: worship times, community events and calls to help with outreach projects. Below the ocean's surface was a long list of all the things churches needed to keep private. That 90% list ranged from private conversations in men's groups, women's groups and Bible studies—to pastoral counseling, intimate details of prayer requests and lots of other very personal services that are a vital part of church life.

And with that unique appeal, CircleBuilder was growing! Almost immediately we had 1,000 churches and ministries leaping into our service. In anticipation of the expansion that we were sure would follow, we planned to add specifically branded domains within the larger CircleBuilder world, including CatholicBuilder, MissionaryBuilder and many more. We could see the appeal emerging beyond Christianity, as well. We offered JewishBuilder immediately and then also snapped up domains so that we eventually could launch a MuslimBuilder, HinduBuilder and other faith-branded networks. By 2010, we had jumped to 6,000 accounts for churches and ministries—and we nearly tripled that number by 2011.

That global vision was reflected in our logo: an abstract image of a person lifting both hands, a universal posture of prayer and praise to God.

We were learning so much so fast about the challenges facing church leaders around the world that we also had a unique opportunity to help them with our growing expertise. As I prepared to lead each one of my hour-long workshops, my intention was to teach more than to make a sales pitch. Even if most of the thousands of men and women who attended my talks at conferences never chose to sign up with us—I still was helping each one of them to walk away better equipped to develop their ministries. That's why they showed up in such numbers—for help in grappling with this confusing new maze of the online world.

My first question, after I was introduced and greeted people, was always: "What's the world's largest social network? Please, just shout it out."

"Facebook!" That always came back right away.

"No, that's not it. Keep guessing. What is the world's largest social network?"

"Twitter!" That usually was second. Sometimes: "YouTube."

I would give folks time to shout out a few more guesses.

"OK, I'll tell you the answer," I would say at length. And you may be surprised at this." Audiences always were visibly startled when I said, "You made some great guesses, but the answer is: Religion is the largest and most underserved social network in the world." Then, I would tick off religious populations as compiled by Pew Research: There are 2.4 billion Christians, close to 2 billion Muslims, about a billion Hindus, then I would go on through the other smaller faiths.

"You know what else may surprise you? As people of faith, we *own this!* We're the people who invented the idea of global connection!" In fact, I would explain, "social media" is just the current digital manifestation of the core principles found in the scriptures of most world religions: a timeless call for men, women and their families to form communities—and to reach out into the whole world.

"This isn't a novel idea. This is an idea we all have owned since the dawn of civilization," I would say. Then, because most of these groups were Christian, I would remind people of just a few of the many appeals in the New Testament, like:

From Ephesians chapter 4: "The gifts God gives us are that some would serve as apostles, some prophets, some evangelists, some pastors and teachers, to equip the saints for the work of ministry, for building up the body of Christ, until all of us come to the unity of the faith."

From 1 Corinthians 12: "Now you are the body of Christ and individually members of it. And God has appointed in the church first apostles, second prophets, third teachers; then deeds of power, then gifts of healing, forms of assistance, forms of leadership."

From Matthew 25: "Whenever you did this for the least of these sisters and brothers, you did it for me."

There were dozens of Christian passages I could share—and I would rotate through them in my talks. As you read the three New Testament examples above, you may be startled that this Jewish guy was so sincerely teaching Christian leaders about the importance of strengthening and growing their communities. In fact, I came to regard myself as a part of their family. They were facing the same problems Jewish leaders were bemoaning. All of us could see the increasing secularization across the U.S. and shrinking numbers of active members. I firmly believed this then and do to this very day: The world would be a far better place if congregations could energize their members to actually follow their own timeless teachings. I truly wanted to help them. This was tikkun olam pure and simple.

In these programs, I would toss out questions like:

"Can we have a show of hands on this, please? How many of you believe your church is really working right now in the way you think it should work?" A minority of hands would go up. Clearly we shared some problems, whether we were Christians or Jews.

"How many of you consider your church a loving community?" A majority of hands would shoot up—but not all of them. There always was room to expand our hearts and service.

"Are you welcoming?" Half the hands.

"Are you growing?" Less than half.

"OK, you've all seen the responses," I would say as I wrapped up that Q&A. "Now, consider this: I've been asking you about whether your church is loving and welcoming. As you raised your hands, I'll bet what you were envisioning was what happens when new people physically show up at your front door. That's one way to evaluate whether you are welcoming. But here's the next question: What happens when new people meet you by coming to your website? And that's assuming you have a website—and I know some of us don't even have one yet. But, if you do have a website, think about it for a moment: Is your online home a welcoming place? Is it easy to find your way around? Are upcoming events easy to find? Or—are a lot of your online postings old stuff, some of them from months ago. Are old Christmas posts still up there in March?" Heads would nod as I listed other common examples of outdated material.

Then, I would move into the middle part of my talk, focused on how various social media services try to welcome and share news with people. I would start with Facebook, then Twitter, then YouTube and I would go on to highlight at least a half dozen others. People often took notes. As I discussed the pluses and minuses of each service, I always started with the great opportunities people can find—and there are, indeed, lots of opportunities we should welcome. That's true to this day.

"You may not like some of the stuff that pops up on these services, but think about how important Facebook and YouTube are, now, to a lot of your members," I would say. "People can keep in touch with their kids, share photos, have fun wishing happy birthdays to their loved ones, watch heartwarming or funny or fascinating videos. Need to fix something around the house? There's a YouTube video that shows you how to do it. So, there's a lot we love about these services—and that's why they're really essential to millions of us today."

Then, after the pluses about each social media service, I would point out all the other wide-open doors these hubs provide to unwanted advertisements, unfriendly viewpoints, vulgarity—on and on. I always sincerely stressed the opportunities they should claim in these free services—and then appropriately warned about the dangers, too.

In the final third of my seminar, I would loop back around to their own hopes for improving and growing their ministry. This often was one of the most popular portions of my presentations—as I focused on how to keep in touch with members online through email or other updates.

"How often should you communicate with your church members?" I would ask, inviting folks to call out answers. People in the crowd would offer suggestions, usually agreeing that a couple times each week was most appropriate.

"You're right about that. Most people involved in ministries nationwide say that two to three contacts a week is just about right," I would say after some back-and-forth with the audience. "You have to strike the right balance. If you communicate too frequently, you become annoying. Not enough, and you become irrelevant."

I would pause at that point for a moment. Some people who had been taking notes would look up at me again and, when I had their full attention, I would say: "But, here's an idea I haven't heard anyone suggest: How about asking each member how often—and the way—they'd prefer to be connected?" No one ever suggested that response in these sessions because it wasn't a common service offered online.

As that idea sank in, I would say, "Well, that's one of the approaches we take to help people participating in CircleBuilder feel more comfortable. They can choose options like that—frequency of contacts. It's just an idea to consider." And from the feedback afterward, they certainly did consider it.

Then, if I had enough time, I would show some sample event pages from real church websites and I would ask people to guess how to sign up for the events they saw listed on the screen behind me. They usually couldn't because there wasn't a link in the examples—an all-too-common error in a lot of church websites.

I would ask people if they had questions about those events. They would flood me with questions—from what to bring to the event, such as food, to what to wear and whether they could invite friends or children to come along.

"Wouldn't it be so much easier if you could ask those questions among your friends at the church in a quick and private way? Then, of course, it should be much easier to register for the event itself—and to set a reminder for yourself about the date and time. And, if you're the host of that event? Wouldn't it be nice to get some feedback afterward about what people thought about their experiences? That way you can keep improving what you're doing." Of course, CircleBuilder offered such options.

Usually, I had a little less than an hour—and got rave responses. Sometimes I was able to give the presentation more than once at a conference and the seats were filled each time.

As successful as those presentations were, our early adopters tended to come for our introductory offers and lower-cost tiers of service. Our team clearly understood the market and knew that we had to score big sales for nationwide and even global networks of ministry. We pursued those deals relentlessly—but ultimately, we met more and more barriers in a market that became ever more crowded as the years passed.

One of our near misses was Rick Warren, pastor of the Saddleback megachurch in California. By the time we were launching CircleBuilder, Warren already was one of the leading Christian evangelists in the U.S.—and he also had become a mega-best-selling author as well. His 2002 *Purpose Driven Life* has now sold more than 50 million copies in 85 languages around the world. When we reached out to him, Rick initially seemed fascinated with our concept. He met briefly with Brent Cohen in Los Angeles, but then never found the time to develop a deeper relationship with us.

"I'll never forget the night we met," Brent told me on Zoom. "I was able to meet with him in person because I was based there in LA when he agreed to be the guest speaker at Rabbi David Wolpe's Sinai Temple one Friday night. That was a huge event, jammed with people, and I have to say this: Boy, did he deliver a message that night! As I listened, I thought: This reinforces everything we're trying to do. Yes, as entrepreneurs, we want to succeed and make money, but what we really want to do is change the world for the better. That really is what drives all of us in this kind of work."

In his talk at Sinai Temple that night, Rick Warren retold the story from Exodus in which Moses was so fearful about his ability to lead people that he wound up having a heart-to-heart talk with God. Moses brought up his anxieties and excuses. Then, God asked him, "What is that in your hand?" It was Moses' staff and God proceeded to miraculously transform that staff to make the point that anything is possible. As Brent recalled the sermon: "He was reminding us that, just like Moses with his staff, God gives us the tools we need to do the work we're called to do. That was a powerful message that certainly hit me hard that night."

After his sermon, Brent had time backstage for a short conversation with Rick—and the pastor was encouraging. In fact, he took the time to write supportive notes to each of us in copies of his book. Brent and I still have them on our shelves.

Brent floated the idea of serving as one of our advisors, just as Craig Newmark had done for PlanItJewish.

"I'd like to do that. Send me the details," he said. So, emails and a couple of phone calls followed—but, despite our best efforts, that intention never materialized. Every entrepreneur knows that we have to extend dozens of invitations for every one that connects in a meaningful way. In this case, we missed, but Brent and I didn't count our experience with Rick as a failure. In a deep way, he inspired us. To know that one of the most media savvy Christian leaders in the world was encouraging us—that was a boost in itself.

The biggest miss involved the world's single largest religious group: the Roman Catholic Church, which the Vatican currently reports has 1.3 billion baptized members. By the time we began to make our appeals to Catholic leaders connected with the Vatican, CircleBuilder was growing and the news media was largely behind us.

One news story that I liked to share began this way:

> Every day, we hear stories about promising new startups in exciting, high-growth industries. These stories make great headlines, but statistically most of them will fail within five years. Those companies that remain after the initial growth spurt are the ones worth noticing. These are the ideas with staying power.
>
> CircleBuilder software is one such company. It's a software-as-a-service (SaaS) provider catering to what CEO Howard Brown calls "the largest social networks in the world"—faith and religion.

As we tried to win over Vatican officials, Brent and I already had years of experience with PlanItJewish and CircleBuilder behind us. It was a huge leap in scale, but it also was the logical extension of everything we had built. We simply had to try to sign the world's single largest religious organization, the Roman Catholic Church.

What we did not fully appreciate was that Vatican decision-making is legendary for its arcane twists and excruciatingly slow turns. In our case, those twists and turns could fill another chapter. At one point, a bishop blessed me, blessed my family, and blessed the code that ran our service. At another point, we were part of a national nonprofit campaign across the U.S. to encourage loyalty and increased activity among lay Catholics. At yet another point, we worked with a team trying to get men and women to recite the rosary more frequently. We were asked to set up a dozen Catholic beta sites, which we did. We were assigned to work with the World Priests organization headquarters in Ireland, which we did. At another point, the deal seemed to hang on whether we could demonstrate our global flexibility in languages, so we set up Catholic sites in a dozen different languages. Unfortunately, for every encouraging bishop and Catholic lay leader, we also found ourselves talking with just as many clergy in key decision-making positions who stared back at us like deer caught in headlights.

"Remind me what this is?" one bishop asked us. "A website? We already have a website."

"No, this is something entirely different," I said. "This is a way to safely and securely help parishes—and church ministries—to energize their members, to have meaningful contacts with them and—" And, to be honest, even as I was saying this, I could tell that my message wasn't registering.

We tried to win over the Vatican for nearly two years. We responded in a helpful way to every request Catholic leaders made of us. During that long campaign, we worked like online mechanics for various partners in the church, building what amounted to one concept car after another for them—inviting them each time to test drive what we were offering. We simply could not get the right leaders to understand the connective power we were offering to put in their hands. Ultimately, the few leading Catholics who did understand the possibilities began making excuses, like, "You guys have to remember that any change is scary. We've been around for 2,000 years precisely because we try not to change."

Of course, the Catholic Church was changing and continues to change to this day. The Vatican made headlines each time the pope's staff set up a new account on one of the leading social media services. We were so determined to become one of those services that we kept raising money to expand our campaign and seal the deal. Investors like Paul kept backing us for years. But, in the end, we never quite reached that explosive tipping point like the other giant social media services. As years passed, the truly transformative deals—like signing a major Vatican contract for CircleBuilder—remained just beyond our reach.

Naturally, in 2021, I wonder what CircleBuilder's potential might have been if our campaigns were reaching their crescendo in early 2020 like Zamir Khan and the team behind VidHug. In the summer of 2021, national news stories heralded a big new deal in which two entrepreneurs from my own hometown—Framingham, Massachusetts—raised several million dollars to buy VidHug. They renamed the service Memento and added it as a star attraction to their rapidly expanding Punchbowl company, which bills itself as "the gold standard in online invitations and digital greeting cards."

All entrepreneurs know that timing is crucial to success. My early work with Avid Technology video systems was perfectly timed and it remains a huge success story. We tried to launch Liquid Audio way too early and it's gone. CircleBuilder was both too early—certainly we were years before the COVID pandemic proved how much congregations needed online services to survive—and too late. Our race began in 2006 with Facebook leaping out of the starting blocks at almost the same time.

What is certainly true in 2021 is this: The wisdom I was sharing in those presentations to church leaders about digital outreach and connection is more valuable now than ever.

There is so much more that entrepreneurs and religious leaders can build together to help the world. In fact, these partnerships span religious history— and will continue in the future. Together, we have built cathedrals and temples, established publishing houses, founded vast health care and educational systems—and the list goes on and on.

Today, I am known by Babson alumni around the world for my tireless promotion of the school's unique combination of values and learning. Yet, few of those alumni know that our founder, Roger Babson, was among the first 20th century American entrepreneurs to devote a significant amount of his work to encouraging what he called an "interchurch movement." In his day, Babson simply could not envision that the proposals he passionately advocated in a series of books amounted to what today we envision as an interfaith movement. In Babson's era, asking Catholics and Protestants to work together was as daring as my work today asking Christians, Muslims, Jews, Hindus and Buddhists to collaborate.

Babson argued in one of his books: "Religion is not only the vital force that protects our community, but it is the vital force that *makes* our communities. And, the power of our spiritual forces has not yet been tapped." He went on to propose elaborate ways to build what amounted to faith-based community circles. He urged the readers of his books to consider setting aside a small portion of the religious donations that came to each church as community funds shared by all congregations to help strengthen needy families and at-risk children. To raise awareness of these plans, he proposed establishing publishing houses that could produce educational pamphlets and books, knitting together communities of public interest. Of course, Roger Babson died the year after I was born. Had he lived in our era, Babson himself might have been an angel investor in CircleBuilder. If you substitute online social media for the regional publishing houses he envisioned, he was arguing our case 100 years ago.

In another book, Babson outlined interfaith principles for healthy communities: God is the owner of all things. As humans, we all are stewards of what we have received in life and must give an account for all entrusted to us. This acknowledgment requires setting apart a portion of our income to give back to the larger community—some of it to support our own religious groups and some to support programs for health and well-being across the larger community. A century later, most of us would want to tweak many of the detailed planks in Babson's plan, of course, but mainly we can say to his heartfelt plea: Amen.

If you take away anything of value from our adventures described in this chapter, I hope it's this: Millions of men and women who care about their religious communities are scrambling to keep them alive after more than a year of forced separation during the COVID pandemic. The principles I've described here—and the questions I was raising in my workshops—are the burning questions in thousands of houses of worships nationwide.

If you care about these issues, consider downloading the free discussion guide on the website for this book and spark your own discussions with friends about the ways you can envision and promote community outreach.

Roger Babson was prophetic because of the truthful clarity of what he saw and expressed about the potential of faith communities to heal our world. Today, we have a wealth of scientific research backing up his instinctive observations, including the worldwide public-health consensus on the "social determinants of health." In developing those lists of healthy practices, researchers around the world have found that our well-being and longevity depend on a whole lot more than specific medical interventions. For example, social determinants of health include the vital need to be part of a caring community with meaningful connections on a regular basis. Or, to put this in the simplest terms: People who are active in congregations, especially as they age, are more likely to be happy and healthy. That's not wistful thinking; that's the consensus of public-health research.

Like Babson, that's where my faith-based instincts led me and my business partners for many years as we circled the globe. I wrote the following about the importance of media in knitting together congregations more than a decade ago, but these words are just as true as I complete this book today:

> Human beings yearn to connect. We want to belong. In our DNA, we are drawn toward something larger. From biblical times, we have formed families and our families have formed tribes that help us define our sense of place in the world.
>
> In today's crowded world, we live everyday among overlapping tribes, many of those connections drawn across the internet. It has never been easier to associate with someone halfway around the world. It has never been easier to communicate with people whose daily lives and cultures differ from ours. At its best, the internet breaks down walls and opens up new avenues of constructive interaction. If used for good, social networking can provide a sense of belonging and connectedness, a place in a community where we can experience shared belief, collective story and collaborative ritual. This is fruitful ground for the expression of God's love—if we choose to use this power in a loving manner.
>
> Combine the timeless power of faith with the ability to connect in meaningful ways from the palms of our hands— and our communities can begin to take on shapes we might never have dreamed were possible. Together, we can inspire, serve, educate, enrich and bring people together for common purpose. Media can form bridges between generations and between those who are geographically distant, drawing people together with common ideals and bonds of faith.
>
> Together, we can spread our wings and expand the shelter of our embrace.

Shining Brightly

The most in-depth, ongoing reports about religious communities around the world are found in the Pew Research Center's online hub: pewresearch.org/topic/religion/ From this hub, you can find reports on hundreds of studies exploring all of the world's major faith traditions as well as many minority religious groups. In my own work over the years, Pew research has been valuable because Pew reporting presents research data in a style that's appropriate for everyday readers. Plus, if you are leading a small group, Pew permits sharing of its thousands of helpful charts and graphs.

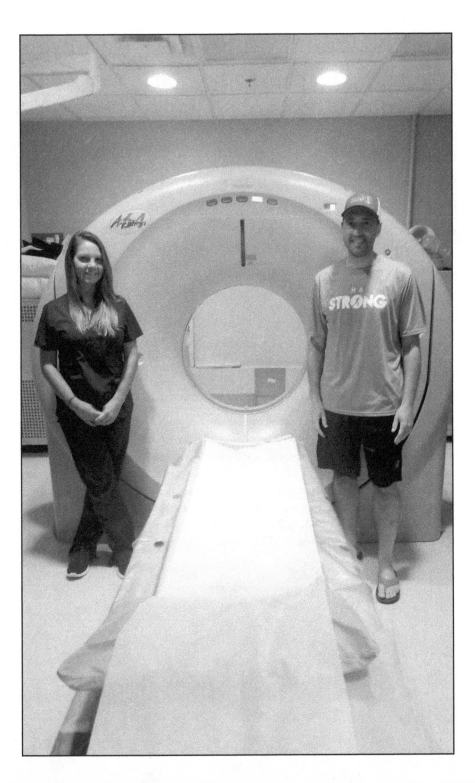

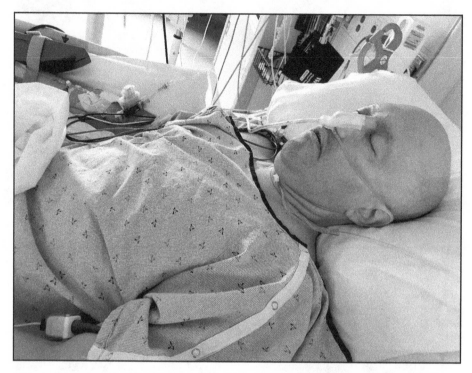

There are many grim photos during my second life-and-death struggle with cancer, but I'm going to spare you most of those images. Lisa took this photo when I finally was wheeled out after 11.5 hours of CRS HIPEC surgery. Then, as the families of cancer patients know, my life after cancer treatment is marked by a cycle of scans. On the previous page, I'm posing next to a CT scanner with which I have regular dates, hoping I will rack up yet another radiology report of NED, No Evidence of Disease. I always ask for Donna Roussey as my radiology technician, because so far I've had an unbroken series of NED scans with Donna at my side.

13

Meeting Death Again

Suddenly, I met death again.

In an instant, the results of a routine medical test as I reached 50 turned my world upside down. If you act on any of the advice in this book, it should be this: Get yourself screened for colorectal cancer, because it is one of the most preventable of all cancers.

How early should you be screened? When I turned 50 in 2016, the American Cancer Society still recommended 50 for a routine first colonoscopy. Thanks to lots of research-based health care advocacy since then, that age recommendation now has been lowered to 45. However, every major health care organization including the American Cancer Society says you should discuss this with your doctor at your annual physical. If you have a family history of cancer, especially colorectal cancer, you may need to begin these scans earlier in your life. While everyone complains about the uncomfortable fasting-and-cleansing process 24 hours before the scan, this is a medical procedure that can save your life—so one day of discomfort is a small price to pay for that reassurance.

Unfortunately, my cancer was found late and, even with surgery to remove portions of my colon, it spread so extensively throughout my body that I should be dead now. I'm not exaggerating. Those are the stark odds I faced. I was absolutely stunned. I had put concerns about cancer in my rearview mirror more than a quarter of a century before that colonoscopy, and I was not even thinking about my potential for a recurrence.

Later, when I had an opportunity to go back and talk to my doctors from Dana-Farber, they agreed that this new cancer was likely a result of the massive treatments I underwent to wipe out cancer the first time. Dr. Robert Soiffer said, "There could be a relationship between extremely high doses of chemo and radiation we used in 1990 and what you found in 2016. Do I know that definitely? No, but the ongoing research on the kinds of treatments you received the first time shows there can be effects much later in life that can include solid tumors, lung cancer, colorectal cancer, pancreatic cancer. Some of these cases may not show up for 20 years or more."

I certainly didn't blame Dr. Soiffer or Dr. Rubin for not warning me more forcefully about the long-term risks—and I told him so as we talked across Zoom. "I'm just thankful for everything you guys did," I said, "At the time you were treating me, we were fighting against almost impossible odds to save my life. I couldn't worry about a chance of something happening decades later. Back in 1990, we all knew I could die in a matter of months. We had to do whatever was necessary for me to survive and extend my life."

"Exactly," Soiffer said, "plus, at that time, there hadn't been as much research into the long-term health effects of those treatments, so we did not know everything we know today about the long-term effects. All of us were focused on finding some way to get you through 1990 and 1991. We weren't even worrying about what might happen in 2016. Now, of course, we've adjusted the kind of treatments you had back then. For example, we've come down on the intensity of some of the conditioning regimen you got back in 1990."

"As you write this in your book, let's be clear that we don't know definitely whether those treatments caused the new cancer," said Dr. Eric Rubin. "Do we suspect that the amount of chemotherapy and radiation we gave you could have contributed to this? Absolutely, yes, we think that may have played a role. But we don't know for sure. Colorectal cancer is a very common form of cancer. More than 100,000 men and women are diagnosed with it every year. You might have developed that even without your earlier treatment even though you had no family history of colon cancer."

So, now I know that I should have been more careful about cancer screening. I should have asked for a colonoscopy years before I did. Whatever the cause of this new cancer, it turned out to be aggressive and within a matter of months it seemed to be killing me. I only survived through the heroic efforts of my doctors, my family and friends—and, of course, my own iron-willed determination to survive. When I stand up to speak at national conferences and seminars, now, I hardly need to say anything to inspire people. Simply by standing up to talk, I'm living proof that extremely long-shot survival is

possible. People look at me walking, talking and telling them about the work
I am doing around the world today and that alone gives them a major dose of
hope. But, let me repeat: I'm the very, very rare exception, not the rule.

Yes, I do mean to scare you when I write this. When I met death this second
time, I flat-out expected to die. Everyone, included my doctors, thought so.

Then, here's some good news you can take away from this story: If I had
been screened at age 40, you likely would not be reading this book. My colonoscopy would have turned up some polyps that would have been snipped.
The cancer would not have become so advanced. I would have cruised onward
as an entrepreneur working very long hours on a host of new projects and
would have had neither the time—nor the life experience with cancer—that
would have prompted this book.

Instead, 2016 became a nightmare from which I could not seem to shake
myself awake and regain my old life. My life, as I had known it, stopped.
PlanItJewish had been shrinking over the years as I poured all my energy into
CircleBuilder—then, we had trouble converting those big CircleBuilder deals
to revenues that would have guaranteed our future. All of our labors to prove
to the Vatican the potential of our service never produced a breakthrough
expansion to Catholic parishes around the world. I had been shouldering both
businesses by the sheer force of my salesmanship and high hopes. In 2016, I
shut it all down—contacting key investors, informing the existing subscribers
to our services and then completing the financial filings that are required in
such closings. I was facing the end of my life. I needed all my energy for this
titanic struggle with cancer.

So, I'm going to ask you to stop reading for a moment. Please, mark your
place in this book and go check on the date for your next physical exam—or
schedule a physical if you are not in the habit of seeing your doctor each year.
Consider whether you should ask for a colonoscopy or an at-home screenings
test like Cologuard™ even if you're not yet 45. Do you have relatives who have
had colorectal cancer? That increases your risk.

I am not kidding about this: If most of my readers take this simple step
right now, it's altogether possible that this book will save some lives. It could
save yours. Thank you to my long time friend and internal medicine doctor
David Rosen for making sure I scheduled my colonoscopy after I turned 50!

Take a moment. Please, do this.

I'm waiting.

And now: "Are you back with us?"

Those are the five words Dr. Philip Goldmeier asked as I roused myself
slowly from the anesthetic that had allowed the doctor to conduct my

50-year-old colonoscopy. As I was becoming alert, I could feel Lisa's hand gripping mine.

Always upbeat, even when very groggy, I managed to form my mouth into a big smile and mumble, "Hey, doc, so everything's good? Right?"

He looked at me with deep concern.

Maybe he hadn't understood what I was trying to say. Maybe I had slurred my words, so I said more distinctly, "I'm in great shape, right?"

His reply was one word: "No."

Lisa gripped my hand even tighter.

Then, the doctor said, "I got my camera all the way to the end of your colon, up into the area we call the cecum, and I saw something there. When I find something in the cecum, it's generally not good news. It could be—" and he paused, pondering what to say next.

"What?" I said. "What?"

"It could be—and I think it probably is cancer."

"Really?" I did not know what else to say.

Lisa sat in stunned silence.

"It's a solid tumor."

"What?" I asked.

"I took a sample of it and we really won't know any more until that sample gets to pathology and they tell us what we're dealing with." The tumor turned out to be 8 centimeters long, a little more than 3.5 inches.

My heart was racing. This was not at all what Lisa and I had planned. I was supposed to have my test, quickly bounce back from the anesthesia—and we were looking forward to seeing our family at our niece Marly's high school graduation party under a big tent. After my 24 hours of uncomfortable fasting and cleansing, I was supposed to wake up from this routine test to enjoy a couple of fun days with Lisa and the whole clan. My parents and cousins had traveled to Michigan for this party. Everyone was ready to celebrate.

I can barely remember our car ride home, except that I kept running through that brief discussion with Goldmeier and mumbling, "Oh shit!"

Lisa remembers more details than my anesthesia-fogged brain retained. "We talked a lot as we drove home," she said. "We realized that we should have seen the signs in the past six months. Something had been going on with you for a while."

"That's right," I said as we pieced together memories of that day. I'd been having some stomach-and-digestive-tract issues for a while. "I should have seen the signs."

"You did. You'd been complaining about it for at least six months," she said.

"Yes, you're right," I told her. "But I just thought it was stress about all the things going on with my work."

"You want to talk about stress?!" Lisa said. "Here I was sitting in the hospital seeing you wheeled back from your colonoscopy with all these wires and monitors hooked to you. You were asleep. You looked so vulnerable. Already, I was feeling very protective of you, worried for you—and then we got this news from Dr. Goldmeier. I was shocked. The only thing that kept me from collapsing, I think, is that he was very kind as he talked with us about next steps. He had already taken action—helping to pave the way for us by contacting colorectal surgeon Dr. Harry Wasvary. Goldmeier's kind, yet straightforward manner helped me to feel a little less devastated."

By the time we finally reached the graduation party, Mom—being Mom—immediately started talking about moving to Michigan to take care of me like she had the last time. I had to insist that Lisa was "my person" now. Mom didn't have to move in with us.

To head up my oncology team, my brother-in-law Dr. Bruce Millman, a Beaumont Hospital pulmonologist, recommended Dr. Richard Zekman, a top cancer oncologist-hematologist. I was happy with that choice when I learned that Zekman also was comfortable working in a collaborative way with patients. That was crucial in my approach to fighting cancer. Battling cancer is a team sport and I wanted a doctor who would work with me, talk with me, answer questions and openly discuss my options.

When I reached Rich on Zoom to talk about this part of the story, I started by telling him why I had selected him in 2016. "I needed a doctor like you who was willing to partner with me—to collaborate with me. And believe me—I know that was asking a lot of you. I'm a handful as a patient."

"No you're not! You're a great patient," he replied. "You've got a great fighter's spirit and that's so important. Then, to put this in context for your book: When we met the very first time, we were looking at a relatively common form of colorectal cancer. The cecum is at the connection between the small and large intestine and the pathology showed a common form of colon cancer growing there. The reason we had so much concern about your case, Howard, is your history of cancer. Right away, we went back through your records and found that your earlier doctors had used just about every treatment known to them back then. They did all the right things. You would have died if they had not pulled out every stop back in 1990—even though that almost certainly left you with long-term toxicity. While we could not definitively link this new cancer to your first cancer, we did suspect it was a *sequela*, a malignancy related to an earlier treatment. And that concerned us because *sequela* cancers tend to be bad actors—and that certainly proved to be true in your case."

The medical team did not mess around. Within two weeks of my colonoscopy, I was in Beaumont Hospital in Royal Oak, Michigan, so colorectal surgeon Dr. Harry Wasvary could perform laparoscopic surgery called a hemicolectomy. He entered through four points in my belly to remove 13.5 inches of colon plus margins and lymph nodes. I stayed in the hospital for two days.

I was so determined to attack this cancer like the Marines or Navy Seals landing on a beach that I urged my doctors to let me play basketball again as soon as possible.

"You've got to clear me to play," I begged Rich as the head of my team. "Basketball is my happy place. I'll know I've beaten this cancer when I'm back full-throttle on the court." In fact, Rich and I became so close during this whole life-and-death journey that he even wound up playing basketball with me a few times.

But his reaction to my plea was cautious. "I asked you to wait at least a month, didn't I?" Rich recalled.

"You did."

"That sounds about right. Your diagnosis was Stage III and, after that kind of surgery, you needed to heal properly. We didn't want any undue stress on your abdomen for a while. But what I really was thinking as we talked was: Just wait until you start chemo and then you won't be so eager to mix it up on the basketball court."

"Well, I knew chemo," I said. "I thought I was ready for it. I was going to attack that like the Marines, too."

"And you did. I don't think I've ever seen a patient take to chemo with such—such—"

"High spirits and mental toughness?" I suggested.

"Yeah," he said. "But even then, remember, the chemo eventually did knock you out physically. We started with infusions every two weeks but then we had to extend the time between appointments because your body just couldn't keep taking it every two weeks."

"Through all of that, I kept telling you that I planned to set records for recovery—and I was absolutely determined to do that. Remember that, when we had removed that first chunk of my colon, we had no idea what really was happening inside my body."

In July, a chemo port was installed in my chest. Then, chemo began in August 2016, with infusions every two weeks. I was so confident that my mental strength and overall health could conquer this that I drew on my memories from 1990, when I was pretty much living inside the Dana-Farber center for what seemed like months at a time. One of the biggest challenges was remaining upbeat in such a somber setting. So, I showed up at the clinic for each six-hour chemo infusion shining as brightly as I could muster—even when the recovery time between the chemo sessions had to be stretched out to three weeks later that year.

I'd walk in for my infusion and greet everyone warmly. It's such a sad place, most of the time, that I was determined to bring whatever cheer I could muster. I'd often show up with a big box of mixed donuts or sweet rolls. Once I brought flowers. I'd bring candy. The nurses had nicknames for me.

"Hey, Hobro!" someone would call out to me. "Donuts today?"

"Yeah, donuts for everyone," I would say.

Men and women getting chemo on my same schedule would grin and welcome me. Even if they didn't want a donut, the impact of one upbeat person warmly greeting and encouraging others could change their whole attitude on those awful infusion days.

Did I hate the chemo? Certainly! No one loves chemo—but, even on our worst days, each of us can choose how we express our discomfort, pain and anxiety. Often, consciously choosing to act out the steps of shining brightly wound up changing my attitude as well as raising the spirits of all those around me.

As the chemo became more physically devastating, did I let it dampen my spirits? Yes, my internal struggle to crawl out of bed and adjust my attitude for the day became agonizing. But I was absolutely determined to survive—and, along the way, to lift the spirits of the men and women around me from the staff to other patients. If you haven't gone through this struggle, or cared for a loved one during this process, then you may find it hard to appreciate how much mental toughness it took to take this approach. To begin with, the chemo not only made me horribly sick and deeply tired—it also began to give me neuropathy in my hands that I've had to deal with to this day. The toughness of this struggle was why my friend Brad "Bubba" Urdan came up with a slogan and logo to crystalize my resolve: "HB Strong!" He had shirts printed with that slogan to proclaim my promise to myself and the whole world—and I began to spread it out across my social media. I needed every ounce of creative energy and mental focus to keep marching through these physical demands with my head held high and a smile on my face.

And I have to say, I was pulling it off pretty well.

That is—until the chemotherapy didn't work. By the early weeks of 2017, it was clear that the cancer found inside my colon had now moved outside my colon. In March 2017, I was back at Beaumont, where Dr. Wasvary removed another 10.5 inches of my colon. Then, the medical team wanted me to go right back into chemo.

"I just need a little break," I said firmly in a series of meetings with my medical team. I told Rich, "Please, I just can't do more chemo again, at least not right away. I need something else."

At that point, I was desperate to find other options. I heard about a clinical trial at the nationally respected Karmanos Cancer Institute in Detroit. Rich helped me apply. I met with a Karmanos research team, was accepted into their study and tried that for a while. I was feeling OK, even though we later learned that this treatment wasn't addressing the issue. The clinical trial did not work for me, cancer still was spreading relentlessly throughout my body.

As Rich and I talked on Zoom, I felt I should apologize to him for taking that dead-end detour. "Looking back, Rich, I know I made a bad choice switching to that clinical trial. I never should have insisted on doing that. I should have followed your advice to do more chemo."

"No, no, as you say, Howard: Let's not have any regrets about that," Rich said. "We talked it over and your choice to go with the Karmanos clinical trial was reasonable at the time. It was a good decision."

"Except that it didn't work," I said, "and I wound up in an almost impossible situation for myself—and Emily and Lisa—and it all blew up when I was more than 1,000 miles away from home."

This is the point in this chapter where I need to emphasize that getting a colonoscopy and avoiding colorectal cancer is not just about saving your life—it's about preventing the trauma that cancer brings to everyone around you. You may think you're indestructible and your positivity will keep you healthy and happy. Hey, that certainly defines what had been my approach to life. Maybe it defines your approach—or maybe someone you love thinks of themselves in that way. Maybe you like to say: "Hey, who needs an annual physical? I'm fine!"

What I'm saying is: If you're wrong, you're not the only one who will suffer. A diagnosis of cancer immediately draws into the struggle all of our friends and loved ones. The bigger your circle of caring companions—the more people who suddenly struggle with you. I had worked for years to build circles as big as the whole world, so lots of people soon were suffering with me. In the next chapter, I will share some good news about that supportive part of the struggle with cancer—but in this story of my life-and-death confrontation with cancer in 2017, all I could see was the tragedy I was wreaking on Lisa and Emily. Worst of all, whether I survived this battle or died, Lisa and I were heartbroken by the trauma this seemingly unending anxiety was causing in the midst of Emily's formative high school years.

As a family, we all had invested lots of money and thousands of hours in supporting Emily's love of soccer and her hopes for a soccer scholarship to college, someday. Just like I had the basketball skills to play collegiate ball, Emily had been playing soccer since elementary school and by 2017 was competing and traveling widely with her team as a top goalie in US Youth Soccer National League. Like other players hoping to receive college offers, Emily had an online biographical page that included photographs of her in action at the goal, logos of the national organizations in which she had competed and her Top 10 athletic achievements so far. That list included winning the 2017 Midwest Region II Championships. She also listed her academic achievements, which—before my cancer—had been well above a 4.0 grade point average even though she had tackled honors courses in science and English. Like other promising high school prospects, Emily also had a one-page student-athlete resume that was distributed to potential college recruiters. The resume included contact information for coaches who could serve as references for the recruiters and a short summary of her college goal: "To excel as a student-athlete at the highest levels of competition commensurate to my goalkeeping and leadership abilities."

In the summer of 2017—as it was becoming obvious to me that the experimental clinical trial was failing—Emily had one of the greatest shots in her soccer career. She was just about to turn 16 and had been chosen as one of two goalies for a team playing in the under-16 division of the United States Youth Soccer National Championships, held that year in Frisco, Texas north of Dallas. That meant she was playing at the top of the National League pyramid. Even if you're not a sports fan, the championship that year was like the final scenes you've seen in those Hollywood sports movies in which a beloved bunch of scrappy kids take on the greatest in the world with soaring hopes that they just might be able to squeak out a big win.

Whatever was happening inside my body, I was not going to let cancer disrupt Emily's soccer dreams. I convinced Lisa that I would be able to travel with the kids for the weeklong event. I promised to phone and text her everyday with updates.

"To be honest, as you got ready to leave, I was afraid every day," Lisa said as she looked back on that summer. "I was praying every day. I knew things weren't right with your treatments. I was—I was just sooo worried all the time."

Nevertheless, Emily and I boarded the plane, rented a car at the Dallas-Fort Worth airport and soon we were focused on the whirlwind of a national championship week.

"This was big time. Given my family, I was very competitive, determined to prove my resilience," Emily said, recalling that week. "It's only now that I realize: After all that happened with cancer and the toll of all those years of fear and stress, I've changed. I've grown. I'm not that same person with this obsessive need to prove myself on the field all the time. My life has moved on—is moving on—in so many ways now. Those experiences with soccer, and there in Texas, really were both wonderful in many ways and also took their toll on me."

We arrived on Sunday July 23, 2017, a week before the finals and a day before the big banquet that kicked off the week. We settled into one of the hotels that was part of the event, a good 40-minute drive from the fields. The week started with warm-ups, training and light practice for all of the teams. Then, the early games determined which teams made it to the semifinals and the finals at the end of the week. Emily's team was very good and they kept winning.

I was thrilled. I was exhausted, too. Even before we left Michigan, I had not been sleeping because of the pains throughout my back and abdomen. I kept it secret, but I actually could feel lumps that had formed in a couple of places. By the middle of the week in Texas, my discomfort was obvious to Emily.

"I knew you were having pains and, at first, you kept trying to dismiss what was happening," Emily recalled. "I remember you said, at one point, 'It may be my gallbladder.' I realized that you were saying anything you could think of so you wouldn't have to mention cancer. You didn't want me to worry, but of course I was worrying."

By Thursday of that week, I could not stand the pain any longer. I had not slept the night before, so it was easy for us to make it to the field by our assigned 7 a.m. starting time (arriving at 5:30 a.m. for warm-ups) that morning. I found a moment to phone Lisa and finally admitted some of my symptoms—and she was so alarmed that she made me promise to phone Rich Zekman. So, as the team was warming up for their game, I rang Rich from the sidelines.

"You've got to go get checked out, Howard," he insisted, and he began Googling my location. Within a minute, he said, "I can see a Baylor University hospital center that's just a few minutes from where you're standing. You've got to get over there and let them run some tests."

"I can't do it right now. Emily's about to play," I said.

"Howard!" he barked at me. "Get over there."

"She's just about to play. After the game," I said.

"Promise me you'll get over there the minute the game is over. Promise me!" Rich said.

"I promise." I didn't say anything to Emily before her game, but I did ask two of the team moms—Leslie Boutorwick, a former nurse, and Rebecca Medalle—if they could drive me to the hospital after the game. Soccer parents become another family and support community. They drove me and waited with me at Baylor Hospital in Frisco, Texas.

"Of course, I'll never forget that day," Emily said. "We played; we did well; we got off the field and we were very happy because we got to go on in the tournament—and we were happy because we had a day off the next day to get ready for the semifinals. So, I was feeling great as I came off the field. Then, the first thing I hear from my dad is, 'I have to go to the hospital to get a few things checked out.' You told me that Emma Bouterwick's and Madison Medalle's moms were going to drive you to the hospital. I wanted to go, but you wouldn't let me come with you. Another soccer dad agreed to take me back to the hotel and get lunch. I gave you a big hug—a big hug. I said, 'I love you.' And you were gone."

When I walked through the doors at the hospital, Rich's call had alerted a whole team to jump on me. It seemed like a dozen people were taking vitals, drawing blood, giving me an ultrasound, then a CT scan—and then the most frustrating thing was they wouldn't tell me about any of the results! All that rushing around was followed by this agonizing wait. They insisted on sending the results up to Rich on Friday. I was supposed to wait and call Rich again before I could get any answers. So, I kept texting him, asking for updates.

Finally, we were in our rental car going to a Panera to eat on Saturday before the semifinals when Rich rang. Emily was driving, so I took the call.

Rich's first words were: "Howard, you've got to get yourself back up here—now!"

My main concern was not letting Emily hear any of this.

"What did you see?" I asked.

"The cancer has metastasized big time."

Recalling that conversation now, Rich said, "I hated talking to you over the phone about this. I'm sorry about that. This is a conversation to have in person—but I had to tell you: You now had metastatic colon cancer, or stage IV cancer, and it was growing and spreading aggressively. I knew this was not going to end well. Of course, you don't want to talk about that over the phone.

I know you're a tough guy, Howard, but that was terrible to have you a thousand miles away trying to deal with this."

Even then, I tried my best to conceal the full extent of the news from my family. Emily sensed that something was terribly wrong, but I refused to give her the details as we reached the Panera and ordered lunch.

"I didn't want you to worry," I told Emily as we both recalled these fateful days. "You had these big games ahead of you—and you went on to win on Saturday and then Sunday. I knew you had a good shot at it and I was right. You wound up as national champs! I couldn't jeopardize that."

"You know what I felt?" Emily said, recalling that week. "I was pissed off! I had been suppressing all of my fears for so long already—and I knew with these Zekman phone calls and the hospital tests that something was very wrong. One of my coaches always told me to worry about those things you can control, so that had become one of my mantras. I mean, I was the daughter of two parents who taught me that you should always remain positive and strong. Well, that moment in the car in Texas with that call from Zekman, it felt like I was falling down a spiral into this darkness of all those fears I had suppressed. Do you remember what I said to you in the car?"

"What?"

"I said, 'Dad, you've got tumors, don't you? The cancer's back, isn't it?' And you refused to say anything. You just sat there silently. So, I knew! I knew right then."

"I didn't want to keep you from playing."

"I know," Emily said. "And we played; and we won both days—semifinals and finals. We were U-16 national champions. I did exactly what I had been taught for years: You have to look fine. You have to look happy. I was breaking inside, and I couldn't tell anyone half the stuff that was going on inside my head. You didn't want me to think about it—but I was constantly thinking about it! That's why I'd listen to music all the time—because I hoped it would numb what I was feeling."

"I'm sorry," I said. But the truth is this: Just like I remained silent in that car after the call with Rich Zekman, Emily had remained silent as well. She never described the depth of the struggle that was going on inside of her—until we talked about it for this book.

"I want to be clear, now that I'm talking about this," Emily said. "You wouldn't tell me if you had a tumor—and I certainly wasn't going to talk about myself. I understood that we were a family who didn't let people see if we were suffering. I was angry, but let me be clear about this: I wasn't pissed off for myself—and I wasn't angry *at* you. I was pissed off FOR you! You didn't deserve to have this happen again. I was angry at the injustice of this. Why was this happening to you? Why would someone have to deal with cancer twice in one lifetime? Of course, in my anger, I was ignoring reality—I can see that now. People get cancer all the time. Every life ends. We don't have any control over when it is going to end. That's why I keep repeating this other mantra: You can get busy living, or you can get busy dying. There's a lot of wisdom in that, now that I've had years to think about this. But, obviously at the time, these experiences were messing with my sense of the reality of the world. I was forced to come face to face with these deep questions that I couldn't get out of my mind. That's why my first major, when I started at U of M, was philosophy. There were deep questions about life and death, justice and injustice, swirling all around me for years and they still are—even though I've changed majors."

I am sharing the raw emotion that Emily poured out in interviews for this book, because most cancer memoirs are so focused on the person with cancer that they don't convey how much our loved ones suffer with us. I admit that I had little psychological or spiritual strength to help Emily that summer when my cancer was literally blowing up inside my body. I was at the center of this cancer struggle. My own mind was overwhelmed with all of the terrible news that unfolded over the next few days, combined with all of my own emotions and the tidal wave of emotions from my loved ones.

Suddenly, I was face to face with death again and I feared that death held all the cards. I was going to lose this time. That became obvious to all of us.

Despite going back and trying to recapture memories of what happened next, the main phrase I keep hearing from everyone involved is: "And then we all cried." That's true of Lisa, Mom, my twin sister, Rich Zekman and the people like Michele Wonch, Rich's nurse practitioner who had become such a vital part of my oncology team. There was one big cryfest that continued for days.

I knew what was coming, so I refused to let anyone come with me to Karmanos Cancer Center in downtown Detroit on Monday morning, where Dr. Tony Shields and the clinical-trial team had scheduled a battery of tests that wound up taking seven hours. Throughout that long day, I kept trying to force my mind into a positive place: This has happened to me before. The cancer didn't win last time. It may not get me this time.

When I had been scanned and probed and the tumors biopsied, however, Tony sat down with me for one of the most terrifying conversations in my life. He began by explaining that I could not continue with the trial. The cancer was so aggressive and advanced that I was at the point where oncologists move toward what they call "salvage chemo," the Hail Mary of treatments when nothing else is working.

Tony seemed as heartbroken as I was but he was a man of few words.

At length, I said, "Am I hearing you correctly? You're telling me to get my affairs in order. I'm going to die."

He said nothing.

I understood, of course, and kept pushing him, "But, aren't there people who survive this? Can't I get back with Rich Zekman and hit this with salvage chemo? Don't people survive when they reach this point?"

I will never forget his long pause and then his one-word response: "Rarely."

BANG! That word "rarely" was like an epitaph etched on my tombstone. After trying to psych myself up to beat this thing all day long, that word triggered a cascade of my darkest fears: I won't see Emily graduate. I'll never be able to walk her down the aisle. This news is as bad as it gets. When Emily described her experience of spiraling down into a pit of fears, I knew what she meant. I lost track of hope. I was depressed. And it did not help one bit that on Tuesday morning, I was accompanied by my twin sister, Cheryl, and Lisa as I arrived at Rich's cancer clinic—and they had Mom on a facetime video connection.

What can any of us remember about that day? Crying. Michele Wonch saw us first, as she always did—and she was overflowing with tears. "Oh my gosh," Michele said. "We're all heartbroken."

Then in the exam room, I saw Rich standing there and for the first time he was withdrawn, sad and pale. He had a hard time looking at us. His head was down and he was somber. Lisa and Cheryl began weeping uncontrollably. I could hear Mom, streaming with us, wailing.

"Michele was right. She nailed it with: 'We're all heartbroken,'" Rich said as we tried to remember that visit. "This was not only heartbreaking for you and your family, Howard—it was heartbreaking for all of us. We'd become so invested in you, we cared about you and your family so deeply, that to have this turn of events—was awful. Awful. Just awful."

The tests showed metastases spreading to my liver, peritoneal lining, omentum, small bowel and outside of the colon. The growths were so aggressive that I was able to feel them through my skin. The only option was a heavy-duty chemo regimen that might slow down the spread. Without any treatments, Rich said I could have three to six months, or less, to live. None of us thought there was much hope at that point—but Rich recommended this course and I agreed.

I thought I knew chemo, but this stuff was a Rock 'em Sock 'em concoction—so toxic that I lost my hair in a week and a half. Among the drugs was

Avastin and Irinotecan, which patients pronounced "I run to the can" because of the extreme side effects.

For months, I did use whatever energy I had to get my affairs in order, as we say. I began a series of interviews with my friend Rabbi Joseph Krakoff, who had become the director of the Jewish Hospice and Chaplaincy Network. He contacted other media professionals, including the staff at the *Detroit Free Press*. Together, we hoped to turn my shining-brightly approach to dying of cancer into an inspiring story that might help other families—especially by prompting people to get checked for colorectal cancer. One story eventually appeared in the *Detroit Free Press* newspaper and online.

Then, a ray of hope shot through all of this darkness in late September 2017—a CT scan that showed slight regression of the metastases. My reward was four more cycles of that chemo with all the horrifying side effects, but my entire family seized on this report of "shrinkage" as a sign of a possible miracle. Once again, our spirits for fighting cancer were supercharged.

Even as I had been working on a legacy story about my approaching death with Rabbi Krakoff, Lisa and I had been scrambling in all directions to make helpful connections. I organized spirit-boosting trips by old friends from across the country. Lisa and I both reached out for psychological, spiritual and therapeutic support. Lisa found a private, worldwide Facebook network called Colontown. She had learned about it from a cancer survivor at the checkout line at our local grocery store. A few weeks later while searching a cancer support app called Belong, I was invited by Vincent De Jong in the Netherlands to join Colontown. Lisa joined the stage IV caregiver's support group within Colontown a few months later. With our ongoing research and Rich Zekman's advice, we all began to move toward what cancer surgeons describe as "the mother of all surgeries" in their field: cytoreductive surgery (CRS) combined with the administration of heated intraperitoneal chemotherapy (HIPEC). The surgery can last all day, sometimes around the clock, requiring shifts of medical personnel to complete it.

"We came to this conclusion that I should try CRS and HIPEC with lots of input from people, including your own advice," I told Rich as we recalled what happened next.

"This is a rare form of surgery," he said.

"It is," I agreed. "But, in a specialized group within Colontown that was called HIPEC Heights, I had contact with a couple hundred people around the world who already had undergone the surgery and knew all about the side effects—and also the possibilities. Do you remember when we first talked about heading toward CRS and HIPEC?"

"Of course I remember that," Rich said. "But we still were talking about very, very long odds. To begin with, it's a very small percentage of people with stage IV colon cancer who even qualify for this kind of surgery. But then, your chemo was showing a little shrinkage and, remarkably, you did meet the criteria to go for this surgery. And while you consulted with CRS and HIPEC surgical oncologists all over the country, you chose to have Dr. Vandad Raofi here at Beaumont Hospital to do it."

"We're talking about miracle-class long odds here, aren't we?" I asked.

"We certainly are."

"But it gave us hope—and hope was really all I had to cling to as I just tried to keep waking up each morning and just surviving on another day," I said. "I was bald and weak and numb and sick and I was starting to look like a ghost of myself. Hope was very important. When we agreed that this was a real possibility, I got to tell Emily, 'We're hearing there can be a big positive outcome if I can just get this type of surgery.'"

Emily sucked in a huge breath of air and let it out slowly. She told me it felt like the first healthy breath of air she had taken since the fiasco in Texas.

Through Colontown and HIPEC Heights sub-community, I was in contact, educated and supported by fellow patients, given guidance on how to interview and select a surgical oncologist, and helped to understand new terminology, like peritoneal cancer index (PCI). Before agreeing to attempt the surgery, a surgeon carefully analyzes your abdomen and pelvis, rating the progression of cancer on a scale from 0 to 39. Patients hope for the lowest possible score and my PCI score was 6, so more good news!

The advice I received from my friends in HIPEC Heights was to choose a surgeon with the best outcomes. At the top of the list internationally, at that time, was Dr. Paul Sugarbaker at the Washington Cancer Institute, who was an innovator in CRS and HIPEC. There also were noted experts in Massachusetts, Pennsylvania and Maryland who had performed more than 500 CRS HIPEC procedures at that time. Before I finally made my choice, I had interviewed five surgeons. I chose Dr. Vandad Raofi, even though I would be only his 41st patient to undergo the grueling procedure. I selected him because he also had performed thousands of successful surgeries related to the abdomen. I also trusted Beaumont Hospital and appreciated that it was five miles from my home, because I knew that family support would be vital.

My own preparation for the surgery took more than a month. We stopped chemo. I had other preparatory tests and procedures. Finally, at 6 a.m. on March 13, 2018, Dr. Raofi and his team began their 11.5 hours of CRS, slicing me open and quite literally cleaning out every sign of live and dead cancer cells he could see through his microscope glasses. Then, the HIPEC took another two hours as heated chemo sloshed around in my abdomen to kill off lingering cells that Raofi could not see during his physical debulking.

"Will you help me explain this surgery to readers?" I asked Dr. Raofi as I was finishing this chapter.

"Most of the time when I talk to people," he said, "I ask them to imagine that their abdomen is the living room of their body. Then, I ask them to imagine that each organ is like a piece of furniture in that living room. Maybe your liver is a couch, your spleen is a recliner, your pancreas is a cupboard and so on. Then, around the walls of this room are thin drapes and that's how to think about the omentum, this curtain-like tissue. Some cancers spread through lymph nodes or through the blood stream—but some colorectal cancers can explode like someone is firing a paint gun in your living room. The goal of this CRS surgery is physically to go through your living room and clean the cancer out of every nook and cranny. If you see some cancer on the liver, you clean or cut or scoop or burn it out. That's why it takes so many hours."

"And in my case, you knew that the earlier chemo had been working because you were pulling out both live cancer and some dead cancer, as well," I said. "So, the surgery and HIPEC really was a chance to get in there and finish off the cancer—to wipe it out."

"Well, to be clear, the CRS is the main surgical part. The HIPEC then puts a heated chemo into that area to finish the cleaning," Raofi said.

"So, a lot of this surgery's success is the result of the physical effort to find the cancer and remove it," I said. "But a patient's attitude and spirits matter, too, wouldn't you say?"

"They do," he agreed. "The best outcomes depend on the overall physical health and performance status of the patient. You were someone who had worked out all your life and you had a very strong determination to recover, to follow everything we asked you to do."

"Well, you saved my life."

He hesitated, then said, "You know, I don't like to talk about saving lives, because no one can stop death. It's a natural part of life. I think about what we do as resetting your body's natural timeline. Humans are expected to live to be much older than you were at the time of your surgery. I like to think we reset your natural clock."

That resetting was the single most painful journey in my life. Waking up in the hospital ICU after that much disruption to my body, my morphine pump became my best friend. It would take another chapter just to detail all of the aches, pains and physical side effects of the surgery—but, in the simplest terms, I was in agony for nearly two months before I could claim our first post-operative milestone: simply starting to feel a little better. I quickly weaned myself from pain killers, but I lived for a very long time on protein shakes. The roller-coaster plunges kept coming. In July 2018, I was back on maintenance chemo and, this time, a drug I had been able to withstand suddenly caused debilitating migraines and dangerously soaring blood pressure, called chemo-induced hypertension. I spent more weeks in the hospital. My ongoing scans looked like I was heading toward No Evidence of Disease (NED), the gold standard for cancer survivors. But for every exhilarating rise in our hopes, there seemed to be another dip. By late in 2018, I was suffering from internal scar tissue and a suspicious little growth had to be removed in yet another surgery. The ups and downs continued.

Flash forward to 2021 as I am completing this memoir and I am thrilled to report an unbroken record of nine consecutive NED reports—and discussions with Rich Zekman about how extensively I need to be tested every three months going forward.

"I know we focus on NED, which is just a factual finding that no disease is visible at the moment, and I know we don't talk about 'cures,'" I said to Rich and Michele.

"That's right," Michele said. "You're in remission. We would not say he's cured. As of right now, we can't see any evidence of disease."

"Biologically, we can't predict what the future holds," Rich said.

"Agreed," I said. "But obviously we pretty much knocked out the colon cancer in a major way. In simple terms for this book, what would you say was the curative part of all those treatments I had?"

"Well, we saw that the salvage chemo produced some regression and that was positive and then Dr. Raofi performed the CRS and HIPEC—and we kept monitoring everything and kept responding to anything we found," Rich said. "I don't think we can point to one single thing, but it really was the result of all of those treatments."

"OK, so I'm not cured, but I am back playing basketball full strength—except for COVID restrictions," I said.

"Yeah, I've played with you," Rich said. "It's clear to me that you tackle everything in life to the extreme—from fighting cancer to playing ball. There's no question: You're an exceptional guy. You take even the worst stuff in life and try to turn it into something positive for yourself and mainly for other people. You're inspiring."

"You are," said Michele. "And I think a word we can use in your case is miraculous. The odds alone say your recovery was miraculous. And what I mean is: I don't know a patient who has been more determined to focus on the positive. It's miraculous to me that, given everything that happened, you never slipped into a period of woe-is-me desperation."

"Well, I felt it more than once."

"But you somehow managed to take whatever was happening to you and find this force within yourself to keep going—and to keep encouraging others," Michele said. "Any time you come back to see us, you're the guy who everyone wants to see. Everybody wants to see Hobro. Just seeing you makes it a better day."

"We're not just talking about good cheer," Rich said. "We're talking about the way you began using your life story, even when we all thought you were dying. I remember making special arrangements during your chemotherapy infusion so you and Rabbi Krakoff could do that story for the *Detroit Free Press* to encourage other people. Yes, you've suffered a lot, and there have been some painful setbacks, but you wear it all like a badge of honor—like it's somehow a privilege to survive it all because you now can understand what other people are going through. Whatever you've experienced, you turn it around and want to teach others about how to navigate those problems. You know, as we get better and better at treating cancer and we wind up with more and more survivors of advanced cancer—we need more national opportunities for people to learn about survivorship. After this process just devastates a person and their families, how do you even begin to think about picking up the pieces again and moving on with your life?"

"We did cry a lot at some points," Michele said. "But as I go on working with patients, you and your family taught me a lot about how to remain positive just one day at a time."

And—one last time—that's why I keep hammering away at the message: Go get yourself checked. One of the national cancer nonprofits I support, the Colon Cancer Coalition, hosts fundraising-and-awareness-raising events called Get Your Rear in Gear. The Coalition—and other nationwide cancer-advocacy groups I support—are relentless in pushing for cancer education, early testing, more research and more support for patients, families and caregivers.

After I faced death this second time, I emerged with a vast worldwide network of contacts, many of whom know me simply as HB Strong. I am humbled by all of the people who love me, pray for me and my family and who have followed our journey. Through all of those online channels, I can't count the times that I have sent these words circling the world:

Cancer sucks, but the beast must be slayed, so that is all I can do each day.
Fighting cancer is a team sport. You can't do it alone.
Keep the faith.
And get yourself checked.

Shining Brightly

Please consider learning about colorectal cancer support organizations that advocate relentlessly for awareness, screening and survivorship. Also, our family will be forever thankful to the Nationals Soccer Club in Michigan, especially the unwavering support from club administrators Charlotte and Steve Shephard, the coaches, all the soccer moms, dads and players that helped our family during our time of need.

+ **Colontown** – Colontown.org
+ **Colorectal Colon Coalition** – ColonCancerCoalition.org
+ **Fight CRC** – FightColorectalCancer.org
+ **Colorectal Cancer Alliance** – CCAlliance.org
+ **Man Up to Cancer** – ManUpToCancer.com
+ **Global Colon Cancer Association** – GlobalCCA.org
+ **US Youth National Soccer** – USYouthSoccer.org
+ **Nationals Soccer Club of Michigan** – NationalsSoccer.com

You can't beat cancer alone. Friends and family always have been a huge part of my support network. They were available to me, when I was in need, because I have cherished friendships all my life. One photo here shows me with my childhood friends sprawled on a Cape Cod beach in the late 1980s during one of our many reunions. When I met cancer the second time, I called for all hands on deck. My friend Rabbi Joey Krakoff sat at my side during chemotherapy. My lifelong buddies showed up from all over the country for such a raucous reunion in 2017 that cops showed up after neighbors complained about the fireworks we were blasting in my back yard. Later, we all wore my HB Strong shirts in a supportive reunion in Las Vegas.

14

A Circle of Lovingkindness

Life is love.

In three words, that's what I have emphasized in many different ways throughout this book. In Judaism, love of others is just as important as love of God. Every year as we approach Rosh Hashanah and Yom Kippur, we know that reconciliation with other people is an essential step toward reconciling ourselves with God. Christians were given this teaching by Jesus, as he taught his followers, "'Love the Lord your God with all your heart and with all your soul and with all your mind.' This is the first and greatest commandment. And the second is like it: 'Love your neighbor as yourself.' All the Law and the Prophets hang on these two commandments." The New Testament places both of those commandments in quotation marks because Jesus was drawing on his Jewish wisdom and was quoting from the Torah.

We need each other. God made the world that way. In fact, all of the world's great religious traditions call on followers to embody love and to care selflessly for others. Thank God, some of the men and women in our lives do this so naturally and so fully that we sometimes describe them with the Christian term "saints." Every religion urges us to follow the examples of such special people. Christians revere these saints, who they describe as faithful men and women of heroic virtue and service. Muslims respect similar noble followers of their faith by calling them *wali Allah*, or friend of God. Hindus have more than a dozen terms for these special people, from *gurus* to *yogis*. Buddhists have *bodhisattvas* and *arhats*.

"In Judaism, we also have many words to describe saintly people," Rabbi Joseph Krakoff told me one day as I was in the depths of my second struggle with cancer. "I think that many of the people who have surrounded you, Howard, can be described by the word *chesed*, which means 'lovingkindness' when it's used in the Psalms. It describes someone who gives themselves fully with compassion and love."

"Like Lisa," I said. "She stepped up and became 'my person.' Thinking about all she's done every day, day after day, month after month—that's chesed."

"It is. And it's so much more than that, too, in your relationship," he said. "But remember there are many other people around you whose lovingkindness we would call chesed."

"Yes, so many others!" I agreed. At that point, I was suffering through early rounds of salvage chemo with no sign of any shrinkage. In those devastating months, I lay dying with that last-ditch poison surging through my veins—so I had lots of time to sit with my friend and talk about these cosmic questions. As he raised one deep question after another in light of my looming death, the rabbi recorded my responses. He is a dear friend. Lisa and I called him "Joey" and considered him our family's rabbi. He had moved on to become director of the Jewish Hospice and Chaplaincy Network. What an auspicious step from my perspective! In those months of salvage chemo when we all assumed that I was dying, Joey and I began working on a documentary film about my perspectives on the journey toward death. We hoped our video might help families going through hospice.

At one point, Joey asked, "Knowing that you are facing death, do you believe in heaven, Howard?"

"Sure. Of course," I said without thinking much.

"What will it be like?"

"I don't know. I can't recall even thinking much about heaven much since my stage IV diagnosis for non-Hodgkin lymphoma over 30 years ago," I said. Frankly, his question threw me. My emotions were raw. I had been told to quickly get my affairs in order, so my thoughts were reeling every day in all kinds of directions. Now, for this documentary, he wanted me to describe heaven to other people? Huge question! Tough question! Finally, I said, "I expect in heaven I'll see those who've gone before me. You were just talking about chesed, lovingkindness, and there are so many people like that who've gone before me. I have no idea whether death will look like a white light or will look like pearly gates. I can't give you that kind of visual image—but, when I think of heaven, I would like to feel welcomed there by someone I've loved. I would like to be reunited with family and friends who have passed and are there to welcome me." Then, I described some of those beloved people to Joey, beginning with Bubby Bertha, whose story opens this book you are reading. I continued with all of my grandparents, Tante Carole and other cancer patients who died.

Another one of Joey's questions that stopped me cold was: "The doctors say you are not likely to survive this, but they don't know for sure. How do you live with the ambiguity of not knowing how long you have left?"

As that Q&A series unfolded with Joey, I would repeat the same questions to Lisa as we talked later. "Today, he asked me how I live with the ambiguity of just not knowing how much time I have. What should I say to that kind of question, Lisa?" I asked one evening. "In these interviews, Joey's not pulling any punches. What would you have said?"

"I would turn the question back to him. I would ask Joey how *he* helps people to live with this ambiguity," Lisa said.

"You want me to turn it around and ask him what he thinks?"

"He's got a lot of wisdom about this. Any wisdom he can share would be appreciated," she said.

"And what do you say? How do we live with this?"

Then, because she is a writer, Lisa typed up a note so I could share it word-for-word with Joey in our next session. "How do we live with this? Every day, we hope for the best, yet brace for the worst. It's so hard not knowing, living in limbo. I want to be hopeful and positive. If there's any chance you will live, then I cling to that—we cling to that—and then it's hard to even think about dying. If we knew that there was a specific amount of time—say one year— then that might be easier because we could accept that and plan for it. But we don't know."

She concluded: "Whatever happens, we are reminded every day to make the most of that day we have together. How should we live like this? Promise to be kinder to each other every day."

Her words were a lot to take in. For once, I had no immediate reply. I sat and read them again. As usual, she was right.

Even more importantly, throughout that long struggle, Lisa was as good as her words. Despite my vow to hit this cancer like the Marines landing on a hostile beach, I was often so exhausted that I could barely get out of bed. The neuropathy that plagues me to this day made it nearly impossible for me to even button my shirt on some mornings. Lisa had to help me dress and that was one of the easiest of her endless caregiving chores. I spent hours either sitting on or hovering over the toilet—and sometimes did not make that destination in time. Cleaning after me was a horrendous chore. Then, part of my treatment, at one point, was a regimen of steroids and in my steroid-fueled frustration, more than once, I became enraged and roared at her with Emily listening in the background. I will forever regret those moments, but it's true that I sometimes shouted at my loved ones, the very people to whom I should have been as kind as possible. Many cancer patients and their families know what I am describing all too well.

And Lisa just kept going. Somehow, she just kept going. This was truly *chesed* taken to an extreme.

As the three-way conversation unfolded between Joey, Lisa and me, one night at 3 a.m. when I had finally nodded off to sleep, Lisa woke up, still thinking about Joey's earlier question about the ambiguity. She sent me a text that I would find in the morning: "How do we live with this? How do I live with this as a caregiver? The reality is you don't even have time to take care of yourself, because you are handling so much that you cannot even stop to think for a moment—and then you just crash. You try to rest, to sleep, to recover—but the roller coaster starts all over again every morning. You can't escape. Mainly you do your best not to even think about the future, because those fears would just ruin whatever moments of peace you can find in your day."

Since I survived this second stage IV death sentence, Lisa and I have been asked many times to share our stories, so she finally wrote her own version—and you really should read this, not in my voice, but directly from her. That's especially true if you are among the more than 50 million Americans who are unpaid caregivers for loved ones. She titled her story with the phrase that now has become famous to fans of *Grey's Anatomy*.

His Person

Ani l'dodi v l'dodi li.

I am my beloved's and my beloved is mine.

I recited these sacred words from the Song of Solomon under our wedding canopy, as have Jewish brides for centuries before me. Howard and I love these words so much, we had them inscribed in our wedding rings and they appear prominently in our Ketubah, our Jewish marriage contract.

In the cancer fight, I was not just Howard's beloved and he mine, but I became his "person"—the one to ensure his medical wishes were followed, that he received the best care possible and that he was well taken care of. I was his ears and mind when he could not process what was being said or done. I made sure to ask doctors and nurses the questions we needed answered to make the best decisions, to understand medical terms, diagnoses and treatment options and to remember what they were saying to carry out their care instructions.

I made sure he was comfortable and that he was well-nourished. I ran to get medications, cleaned up after him when his body reacted to the meds, and made sure he sought medical care when needed, including when he was trying too hard to tough it out. I tried my best to comfort, encourage and care for him through some very tough times.

Being his person was a role I took seriously, naturally. As his person, I also shouldered the worries, the day-to-day obligations, the financial stress and took care of our daughter so he could put all of his attention on healing. All while dealing with my own health challenges and the constant cloud of fear, anxiety and dread hanging over our heads. This is the unspoken role of all caregivers and just what you do when you are someone's person, someone's beloved and he yours.

Still, it was and can be physically exhausting, mentally draining, frustrating, lonely and scary. Even though we are not the patient, we can make ourselves run down, sick with worry and inattention. It is common for caregivers to neglect themselves while their loved ones are dealing with cancer.

Often, we live in a twilight zone, watching our lives crumble as life goes on for others, who are blissfully unaware of this seismic shift. We live in limbo not knowing what will happen, hoping that our person will beat the odds, pursuing every medical avenue, but wondering at times whether we are simply deluding ourselves that things can turn around and if we should just accept a dire prognosis and be better prepared for the worst.

Ultimately, we learn to accept what is and what is not within our control. We find—embrace even—a new normal. It may not be how we envisioned our lives, but unless we adapt, we will be paralyzed or consumed with fear and grief. Once we accept what is, we may even find there are some positives and silver linings in our situation.

Luckily, we were blessed to have incredible support from family, friends, our daughter's teammates' parents, her teachers and school, the Jewish community we served through all of our adult lives, and the HBStrong community that Howard cultivated. With only disability income, both sets of parents stepped up to help sustain us. We are forever grateful.

Neighbors and friends brought over homemade green smoothies and raspberry bars, gourmet Chinese feasts and home-cooked meals. One couple bought ACT tutoring sessions for our daughter when they heard that her dream to play soccer at Princeton could rest on her ACT score. Others drove Emily to school when we couldn't. The Nationals soccer team did a meal train for us, delivering warm meals and good wishes several days a week after one of his surgeries. The Babson community, while remote, set up meal deliveries at local restaurants and sent gift cards to Panera and our favorite grocery market. The school also sent home gift cards and Emily's teachers rallied around her. Scott Kaufman and Allan Gallatin, friends from the Jewish community arranged for us—and Howard's mom and his sister's family—to go to a pre-season Patriots game when they were in town to play the Lions, complete with field passes, a suite, catered meal and 50-yard-line seats.

Bubba Urdan had the first round of HBStrong T-shirts made up and Alan Gallatin got the three of us Tom Brady No. 12 game jerseys, which we wore to the pre-season matchup. The next day, one of Howard's sister's friends, Jodie Kley-Marvin, did a family photo shoot of us—a request by Howard as his hair was quickly falling out. In fact, the next day he was completely bald. Bobby Powell from Framingham South High School and his Babson College roommates Ed Sherr and Greg Tufankjian started a GoFundMe for us. His high school friends, then his California fantasy football buddies, came out to Michigan for "last hurrahs."

It was all very humbling. Both of us had always been more comfortable giving than receiving. Although we were always grateful and deeply touched by people's generosity and acts of kindness, it was not as easy to accept—or to admit—that we needed help. One thing that helped me to accept assistance more graciously was to remember how good it feels to give, which helped me to think about how important it was to allow others to have that feeling.

Through sharing in this way, we feel less alone, which is incredibly healing. That's why the most helpful and hopeful words we heard from friends and family were expressions of true empathy—acknowledging our pain. Among the most comforting words I heard were:

"I'm sorry you're going through this."

"I get it."

"You are not alone. I'm here for you."

"What can I do to help?"

We needed to hear those empathetic voices at so many crisis points in our long journey. One of those milestones I discovered was "scanxiety"—worrying about the outcome of a diagnostic test, like a CT or PT scan. Somehow, I came to realize that no amount of worrying on my part would change the outcome or make me better prepared for bad news. Worrying only made the present moment worse. It's natural to worry—but constant worry is devastating. Eventually, I learned to live more in the moment, push away the what-ifs and worst-case scenarios and wait to respond until we had the results. As a natural worrier, this was a valuable lesson and it applies to many of life's situations, not just scan results or cancer.

Another key lesson was the importance of practicing self-care. This looks different for everyone, but can include: meditation, yoga, exercise, spending time in nature, getting adequate rest, staying connected with friends, joining an online support group or talking to a professional therapist. It can mean volunteering—getting outside of yourself by helping others. A particularly hard concept for me and other caretakers was feeling it was OK to have happy moments when our loved one is suffering. No matter how grim things get, we must find ways to cultivate joy.

We were especially fortunate to find and become a part of Colontown, a private, invitation-only Facebook support group for patients and caregivers. The men and women around the world who populate Colontown truly became lifelines. They use their own experiences with colorectal cancer to serve both as supportive friends as well as a vast reservoir of medical knowledge and firsthand experiences of what worked, what didn't—and what to expect. Colontown is a place to give and receive comfort—and hope. It's a haven where humor, compassion and honesty pulled us through and lifted us up. Yes, humor was part of that lifeline, including bracelets, T-shirts and even tattoos that said KFG, short for a mantra Howard and I certainly shared: "Keep Fucking Going."

How did I find those friends at Colontown? I first heard about Colontown in April of 2017 in a supermarket check-out line. I had quite a pile of fruit and vegetables heaped on the conveyor belt and confided in the cashier, Carrie Morse, that I was trying to get my husband to eat healthier foods because of his cancer. That's when I discovered that Carrie was a colorectal cancer survivor. She told me about all the support she had found in Colontown. Carrie even recommended one of the doctors who later consulted on Howard's case—all through a casual contact I had made over groceries.

Howard joined Colontown through an invitation from Vincent De Jong in the Netherlands of all places. I joined the caregivers group within Colontown when Howard reached metastatic stage IV, receiving last-resort salvage chemo. At that point, when there seemed to be little hope, I was desperate for a lifeline.

I was welcomed to the Stage IV Carepartner Corner of Colontown in January of 2018 by a woman with two young children who was the "person" for her husband. And therein lies the bittersweet truth of these supportive relationships. Like many of the stage IV caregivers I met and bonded with so closely—that woman has since lost her husband. My heart breaks for each person struggling with such loss. Now, I go on the site mostly to give hope, using Howard's incredible recovery and sharing the steps that worked for him to encourage others, as they fulfill their role as their loved one's "person."

The risk of writing this chapter is that Lisa and I could not possibly name and thank all of the individuals who embodied chesed from my diagnosis in the summer of 2016 through my CRS and HIPEC surgeries in 2018—and during my long recovery after that. Lisa listed some groups of friends in her story, but there were many others who performed all kinds of services that any family dealing with cancer can appreciate.

That includes driving when I wasn't able to get behind a wheel for any extended period. Ross Leonard is a financial advisor I met because we were both soccer dads. Now, looking back, more than half of the years I've known Ross involved cancer, although that will change in the future as our relationship continues to deepen. In fact, as I finish this book, Ross's daughter Anna is a sophomore studying at Babson College.

During my struggle with cancer, I was the manager for our daughters' club soccer team, which was part of a league that required countless hours of travel to games. That meant the Browns and the Leonards often shared long stretches on the interstates. Ross did the lion's share of that driving. Sometimes, especially during chemo, I slumped in the back seat, tried my best to nap—and to avoid complaining.

"You took such good care of me, Ross," I said when I asked him what he recalled about those road trips. "You are a great friend."

"Oh, it was a pleasure," Ross said. "After all, we became friends in the first place because we shared so much, Howie. We both love sports. We both love to talk about new ideas in business. I always knew that, if I was thinking about a new idea in my work, I could share it with you on one of our drives and you'd have a really good perspective on it. Our families became friends. Emily became like a second daughter to us."

"Well, during the worst months, I wasn't much of a good conversation partner. I remember that sometimes I was pretty much out of it in the back seat," I said. "At least you always had lots to talk about with Emily, too."

"Oh, sure! Sports. Trivia. Music. No shortage of subjects with Emily. Those were great trips. And you were always so positive, Howie. That's what I remember. And that certainly rubbed off on Emily, too. She was one tough, tough, tough kid, both on and off the field."

"I can't begin to thank you for all you did," I said. "There are so many people I should thank for helping me through those years."

"You don't need to thank me. I treasure those memories," Ross said.

That's the kind of response I heard from all of the friends who I contacted as I reconstructed these experiences for this book. Most acts of chesed amounted to simple acts of service: Driving, bringing us meals, cheering up Lisa and me with a call or visit—but some were huge. Among the real pinnacle experiences were the big, loud, boisterous gatherings of my old buddies that Lisa describes as my "last hurrah" weekends.

From Joey's perspective? "Those times when groups of your friends came from across the country—that really is the Jewish *mitzvah*, or commandment, known as *bikur cholim*. It dates to the ancient times of Abraham and Sarah. When we talk about chesed and acts of lovingkindness, bikur cholim is the specific calling to visit the sick and to care for them. We're all expected to do that, but obviously, there's a huge range of responses to that calling. We learn that someone we know is sick and we might choose to do the lowest-common-denominator thing: We might drop a 'Get Well' card in the mail. Then, some people go to the next level. They might bring food to the family for dinner. And the levels of caring progress until some people choose to go to the *nth* degree of caregiving. The truth is: We can't do everything for everyone. We all know many people who are sick, and we can't go to the *nth* degree for every one of them. But we all do have that calling, that obligation to visit the sick. Even if it's difficult, it's still an obligation."

An obligation, perhaps, but I was asking for far more than that in these "last hurrah" weekends. That's why my exhausted spirits soared when I put out calls nationwide to old friends to visit—*and they came!*

I'm an extrovert and people are my most potent medicine. That's one reason I have nurtured these friendships throughout my life. In the darkest days of my salvage chemo, when we all were sure I would not last long, I summoned my remaining strength and threw these Hail Mary invitations to various groups of friends. First and foremost, I reached out to the boys from the old neighborhood in Framingham: Bobby Bunny, Ozzy, Thews, Monkey Boy, Cappy, Wayne-o, Beak, Johnny-Ray, Wheels, Deano, Pow-Pow and Mitch. If that sounds like the cast list from *Happy Days*, well, that's what we still call each other, even as adults. In their professional lives, these boyhood friends were better known as Bobby Hoyt, Kurt Jones, Greg Matthews, Robby Dlott, Jeff Capobianco, Wayne Pass, Jeff Cohen, John Cannistraro, Andy Wheeler, Dean Scott, Bobby Powell and Kevin Mitchell, who later died. Today, these guys are a virtual Who's Who of community leadership scattered from Arizona to Florida to New England, including a one-time city planner, an assistant district attorney, an insurance executive, a marketing director for an auto company, a couple of military veterans and small business owners.

I hoped at least a few of them would catch the desperate invitation I threw out there and run with it to Michigan.

"Hell, yes, we would!" said Bobby Hoyt, a retired U.S. Navy Seal commander who now works for an engineering firm in Florida. "What did you think we'd do when we got that message: 'I'm dying. Get your ass to Detroit. Now.' Just sit at home on our asses? Hell, yes, we came."

In preparing this chapter, I talked with the old gang in a big Zoom gathering.

Some thought our lifelong bonds were unremarkable. "Why wouldn't we still be friends?" said Robby Dlott, who owns an insurance agency. "After all, we've known each other since middle school. Why would we stop being friends?"

"It's not that easy," said Jeff Cohen, a marketing executive. "When I tell people that I have you guys, good friends all spread out across the country now, and we're so close that we can still count on each other at times like this—they're amazed."

"Like I said, 'Why would we stop being friends?' We made a promise—a strong promise—to stick with each other," Robby said. "And talk about strength: I've got to say that Howie is the strongest frickin' human being I've ever met. So, when he called us, there was no question about it. We needed to go. With stage IV colon cancer, he still was stronger than any of us. He's such an incredibly inspiring person to have gone through this once in life, and beat the odds, and then he's battling it again? Who wouldn't want to go be with him?"

"Well, there's no question that strong relationships, friendships like we've got, are critical to a person's well-being," Bobby Hoyt said. "Your emotional well-being is so linked to your physical well-being that what Howie was asking us to do—of course, we did it. We knew what was at stake. We showed up determined that, while we were with you, Howie, we would never allow you to feel like you were dying from cancer. And that started the minute we arrived with all the joking around and harassing you just as much as we've always done. You never want to allow someone to slip into feeling they're a victim. Of course, we're all empathetic, but we also were determined to have a great time when we went to see you—because that's exactly what you needed from us, right?"

"Right," I said. "That's exactly right."

"We decided to party just as hard as we did when we were kids," said Kurt Jones, who was city planner in Scottsdale, Arizona, before moving to a law firm as a zoning specialist. "And that definitely involved a lot of drinking."

"Definitely," said Bobby. "The message we brought to Howie's house was: 'You better live, you son of a bitch! So, let's live it up.'"

The moment they all agreed to come for an autumn weekend, I knew I had to move Lisa and Emily out of the house. Things could—and did—get crazy. When the guys all arrived, our first stop was at a liquor store called The Bottle Shop, which was owned at that time by my sister, Cheryl, and her husband, David Gingras.

"I couldn't believe it when I saw this whole gang drive up—all the guys from the old neighborhood!" Cheryl said, recalling that afternoon. "So typical! The first thing they did when they got here was drive to our store to load up on the liquor and cigars they needed for the weekend."

In fact, that weekend alone could wind up as a stage play or film someday like so many other bittersweet dramas you may have seen about such dramatic reunions. From the opening hours, this one was liberally bathed in alcohol and smoke. I wasn't smoking any cigars, but the guys like to chomp on a good cigar. We told stories. We laughed. We argued. We played poker. They wrestled. We teased each other relentlessly. We watched football on a big-screen TV and our all-time favorite movie, *This Is Spinal Tap*.

"Who can say that laughing along with *Spinal Tap* isn't good for you? I know it is!" Kurt said. "*Spinal Tap* is the most genius movie ever made. And, you've got to understand, that's how a lot of our communication works—you know, with code, and lines from movies like *Spinal Tap*, *Caddyshack* and *Stripes* with the old nicknames and so much other stuff we share."

"You know, cancer already was a part of our story as friends, way before that trip to Michigan," said Greg Matthews, assistant attorney general at the Massachusetts Attorney General's Office in Boston. "One reason we all wanted to hang onto these friendships, in the first place, was that all of us were so young when Howie went through this the first time—and we all confronted our own mortality along with him. That's where we all learned how important it was to be available to each other, when we needed it, and to be absolutely honest with each other."

"Hey, we're nothing if not honest," said Jeff Capobianco, an insurance executive. "Brutally honest."

Greg nodded, "Talking about honesty, Howie, I don't think you'll ever forget that wig, will you?"

"Ohhhh, the wig," I groaned and rolled my eyes. "When I lost all my hair, my mom got a wig through a service that provides them for cancer patients. She thought I might like it, but I wore that wig for *like a minute*—until these guys got one good look at it and—"

"And we told you honestly, 'Howie, that's the dumbest shit ever. Get that thing off your head!'" Greg said.

"I did. I heard you! I re-donated it immediately."

We used every single available hour that weekend, even though some of us slumped off to sleep at various points. We watched sports, played sports and even jammed ourselves into cars for local road trips to compete at everything from video golf and foot golf with soccer balls—to croquet and bocce ball. Well, at least I had booked some bocce courts, but we never got there. We were wiped out at that point!

I soaked up every minute of it like the world's most potent medicine, but to be honest: I was so physically devastated that, more than once, I pretty much collapsed and slept through several stretches of the gathering. That meant I occasionally woke up to a surreal scene like an all-night poker game that became so heated in the wee hours of one morning that one guy tried to turn over the table, sending chips flying all over the house. Lisa and I kept finding poker chips for weeks afterward.

Another time that weekend, I woke up to a half-drunk Bobby grabbing my shoulders and shaking me, crying, "What are you going to do, Howie? Die on us?"

"I can't tell you," I said, half-awake as Bobby kept shaking me. I began crying with him. "I don't know! I just don't know!"

"You better not fucking die on us!" Bobby said and enfolded me in his arms.

All of us were turning into the kids who once had bicycled all over Framingham and later drove our cars all over New England at all hours of the day and night in search of a good time. We loved to laugh and court a little danger. In fact, in the middle of the long weekend, Wayne-O pulled out Halloween fireworks and started lighting them and tossing them around the backyard until neighbors called the police.

"You remember that scene?" Greg said. "We're sitting in the back yard like dummies lighting off all these M80s that we had no business firing off in those close quarters. And here come the cops! And, as I remember it, they actually turned out to be guys you knew, Howie."

"Well, there actually weren't many cops in that little town where we were living at the time," I said.

Greg said. "I'll never forget that. Talk about embarrassing! I'm like: 'Well, I'm actually a district attorney myself.' Then, next to me was a former Navy Seal commander, a city planner and—"

"I remember!" I said. "I remember that we couldn't stop laughing, even when the cops showed up, yet somehow we managed to sweet talk these guys into showing us some sympathy. Remember? In the end, they even posed for a photo, which was posted to Facebook, with us in the back yard. That was photographic proof that all of us got busted that weekend."

"We all thought it was our last time with you," Greg said and the conversation fell silent for a long moment. "Well, we did."

That's why Lisa calls that weekend, and a couple others like it, a "last hurrah."

My doctors say that my CRS and HIPEC surgery, combined with further chemo, was a possible curative key to my survival. I know the truth: All of that heroic medical effort was needed, but my friends and family gave me the strength to survive the agonizing treatments. As Lisa pointed out in her story, other friends came to Michigan to see me. College friends. California friends. And friends from various corporate connections. There was a long wave of last hurrahs that autumn.

I needed to thank—and have thanked—every one of those friends. So, why did I choose the weekend with the Framingham boys to share in this chapter? First, it was the wildest of them all. But the person who finally convinced me to include the Framingham friends' story in this book was Greg Matthews' wife Jeniene, an attorney herself who later changed careers to teach English at a New England boarding school. Jeniene urged me to tell this particular story. She said, "Greg and I met in law school and, as soon as I got to know him, I kept hearing all these stories about his boyhood friends—so many stories, so much accumulated lore among you guys that it began to take on these mythic proportions. A lot of times you guys have allowed yourselves to get downright silly together. You're now these respected professionals spread out all across the country and yet, when you get back together, you somehow are able to become those fun-loving Framingham boys again."

Jeniene paused and then pointed at me across the Zoom screen. "Howard, the love you share with these guys is a beautiful thing and I have to say: I'm envious. I don't have a circle like that. Most people today aren't able to go back home like you guys can wherever you meet up somewhere across the country."

In short: Jeniene was right about including that particular story, God help us all.

There is one final obligation in Jewish tradition that, so far, these guys have not had to perform for me—but I have performed myself for others.

"It's always a higher form of chesed if we do something with no expectation of receiving anything in return," Joey said. "And it's the highest form to do something for another person who could not possibly give you anything in return—and could not possibly do for themselves. I'm talking here about burying the dead. In the end, whenever it comes, we all face that moment. Caring for the dead is the highest form of lovingkindness we can show to others."

Just like my guys came running from all points of North America when I needed them, I have made a commitment over the years to drop everything and do likewise when others need me.

Remember Jay Rosen? He was the first real friend I made in Los Angeles, thanks to my father's relentless matchmaking. Remember how Dad told that story? "You didn't know anybody out there when you first got to LA, so I thought: Howard should get to know a good Jewish kid. I remembered that Morty and Sydell and Wolfie had a boy out there, too. I'd known them for years. Decades! They were a family who started with one shoe store up in Manchester, New Hampshire, and then they opened more stores around New England. I'd go see them regularly because I supplied boots for their stores. We'd talk. Morty and Sydell were husband and wife, you know, and Wolfie was the uncle—Morty's uncle."

Remember those guys? I certainly have, all my life. That's why it felt like a blow to the gut when I got the call from Jay on July 20, 2006, that Morty had died of a cancer that had been largely undetected until it was far too late to save him. He was only 66—and died only six weeks after Jay's wedding day. I was a groomsman with David Infante and Adam Drescher at the wedding.

"When Dad died in 2006, there was so much emotion mixed with joy that it was just overwhelming. I can only describe it as the most bittersweet year in my life," Jay said as he recalled 2006. "That's because it was also the year I married Rebecca. They found Dad's cancer as the result of a blood test and then realized it already had spread in his body. So, he went very fast. That meant: Right in the middle of our preparations for our wedding in California, Dad was dying out East. I can remember Rebecca and I had scheduled some Arthur Murray dance classes so we could manage to do a decent box step at our wedding reception. There was one day when I spent some time talking with Dad on the phone, then Rebecca and I had to go to our dance class, and then we sat down to dinner that evening—and all Rebecca and I could do was just cry and cry and cry."

I said, "When you called to tell me that Morty had died, all I can remember is your saying two words: 'Morty passed.' Then, there was just a whole lot of silence between us. I don't think we said a whole lot on that call."

"That's right. Mostly silence. And we cried. And I said, 'Howard, I just wanted you to know this so you can tell your parents. Don't feel you have to fly in for the funeral.'"

"Right away I said, 'Jay, I'm going to be there.'"

"We both knew this was one of those defining moments in a friendship," Jay said.

"And we've shared a lot of moments," I said. "Like when I showed up in California as this frail skeleton who had just barely beaten cancer the first time and was obviously not at my best. When our parents told us to meet, you very easily could have taken me to dinner and, you know: one and done. But that's not what happened. You were very kind to me and our friendship grew."

Then, much later, when I was in those darkest weeks of salvage chemo, Jay was another friend who flew across the country to cheer me up. "Lisa could barely believe we were going to try it, but we made quite a road trip," I recalled about Jay's visit in November of 2017. "After your career in media, you knew all kinds of things about music, so we drove all the way to the Rock & Roll Hall of Fame in Cleveland! It probably was insane to even try that, but we did and it turned out to be absolutely wonderful. We spent all day in the museum. You knew so much about everything. It really lifted my spirits. I was feeling so good about this that we even added on a trip to the Pro Football Hall of Fame in Canton, Ohio."

"And then you crashed."

I laughed, "Yeah, I crashed. I drove myself until I had not a single ounce of energy left. The rains began to fall, and we had a long, stormy drive back to Michigan—and I pretty much collapsed in the passenger seat, leaving you to drive through that storm for hours."

"It's what we do for each other."

"It is and that's exactly why in July 2006, right after you called me about your father's death, I called my parents and said, 'Morty has passed—and I'm coming for the funeral.' We all knew how fast this was moving. Jews always try to bury quickly. That's our tradition, so I had to hop on a plane the next day into Boston. I went to my parents' house in Framingham and then we drove up to the funeral in Manchester, New Hampshire."

"Dad was so well known in the community that it was standing room only," Jay recalled. "There must have been 500 people on that hot July day all to honor Dad. You know, in his prime, he was a model salesman, a guy who could walk into a room and light it up, a guy who could make people laugh and they'd always feel better after having spent time with him. There was so much sadness in that room that day. He was only 66. Later, as is our custom, we would sit *shiva* and people could come visit with us, have some food and share stories. But, right after the service, the immediate family and friends had to make this hour-and-a-half drive south to the cemetery in Sharon, Massachusetts."

"That was quite a funeral procession!"

"And eventually at the graveside, after the brief service there, we wound up with just three of us standing there along with the funeral home staff," Jay recalled. "It was you and me and Jeff Novak, whose family had been friends with my family since the 1960s."

"That was the scene: Three guys, three shovels and a mountain of earth."

"It may be hard for non-Jews to appreciate that image," Joey said. "But the mitzvah of chesed you're describing in this last story goes all the way back to Genesis chapter 47. That's when Joseph is still in Egypt and promises to bury his father, Jacob, called Israel at that point, not in Egypt where they have been living, but back with their ancestors. It's an incredibly difficult request that Jacob is making—and he insists that Joseph firmly promise that he will do it. That's why we say this is the highest form of chesed. Jacob couldn't do that for himself. In fact, that's why the Jewish charities today that will help bury Jews when they die are called *Chesed Shel Emes*, or Charity of True Lovingkindness."

"Of course, I knew about mourners putting some soil in the grave as a symbolic sign of helping with the burial," I said. "But to be honest, I had never heard of the custom of literally filling the entire grave by hand to honor the dead. That's the day I learned about that tradition."

"Not everyone does it. Most people don't. But it is a well-established tradition, especially in the Orthodox community," Joey said. "You have to understand that in Jewish tradition, we are not throwing dirt on someone, we are spreading over them a blanket of earth as they rest in eternal peace. You might think of it like tucking your child into bed at night. At the grave, we are tucking in our loved ones for eternity. I encourage family members and friends, if they are physically able, to at least do a few shovels. Then, there are people who will stay and do the entire mitzvah. It's quite a challenge. You spread some of the earth right over the coffin, then usually a vault lid is placed and more earth is added. When you're bereaved and grieving and you've reached the point where there are no more words to be said, this becomes a physical expression for your grief."

"It's what Dad had shown me," Jay said. "I'd seen it all my life. Dad would be one of the last ones remaining after a funeral. My father and his father before him had done this for others. Now, I was going to do this for Dad."

"We were wearing nice suits, but it was just so hot that we were sweating through our clothes. I remember taking off our coats, but pretty soon all three of us were covered in dirt. We were really muddy at that point," I said. "We didn't even talk, did we?"

"No, we focused on the work," Jay said.

"We were on a mission, just pounding away at moving that huge pile of earth."

"I've got a hole in memories of that day. I can't recall some of the other things that went on, but I will never forget that time we spent at Dad's grave."

"As it should be," I said.

"When we moved from the grave to shiva, the whole point was to remember and share stories," Jay said. "We tell the stories because that's how we keep the blessed memories of our loved ones alive."

We tell the stories.

That's how we keep our memories alive.

I hope that at least some of the stories in this chapter echo moments in your own life so that you might be inspired to go and do likewise.

Shining Brightly

Please consider volunteering, giving or learning about these or similar organizations that touched my life. There are so many compassionate organizations that helped me and can help you.

Finally, "Tap into America" with *This Is Spinal Tap* for some humor.

+ **Jewish Hospice and Chaplaincy Network** – JewishHospice.org
+ **Paltown** – Paltown.org
+ **Colontown** – Colontown.org
+ *This Is Spinal Tap* – en.Wikipedia.org/wiki/This_Is_Spinal_Tap

Finding a personal happy place is a key to surviving long-term traumas like those associated with cancer. Basketball is my happy place. I've played since I was 6 years old. One photo shows me shooting a basket as a point guard for Framingham South High School in 1984. I still play regularly with a diverse circle of friends. The final photo, sporting a Babson College shirt, was shared along with a story about the importance of basketball in my resiliency.

15

Now in My Court

My favorite photo from the spring of 2021 shows me on an outdoor basketball court fully masked against the COVID pandemic and proudly sporting a Babson College jersey as I hold up two basketballs, one in each hand. The caption reads: "I, Howard Brown, Stage IV Colon Cancer and now No Evidence of Disease (NED), celebrate survivorship by going to my happy place: the basketball court!" That photo and caption soon spread worldwide on social media—and that little ray of sunshine still is bouncing around various social media platforms, spreading smiles to this day.

I created it in response to a request about cancer survivorship from Carrie Treadwell, director of Strategic Patient Advocacy and Engagement for the American Association for Cancer Research (AACR), one of the cancer advocacy groups I have supported over the years. The AACR is the world's oldest and largest professional network of cancer researchers and, in recent years, has become an advocate of increasing patient-centricty in the ongoing battle with cancer. In addition to supporting research and advances in treatment, AACR hosts rallies and teaching events, builds supportive networks among celebrities as well as everyday patients and their families, and uses every form of media to spread awareness. After Siddhartha Mukherjee won the Pulitzer Prize for his book *Emperor of All Maladies: A Biography of Cancer*, which sold thousands of copies, AACR co-sponsored the six-hour PBS documentary based on the book so millions of families would learn more about the ongoing struggle to defeat this disease. Currently, my primary role with AACR is participation in their seminars for patient-centric learning, called the Scientist⊠Survivor Program®. It's demanding. Each year, I've got a stack of advance reading to complete before I attend the lectures by researchers, doctors and other health professionals about cutting-edge issues in the fight against cancer. Then we discuss the findings and AACR encourages our collaboration in promoting awareness.

While I'm honored to be part of those annual meetings, because I always learn a lot, my most valuable contributions extend in other directions, mainly in expanding the supportive network around the world. The campaign to defeat the Emperor of All Maladies can be described as the world's biggest team sport. That's especially true if you think of the millions of families worldwide in which patients and unpaid caregivers are tirelessly keeping up the good fight every day. What those of us on the home front in this world war against cancer can contribute is increasing awareness of all the ways people can survive these treatment regimens—and keep their spirits shining brightly enough to remain in the game. In the stories I already have shared with you in this book, it's obvious that successfully beating cancer starts with finding that ounce of energy, that spark of light, that allows us to climb out of bed each morning.

For me, the mountain of accumulated medical records and test results chart my journey toward NED for my doctors—but my own personal benchmarks of survival have always been on the basketball court. For that, I will be forever grateful for my teenage years under the strict mentorship of Massachusetts Basketball Coaches' Hall of Famer Phil "Smokey" Moresi. In fact, as I was finishing this memoir, Moresi and I both contributed stories to a new book by Martin Davis, *Thirty Days With America's High School Coaches*. The theme that runs through those two chapters in Martin's book is Moresi's focus on developing the minds, the hearts and the physical talents of his entire team—including players who often had to wait their turn through an agonizing period of warming the bench.

I'm talking about myself.

From my youth, Moresi drummed into me that life is a long and arduous struggle—so that the relentless training while we sit and wait to get into the game is often just as important as winning in the end. In fact, it's the years of training that make the winning possible.

"Under Coach Moresi, you busted your butt, even though you knew you may not play. That allowed you to develop the resiliency and the skills to move on through life," I say in Martin's book. Here is more of the story that Moresi and I shared:

July 4, 2020: A short video clip on Howard Brown's Facebook page shows a middle-aged man wearing a Babson College basketball jersey, dribbling from the top of the key toward the basket—stopping and popping from 15 feet away. Howard's parting words?

"That's how we do it. I want to wish everyone a happy July Fourth. Be safe. Put on a mask. Cancer sucks."

Anyone who knows Brown understands that one of the persons who built his foundation—and sparked a light that keeps him burning brightly—is his high school basketball coach, Phil "Smokey" Moresi. What Brown appreciates most about Moresi is not what he learned while leading the high school team as the starting point guard in his senior year. No, it's the lessons Moresi taught him the preceding three years, when Howard either wasn't on the varsity team or was sitting on the bench.

Howard could have started on a lot of teams his junior year, but Steve Niccoli— the returning starting point guard—was a senior. "We went 6-12 that year," Brown says. "Niccoli won the MVP of the Bay State League for a team with a losing record." Niccoli had to earn every minute of his playing time, though, because in spite of the fact that Brown wasn't playing, he was riding Niccoli the whole year—in practice.

That effort didn't go unnoticed by Moresi, who pulled Brown aside at the year's end.

"Howie, I got to tell you, one of the main reasons Stevie won that award was because you were so good that you pushed him every day and every minute of practice," said Moresi, "and you became a pain in his ass."

Howard took it as the highest possible compliment. "Moresi knew that being second-team was really difficult," Brown says. "You busted your butt, even though you knew you may not play."

Moresi continued. "Remember, Howie, during your own senior year you led the team. Your hard work and patience did pay off." That year, Howard was named team MVP, Bay State League All-Star, and came in second for league MVP with a team that went 8-10.

What Howard could only partially appreciate during Niccoli's senior year was how important that second-team lesson would be. Just how much Brown would come to depend on those learned skills was something that he could not know at the tender age of 17, or even 18. He couldn't see the two bouts with cancer in his future; he couldn't see the ups and downs of being a serial entrepreneur, an interfaith leader and a cancer survivor/advocate. Today, some 40 years after Brown last dribbled a ball on his high school court, the lessons that Coach Moresi taught are still with him—for example, how to shoot a free throw.

"For foul shots, he taught us BEEF," Brown says. It's an acronym for: Balance, Elbow-in, Eyes on the rim, Follow through.

Such a skill is certainly important in basketball, but is it in life?

When Brown was facing cancer for the second time, he used BEEF to fight for his health and life. Brown knew that he had to do four things:

First, he had to maintain his balance. "We learn to lean on others, to depend on others—and eventually to reach out and let others lean on us, depend on us," Brown says. For many of us, leaning on others is a sign of weakness. For Howard, learning to lean on others was simply a way to maintain balance in his struggle.

Second, he had to keep elbow-in. When shooting a basketball, it's natural to let your elbow fly out. Learning to control it, keeping it tucked in, is the secret to consistently making shots. It keeps the ball flight straight and produces the proper arc. Through numerous bouts of chemo and four major surgeries, Brown kept his elbow in. He was doing the difficult mental work of just waking up every morning and doing what had to be done, even when his body had other ideas.

Third, he had to keep his eyes on the rim. The goal was beating cancer via laser focus and mental toughness. "Eyes on the rim" is the visualization of the basketball swishing through the net. Brown could not allow an air of defeat to distract him from his goal. Death was, of course, a very real possibility. Along the way Brown had met and then lost many friends and acquaintances who were also struggling with cancer. None he met, however, took their eyes off the rim.

Fourth, he had to follow through. Now ranked among the luckiest of colorectal cancer survivors, Howard has become a national advocate, spokesperson and leader in the fight against this dreaded disease. He frequently reminds everyone to get screened in efforts to prevent colorectal cancer.

Today, when Brown talks about his old coach, "fiery" is a term that inevitably comes up. After all, Moresi was tough. He would get into it with the referees. And, yes, he would even sometimes get thrown out of games. Yet it was that fieriness that drove Moresi and his players to keep striving, to keep improving—whether they were undefeated and hoisting state championship trophies or fighting through 6-12 seasons.

It's the little things, in sports—the little things that great coaches drill into their young players—that stick with them. At 18, BEEF was Howard Brown's world. Forty years on, BEEF still helps to define Brown's world. The great lessons are hard-learned—over, and over, and over again.

"That's how we do it ... cancer sucks."

Fiery.
In interviewing all of us for his book, Martin Davis recognized that quality—a fire in our hearts—was an essential ingredient we shared back then on Moresi's team. That extended from the coach himself on down to the last player left warming the bench. Fiery also describes how I approach every game among friends to this day. When I hit the court, the hospitable, kind and socially gracious Howard Brown becomes a fiercely directive point guard, trash talking, sweating and pouring every bit of energy I can muster into the game. Everything else in my life recedes—all the cares, complaints, concerns and chronic pains and disabilities. I am certainly not the only basketball player

to describe the zen-like focus of playing all-out basketball. I may be the first to write about it while playing with chronic neuropathy in my fingertips and feet, where my all-consuming focus on getting our team to the basket includes my inability to even feel the ball in my hands much of the time. The sheer energy it takes to will that basketball into the basket and trust in my body's overall muscle memory to propel it accurately—now that's a fiery focus!

The fact is that I forget about cancer for a precious few hours while playing basketball—just the respite I needed to get me through the battles I was facing daily.

One of my close clergy friends is Rabbi Josh Bennett, who I met one night while playing poker with friends. I had no idea what he did for a living. In fact, among the hundreds of guys who I interact with in various forms of recreational sports, I have to admit that I know a number of them only by nicknames. So, Josh and I struck up a friendship without any deference to his scholarly and pastoral role as a leader at Michigan's Temple Israel, one of the largest Reform congregations in the country.

"We hit it off right away," Josh said as I talked to him for this chapter. "I think what ties your many pursuits together—whether it's your entrepreneurial spirit in business or your love of working throughout the Jewish community or your passion for sports—is that you quite simply are comfortable with conflict. In fact, you embrace conflict in a way that not many people are able to live with for long. In the Jewish world, I've seen you step into some very challenging encounters that bridge interfaith gaps in our world. You've formed relationships with people who other members of our Jewish community are not willing to even engage. It's because of that willingness to step into very uncomfortable, challenging situations that you sometimes find answers that other people have never been able to uncover. And, Howard, I have to tell you: I have learned a lot about that from your embrace of conflict."

After we ran into each other playing poker a few times, our shared sport became soccer. Our children loved and played soccer. Neither one of us can claim to be stars, but we enjoy both the athletic and strategic challenge of reading the other team's game plan and trying to position ourselves to counter it.

"Let's put this simply, Howard," Josh said. "You're always looking at soccer like it's a chess match."

"Well, that's how I was taught to play basketball. I play soccer goalkeeper like a point guard or a floor general in basketball," I said, smiling. "Half the fun is understanding the X's and O's of the game as it unfolds in real time."

While I have played a lot of men's over-40 soccer with Josh, my closest ongoing basketball buddy is Alan Bakst. Like Josh, I met Alan at a game, a basketball game in this case. His childhood fascination with science led him into the business side of health care as a representative for a medical devices firm.

"Like you, Howard, I grew up in a modest home and one thing that's great about basketball is that it doesn't cost much to play," Alan said. "Think about all the equipment you need for football or hockey. All you need for basketball is a ball and a pair of sneakers. Even if you don't own a good ball yourself, you can go play with other guys if there's a court near your house. And, like you Howard, I've always found that basketball is a great way to meet new people, develop friendships and exercise."

"That's true, even though on the court we may not sound that way," I said. "Trash talking is part of the game."

"On the court, we all know what a really big mouth you've got, Howard," Alan said. "That's where it all comes out. You just keep chattering. You're telling everybody else what to do."

"We all know it's in fun."

"We do, but it's more than that," Alan said. "I grew up just playing street basketball, you know. I wasn't on a high school or college team like you were. So, when I began playing with you, one of the things I realized is that there are different levels of playing this game. I realized that you were fundamentally a better player because you were able to see—as we were playing—the deeper strategy in the game. You were directing and shouting at us because you could see where we should be going like you were planning three moves ahead of the other team."

"That's true, I do like to play at that level," I said. "But there are a lot of reasons people enjoy playing basketball. And that's just fine. Some guys just like to run up and down the court a lot and they're not even thinking about the X's and O's. Guys who've played a lot of street ball tend to think of it more as dominating another player one on one. In street ball, there's less passing. Some guys just want to get a good workout, sweat with us for a while, and that's the extent of it. Lots of reasons people play and lots of approaches to the game."

"But as point guard," Alan said, "I think of you, positioned at the top of the key. You're looking around even as you're moving, looking to set screens and picks so a guy can pop open—like a checker piece popping over another one to a square where suddenly you can score. Success in basketball depends on your vision, seeing and understanding what's happening as everyone is in motion around you."

"Court vision," I said.

"I don't know how many times you've yelled at guys, 'Get your head up! Get your head up! Court vision!' For instance, if you have a habit of looking at the ball before you shoot or when you are dribbling, that's a bad habit you need to break. Your head needs to be up—always looking at what's happening all around you."

"That's how a guy who's 50 or 60 has a chance at beating a guy who's in his 20s," I said. "Now, let's be honest. A guy in his 20s probably can run right over us and win—but not necessarily. It may be the older guy who has better fundamental skills and better court vision. Think about this: When you get into your car and start it, you think about what's going on around you. What's in front of your car and what's behind it. Weather conditions. Is the car running smoothly? Is the radio too loud? Is that guy in the driveway in front of you aware that you're coming or is he going to pull out in front of you suddenly? As the point guard on a basketball team, you're driving this team of five players who are supposed to act in a complementary way to score one basket more than the other team before the whistle blows. That's court vision and court awareness."

"You can still get knocked around a lot," Alan said.

"Sure!" I said. "We both know guys who have made a conscious decision to stop playing basketball in their 50s and stick with tennis or biking or golf. Basketball can beat up your body, especially if you're playing on concrete. But I'm not planning on stopping anytime soon, are you?"

"No. No," Alan said, then paused. "Howard, I think of us now as sort of elder statesmen among the guys who play with us. When the weather's good, we tend to organize our little games from our phones. We'll get a text from Dan Serlin: 'Is there a game today?' 'Is there a game at Norm Markowitz's or Dan Butler's courts?' 'Can you fit me in tonight?' And we keep everyone informed and coordinate who's playing."

"We're the statesmen organizing the games for so many others," Alan said. "And I'm also proud that we've been successful in the mix of players. A lot of Jewish people I know think it's amazing that we regularly play with Chaldeans."

Chaldeans are Iraqi Christians, who have migrated to communities like Macomb County north of Detroit over the decades because of persecution in Iraq. They prefer to call themselves Chaldeans, but they are ethnically within the Arab world in the Middle East and Alan is correct: There aren't many regular Jewish-Arab basketball leagues.

"There's a beautiful chemistry on the court," Alan said. "On my phone right now, I probably have 120 guys we've played with in recent years. What do we share? A lot of the guys we play with—Jewish or Chaldean or Black or from some other ethnic or religious group—tend to be professionals or business owners or entrepreneurs. Another value we share: Most of us have had solid families around us from the time we were kids."

This conversation prompted Alan and I to look over the long list of our Michigan basketball brothers, who we call the Boyz:

Alan Bakst, Dan Serlin, Dan Butler, Norm Markowitz, Andy Markowitz, Ryan Markowitz, Danny Kallabat, Bryant Kallabat, Jeff Kallabat, Mahmoud Baydoun, Mike Romaya, Arvinder Sooch, Dylan Putrus, Tim Somero, Justin Hermiz, Dave Arafat, Chris Arafat, John Arafat, Lance Denha, Justin Bennett, Jason Jucius, Jon Lauter, Adam London, Dave Leak, Adam Ellis, Ron Hirsch, Greg Hirsch, David Kam, Craig Bauer, Ken Sachs, Adam Fishkind, Jeff Blackman, Jason Ingbar, Craig Hysni, Dave Gach, Marc Cohen, Isaac Sternheim, Yarden Blumstein, Matt Freed, Rob Ballinger, Zach Manni, Pierre Rishallah, Ozzy Naser, Eric Kovan, Yoav Raban, David Contorer, Amine Zein, Daniel Schwartz, Jeff Comeiner, Geoff Kretchmer, Lee Hurwitz, Jeff Pitt, Eric Michaels, Danny Singer, Rich Kligman, David Jacob, Howard Eisenshtadt, Josh Charlip, Bubba Urdan, Corey Sparks, Richie Grison, Dave Jovanovich, John Jovanovich, Jason Watson, Jordan Stav, Malik Basha, Alex Bennett, Arvin Sooch, Brent Saperstein, Yoli Silverstein, Rick Sherline, Brandon Nunn, Craig Brown, Daryl Nafsu, Mo Hutton, Darrec Muraca, David Banooni, Don Meade, David Domstein, Aaron Fogarasi, Dale Halpin, Michael Stein, Howard Krugel, Mike Yaker, Josh Yaker, Daniel Yaker, Jacob Rashty, Justin Jacobs, Zach Manni, Mike Wolf, Andy Mayoras, David Karp, Mike Fedorchak, Scott Sonenberg, Mo Hutton, Ed Perez, Pete Toma, Tom Toma, Mike Feld, Terrance Burkette, Derek Weiss, Norm Torrey, Erich Tavadia, Rob Feldman, Mike Bernard, Josh Mershman, Zack Cohen, Lou Aguinaga, Brian Mulcahy, Mitch Schecter, David Jacobson, David Epstein, Jon Colman, Mike Curhan, Bob Schwartz, Gary Ran, Brian Witus, Sharif Kurtovic, Levi Shemtov, Dov Stein, Anthony Boji and Rich Zekman.

As Alan and I pondered that roster, I said, "It's the huge diversity these guys represent that caused Alan Muskovitz of *The Detroit Jewish News* to come to a game one morning—then write a feature story about us. I love the photo they published of all of us."

After watching us play, Muskovitz wrote:

Cross-Cultural Cagers

Jewish and Chaldean basketball players enjoy long-term friendship

"It's not just about the sport; it's about deep friendships. We live parallel lives, and we don't intersect all the time, but basketball was the mechanism for us to interact. And our lives are richer because of it."

Who said it? Lebron James? Give up? Actually it was Rick Sherline, Southfield insurance agent and pick-up basketball fanatic, describing his 15+ year relationship with a group of Chaldean (Iraqi Christian) basketball players with whom he shares "a special kind of relationship." Rick thought our readers would enjoy hearing this feel-good story.

From the moment I heard the first heartwarming details, I understood why Rick felt it was a story people could learn from as well.

Two cultures, one sport, countless hours of fun. There are a few versions of exactly just how it all began. By most accounts, it came down to two different groups of players showing up at a court, one Jewish, one Chaldean, each in need of extra players to field two teams for a game of pickup basketball. Game on.

It was there, Sherline recalls fondly, that we "cross-pollinated, melded our two games together" and, in doing so, the players discovered they shared the same passion for family, education and friendship. As the years passed, the friendships grew and so did the number of players with the games moving from the school yard to the backyard of West Bloomfield physician Dr. Norman Markowitz.

"The guys meshed from day one," Markowitz says. "There were never any issues regarding our different cultures or any awkwardness whatsoever."

Chaldean counterparts Justin Hermiz and Tim Somero echo those exact sentiments. "It has been a great Chaldean/Jewish social connection we have developed," Justin says.

Tim adds, "I love the guys—like they're my own brothers—I don't make a distinction between who is Jewish or Chaldean."

The relationships have extended to off the court as well, both personally and professionally. Players meet for lunch, attend simchas, even check up on the health and wellbeing of each other's family members. Recently, Tim Somero took his basketball devotion to a whole new level, admitting to me that one of his "primary considerations when looking for a new home for my family is the drive time to Norm's court."

This story reminds us that sports offers a unique and profound way of changing the course of human interaction, where differences are celebrated and where understanding is born. It can happen even on a backyard basketball court.

Basketball is a lot more than just a game to me. Basketball is a cerebral sport, a community sport, a sport of relationships, respect, chemistry and teamwork. Each time I have been knocked down by a physical disability, a surgery or a chemo series, one of the goals that gets me out of the bed each morning is getting back onto the court as a milestone in the healing of my mind, body and soul. I've had a chemo port installed, neuropathy, chronic diarrhea and the fogginess that I call chemo brain—and I've played through all of that. I don't know too many stage IV cancer patients who've kept playing before, during and after treatment. It's hard playing full-court basketball several times a week with all that running, zigging and zagging. It's even risky. I sometimes worry that a hard hit to the chest might disturb my chemo port.

This is simply a part of my healing journey. The blueprint to my own survivorship. Basketball was the light that got me through some of the darkest periods of my life.

And that's the story behind that little photo caption that keeps bouncing around the internet: "I, Howard Brown, Stage IV Colon Cancer and now No Evidence of Disease (NED), celebrate survivorship by going to my happy place: the basketball court!"

No, I'm not trying to convince you that you have go out and shoot hoops. Maybe some people will be prompted to get out on the court again after reading this chapter. Most won't. The whole point of this chapter is to tell you about *my* "happy place."

We each need to find at least one of those for ourselves.

My happy place is anywhere I'm playing with my hoops with my boyz.

What's your happy place?

Shining Brightly

Finding my happy place on the basketball court helped me fight, heal and grow stronger. Yours could be yoga, meditation, nature walks, art, music. Find that place of joy.

- Nerd Balls on Strangers (Hoops Trash Talking) – youtu.be/JM1HuI0UMVA
- 5 Tips to Find Your Own Happy Place – livehappy.com/self/5-tips-find-your-own-happy-place
- American Association of Cancer Research – AACR.org/ About-the-AACR-Foundation/
- FriendshipCircle.org – this amazing nonprofit is our indoor basketball court in the winter months.

Roger Babson, an "angelic troublemaker" and a hugely successful entrepreneur, is a life-long mentor because his Babson College was such a formative part of my life. In this famous news photo from early 1929, Babson stirred up trouble nationwide with his enormous chart that he said predicted a stock market crash that autumn. For months, critics called him crazy—until they realized he was right. Never one to hide his accomplishments, Babson symbolized the global significance of his ideas by installing an enormous globe on campus. When I became the president of the Babson Alumni Association, I passed out "shining brightly" sunglasses to homecoming attendees. I kept going as president, even when I was struggling through my chemotherapy and surgeries.

16

'Babson, You're Shining Brightly!'

Roger Babson would have been a master internet influencer. He loved to turn his most heart-felt messages into vivid images designed to surprise, amuse, fascinate and drive home the point of whatever campaign he was waging.

In September 1929, he issued the most audacious warning of his career: The stock market was about to crash. He warned American investors to pull back before that happened—and he knew exactly how to get their attention. First, he waited to deliver this news until the 16th annual National Business Conference, which was held at his college early that September and drew lots of corporate leaders. Then, he chose to proclaim his warning with the aid of a wall-sized timeline jam-packed with stock market data. Of course, this gigantic chart prompted media professionals to snap photographs of Babson standing in front of it, dramatically raising his arm to aim his prediction with a long wooden pointer at the fateful final months of 1929. *The New York Times* felt compelled to report this news under a headline: "Babson Predicts 'Crash' in Stocks." After all, Babson himself was a nationally syndicated columnist, at that point. They could not ignore the stunt, so *The Times* reporter quoted him extensively. Babson described the stock market as a house of cards that was going to collapse like an earlier boom-and-bust in Florida land speculation that ruined thousands of middle-class American families. However, *The Times* staff was so skeptical of Babson's bombshell that editors quickly assigned and published a second news story that appeared next to the one about Babson's claim. This sidebar quoted the prestigious Yale University economist Irving Fisher denying that any crash was looming.

Babson alumni know that our founder occasionally was prone to quirks and gimmicks, including a few way-off-the-mark predictions throughout his lifetime. Nevertheless, every incoming freshman hears the story of how Roger Babson caught the nation's attention in September 1929. He forecast the infamous crash and, for the next two months, the leading lights of his day sneered at him—until October 24, 1929.

Students and alumni hear a lot more about Babson these days since he greets students in the form of a new life-size bronze statue that's permanently poised near another of his audacious creations: a 25-ton rotating world globe. He personally paid to have this monster orb designed, built and installed on campus just after World War II to "impress upon students and other viewers an appreciation of the world as a whole … stimulating an interest in world geography, history, economics, transportation and trade." With a bit of P.T. Barnum razzle dazzle, Babson claimed that his 28-foot-in-diameter sphere was the world's largest globe—and it does rank *among* the biggest. Guinness currently ranks Eartha, a landmark in Maine as the world's largest *rotating* globe at 41 feet in diameter; and the so-called Daily Planet in Raleigh, NC, is the largest fixed globe at a whopping 71 feet wide. Of course, none of these matter to Babson alumni, who regard our founder's globe as a beloved symbol of our school. By the 1980s, however, Babson's big blue showpiece was crumbling. Trustees were on the verge of demolishing it when a campus-wide campaign moved board members to save the globe. Good thing, too! In 2019, a fully restored globe with a new high-tech surface guaranteed to withstand future years of inclement weather became the eye-popping focal point of Babson's new Centennial Park. Along with flags to honor the nearly 100 nations our students call home, the park honors both Babson, the school's long history and President Kerry Murphy Healey, who retired that year.

If Babson alumni occasionally roll their eyes and sigh at yet another Babson story, it's because the further one digs into his history of publicity stunts, one finds a few that got him into trouble.

Like the carved rocks.

Babson described himself in his many books and public talks as a man of both deep faith and equally impassioned insights into American capitalism. He saw himself as destined by God to stir up the entrepreneurial enthusiasm of young Americans. The two most-used adjectives associated with Babson's name in biographies both begin with "e": evangelical and eccentric. He was a self-styled angelic troublemaker who often risked taking decisive actions first—and asking for forgiveness later, if things did not work out quite as planned. I've always admired that daring spirit. As an entrepreneur, one could do worse than claim a title like angelic troublemaker.

That's precisely what happened when Babson carved the rocks. Or rather, when Babson hired some of the finest stone carvers in Boston to etch inspiring words into enormous boulders. Beyond his faith and his college, Babson's other source of pride was his family's deep roots in a small patch of ground near Gloucester called Dogtown. Starting in the mid-1600s, that patch had been known as Common Settlement, a modest village of farmers, artisans and people who made their livelihood at sea. Most of them aspired to move their families to better spots right along the coast—and they did so until only remnants of the original settlement remained. Before the village entirely vanished, a handful of the poorest people clung to their modest homes with dogs to help protect them from predators, hence the name that stuck. Babson developed a lifelong romantic attachment to what had become rocky cow pastures by his own childhood. Despite his fame and fortune, this was his happy place—the spot where he could putter around and renew his spirits. He loved this rocky patch so dearly that, along with a cousin, he bought 1,150 acres of Dogtown a few years before the Great Depression hit. Among other things, this allowed him to fund an archaeological dig at the original settlement site.

After the stock market crash, Babson did not gloat about his prophetic forecast. He took the Great Depression in stride as an opportunity to train the next generation to emerge from such a dark era. He didn't hoard his own wealth. He doubled down on giving back to his beloved communities, including Dogtown and Gloucester. Why? Because it was the right thing to do—and it was flat-out "fun," he said. No kidding. He wrote, "There is nothing which so develops the spiritual side of a person as wholehearted, unselfish giving. The person who leaves pure charity out of their life misses a tremendous lot of fun. God made this old world on peculiar plans. One of these plans is that while He put into the hands of humans almost everything we want, He asks that we turn back or dedicate a certain part of it distinctly to Him. Why? The reason is simple if we but look and see how much happier and fuller is the life of the person who gives, rather than of the one who does not."

In Dogtown, Babson's philanthropic passions coalesced in a brainstorm, a crystal-clear vision for bringing new life to these largely empty pastures. Through the Works Progress Administration, he hired 35 unemployed Finnish stonecutters to create a visual reminder of life's most important values by etching inspiring words and phrases into the huge boulders strewn around Dogtown. In Babson's mind, this was a win-win-win idea. He would provide desperately needed employment to the workmen, encourage the economic benefits of tourism and inspire anyone who wandered through his wooded park to live a better life.

Soon, the ringing of hammers and chisels woke the neighbors early each morning and his slogans emerged in huge block letters on dozens of enormous boulders, including:

KINDNESS

INTEGRITY

SPIRITUAL POWER

KEEP OUT OF DEBT

BE ON TIME

NEVER TRY NEVER WIN

PROSPERITY FOLLOWS SERVICE

HELP MOTHER

INITIATE

USE YOUR HEAD

IF WORK STOPS, VALUES DECAY

Unfortunately, Babson miscalculated. When they discovered what he and his stone carvers were doing, lots of people thought he had gone way too far. His single loudest critic was a neighbor who was infuriated because Babson had not properly checked his property lines when dispatching his Finnish carvers. Leila Webster Adams was livid when she found words carved on a boulder situated on her land. "Just look at that horrible thing," Adams told reporters. "Why the idea of a man like Roger Babson, so well-known and popular, going about carving such things as 'Prosperity Follows Service,' 'Keep Out of Debt,' and 'If Work Stops, Values Decay.' Whoever heard of such foolish notions?"

This time, the growing chorus of critics included members of his own family—which really stung. He later wrote about the controversy in one of his books, arguing that it all turned out for the best. "My family says that I am defacing the boulders and disgracing the family with these inscriptions, but the work gives me a lot of satisfaction, fresh air, exercise and sunshine," he wrote. He described the winding pathways among these boulders as if they represented yet another volume in his inspirational library, a real-world *Life's Book*.

Most importantly, Babson acted decisively to reconcile with his wounded neighbors. Among other acts of reparation, he sold back a stretch of land that

Gloucester wanted for a tiny fraction of its worth. Time has judged him warmly for what at the time seemed to be an outrageous act. Today, like Babson's globe, his creation has become a trendy tourist destination—just as he hoped. The new international Atlas Obscura guide to the best out-of-the-way spots for travelers calls the Dogtown & Babson Boulder Trail "an eerie presence strewn in an overgrown forest with many footpaths scattered throughout and a popular hiking trail."

Angelic troublemaker, indeed. More than half a century after his death in 1967, Roger Babson turns out to have been right about the stock market crash, his globe and his carved rocks. He also was right about enthusiastically embracing a happy place where one can reliably renew one's spirits in the midst of life's inevitable downturns.

After I graduated from the college, started to work for NCR and beat cancer the first time, I consciously put some parts of my life in the rearview mirror as I headed west. At the same time, I grasped even more tightly certain beloved pillars of my life, including my Judaism and my thankfulness for the trajectory on which Babson had sent my life. Although I was often overwhelmed with work in California, I carved out time to help my alma mater. That started with a low-key offer to voluntarily represent Babson at occasional college recruiting evenings at local high schools.

I initiated the idea, since giving back was so engrained in me. This was before there was any internet presence, but I managed to reach someone in the college's admissions office via phone and offered to help recruit new students. A few days later, a box arrived containing a Babson flag to use as a table skirt, some brochures and postcards that prospective students could mail to Babson to request further information. There was also a brief note of thanks—but the staff obviously held out little hope for my efforts, since recruiting in Los Angeles 3,000 miles away from Babson's campus was unknown to many at that time.

To equip me for college recruiting, the box held a total of 10 postcards. Their skepticism turned out to be well founded. In my first outing, I showed up at 5 p.m. at a converted school gymnasium in my suit and tie, hung my Babson banner along the edge of the table that would serve as my booth and beamed in a friendly way at the first families wandering through the college fair.

"Ever hear of Babson?" I asked one young guy who made eye contact.

"Is that Baptist?"

"No," I said. "It's all about becoming an entrepreneur, learning how to start your own business, set your own—" But he was gone. Further down the line, Bard College has caught his eye.

A while later, a girl walked right up to my table. Good sign! Then, she asked, "Does it snow there?"

Well, this was Los Angeles, after all. A lot of the students wanted a change of climate with their college admission.

By 10 p.m., I was back at my apartment with two completed postcards. I followed the instructions in my recruiting package, folded everything back inside the shipping box, mailed it to Babson and, for a while, those occasional evening fairs represented the sum total of my impact on campus.

That changed when I moved to Silicon Valley and settled in the San Francisco area. I maintained my college-recruiting commitment to set up booths at a couple of events each year. As a visible Babson representative in the area, I also learned that there were more alumni neighbors than I had realized, including a half dozen who had started to meet occasionally. I joined them. At first, we called ourselves the Babson San Francisco High Tech Affinity Group, because it reflected our shared interest in technology and business. Craig Newmark was one of the most popular speakers I recruited for our gatherings. However, because we wanted to identify ourselves more clearly as part of the national network of such chapters, we switched our name to the Babson Alumni Club of the San Francisco Bay Area. We interacted with some of the big Silicon Valley firms on behalf of the college, including a tour I helped to organize for 40 Babson graduate students who flew out for the opportunity with their resumes on floppy disks. We arranged tours with several high-tech and venture capital firms and encouraged the students to network in part by leaving their floppies with representatives at companies where they hoped to work one day.

In the summer of 2005, when Lisa and I moved to Michigan, a couple of leaders in the alumni association recruited me to help with a complex transition. The association was growing, but a structural flaw had emerged from the college's perspective. The alumni had established the group originally with modest aspirations to organize homecoming reunions and a few other occasional programs. No one had questioned the association's leaders when they filed to become an independent 501c3 separate from the college. I was asked to help navigate the potentially controversial process of merging that nonprofit under control of the college's board of trustees, which was a more common arrangement among colleges. My involvement in this project grew out of a phone call I got one day from the current president of the alumni association

Patrick McGonagle, an old friend from my graduating class. Patrick wanted to pick my brain as an active alum and a successful entrepreneur. Then, he kept calling and eventually asked me to volunteer and consult on the process. I found myself involved in the merger, which successfully moved the alumni association's bylaws and assets under the management of Babson's alumni affairs office. By 2006, I was nominated to a formal seat on the alumni board of directors to continue this kind of work. From the start, then, I was seen as an agent of change and also as an outsider because I lived far from Babson. As a small college, a lot of the other alumni board members lived within convenient driving distance of campus. Because of my involvement in the merger, I understood the inner workings as well as the untapped potential of alumni. I was ready to push the board to launch new programs and new approaches to engage alumni around the world. After all, global networking was my expertise.

By 2008, my eagerness to kick start the board led me to risk jumping the customary line of board succession. I ran for president based on my entrepreneurial resume—and narrowly lost to the person who had been in line for the job through the custom of having served first as the board's clerk. At that point, after a brash presidential bid and a humbling loss, a few of my colleagues in the alumni association assumed that I would pack up my Babson mementoes and vanish.

That was a misreading of my character and that's why I told you the stories about Roger Babson. He never seems to have held a grudge, even when one of his ideas flopped or backfired. So, yes, I was styling myself as an angelic troublemaker in the model of Roger Babson, trying to stir the board to new levels of outreach—but, also like Babson, everything I was pushing was aimed at the greater good. Just as Babson had done after his rock-carving dream turned to disappointment, I was ready to go right back to serving the community and mending relationships.

"That surprised all of us," said Anne Heller, who is considered royalty among Babson alumni. In 1970, she was the first woman graduate from our college, a pioneering role which she followed with a successful career in business. Then, in the late 1980s, she was recruited to help develop Babson's outreach among alumni. That staff assignment grew until she was named director of alumni relations and became a chief architect in merging the independent nonprofit under the college's supervision. Through Patrick, I was soon working with Anne.

"We didn't know a lot about you, at first," Anne said. "We knew you'd been active out in California in a largely independent way. We knew you'd been involved with startups, so it was natural to ask for your help. We invited you onto the board. Then, you wound up running for president when it wasn't your turn. I was very concerned about that; and I honestly wasn't in your corner when you ran. I thought you had a lot of ego tied up in what you were doing. When you suffered a really tough defeat, I figured that you'd either just leave—or, worse, you'd gather forces in opposition to the new leadership and become this ongoing thorn in our sides. But you didn't do either of those things. I had not understood how deeply you felt about Babson and about the value of giving back."

"What changed your mind?" I asked.

"It was a simple thing," she said. "We talked after your defeat and you said to me in all sincerity: 'Anne, what would you like me to do now?' You honestly wanted to serve in some other way. That was music to my ears! That's the moment we started to become friends. I learned that I could turn to you for important things, even if it was just to seek some private counsel about something we were planning. Every question I asked you, you tried your best to answer. Every task I assigned you, you accepted and did a great job. So, I wound up giving you the toughest jobs."

"I know! Like rewriting the bylaws!" I said and we both chuckled.

"Ohhh, the bylaws. Right. You took that thankless assignment. And, like everything else, you did it very well."

"When you asked, I could tell you were thinking I would refuse, but it was a job that no one else was eager to take. We needed those new bylaws to unlock the association's growth. It had to be done, even though it certainly was no fun."

"You didn't complain. You did a great job. I was happy."

"We should make it clear that I didn't do the bylaws alone," I said. "Among all the other people involved in the process, I certainly relied on you a lot, Anne. At that point, you were coaching me in several important ways. For instance, you told me I should wait and run for the clerk's office in the next elections, then serve as clerk, do a good job in that role, and move up to the presidency that way."

"You took my advice. You waited. You did it."

"Along the way, I had lots of time to talk over some of my own plans with you. I admit that I had my deficits from the board's perspective. First of all, I was an outside activist, because I didn't even live in the region—and I always was eager to push the association to tackle next-level projects. In the end, though, I wound up as the only alumni president to be elected to two consecutive terms, so people must have come around to seeing that my motives were pure."

"They did and that's why I agreed to delay my own retirement from Babson. I stayed on for your second term."

"We both were determined to change how the association did business," I said. "The goal was to find projects that would give the alumni association standing and credibility and would spark growth. Even if some ideas flopped along the way, we would just put a Band-Aid on our scraped knees and get back in the game. That's a very Babson way of doing things."

"I loved those years. We became a force multiplier on campus."

I basically flipped the way the alumni association did business. Before, we were mainly the keepers of campus traditions and managed long-established customs like volunteering at class reunions. Under my leadership, the alumni board became more entrepreneurial for and on behalf of our alums worldwide. We added value to the campus departments in a wide variety of ways, like agreeing to sponsor some new annual events that gave us a bigger footprint and brand. We pushed the alumni association to grow, to draw more alumni toward making annual donations to Babson and in partnership with the alumni office more alumni clubs were started around the world. We raised funds. We got people engaged across social media. We welcomed new students. We supported athletics. The annual reports from those years show steeply rising lines on a whole range of alumni engagement and participation metrics.

This was possible, in part, because the role of Babson alumni board president was an opportunity to interact with the college's leadership at all levels. The board president also was appointed to the college's board of trustees—yet another huge job but also a valuable window into how the nation's No. 1 school for entrepreneurship runs. It was an honor to serve as a trustee for four years during tremendous growth on campus from new buildings and record-breaking fundraising.

I was reelected in 2016, the same year as my colon cancer diagnosis, but there was so much work to be done that I was not about to step down. I just kept going, even when that meant I was slumped on my back somewhere, summoning what strength I could still muster to conduct alumni business online and via my phone.

"Oh my Gosh! I worried about you so much!" Anne said. "There were periods when we were talking by phone almost every day. After your diagnosis, I would start those calls by asking, 'Where are you, Howard?' And sometimes I got silence. Do you remember that?"

"Yeah, the silence usually was because I was driving—talking hands free, of course—but I didn't want to admit that I was driving."

"More than once, I would say: 'Howard, I think you're driving! You're driving, aren't you? Should you be driving right now at this stage of your treatment? Does the doctor know you're driving?'"

"Ohhh, I remember," I said. "And, as a last resort, you'd go for the big gun."

"I'd threaten to call Nancy! I knew your mother, had her number right there in my contacts and more than once threatened to call her."

"But we never lost a beat on alumni business during my cancer treatments and surgeries."

"No, somehow we never stopped. We were fully functioning as an association, although I don't know how we pulled that off with everything going on in your life."

I paused for a moment, then said, "Anne, I've been thinking about this phrase 'angelic troublemaker.' That phrase describes Roger Babson. He was so full of energy and his ideas sometimes were wonderful, but sometimes they were kind of crazy."

"Angelic troublemaker," Anne repeated the phrase, mulling it over. "I think that could describe you. There was no question that, when we first encountered you out in California, we were puzzled about you. Among the Babson staff, you were known as someone who was a lot to handle. You always were pushing a lot of ideas."

"I was an acquired taste, let's say."

"Yes, you hit the nail on the head. First, we realized you had so much energy that we just couldn't stop you. I certainly couldn't control you. What I could do was collaborate with you. And, I have to say: I was so impressed with the gentlemanly way you worked with others, even those who were pretty much opposed to what you wanted to do. I never sensed you had an underlying selfish agenda. You really were interested in what was best for all of us and the college. If an idea didn't work out, well, you moved on to the next idea."

"That's the entrepreneurial spirit as Babson taught it," I said. "That's how I learned to do it."

"One of your lines that I'll never forget was: 'OK, then, let's just move on.' Without anger, but very firm. You used that a number of times in key situations through those years. And, I have to admit, Howard, that kind of calm commitment to carrying on—even in the face of a very frustrating problem or person—was foreign to me. I'm Irish, so I know how to hold onto a good *mad* for a long time. But it's not in your DNA to react like that. And I think that says a lot about your adaptability in beating cancer not just once, but twice."

"There's nothing to be gained by grudges," I said. "Nothing to be gained by obsessing about setbacks. You just move on each and every day."

"I certainly agree, but that's a very hard lesson to learn," Anne said. "It's one reason we worked well together."

"That—and your capacity for putting up with my occasional troublemaking."

"Let's call it eccentricity," she said. "We were able to become good partners because I've got a high tolerance for eccentricity—if someone can really deliver, that is. You definitely were powerful on the delivery," Anne said, then paused and laughed. "You definitely were eccentric! Like those thousands of sunglasses you had made up and brought to campus for Back to Babson Homecoming reunions? When I got a glimpse of those sunglasses at that big alumni meeting, my first reaction was: Oh my God! He is so crazy! Totally crazy!"

"Yeah, but you wore the glasses with me."

"Well, once I got over my surprise, it really turned out to be heartwarming. Now, after that morning, who can forget the sunglasses? Who can forget: 'Babson, you're shining brightly!' It's moments like that, Howard, that made me start to think of us as Butch and Sundance. Sometimes we'd win. And sometimes we'd jump off a cliff together."

"Or put on shiny sunglasses."

Like Roger Babson, I wanted to mark the dawn of this new era of growth in an unforgettably visual way. I had just been elected and came to the Homecoming 2014 conference bursting with ideas. This was an auspicious moment in other ways, as well. My first official acts included an introduction to the alumni of the new Babson President Kerry Murphy Healey, the first woman ever to lead our college. Her delivery of the annual state-of-the-college address would be the highlight of our gathering. A new dawn was spreading across campus. As we approached our centennial just a few years down the line, we already were shining.

So, like Roger before me, I had a vision and I acted without asking for anyone's permission. I designed and ordered 1,000 reflective sunglasses. I chose white frames stamped with a green: "BABSON ALUMNI ASSOCIATION." Each pair came in a white cloth carrying case that bore the same slogan—plus a green logo of Roger Babson's giant revolving globe on one corner of a lens.

We held our Homecoming gatherings on Saturday mornings, each year, in the big amphitheater inside Babson Executive Conference Center and Hotel. As people arrived, I was in the lobby handing out the cloth cases, greeting old friends and enjoying the smiles as people unfolded their glasses.

"Put them in your pocket for now," I said to everyone. "There's a cue in the program."

When the annual meeting was called to order, we moved swiftly through our business agenda. I wanted to give our new president plenty of time to talk. Then, just before her address, I rose and said, "OK, now put on the glasses."

Everyone did.

As I introduced our new president, I held my hands wide like a maestro, offering the concerted attention of the alumni association to our new leader. As the auditorium's house lights gleamed a warm gold glow off all that reflective glass, I declared, "Babson, you're shining brightly today!"

Throughout the Homecoming weekend, those glasses were the hottest items on campus. Only the alumni got them, at first, but soon everyone seemed to be sporting a pair. I returned home with just a handful left—and that was only because I was determined to keep at least a few of those mementos.

From there, working shoulder to shoulder with Anne Heller, we spent the next couple of years gradually changing expectations among longtime board members about what such an organization could dare to do. While we hit a few stone walls, Anne and I overcame the opposition by meeting any temporary defeat with new ideas. Pretty soon, even if you were resistant to change, it became easier to let us try various proposals than to see them multiply.

One of the board members who became a dear friend is Sharlene Sones. She graduated in 1986 and has had a long career in marketing and branding. I had first worked with her briefly when I was looking for input on the launch of CircleBuilder and was introduced to Sharlene by another Babson friend, Michael Weissman. He thought she might have a valuable perspective on CircleBuilder because, at that time, she had just finished marketing work for an early virtual-world technology with a religious theme. As a former marketing director for a Christian record label in Nashville, she understood media marketing in religious communities and was one of the influential people who urged us to launch our new company. Later, I nominated her and others including my own roommate, Greg Tufankjian, to serve on Babson's alumni association board (BAA).

"Like you, Howard, I joined the board because I was grateful for Babson's impact on my career and wanted to give back," Sharlene said as I talked with her for this book. "I started out as the first person to earn a four-year college degree in my family and ended up working in what I can only describe as my own personal dream jobs in the sports industry.

"And again like you, Howard, I had relied on that Babson network throughout my career. Around Babson, we like to say: Your network is your net worth. That concept is engrained in everyone connected with the college to the point that you actually have to be careful if you ask a friend from Babson about some new project you're considering. You have to be careful, because you're going to get answers! So many answers! Did you talk to this person? Have you done this? Have you reached out this way? Have you—The helpful tips just keep flowing. And here's what I've found is unique about the best in Babson networking. There's no chit system."

"That's right," I said. "There's no scorekeeping. Anne Heller talked about how impressed she is when she finds Babson alumni who truly take that to heart. It's about the overall good. Not everyone learns that lesson, to be honest."

"No, but it's in our Babson DNA. We're asked to sincerely believe that working together produces more than any one of us could accomplish. It's about the entire community succeeding. Anne Heller was right to highlight that. It's a rare enough commodity in the business world. It's a powerful idea. If we truly believe that, then we can open ourselves to learning from each other. And, Howard, I learned a lot from you as the new board president. Did you know I took some of your lessons and applied them directly to a nonprofit board that I was asked to lead?"

"You applied lessons I taught you? I don't remember listing a bunch of principles."

"It's the way you did things. We saw what worked. We caught the lessons." In fact, Sharlene actually wrote a column about five lessons she had applied in her own leadership. So, to close this Babson chapter, here is Sharlene's perspective on the principles we shared in those years when I led the alumni board. I laughed when she sent it to me because of the way she headlined the column:

Lessons on Running a Board of Directors

"What would HB (Howard) do?"

By SHARLENE SONES

Have you ever been part of a board that could have been more effective? Where meetings were more about bureaucracy than meaningful impact? Have you ever reflected on your team's "what if's" and "if only's"? If so, here are five guidelines that contributed to Howard Brown's success in leading the Babson Alumni Association board of directors. They are lessons that you can apply, no matter what kind of team you are leading.

I recently was asked to serve as president for a nonprofit board of Cape Cod-area sporting enthusiasts. We were a small organization with a small budget, very big needs and few processes for development in place. Among my colleagues, though, we had lots of independent thinking and plenty of heart. Contemplating the job, I wondered if I would be up to the task. That's when a question popped into my mind: "What would HB do?" I had been a part of the Babson Alumni Association board for a decade with a front row seat to how Howard reinvigorated the group to embrace exciting new ideas. Thinking about his example led me to consider what I could borrow from his approach that made fast progress from the start of his first term.

The following five considerations helped me do just that— and I believe can serve anyone leading a board or any other team toward inspired goals.

Show Up Prepared.

With a new board that was open to fresh ideas, how could I inspire a culture focused on achieving results, while feeling good about our work together? I leaned back on my experience as part of the alumni board while Howard was at the helm. The first thing I appreciated was the tone he set by the way he showed up and engaged with everyone. Right out of the gates, he took great care in preparation.

Board meetings suddenly had energy and momentum. Agendas were clear. Learning was carefully incorporated. A new discipline and focus kept the board on task, provided opportunities for meaningful dialogue and exploration of ideas. Gone were meetings that bogged down in bureaucracy. In their place were considered, thoughtful and productive gatherings where members contributed and received value in equal measure. That upfront care before any meeting opened made the most of everyone's valued time together. Howard's consistent preparation and engaging presence also set the tone for the way everyone should approach their own assignments. Our work was important. Everyone's input was needed. We wasted no time.

Illuminate a Positive Path Forward.

So, first, I committed myself to being buttoned up and disciplined as I approached each meeting, then actively focusing on the participation of each board member during our gatherings. But how do you get a team to catch that vision and do likewise? How can you draw a team toward a common goal and vision? Howard's arrival at his first alumni meeting with his "Shining Brightly!" sunglasses was a signal that we all had become part of a campaign that he was inviting us to embrace. Those glasses represented a future so bright that we would have to wear shades! The moment we all put on those sunglasses, we were taking a committed first step on board—whether we liked it or not.

To be honest, the moment Howard invited us to raise those sunglasses, I didn't like it! The sunglasses felt forced on us—and a little silly. Then, I was astonished that the gimmick worked. Those little glasses that might have cost a few bucks a pair became a call to action none of us forgot for a new and higher standard of working together.

Howard did not stop with the glasses. Soon, I was amused to find that his email signature was "With Babson Pride and Spirit." At first, I thought: Over the top! Then, it grew on everyone, including me. Pretty soon we felt more pride. Those ideas from the glasses to the email sign offs were simple and clear encouragements to all of the alumni he reached.

I never developed a signature item as clever as the sunglasses, but I took to heart the need to share a common theme. Throughout my term as a board president, my nonprofit supporters always knew what theme we shared—often focused on our bright, shiny potential.

Bond through Vulnerability.

I'll say it again: I will never forget that moment of feeling silly when Howard ordered us to raise those glasses. But what it taught me was how potent a little dose of silliness can be in building bonds. Howard's sincerity was critical to pulling off that stunt. He really believed in his message. It was his ability to lighten it up and to encourage us to laugh at ourselves a little bit that convinced us that we could pitch in with just as much enthusiasm. He knew what he was doing. His orchestration of that moment of shared vulnerability—at the very low stakes of simply wearing a pair of plastic glasses—united us for that instant.

The long-term result of these efforts was that Howard kept inviting everyone to claim the permission to try something new. To dream. To ideate. To give things a go and be unafraid of things not working out. He consistently came to the table with new ideas and initiatives. Some worked. Some didn't. But our goal was not to count failures or blame each other. Our goal was to move forward together.

Then, in his second term, Howard embodied that vulnerability in his personal life. Howard shared highs and lows in his struggle with cancer. By his own example, he reminded us that we had pledged to show up with all of our available energy. That's what he did, even when he was struggling. At the end of the day, he reminded us that the board was really a team of people—each one of us trying to navigate our lives with our own struggles, trials and triumphs.

Nurture the Individual.

"We can't do this alone." "This is a team sport." "We need each other." All of these were among Howard's go-to encouragements—and you have probably heard all of them countless times. The key to Howard's use of these lines was: He actually believes and lives them. Crucial to Howard's knack for empowering people is the fact that he could see the value, the special skills and knowledge in each board member. We weren't invisible members of a team—the team only worked because of each unique person's talents. The proof that he was listening was his willingness to let each of us surface our own ideas and actually run with them.

Beyond board business, he surprised many of us by taking time to check in with us as individuals. To listen and nurture relationships. To truly show how much he cared and was willing to help each of us if he could. Our meetings took on a new personality. Each gathering ended with time reserved for "good and welfare" celebrations of baby births, family and career milestones and important achievements.

Celebrate Our Wins.

At the end of the day, people want to be a part of something that has real purpose in the world. In the simplest terms: We want to be part of a team that feels like we are winning more than we are losing. Howard understood that results and metrics matter, consistently reinforcing them and measuring progress along the way. Seeing the fruits of our own labor energized us to keep forging ahead.

Howard made it a point to celebrate the successes and acknowledge the effort of board members in doing so. He sang the praises of others, often surprising people as he highlighted the value of their work. He was generous when praise was warranted. My favorite example was the creation of an award Howard called "The Annie Award," named in honor of Anne Heller's example as a mentor to all of us. What a small thing it was to create and bestow those little awards—yet how memorable it was to stand briefly in that spotlight among our peers and feel that we had earned an award invoking Anne's example for excellence.

In my own experience now, I can tell you: These five principles are invaluable. I knew they would work because I saw them in action when Howard was head of the alumni board. As I am now sitting at the helm of my own regional board, I try to embody every one of these values as facilitator, visionary, encourager and overall as a leader who knows how to step out of the way and enable people to run with their best ideas. We're all better for it.

Now, I know that my goal at the helm is to remain as good as my words. My board is eager to do more.

Perhaps it's time to order a box of sunglasses and share Howard's call to shine.

Before you order your own sunglasses, and I'll share a merchandise link below, I need to add to Sharlene's gracious summary that none of this important and creative work would have been possible without a huge team of equally committed professionals both on the Babson staff and among the volunteer members of the alumni board. As I was finishing this book, the Back to Babson homecoming in the autumn of 2021 featured green T-shirts that proclaimed: "No. 1 for Entrepreneurship 25 consecutive times," referring to the *U.S. News* rankings. Together, our entire past and present faculty, staff and alumni has played a role in that success story among our more than 42,000 graduates in 127 countries around the world. Jason Rueben, Amy Reich-Weil, David Pina, Laticia Stallworth, Mikki Wosencroft, Terri Monjar, Anne Hastings, Priscilla Christie, Terri Radcliffe, Jeremy Hill, Russel Kelner, Karl Ferguson, Susan Drew-Brouillette, William Nelson, Wilma Miranda, Alvaro Peña Ospina, Rick Loewenstein and so many others inspired my Babson pride and spirit!

I need to recognize the other alumni association presidents who have inspired me with their dedication and hard work on behalf of the alumni and the college: Patrick McGonagle, Steve Gaklis, Ann-Marie Copland, Jacqueline Giordano-Bedard, Marco Gargurevich, Alexandra Piccirilli and Patrick Baird. Success is built on the shoulders, experience and work of others. I benefitted in countless ways.

Winning teams get it done repeatedly. Babson's staff has formed truly outstanding volunteer-professional partnerships. Thanks to Edward Chiu, Gerri Randlett, Effie Parpos-Marthinsen, Anne Heller, Carol Hacker, Anjali Wali, Grace Carew, Christy Cisneros-Lagos, Aine McAlister, Serghino Rene, Peter Latvis, Paula Weafer, Diana Prescott-Zais, Dara Dalmata, Sandra Anthoine, Ben Chevrette, Sharon Mintz, Bonnie Lester, Julie Snow, Erin Crowley-Martinovich, Judy Curley, Emily Groccia, Lola Norman-Salako, Courtney Minden, Susan Duffy, Sarah Sykora, Kerry Solerno, Debi Kleiman, Lawrence Ward, Ian Lapp, Will Lamb, Jonathan Moll, Michael Layish, Katherine Craven-Kryzanski, Kelly Lynch, George Recck, Amir Reza, Annette Robinson, Michael Chmura, Woody Lappen, the late Ellen Solomita—and so many more.

My service as a Babson trustee was a high honor that I will always cherish. The dedication, passion and excellence that I was privileged to be part of for four years gave me a lifetime of learning, mentorship, friendship and experiences with the "best of the best," including Robert Weissman, Governor

Craig Benson, Joseph Winn, Marla Capozzi, Jeffery Perry, Deborah De Santis, Amanda Strong, Bruce Herring, Eric Johnson, Fred Kiang, Jeffrey McLane, Kenneth Romanzi, Rick Renwick, Len Green, Martha Vorlicek, Richard Snyder, Warren Cross, Brett Gordon, James Rullo, Timothy DeMello, Shatiek Gatlin, Paul Chisholm, Richeleau Dennis, Thomas Gilbane, Carmela Kleijten, David Lamere, Narender Manoj Madnani, and Babson College presidents during my terms: Leonard Schlesinger, Brian Barefoot, Kerry Murphy Healey and Stephen Spinelli.

I am grateful for all the wisdom, kindness and friendship you have bestowed upon me and my family.

Finally, I have to give a shout out to all the Babson students and alums from Michigan and Babson Athletics: I love ya! Let's Go Beavers! Defend the Dam!

Shining Brightly

Babson College changed the trajectory of my life. Thank you, Marilyn Snyder, for seeing that potential in me. For the launch of this book, I ordered more of those reflective sunglasses, this time with "Shining Brightly" on the frame. If you would like a pair, visit the book's website at ShiningBrightly.com.

Lastly, please consider learning more about a small college outside of Boston, Massachusetts in the town of Wellesley that changes the world for good everyday:

+ **Babson College** — Babson.edu

+ **Babson College Alumni Network** — Babson.edu/alumni/

+ **Babson leadership** — Babson.edu/about/presidents-office/leadership-and-governance/

+ **Entrepreneurship of All Kinds** — Babson.edu/about/at-a-glance/entrepreneurship-of-all-kinds/

+ **#1 for Entrepreneurship** — Babson.edu/about/at-a-glance/rankings/

+ **Babson World Globe** — Babson.edu/glavin-office-of-international-education/kerry-murphy-healey-park/

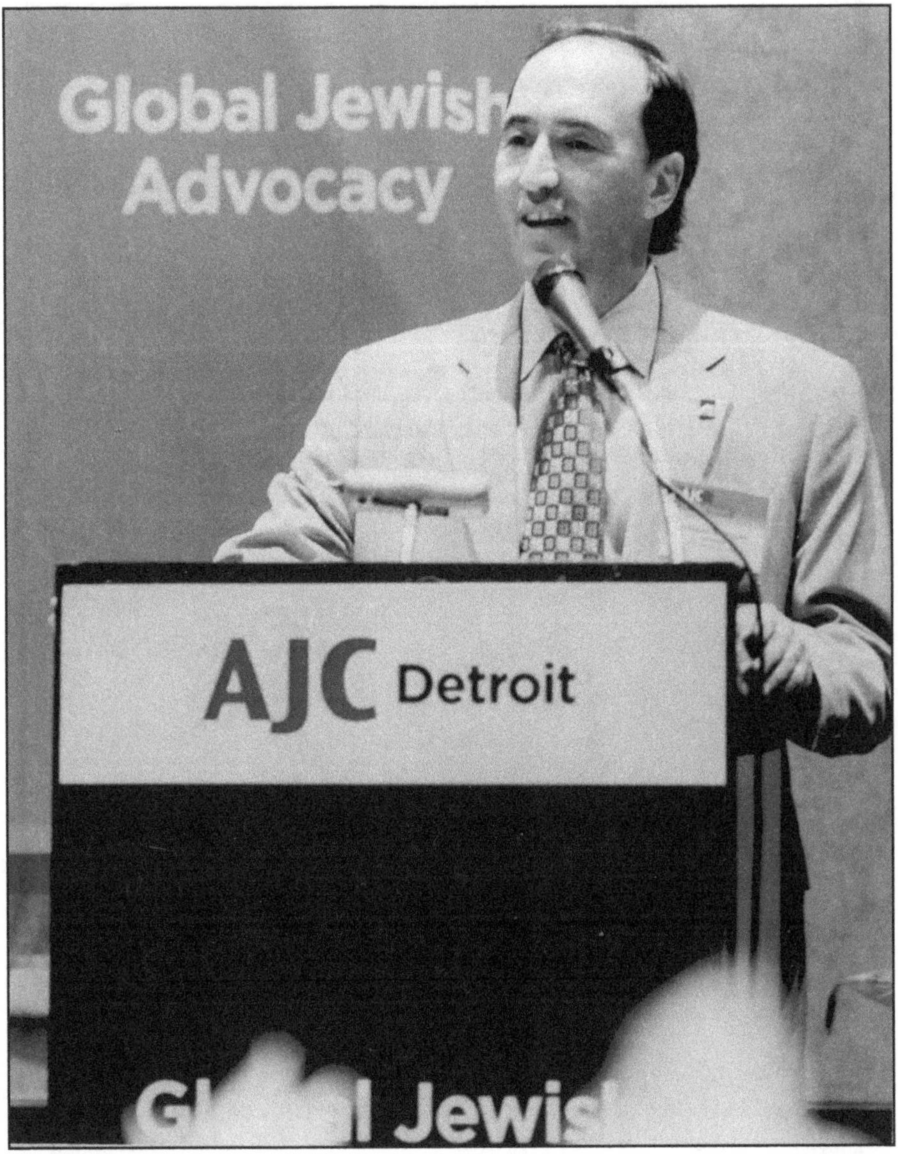
Global Jewish
Advocacy
AJC Detroit

PERSON OF THE WEEK

I'm known for my colorful public presentations—but I have accomplished more with whispers in conversations that were never reported to another soul. One of my whispering mentors is Dr. Yahya Basha, who is an accomplished peacemaker behind the scenes. When WXYZ-TV in Detroit honored me as a "Person of the Week" in November 2017, I made sure to include him as my mentor. To show the ongoing influence of mentors, I also included the then-current JCRC-AJC President Alicia Chandler, who I mentored as a past president of AJC. Like Dr. Basha, who is Muslim, I care deeply about repairing the world. I'm Jewish. I care about Israel. But I know that peace is only possible by reaching out to interfaith partners.

17

Whispering in a Deafening World

"Have you got a minute for me?"

Not a day passes when I don't get some form of that question from people I care about via text, email, phone and social media messaging. Before the pandemic, these friends might have gently laid a hand on my arm in the midst of a busy day to ask that question. That's because they know I always try to respond. Throughout my entire career in high-profile leadership roles, my most important work often was behind the scenes and never shared with others.

People certainly know I can pull off high-powered speaking presentations when they are needed. My doctors know that I can be a collaborative and driving advocate for my health care. On the basketball court, my teammates know that trash talking is a part of my game. But I have accomplished more with whispers in conversations that were never reported to another soul than with outspoken proclamations. This should not be surprising. In fact, it's the consensus in the best leadership training courses that success depends on authentic relationships that are built on honesty, hospitality, empathy and humility. All are hallmarks of whisperers. For every flashy program I've engineered over the years, there are a thousand quiet conversations. While I remain a colorful promoter of Babson at certain times of the year, my most valuable work for the college now is among the students I mentor, the private consultations and my quiet encouragement of ongoing programs. I am both a Babson cheerleader—and whisperer.

When you whisper, people tend to lean in and listen.

I have become a whisperer among entrepreneurs, as well—and they whisper back. Even as I was working on this book, I helped old friends Bob and Ginger Penfil navigate the complex process of filing a U.S. patent for a new kind of home-safety device to prevent flooding. I partnered with another colleague, Cristian Valencia, in an innovative approach to COVID prevention by quickly sanitizing people and products as they pass through the entrances to buildings. And there are many others—including Roy Kessel with his nonprofit the Sports Philanthropy Network, Larry Nusbaum discussing entrepreneurship every week, Jon and Brett Rappaport, David Hawk and Bradley Gibbons, Mark Wright, Eugene Barlaz, Stuart Kay and my brother-in-law Larry Kirshner—who I am talking with on a weekly basis about everything from inventions to programs that provide humanitarian aid in global hot spots.

I am a whisperer among cancer patients. I learned through the online private Facebook colorectal communities that the single most important response when someone is going through a cancer crisis is to pick up the phone—whatever the hour it rings. In the depths of my own stage IV struggle, Colontown friends more than once talked me through dark moments in the wee hours of the morning. That's why I always try to answer the opening question in this chapter with "Yes," no matter what time of day or night friends may call about their struggles.

I am also a whisperer and avid listener among religious leaders trying to form interfaith bonds that encourage world peace. I have never forgotten my dream of forming a circle as big as the whole world. I am a realist about the dangers that loom among extremist groups around the world, but I am willing to pick up the phone anytime to help longtime colleagues in interfaith work. Sometimes, especially in cases of refugees or hate crimes, a day's delay in intervention can miss crucial opportunities, deepen trauma and even risk lives.

I learned that lesson from my own mentor in global interfaith relations: Dr. Yahya Basha, a name that you almost certainly have never seen in news stories. Even though he is one of the most influential peacemakers in Michigan, his photograph rarely appears in news stories and his name almost never appears in headlines. When Basha's name does show up in occasional news reports, it's often in the second half of the story as background. One example toward the end of a news report explained: "During his visit, the Secretary also held private meetings with community leaders, including Dr. Yahya Basha." Another news report shared the concerns of refugee families from the Middle East, then closed with: "The refugees spoke to reporters in the offices of Dr. Yahya

Basha who had gathered them to voice their concerns." From the conclusion of yet another story: "The event was co-sponsored by Dr. Yahya Basha, who is one of more than 10,000 Syrian Americans in Michigan."

Basha was the oldest of 11 children, born in Syria. He earned his medical degree in Syria before migrating to the United States in 1972, where he soon was leading radiology teams at medical centers in southeast Michigan. Because he is a lifelong entrepreneur like me, he eventually went independent to provide his services to any doctor or medical center in the region. His Basha Diagnostics company now employs dozens of radiologists working at multiple sites. From that financial base as a successful businessman, Basha then devoted himself to peacemaking and human rights on behalf of Middle Eastern communities. Over the years, he became known for his close-mouthed style and wound up as a private consultant to several Democratic and Republican administrations in Washington, D.C. He always has worked closely with the FBI and other federal agencies, as well. He devoted a great deal of his financial resources to directly helping refugees—and is proud of his role in bringing more than 100 members of his extended family to this country.

"If I am alone, I am weak," he likes to say. "If I am part of a community, then we all can work together to improve humanity, starting with the people closest to you: your family, neighbors, colleagues and then all those who share your spirit for cooperation and peace."

When Lisa and I first arrived in Michigan in 2005, both of us were known for our work with Jewish boards and agencies, so we immediately were invited to serve with several Metro Detroit groups. Given her professional expertise, Lisa joined the board of Jewish Family Services. I agreed to take a seat on the overall Jewish Federation board of governors.

What we did not realize was that we were landing in southeast Michigan on the eve of a host of innovative interfaith projects that soon would become national models for cooperation across religious boundaries. Peace activist Brenda Rosenberg already was crossing over from her long career in the fashion industry to launch a high-profile series of programs called *Reuniting the Children of Abraham*. The concept was based on the sacred history Jews, Christians and Muslims all share in revering the ancient patriarch. As we were moving into our Michigan home, Brenda already was pulling together university scholars, students, religious leaders and arts professionals in a collaboration that created a full-length stage play written and performed by students from all three Abrahamic traditions. Eventually, the CBS network produced a special broadcast of the play—and the concept evolved into two books as well as a *Children of Abraham* spin-off project with the Girl Scouts that continues to expand. The debut of the original play in 2006 also sparked the launch of WISDOM, a coalition of women from eight different religious backgrounds that also has sparked national headlines. WISDOM has presented its trademark program, Five Women, Five Journeys, in many venues. Then, that group spun off its expertise in fostering groundbreaking friendships into another book called *Friendship & Faith* that has been discussed by groups coast to coast. Some of those pioneers now are supporting other innovative projects, including Religious Diversity Journeys, a first-of-its-kind curriculum for thousands of seventh-grade students in public middle schools. Southeast Michigan now is home to some of the leading experts in interfaith relationships. Some of them also serve as consultants for the Michigan State University School of Journalism's series of more than a dozen books about religious and ethnic diversity. The sheer number of interfaith innovations produced in the Motor City is astonishing.

Lisa and I were settling into our new home before the full scope of that creativity had emerged publicly. Scott Eisenberg, a neighbor who lived just down the street from us, urged me to get involved with the American Jewish Committee (AJC). Of course, I knew that the AJC was one of the oldest of the Jewish advocacy groups, started in 1906 and famous for its long history of protecting civil rights in the U.S. and promoting human rights around the world.

At first, I protested. "Scott, I'm knee deep in work right now. I'm trying to grow my startup CircleBuilder. And Lisa and I already are serving in the community. I can't take one more role."

He brushed off my hesitancy. "Given the scope of your work, Howard, you would find AJC absolutely fascinating," Scott said—keeping after me until I finally agreed to at least look into his recommendation. I found immediately that he was right. Today in Michigan, AJC champions many forms of outreach and community building—as well as partnerships between Jews and the largest community of Muslim and Christian Arabs outside of the Middle East. So, I finally accepted Scott's invitation to nominate me for the regional AJC board.

I landed on that AJC board just as Brenda and a handful of other interfaith activists were beginning to cause a stir with their entirely new ways of connecting communities. There had never been an interfaith theatrical production like *Children of Abraham*. Fresh interfaith ideas were bubbling up in southeast Michigan and flowing coast to coast. In the Jewish community, a lot of that work connected with the AJC's agenda.

I began to ask around: "Where is all this new stuff coming from? The AJC isn't starting it. We're reacting to it." And I quickly learned that a lot of the heavy lifting was shouldered by activists, like Brenda, who accomplished as much work behind the scenes as they did in their high-profile public programs. As I raised questions at AJC board meetings, Brenda and her close friend, now deceased, Sheri Schiff, immediately tugged on both of my arms to join them in this quieter side of networking.

"I realized immediately that we could work with you, Howard, because you are an entrepreneur," Brenda told me as we talked about these forays aimed at building new relationships. "You understand that nothing is accomplished without taking risks."

I said, "For readers of my book, I think we have to explain this: When you and Sheri and I and the WISDOM women all began making new Muslim friends, that was considered a risk in the Jewish community."

"Oh yes, of course. Some people flat out told us not to do what we were doing. Some people thought we were crazy, so they just let us do what we wanted to do," Brenda said.

"Reactions to what we were doing ranged from support and curiosity to some hostility," I said. "Remember that, when I moved to Michigan in 2005 and asked Jewish friends what they knew about the Muslim community in Dearborn, I got the impression that it was a foreign land on our doorstep. My own first instinct was to accept your invitations. I was eager to go where you were leading me. It did feel like we were opening up a foreign land to the Jewish community—and finding new friends as we traveled together."

"That's right. And the key to that, Howard, is that you understand relational equity—real, authentic relationships that go both ways," Brenda said. "That's a big part of this work we are doing. I think that broader vision is natural for us because of our years in the business world. I was traveling around the world marketing fashion. You were doing the same thing marketing your companies. We both know that our best work requires us to take risks—and form real partnerships. We have to cross these seemingly impossible gaps. Sometimes that's so difficult that I describe it as trying to move gigantic tectonic plates—like whole continents! In fact, that's the title of one of my books, *Tectonic Leadership*."

"What you're describing is the entrepreneurial life. We are not just taking risks for the thrill of it," I said. "We're reaching out because we actually want to make the whole world a better place for everyone. We can't do that without building friendships among our neighbors. We need to get to know each other, even if it feels like the next community is foreign to us. When we do risk that, we often discover that we already share more than we realize. And you're right, Brenda: The goal is relational equity—sharing equally." Then, I smiled at her and added, "Brenda, you just mentioned your title, so let me add the title of the big report that was a culmination of a lot of our work with the AJC: *A Shared Future.*"

"That opened a lot of eyes," she said. "It takes a lot of time, a lot of relationship building and a lot of different kinds of programs and shared experiences to build a better world. If one idea doesn't work, then we try another idea."

"Agreed. It's a marathon, not a sprint," I said. "I had worked all around the world before I moved to Detroit yet there was so much that I didn't understand about this region. For example, I had no idea there were Iraqi Christians who called themselves Chaldeans and they represented another huge community with ties to the Middle East, living in yet another area of Metro Detroit. Today, I play basketball all the time with Chaldean friends—and I have had business partnerships with Chaldean friends, too. But when I first got to Michigan? I don't think I had ever heard the word Chaldean."

"It can be confusing. There are so many different groups of Christians and Muslims with ties to the Middle East—and so many Muslims with no connections to the Middle East!" Brenda said. "The whole *Children of Abraham* project came from an idea at a casual lunch I had with an African American Muslim friend, Imam Abdullah El-Amin."

"You introduced me to all these men and women who were out there breaking the old molds: El-Amin and other imams, Victor and Shahina Begg, Saeed Khan and Dr. Basha and Gail Katz, Steve Spreitzer, Bob Bruttell and—oh, the list could fill a whole chapter."

"Yes, I did," she said, smiling. "That's what I do. I listen to people and I introduce people. El-Amin's suggestion really sparked all my work on *Children of Abraham.* Then, Victor's wife Shahina and their whole family were big supporters of creating the play. Then, Shahina became a co-founder of WISDOM. We all became friends empowering each other to create new things that had never existed before."

"You know that my book is called *Shining Brightly.* And, Brenda, I have to say that has always been one of your keys to success."

"I shine! I shine!" she laughed. "Well, I try to!"

"The first thing I noticed about you during our adventures together was: Everybody loves Brenda!"

Now, she laughed long and hard. "Of course! And now everybody loves Howard, too! We both love working with other people, right? So that love we feel shows naturally in this infectious way. People respond to that."

"They do! But I have to admit that I felt a little bit like window dressing at some of the first events you dragged me into attending," I said. "We all know that the culture in the Muslim world still tends to be pretty male dominated. Some parts of the Jewish world are male dominated, too, but the Muslim community still has more events where it's pretty much all men sitting up front in the prominent seats. So, I caught on right away why you and Sheri wanted me to go with you. Even though you were doing the heavy lifting, you and Sheri were often prevented from sitting at the head tables, because those seats still were all reserved for men. With me along, you finally had a Jewish face on the dais."

"You were a token male!" she teased. "Let's be honest: I broke through on my own by sheer force of will. I was invited to speak at good number of Muslim gatherings. But, yes, when you eventually became president of AJC Detroit board of directors, you really did embody a symbol of serious Jewish commitment to crossing these chasms and the fact that you were a man didn't hurt."

"Some of our work eventually was sanctioned by AJC, but a whole lot of what we did wasn't sanctioned. We did it on our own as individuals."

"That's right. Whatever your official status was, you were one of the few Jewish leaders willing to even meet some of the Muslim leaders. Then, the relationships we built led to lots of good things and some of those did become official AJC programs. Because you were willing to back me up—unofficially or officially—I was able to go even deeper into the Muslim community. Friends we made back in those first visits now are some of the biggest supporters of where we're taking *Children of Abraham* today. I wouldn't be working now with the Girl Scouts on proposals to build a new interfaith program for girls without support from Dearborn Girl Scouts who are Muslim and their families!"

"That's why, when you called, I always picked up the phone—even though sometimes I have to admit that I almost wished I hadn't answered," I said, teasing her again.

"Be honest! You *had* to answer," Brenda said. "We needed you. To build a community, we all have to put in the time and energy and resources. You *had* to show up. That's the whole point of this. We're not just making a public show of caring—we really care!"

"Well, that brings this conversation full circle and connects back to your first introducing me to Dr. Basha," I said. "He's the real master of making time to help other people. And what amazes me is: He does almost all of his work outside the public eye. He's an interfaith whisperer."

"I like that phrase: an interfaith whisperer!"

Very soon after I first met Brenda and Sheri through the AJC, I found myself on the standing list of invitations to dinners hosted by this Muslim Syrian American medical entrepreneur named Dr. Yahya Basha. For many years, he has scheduled, organized and paid for occasional evenings at local ethnic restaurants—orchestrating every detail right down to the seating charts. Our most important conversations always have been private over the phone or over coffee. At a Basha-hosted event, I would rarely spend time with him. Instead, I would find myself seated next to imams, community leaders, elected officials—and sometimes FBI agents or professionals from other government agencies whose portfolios included outreach into ethnic and religious communities. Within that first year, I quickly learned that most of the groundbreaking work we were doing was unfolding in what I consider whispers—conversations in twos and threes and fours that no one else would ever hear. In the business world, I had always known that private contacts were the key to entrepreneurial success. Basha certainly understood that in building his own chain of imaging-diagnostic clinics. What I learned through Basha's interfaith coaching was the power of these private interactions to bridge some of the world's deepest religious and ethnic chasms. I picked up that lesson from him right away—long before we were able to secure a grant to turn the truth of this principle into convincing, research-based data.

By 2013, our chapter in southeast Michigan already was becoming known throughout the international AJC network for daring to reach out and work with Muslim groups. That year I began a two-year term as president of the chapter—but, even before my term began, I had served as a strong supporter of all the background work to launch the *Shared Future* research project. My predecessor, AJC President Bryant Frank, negotiated with the Michigan Muslim Community Council Chair Dr. Muzammil Ahmed to jointly request a research grant supported by the Ravitz Foundation. This was a groundbreaking idea and many allies came aboard to help. The foundation finally agreed to fund a major research project studying everyday Jewish and Muslim life in our part of the country. The study was designed and conducted by the University of Michigan-Dearborn iLabs. As other allies from other universities and institutions came on board, the project led to an annual series of cross-cultural events.

The first big event, a daylong conference to present the results, featured two scholars: Wayne State University Professors Howard Lupovitch and Saeed Khan. All of us were anxious about what they might say and how they might interact.

As it turned out, "they were so similar and their level of intelligence, respectful disagreement and ability to have really challenging conversations framed in history was astounding," said Kari Alterman, regional director of AJC Detroit at that time. "Recognizing potential in the present and the future, their narratives were remarkable, leaving everyone inspired and informed."

What did we find?

We found that the vast majority of interfaith relationships did not revolve around grand-scale conferences or theatrical productions or annual community-wide worship services. Each and every day across our region, thousands of interfaith interactions already were unfolding.

Here is just a brief excerpt from the report:

> The study was based on a survey developed with iLabs, the University of Michigan-Dearborn's Center for Innovation Research, designed to examine the attitudes and experiences of members of the Jewish and Muslim communities. Between July and August 2013, 600 individuals completed the survey.

> The survey included seven questions asking respondents about their religious observances. Overall, respondents agreed that they observe the important holy days of their faith (89%), regularly apply the teachings of their faith in everyday life (77%) and observe the fast days (either Jewish fast days or the fast of Ramadan) (76%).

> Of 19 activities asked about in the survey, the top six most common that individuals had actually done were very similar for both communities. Overall, respondents say they: Had shopped at an establishment owned by a person from the other community (88%), had eaten with a person from the other community (78%), attended a religious service of a different faith (73%), had engaged in a discussion with a person from the other community about religion, culture, ideology and global events (72%), had interacted with a colleague at work from the other community (72%), and had friends from the other community (63%).

> The section asking about working on multi-faith initiatives included 10 potential program topics. Each of these topics had at least 57% of respondents agree they would be interested

in working on them. Overall, respondents say they are most interested in working on multi-faith initiatives related to: protecting women and children from violence (82%), education (76%), and distributing food to the homeless (74%).

Individuals who regularly apply their religious teachings and who are regularly influenced by their religion, regardless of community, are more interested in a wide range of activities and program possibilities to build a shared future.

Why was this report so influential? Two reasons. First, it opened eyes, including my own. I had not realized how wrong I had been to think of the predominantly Muslim area of Dearborn as a foreign land on our doorstep. In fact, we already were one community, sharing in each other's lives in countless ways every day.

Before the pandemic hit, I made a point of attending UNITY Banquets, the single biggest event each year sponsored by the Michigan Muslim Community Council. It's such an influential gathering that Michigan's gover-nor often shows up along with our U.S. senators. All three were there for the last banquet before COVID. As I was enjoying dinner, I saw a man making his way in my direction through the sea of white-draped banquet tables. A few minutes later, I felt a gentle hand on my shoulder. I turned and saw a bearded Arab American whose face I could not place.

"Howard, how are you doing?"

"Fine. Fine. And how are you?" I was trying desperately to recall his name—and failing.

He nodded and patted my shoulder as if reassuring himself that I was healthy. He said, "I'm fine. And I'm so glad to see you here looking so well."

"Thank you for coming over to ask about me." I was wracking my brain to place him, determined not to let him know I could not recall his name.

"My family's here with me tonight," he said, motioning to the far side of the huge hall.

"And are they well?" I asked, still without a clue to his identity.

"Oh, yes, thank you for asking."

Perhaps 60 seconds passed. We both were smiling, clasping hands. Then, he nodded and backed away, headed toward another table to greet friends.

That's when it hit me! That was Dr. Mohamed Al Sibae! *My* Dr. Al Sibae, my liver specialist when my liver was about to stop working. Oh, I felt terrible. I watched his progress back to his family, and this time I set out on the slow, weaving path among the other guests. As I approached his table, he smiled up at me.

"So this is your family?" I asked.

He was pleased to introduce them and I found an empty chair next to his wife so I could tell her, "Your husband was part of the team that saved my life. I'm a survivor of stage IV cancer and during the worst months of my medical treatments, my liver nearly failed me. Your husband was my hepatologist at Beaumont. He stepped in right away. He was there for me at exactly at the moment I needed him. You should be very proud of the work he does."

The whole family was beaming. I was both ashamed that I had not recognized him in this context—and so pleased that I could thank him this way before the evening ended.

After *A Shared Future*, many of us were looking at the men and women we interacted with on a weekly basis in a whole new way.

The second reason *A Shared Future* was such a milestone was this: Our courage was renewed in breaking down more barriers, even at the highest levels of community life. In 2014, the Islamic Society of North America (ISNA) held its annual conference in downtown Detroit. ISNA is the largest Muslim organization in North America, mainly known for hosting the biggest Islamic gathering in the U.S. each year. To improve interfaith relationships nationwide, my friend Dr. Basha was determined that ISNA and AJC leaders should get to know each other. This was a controversial idea on both sides, to say the least. The working relationship of ISNA and the AJC continues to be a work in progress with occasional tensions fueled by international crises—but, in 2014, the two groups' leaders were not even in regular contact.

"Howard, I need a moment of your time," Basha told me one day, as I picked up my phone. "Actually a few moments. I need you to take a drive downtown Detroit to the Renaissance Center with me while ISNA is in town."

"ISNA!?" I said. "We're not connected with them. I mean, the AJC isn't connected with them."

"I know," he said, "but I know the current president of ISNA and he has agreed to talk with us privately." The ISNA president at that time was Imam Mohamed Magid, who was born in Sudan, migrated to the U.S. in 1987 and currently leads a Muslim congregation in the Washington, D.C. area.

"I'll go," I said. "As myself. I can't call it an official AJC meeting."

"I know. I know. Private," Basha said. "What matters is we'll meet."

So, we drove to the towering hotel along the Detroit River—and we wound up talking for a couple of hours with Magid and his colleagues in his suite. One of our suggestions was that Magid consider visiting Israel through an AJC-approved program called Project Interchange. He was hesitant, but eventually said he was open to this possibility. Later, he took that trip and began to participate in other programs connected with the AJC.

"You worked magic that day," Basha said when I asked him to recall that morning meeting in Detroit.

"It wasn't me," I said. "You dragged me down there. You knew what was possible. And then it remained totally private for quite a while. We certainly didn't say anything about it to other people."

Several years later, Imam Magid played an influential role in forming the Muslim-Jewish Advisory Council, a nationwide nonprofit organization of business, political and religious leaders co-sponsored by both AJC and ISNA. The council's stated objectives are: "to combat hate crimes and to promote the positive image of Muslim and Jewish citizens of the United States." In 2021, the council still is so new that no one can predict its longevity. Whatever becomes of the council, the fact remains that an ever-growing array of Jewish and Muslim leaders have experienced interfaith relationships through the council and feel personal commitments to support each other. At least some of the seeds for these relationships were planted years before the organization was founded during a couple of hours of private conversations in a hotel suite in Detroit.

Those seeds we planted in all of those joint efforts more than a decade ago keep growing and blossoming to this day. One of the mutual interests identified in *A Shared Future* was food distribution and Muslim and Jewish groups have turned that into a wide range of projects over the years. During the pandemic, we jointly focused on our overworked health care professionals—highlighting in particular the significant numbers of Jewish and Muslim medical workers. That effort was called Food for the Front Lines. Co-sponsored by both communities and again via Dr. Mahmoud Al-Hadidi, the board president of the MMCC and the Ravitz Foundation, we provided both kosher and halal meals to frontline health care workers of all backgrounds.

"One step leads to another," I told Basha as we talked about our behind-the-scenes adventures together. "Food for the Front Lines was a big public effort because we wanted to raise awareness. But for every public event like that—"

"There's a lot of work no one ever sees," Basha said, then paused a moment. "Howard, do you know why I work so hard to bring people together? It's because, since I was a boy in high school, I have read about and studied world history—how tyranny can arise, how violence can start. And it all stems from people who are afraid of each other. They are afraid because they do not know each other. This work we keep doing, Howard, really rests on the relationships we have fostered. And, like you say, the quiet things we do are some of the most important things we do."

"Whispering," I said.

"You could call it that," he said.

"You are so good at this, in fact, sometimes you don't even need to utter a word to make an important point," I said. "Do you remember that day you called me on short notice to show up at your offices to meet some guests from Syria?"

"I do. And you were very good about picking up the phone and rearranging your whole day to show up for me."

"You call. I answer. I call. You answer. That's our relationship," I said. "What was so different that evening was you wanted me to show up at 7 p.m. to see this very important little delegation from Syria—guys who were involved in the Syrian opposition to Assad. And I was absolutely clueless all evening long. The event didn't even formally start until 9 p.m. You told me to sit right beside you at the head table and then all of the talks and PowerPoint presentations turned out to be in Arabic. You provided me a translator but I had no idea what was really going on. Afterward, I asked you why I needed to be there at all—and you said that you wanted these visitors to understand that Americans do things differently. We partner across religious lines. You wanted me, your Jewish friend, as a visible symbol of that, right?"

"Absolutely," he said. "I had learned that the main guy in that group had never actually met a Jew. I wanted him to see how I work with community partners—and also I was watching him carefully all evening. I wanted to see if he was nervous at all having you at the head table. You played an important role that night."

"Without ever saying a word."

"Right. No words were needed in that case."

"One thing that always impresses me about your work with political leaders from around the world is that you aren't really interested in political power yourself," I said. "Your real goal is to use those relationships to help people who are some of the world's most vulnerable."

He nodded and paused for a moment. "That's right. One of the most important things I have done throughout my life is helping refugees to find a safe place to live. I have known so many men and women and children who have lived through horrific conditions—ordinary people who did nothing to deserve to be oppressed like that, or to find themselves as homeless refugees. When we first see these vulnerable people, there is a temptation to look away. But I keep telling people: We cannot look away. We must try to understand each other. We must earn each other's trust. We must show compassion. And I am well aware that there are many Muslims around the world who have never even met a Jewish person, yet they are suspicious or even hostile. That's why I make such a point, Howard, of inviting you to be with me. I want people to understand that I have Jewish friends. Maybe seeing us together, someone else will dare to start having such a relationship. So many things in this world are beyond our control. So many things happen that bring fear and violence to people who do not deserve to suffer the tragic results. All we can do is form friendships with people who trust each other so that, when horrible things do happen, we can work together to respond."

One other friend Brenda Rosenberg and I share is Rabbi David Rosen, who now lives in Jerusalem and is widely celebrated as the world's most influential Jewish interfaith activist. Currently, he is the AJC's international director of interreligious affairs. He has been honored for his work by the Vatican and the worldwide Anglican Communion—and, like us, he dares to cross chasms others are hesitant to approach. For example, he has been the only Jewish representative on the board of directors of the KAICIID interfaith center in Vienna, founded in 2012 by King Abdullah of Saudi Arabia together with the governments of Austria and Spain and the Vatican.

"I'm very proud of the AJC, because of its unique role in the world," Rosen said by Zoom from his office in Israel. "The AJC is the only Jewish organization with a freestanding professional position dedicated to international religious engagement."

"That's what drew me to AJC in 2006," I said. "I've been fortunate over the years to be invited into some fellowships and programs for further study, including some travel abroad, but I certainly don't move in the global circles where you do your work."

"That's not how I would describe your work," he said. "Yes, of course there are interreligious dialogues and negotiations at Olympian heights in the world that have taken place over the past half century. But you are living and working in a unique and vitally important corner of the world yourself."

He continued, "I don't think there's anywhere in the world where one has a concentration of Christians and Muslims from the Middle East interacting with people of other faiths as you have seen in Detroit and its environs. That makes it a unique place not just in the United States, but actually in the world. I'm not sure you could find transplants of communities on this scale anywhere else—certainly not with such a vibrant Jewish community alongside it. Now, that makes what you are doing critically important.

"Let's consider a parallel from the Jewish-Catholic relationship," Rosen continued. "It's all very well that there are transformations in this relationship at Olympian heights, and some of these developments have been revolutionary. But if you don't have the sociological conditions at the grass roots, then the impact is very limited. What do I mean by that? Where you have Catholics and Jews living alongside one another and interacting with one another, the result is that you have the sociological context for the internalization of these steps at Olympian heights. Proof of that is the fact that you've got almost 40 academic institutions in the United States that are centers for Christian-Jewish studies—and there are maybe two in the rest of the world. You have an amazing cross fertilization both from the top and from the bottom.

"Then in Detroit, in addition to Christian-Jewish relationships you also have Eastern Orthodox Christians, including many from the Middle East, and the Muslim communities as well. If interreligious dialogue is limited to scholars and religious leaders, then the impact is limited. But when you have daily interaction among people in the grassroots as your neighborhood businesspeople, as your medical practitioners, as people of many different professions—as husbands and wives who are neighbors, for instance—then they begin to get to know one another. And the impact can be quite dramatic. And that's why Detroit and its environs is not only a kind of laboratory with regards to these relationships—it actually has significance globally. What has been achieved by people where you live, Howard, has ramifications for the rest of the world. First of all, it is evidence that we can have these positive relationships in daily life, even though there still are issues around which we disagree. It shows that communities can be integrated on the basis of mutual respect. It is evidence that there does not have to be a clash of civilizations. We can see through your examples that it is entirely possible for these communities to be integrated with one another and still retain their individual identities.

"This is enormously important, as well, for me in the work that I do. When I am out in the Arab world, it means that I am not simply acting as a lone ranger. I can actually point to specific examples, including those through the auspices of the AJC, where this work is being done in communities around the world. This becomes a source of inspiration that we all can share. I'm not just a lone ranger with my own personal ideas to advance. I'm someone with whole communities of good-hearted people behind me, showing the world what is possible."

I was humbled to hear him say that. All of the countless hours we all have spent with each other across southeast Michigan—a list of friends and colleagues that would fill an entire chapter, if I tried to list every single one—truly makes a difference in the world. We always hope our little rays of sunshine will help. Rabbi Rosen can see where those bright points of light are reflected in distant lands.

The message of this chapter is that, if we hope to make such a difference in the world, we have to learn to whisper—to talk and to truly listen slowly, carefully, quietly and hospitably. Why is that so important to emphasize near the close of this book? Because in our deafening world today—surrounded by booming media and terrifying news—the simple act of pausing to spend quiet time with friends is an endangered art.

It's also a lifesaving art. Cancer whisperers literally saved my life. Entrepreneurial whisperers connected me with some of the most exciting projects in my career. Interfaith whisperers aspire to help save this fragile planet for our children.

When we speak, we may need to start by turning down the volume. When I urge people to shine brightly, I never want them to blind people.

Dr. Robert J. Wicks devotes several passages to these themes near the end of his book *Riding the Dragon: 10 Lessons for Inner Strength in Challenging Times.* He urges readers to "be a dangerous listener" and to "find love in small deeds." He coaches his readers to slow down, turn down the volume and be thankful for the countless kindnesses each of us receive from other people every day. Usually, we are not even aware of those kindnesses showering all around us, he says. Like the findings we discovered in our *Shared Future* study, we may be astonished at how many boundary-crossing relationships we already enjoy. That's why I was so eager to talk with Wicks as I prepared this book and why I was so pleased that, like Rabbi Rosen, he urged me to drive home these themes.

Wicks told me, "Truly appreciating the other person we meet, perhaps in person or on the phone, means that we are willing to take the time to listen closely. Sometimes, I like to say, we have to listen dangerously—to listen as though our lives may depend on our conversation. And, when we are able to do that, we truly are opening up our hearts to that other person and to new possibilities."

Sometime soon, you will hear the question: "Have you got a minute for me?"

Next time you hear that, first be thankful that someone asked.

Then, dream of all the possibilities you may discover by simply saying: "Yes."

Shining Brightly

We are sons and daughters of Abraham. Together, we share a dedication to local and international relations, diplomacy, interfaith advocacy and reducing hate in the world. Among my own inspiring mentors within the American Jewish Committee (AJC) are: David Harris, Jason Isaacson, David Rosen, Julie Schair, Victoria Schonfeld, Noam Marans, Ephraim Gabbai, Rick Hyne, Kenneth Bandler, Ari Gordon, Daniel Elbaum, David Bernstein, Melanie Pell, Kim Kamen, Lee C. Shapiro, Nancy Lisker, Nadine Greenfield-Binstock, Simon Rodan-Benzaquen, Avital Leibovich, Deidre Berger, Stanley Bergman, Harriet Schleifer and my amazing 2008–2010 Comay Fellowship cohort. Locally in Michigan at the JCRC-AJC Detroit, I am thankful to: David Gad-Harf, Sharona Shapiro, Kari Alterman, David Kurzman, Asher Lopatin, Corey Young, Lauren Garfield-Herrin, Sandy Lippitt, Joy Alekman, Fred Frank, Andy Doctoroff, Ken Gold, Jon Frank, Bryant Frank, Jeannie Weiner, Richard Krugel, Alicia Chandler, Seth Gould, Carol Ogusky, Sheri Terebelo-Schiff, Nancy Bechek-Bluth, Ariana Mentzel, Francine Wunder, Judge Walter Shapero, Kathleen Straus and so many others who continue to build bridges every day.

Together, we are committed to welcoming the stranger into our tents and to extending sincere hospitality that can lead to new friendships and understandings. Let us all use this life lesson to meet and welcome others in our neighborhoods.

+ **American Jewish Committee** — AJC.org

+ **Jewish Community Relations Council / AJC Detroit** — JCRCAC.org

+ *Reuniting the Children of Abraham* — BrendaNaomiRosenberg.com/childrenabraham/

+ *Our Muslim Neighbors* — OurMuslimNeighbors.com

+ *Friendship and Faith* **by the women of WISDOM** — InterfaithWisdom.com/friendship-and-faith/

+ **Michigan Consulor Corps** — ConsularCorpsOfMichigan.org

You've reached Chapter 18, a number that symbolizes our hope for a good life in Judaism. That's always a challenge. When I look at the group photo of friends in goofy hats, my heart breaks at all those lives we have lost to cancer. But there also is hope in this photo, which includes two of my own mentors as cancer whisperers: Vincent DeJong in the red Mario hat peering over the shoulder of Kim Sully. I am thankful to have received so many gifts of hope, including a shofar from my friend Dr. Al-Hadidi and running bibs from friends who competed in my honor. Our survivorship and wellbeing depend on such gifts from so many people around us. Now, I hope that this book is a gift and inspiration in your life.

GET YOUR
REAR
IN GEAR

COLON CANCER
COALITION

SURVIVOR

printed by emediagroup, inc. • www.emediagroup.com • 1-877-765-XXXX • general...

R RUTGERS
UNITE
HALF MARATHON

#HBSTRONG

360

ANDREW WHEELER   AGE: 51   GENDER: M   T-SHIRT: M-MD

18

Sharing Hope

We can share hope with others.

It's a powerful pillar in my life. In other words: Hope is not merely one person's dream in isolation. From the very beginning of human life on earth, hope has been a currency we can give and receive.

At our best, we can do this every day in many ways.

For three decades, people have been talking about Gary Chapman's *The Five Love Languages.* What Chapman did in his mega-bestseller was name five kinds of currency people use to share love: giving gifts, words of affirmation, quality time, acts of service and physical touch. The value of his wisdom is obvious in the more than 10 million copies of his book that have sold worldwide.

Now, we need to learn that hope also is a currency and it takes as many forms as love. Just as Gary Chapman did not invent the idea of sharing love in various forms, I did not make up the idea that we can share hope in many ways.

The rising dove on this book's cover is widely recognized today as a symbol of peace—but for thousands of years in Judaism the dove has meant far more than that. Doves are associated with the deepest hope that suffuses both the human soul and the spirit of God. A dove brought Noah news that the catastrophic flood finally was subsiding. Early Christians saw those same hopes in dove symbols. That's why Vatican designer Gian Lorenzo Bernini chose a dove with outstretched wings to symbolize the spirit of God for his central stained-glass window at the Vatican. In Genesis, Christians and Jews read that, during the Creation, God's spirit hovered over the waters. The Talmud, the Jewish collection of rabbinic wisdom, compares that vision of God's spirit to a dove hovering over its young. In traditional Jewish storytelling, doves are associated with the resilience and flourishing of the people of Israel.

As an entrepreneur, cancer survivor and interfaith peacemaker, I have found it helpful to sum up these ideas as the currency of hope. A century ago, Roger Babson wrote about this idea in his inspirational books. In fact, each morning he wanted to equip himself with fresh words of hope he could share with others. That's why he was an avid collector of inspirational books and organized them into what he called his "good cheer library." Every day, he took quotations from these books to pass along to friends, colleagues and students to boost their spirits. Sometimes, he wrote out favorite quotations from his good cheer library on slips of paper that he could share during his day—literally stuffing his pockets with a paper currency of hope. Can you imagine what a powerhouse Roger Babson would have been in the age of the internet?

What I have tried to illustrate through my own life story is that, when we shine brightly, we can give many forms of hope to others. Chapman had his five labels: gifts, affirmations, time, service and touch as forms of love. We can learn a lot about sharing hope by starting with that list. For example, during both of my life-and-death struggles with cancer, I experienced the power of physical touch to revive my hopes. Effective cancer treatment depends on the compassionate physical care of countless doctors, nurses, technicians, aides, caregivers and loved ones.

At other times, the currency of hope takes a tangible form—the giving of gifts. Gifts of volunteer time and donations can change and inspire lives for the better. In Chapter 17, I described my hope that the world's often-divided religious groups can find ways to work together for the common good. In Judaism, we call it tikkun olam, or repairing and healing the world. Given the violence that seems to erupt over religious and cultural divisions on an almost weekly basis, those of us who work on this kind of peacemaking need regular infusions of hope.

One of the most hopeful shots-in-the-arm I ever received took the form of a ram's horn, a *shofar*. I received my favorite shofar as a gift from a Muslim physician who carried it halfway around the world to present to me.

Of course, I have other shofars. Many Jews do. We think about these horns as we approach the Jewish High Holy Days when the unforgettable blasts of shofars summon our fresh commitment to renewed life. Now, I think specifically about this particular shofar that sits in my office near my desk—the shofar brought to me from Morocco by my friend Dr. Mahmoud Al-Hadidi.

As Jews approach Rosh Hashanah and Yom Kippur, which follows 10 days later, we are required to make amends—as best we can—with anyone we have harmed in the past year. In interfaith settings, I have asked non-Jews to ponder for a moment how they could approach such a solemn challenge by making a list, then reaching out to everyone on that list to make amends. What a challenge! We do it because this tradition of asking forgiveness and making amends is one of the most powerful annual obligations in Judaism. This is a core part of our affirmation that our broken world can be healed, repaired, made whole again—if each of us plays a role.

The services for Rosh Hashanah and Yom Kippur normally draw the largest attendance to Jewish congregations every year. While these services are so long that they try the patience of children—and to be honest, many adults—there are moments of great wonderment that even the youngest girls and boys never forget. As a small child, I didn't know too much about the ancient traditions unfolding around me in those services. I was too young to understand all the tensions circling our globe in the iciest depths of the Cold War. I couldn't have explained the crucial obligations of tikkun olam. I was just a little kid who had a chance to sit next to my father waiting, waiting, waiting for that moment when the shofar was blown.

I would stand up in our pew, holding onto Dad for balance to see the shofar raised—and blown.

What sounds! Eventually, I learned their names.

+ *Tekiah*, a single long blast
+ *Shevarim*, a trio of sounds
+ *Teruah*, a whole series of sounds

And then the *Tekiah Gedolah*—the great blast was held, and held, and held. I would check Dad's watch to time it.

The blowing of the shofar is a call to the Jewish people to awaken, repent and bless God—and all that follows from that reawakening. The shofar summons what artist Marc Chagall described as "The Yearning of Exiles," the name of one of his famous wall-sized mosaics in the Knesset, Israel's Parliament building, that shows the blowing of a shofar near Jerusalem's Western Wall as a dove-shaped angel hovers above the city. That kind of visual imagery of hope for a peacefully healed world was picked up by others. The Bulgarian-Israeli artist Nahum Gilboa painted the blowing of a shofar as summoning a colorful vision of a restored Jerusalem hovering in a cloud of doves.

The shofar is a powerfully evocative symbol of our faith. So, to receive any shofar as a gift is truly an honor. The reason I hold this shofar from Dr. Al-Hadidi so dear is the impulse that led him to reach out toward me with this gift. This was no casual souvenir from an overseas vacation to a colleague in interfaith work. This shofar was given with sincere intention. One night, I was invited to Dr. Al-Hadidi's home to hear Michigan's Senator Gary Peters speak to an interfaith audience of Muslims, Christians and Jews. During the program, I was asked by Dr. Al-Hadidi if I would say a few words representing the Jewish community of southeast Michigan. I thanked Senator Peters for the U.S. senate's adoption of "no-hate" legislation to crack down further on antisemitism, because we all were concerned about the huge increase of harmful acts against Jews across our country. But I went a step further and urged that the legislation also target Islamophobia because both religious-ethnic minority groups face the same forms of hatred. Jews and Muslims must shoulder this hateful burden together—along with all Americans.

"Hate cannot be tolerated," I said. "Our children are born to love. Hatred is not born in us. Hatred is learned, acquired and a choice that is propagated in our communities."

As that event was ending and we were getting ready to leave, another dear friend Bushra Alawie, former Detroit FBI Community Outreach agent, asked me to come speak more privately with Dr. Al-Hadidi for a moment. To my surprise, Dr. Al-Hadidi told me of his family trip to Morocco. While visiting a small Jewish area of Marrakesh, the doctor met one of the last Jewish street vendors in that landmark city whose history stretches back thousands of years. When he saw this vendor's wares, the doctor immediately thought of me, he said.

Even though he is Muslim and was traveling in one of the world's great centers of Islamic culture—he was thinking of me. He wasn't my doctor, but he had become a dear friend through our peacemaking work across our religious boundaries. And he was aware that I had been struggling with—and thankfully was recovering from—stage IV colon cancer.

What did the doctor know of our Rosh Hashanah and Yom Kippur traditions? Not a lot. But he did know that the shofar was a potent symbol of renewal, a cherished reminder of hope—and the commitment to keep reaching out to others.

I was so surprised and humbled as he presented that shofar, I barely recall what I said to him. Did he know our customs and liturgies and traditions? No, he said. But he explained that he understood the foundations of both of our traditions in his mind and his heart—a call to mend the divisions that separate us.

That's why I display the shofar in my home office. That's why I look at it, not just during the high holy days—but every day.

Half a world away from Michigan in a tiny market stall in the midst of a family vacation, Dr. Al-Hadidi suddenly thought of me and, from that spark, he made a simple decision to buy a gift and carry it halfway around the world.

His choices continue to shine brightly in my life—and in the lives of all who know him. As a doctor saving lives, Dr. Al-Hadidi is a master at sharing hope, including his generosity with thoughtful gifts.

The currency of hope can take so many forms! Beyond gifts, then—what about the power of words of affirmation and quality time as a currency of hope?

Two dear friends I met almost by accident during my second war with cancer have taught me valuable lessons about those two forms of hope. They are Vincent De Jong, who lives in the Netherlands with his family, and Kim Sully, who lives with her family in Pennsylvania. Both are survivors of stage IV colorectal cancer and underwent extreme treatment regimens like I did. Vincent works for an insurance company and is an expert at analyzing and managing data; Kim is a nurse.

I stumbled into these friendships while I was searching online for more information about my cancer and the treatments my doctors were proposing. I was looking around one of the larger cancer support websites for people with similar experiences—and I was not getting answers to my questions—when Vincent noticed my unanswered posts and befriended me. He invited me into a private Facebook support group called Colontown that proved to be a lifeline for me and for Lisa. Eventually, as I explained in an earlier chapter, I became deeply involved in Colontown and other nationwide cancer support groups. That journey started with the quality time and the words of affirmation from these two friends I found online.

I was lucky to find them. One of the first things Vincent warns cancer patients, especially stage IV colorectal cancer patients, is this: "Don't let Dr. Google scare you to death!"

Kim, who I soon met through Vincent, echoes his warning: "If you go to Dr. Google hoping to find some hope—you'll wind up calling the undertaker!"

"Fifty percent of healing from this disease is attitude," Vincent said as the three of us Zoomed to talk about our friendship. "If you rely on Dr. Google, you'll discover he's one of the most uber-pessimistic guys in the world. Dr. Google is the grim reaper! One of the big problems in Googling for help is that a lot of the most popular links will take you to old stuff—some of it com-pletely out-of-date stuff. You have no way of evaluating whether what you're seeing is still accurate. If Google is your only friend in this struggle, you can easily get overwhelmed, give up and decide to wait passively for your death sentence to come due."

"What you really need are friends who have gone through this, a few steps ahead of you, and who are willing to take the time to guide you through it," Kim said. "Or, I should say, who are willing to *pull* you through some of this, even when you don't feel like taking the next step. No one knows what you're going through like someone who has gone through it."

Simply discovering Vincent's presence online was a huge source of hope for me. Here was a guy who was roughly my age and, like me, was athletic and had a family. I thought: If Vincent can beat such overwhelming odds, then he's living proof that I can beat them, too.

"You know, Vincent, just your presence as a living, breathing survivor made a huge difference in my life," I told him. "I can't thank you enough."

I could see him nodding on the Zoom screen, but he said nothing for a long moment. Then, he said, "I am getting a little emotional here, because the same thing happened to me, Howard. When I got my diagnosis in 2015, I met a woman who had gone through this the year before, and I discovered her daughter was the same age as my eldest son. She said, 'As parents, we have to beat this. We *must* beat it.' She and I shared so much as I was going through all of this, step by step. Her presence and her words gave me hope over and over again. She helped me to beat it. Then, I strongly believe that we have to pay forward such acts of kindness. I am a Christian, and I know my talents and my weaknesses. I don't have talents as a preacher and I'm not even very good at prayer. But I do believe that every one of us has some capacity to pay it forward in some way to express our thanks for the many gifts the Creator upstairs has given us."

Vincent paused a moment, collecting his thoughts, then continued, "You both know that I'm not usually an emotional guy as I help others, but what I can do is help them take control of cancer by finding the best—the most current—information I can possibly find for them."

"Maybe Vincent's not the most emotional person," Kim said. "But that's why, together, we're a perfect partnership. Vincent is relentless in finding data. That's because analyzing data is his profession, his talent. If you've got a question, Vincent will search far and wide until he finds you an answer you can trust. And I know how valuable getting the facts can be. As a nurse, I'm all about the science, too. But as a nurse my talents also run in the direction of caregiving. I'm the more likely one to actually pick up the phone with you when you're in a dark place."

"What I remember most is those times you picked up the phone to lovingly *yell* at me!" I said, laughing.

"And you would lovingly yell back at me more than once!" she said, smiling broadly.

"I guess I did," I said, recalling some moments when I vented my frustration in full-throated rants. As I thought about it for a moment, I knew Kim was right. "Yes, I certainly did yell sometimes, didn't I? I simply could not unleash some of my anger and frustration on Lisa or Emily or the rest of my family and friends. But you let me vent, Kim. And for that—well, I'm forever thankful."

"And remember, Howard, that I quickly got to know both you and Lisa. We were a team: Vincent and me and you and Lisa. Sometimes, it took all of us on the phone to get you through a bad day."

"Or a bad night," Vincent said. "I can remember talking with you Howard, and because of the time difference in our parts of the world, it would get to be midnight here where I live. I knew we had to stay with you on the phone line to support you, so I would call Kim and explain that I needed to get to bed. I would say: 'Kim can you take over with Howard?'"

"That's true," I said. "And what were we talking about all that time? Sometimes we were talking about very, very basic stuff. Do you remember how bad it was when I was refusing to eat anything? One time, I had this plate of eggs and cheese Lisa had made for me and a protein shake. But I was shutting down. It seemed impossible to take even one bite. I knew I'd just throw up again. I was desperate."

"Oh, I could hear the despair! I could hear it!" Kim said. "But there I was, not hanging up that phone line, and I kept coming back with those simple words: 'Eat just one bite, Howard. Just one bite.'"

"And I couldn't! I wouldn't!"

"But I wasn't about to hang up on you, Howard, until you got a couple of bites down. Remember, at one point, I said, 'Put Lisa on the line. I need to talk to Lisa now.' And eventually—"

"You wore me down. I handed her the phone. You talked to Lisa. You all kept at it. Eventually, I ate that bite."

"You had to!" Kim said. "As horrible as it seemed to face that bite, you had to keep eating. Howard, those of us who have been through this and come out the other side know how impossible it seems to even think about taking those bites, sometimes. But that's what you've got to do. We know it. Others pulled us through this and now we're paying it forward, helping others through it."

"You two taught me how to become a cancer whisperer," I said. "You taught me so much about inspiring and giving hope to others by your presence, by giving me space to rage sometimes, and by always coming back—always being there for me. Now I would describe my role as a whisperer as somewhere between the two of you: I'm a nurturer like you Kim, but I'm also a techie like Vincent. Now, on any given week, I've got four or five people I'm helping, sometimes at all hours of the day and night."

"It's hard work because we lose so many people we care about along the way," Kim said.

"We do," Vincent said. "Death is a part of this work. So many people we care about just don't make it."

"But we don't give up—that's the thing with this commitment to being there for people," I said. "Because friends like you two didn't give up on me, now I won't give up on others. Even if I call someone to check in and they refuse to talk to me at the moment—or they're angry at whatever is happening in their life—I don't give up. It's OK if they don't want to talk at any point. They always have the reassurance that I won't abandon them. And, most often, in the next call, you can feel the hope flowing again."

Words of affirmation and quality time are valuable currencies of hope.

So are acts of service big or small. How often have you seen or read stories of individuals who tackle a heroic act of service in honor of another person? If those stories touch your heart, imagine the powerful dose of hope that gives to the person actually being honored. I know the potency of such a gift of service because it has happened to me on a number of occasions. I am blessed with friends who have boosted my hopes with many kinds of public affirmations.

My high school friend Andrew Wheeler decided to turn his own life around after years of neglecting his health.

"I was overweight and I was smoking about a pack of cigarettes a day," he told me. "I went to see my doctor and he asked me this question: 'Do you love your children?'

"I said, 'Of course I do!'

"He said, 'Well, right now, you're on a path that may take you away from them.'

"That doctor put the fear of God into me and, that day, I decided I was going to change my life," Andrew told me. "When I thought of who could inspire me through this struggle, I thought of you, Howard."

Eventually, he reached the point of tackling the extreme rigors of Ironman triathlons.

"The amount of pain and suffering you have to endure to make it through the Ironman is extreme," Andrew told me. "But it was part of turning my life around. For me, it was all about making sure I would be healthy; I would be there for my family. So, my goal was to go big with this—to complete the Ironman Lake Placid."

I told him, "I remember that so clearly. It was the summer of 2018 and I was trying to recover from the CRS and HIPEC surgery. I was going through a long and tough recovery."

"Well, I wanted you to know that my struggle to finish that Ironman was dedicated to you, Howard," Andrew said. "You've always inspired me by your own courage to persevere, so I was thinking of you, Howard, through that whole swim and bike ride and marathon. Whatever agony I was experiencing, I kept thinking: Howard has experienced much worse and got through it without complaining."

Even though I was not involved in Andrew's tireless training and was nowhere near his Ironman route in 2018, this was a powerful sharing of hope that flowed both ways. He took inspiration from me; and I took inspiration from him and the official running bib he wore that day proudly labeled "HB Strong!"

Then, some friends added fundraising to combat cancer to their acts of personal service.

David Contorer, executive director of Hebrew Free Loan in Metropolitan Detroit, is a colleague with whom I've worked on various Jewish community projects, and a fellow basketball player. He decided to ride in my honor in the annual Pan-Mass Challenge bike-a-thon to support the Dana-Farber Cancer Institute. That year, the 40-year-old event raised more than $64 million.

"I had done charitable Make-A-Wish rides before," David told me. "But when I got involved in the Pan-Mass Challenge, I was joining a very dedicated bunch. Everyone who rode with us on our team was carrying the name of someone they loved who had experienced cancer. Some of them had the names on their bicycles, or even tattooed on their arms. That's how I decided to ride in honor of you, Howard."

"That meant so much to me," I told him.

"Well, I think it really goes the other way," David said. "You're like a freakin' nuclear bomb of hopeful, positive electrons, Howard, and you're always giving off that light to others. You've brightened my heart so many times. This was the least I could do."

Again, hope flowed both ways. Look at this book's cover again. I hope you will carry with you that image of a bright white dove rising out of the light bulb we switch on when we make such commitments.

My Babson College roommate and close friend Ed Sherr helped me to understand the blow-by-blow struggle of competing in one of these epic challenges. After he ran the Boston Marathon in memory of his childhood friend Marc Levine, who died of cancer, and in honor of me, Ed sat down and wrote a detailed account.

> On the morning of April 18 at 10:40 a.m., I was standing in Corral 5 with thousands of people around me waiting to start our wave of the Boston Marathon. As I stood there anticipating the sound of the starting gun, I looked at my running shirt to remind me why I had just spent five months in training and now was going to set out on one of the world's most famous athletic challenges. I was wearing a singlet for the Leukemia and Lymphoma Society team. For the back of my shirt, I had chosen two names: Marc Levine and Howard Brown. This was a tribute to two of my closest friends and to raise awareness for blood cancers.
>
> I raised close to $32,000 in memory of Marc and in honor of Howie. Our team's overall goal was to raise $1 million for the Leukemia and Lymphoma Society. I could never have done my part without the generous support of many friends whose phone calls, emails, personal notes and donations inspired me to get through the training and then run the race.
>
> The months of training were hard because I was pushing through a harsh winter season. My teammates—nearly 150 runners—ran our training runs in all sorts of harsh elements— and we even dodged a few oncoming cars! I especially looked forward to my Saturday long runs. We would meet as a team in Wellesley to run on a course there. But before we set out, a member of the team would stand up and tell us why they were there. As tough as we were, we could not hold back the tears that flowed from these stories. Some of my team members were survivors. Many were running in honor or memory of friends and family. I decided in March that I would tell

my own story at one of these gatherings. I wound up telling how I lost Marc so early in our lives and how Howard had kept going through his stage IV struggle. As I concluded, I explained that it was especially meaningful to me that we were running a training course of 18 miles that day. I talked about the Hebrew word *chai*, or life, which is made up of the letters *chet* and *yod*. In Hebrew, those two letters also have the numerical values of 8 and 10, or a total of 18. I told them how the number 18 reminds Jews of our collective hopes.

I closed by saying: "You may have heard 'L'chaim!' as a toast 'To life!' So, during this training run today of 18 miles, I toast my friend Marc who lived a short but a good life; I toast the people like my friend Howard who have overcome the challenges in life that they have faced; and I toast all of you because you are volunteering and running every day to save lives!"

Emotions rose as each of us thought about our own loved ones—and, in response, the whole team burst into applause.

When I finally took my first steps in the Boston Marathon, I was surprised and inspired by so many friends and family who came to cheer me from the start all the way to the finish line. My wife Resa, our daughters Rachel and Rebecca and other family members made a point of greeting me at Mile 9 and Mile 24.

For more than 18 miles, I felt strong and was taking in everything I saw around me. But, when I got to the second hill of Newton, my right leg started to cramp up and I felt something stabbing at my toes. I suspected that my toenails had come off from the pounding they had taken inside my shoe, but I found out later the piercing pains were coming from blisters. I refused to stop. I battled through all of this and got over Heartbreak Hill, but the last few miles were agony.

By Mile 24, I had nothing left in the tank. That's when I saw Marc's mother Faye and his brother Ken. Somehow, I managed to show them the names on the back of my shirt. Although

Marc is not with us anymore, he was on my shoulders all the way through the rest of the 26.2 miles. I reached the finish line at 4:20:21. I could not believe I had beaten the time I had set as my goal.

What's next? My commitment simply could not end at the marathon's finishing line. I have joined the Leukemia and Lymphoma Society regional board. I have learned so much about the importance of trying to find a cure. What I learned is that Marc and Howie truly are my heroes on this team. They helped me finish the marathon. Now, I keep telling everyone: Let's all work to find a cure!

Do you see how hope can flow both ways? Do you see how many forms this life-giving currency can take? Don't be intimidated by the huge commitments of time, talent and energy that heroes like Vincent, Kim, Andrew, David and Ed have committed themselves to expending. Don't give up on giving a gift of hope to a friend just because you aren't a world traveler like Dr. Al-Hadidi who can bring home a meaningful gift.

Sharing hope can be an easy, everyday part of life. Think back to that Norman Rockwell-like neighborhood in Massachusetts where my Papa Leo formed life-and-death friendships with the men and women who frequented the local park and soda shop. Those relationships extended all the way around the world to battlefields in Europe. What Papa Leo reminds me to this day is that sometimes you don't have to look any further than your next-door neighbor if you want to exchange a little hope.

In my two years of preparing this book, Emily went off to college, and Lisa and I moved into a smaller home in Birmingham, Michigan—where one day our little dog made friends with the 4-year-old boy named Aiden who lives next door. And I already know what you may be thinking: A boy and a dog? That's such a common neighborhood story of friendship that it's hardly remarkable.

But do you remember Dr. Wicks' wisdom from the last chapter? He tells people: "Truly appreciating the other person we meet, perhaps in person or on the phone, means that we are willing to take the time to listen closely. Sometimes, we have to listen dangerously—to listen as though our lives may depend on our conversation. And, when we are able to do that, we truly are opening up our hearts to that other person and to new possibilities."

Of course, that's what Lisa and I have done all our lives. We listened. We watched. Aiden enjoyed playing with Cody and even, on occasion, would take him for a walk. So, naturally, that led to our meeting Aiden's mother, Imelda. We learned that she is a documentary filmmaker, producer and community leader in the cultural arts. She's a media professional and, now, I am publishing a book along with a website and podcast series of videos. That's another point of connection. We're both in media.

Then, Lisa and I learned that she too has health concerns, and we even shared one particular doctor! More connections. Then, I offered service. Being a good neighbor to a single mom, I began picking up a few simple chores that I was easily able to complete for her—like mowing the lawn. Our yards are small, so mowing my lawn takes less than 20 minutes and I only need to spend another 20 minutes to finish her lawn.

Then, one evening, there was a knock at our door.

It was Imelda and her mother, who doesn't speak much English, carrying a freshly baked loaf of bread—a universal symbol of hospitality and friendship.

"We thought you might like this," Imelda said. "It's a traditional Albanian bread."

We loved their *kulak*, a crusty loaf of soda bread made with buttermilk.

So, we fell into a friendly pattern of mowing, baking and Aiden playing with Cody. A couple of times, I gave a car ride to her parents. A couple of times, Imelda's mother baked a special Albanian sweet cake for us.

As we talked, I learned Imelda was born in Tirana, Albania, into the small centuries-old community of Bektashi Muslims who live there. So, there was an interfaith connection. Lisa, Emily and I were a family of Jews living next door to a Muslim family, all of us connected in our Abrahamic roots. Then, we began talking about family history. We share roots in other parts of the world. Imelda came to this country on a student visa and became a dean's list student at Wayne State University in Detroit. She decided to stay to make a new home and better life for her and her family.

As we got to know each other, I wound up talking about tikkun olam and the Jewish value of knitting our broken world together by helping each other. I talked about building a healthy community one life at a time.

"It sounds like our *besa*," Imelda said. "The word can mean 'faith' or 'oath' or 'keeping your promises.' It's a word that describes how seriously we take our community commitments."

That's how we eventually touched on memories of the Holocaust. Yad Vashem, the world Holocaust remembrance center in Jerusalem, lists Albanians collectively among the "righteous" for their preservation of Jews after Germany took over Albania. Leaders in Tirana refused to give up Jewish families to the Germans and, instead, sent them to live with Albanian families. After those strong family-to-family connections were formed, the Yad Vashem record says, "We know only of two cases where Jews were captured and deported. ... All the other Jews survived the war." Why were Albanian Muslims so determined to save their Jewish guests? Besa. As Yad Vashem describes it: "Besa literally means 'to keep the promise'; its significance was that once a family was hosted by Albanians, they could trust them with their lives."

Wow. There we were back in memories of World War II—like the Papa Leo story I described early in this book about his mixed-religion neighborhood, where friendly connections wound up circling the globe during the war. Flash forward to 2021, and here we were sharing a dog, loaves of bread, lawn work and conversations about our own connections that reached around the planet.

Throughout this book, I have shared dozens of inspirational stories from Silicon Valley to Eastern Europe, from family vacations to bedside vigils in hospitals, from births to burials. I have tried to offer a wide range of invitations to readers. Maybe you are inspired by neighborhood stories like those with Papa Leo and Imelda? Maybe you were inspired by the religious connections I have made throughout my life? Maybe you take heart from my stories of beating impossible odds against cancer? Or maybe you are moved by questions like the ones my daughter, Emily, poses to young campers she supervises in the wilderness: If today was the last day of your life, what legacy would you leave behind?

What I realize, as I complete the two years of research, interviews and writing that went into this memoir, is that as a little boy my Bubby Bertha taught me a deeper truth than I was able to fully appreciate at the time. Yes, found money is God's money—but that means far more than the destination of an occasional coin we find along the way. It means that this world was given to us—to all of us—by God so that we could share it and share of ourselves.

This isn't my world.

It isn't your world.

It has always been God's world, given to us to enjoy for the little span of years we are given.

Learning to share this world—and to share the hopeful message that peace is possible—is not a matter of personal preference. It's not a choice. It's not a hobby. It's our purpose here as we walk the earth. Tikkun olam, the Jewish calling to repair the world, is our name for a collective mission we all share.

And, while it may sound like a burden, that call to spread love and hope turns out to be the key to our happiness.

Without hope, there is no happiness.

And there is no hope if we are isolated, if we are excluded, if we pull away from our neighbors.

Hope is never mine.

Hope must be ours.

I guarantee that if you shine your light on the people you meet—you will find hope glowing all around you.

It's true. Shining brightly makes the world a better place.

Afterword

By Rabbi David Rosen

Towards the end of this inspiring book, Howard Brown sums up its central message as "welcoming the stranger into our tents and to extending sincere hospitality that can lead to new friendships and understandings." He refers to us all Jews, Christians and Muslims, as the childrenof Abraham.

Indeed, our respective religious traditions all present Abraham as the embodiment of the value of hospitality, whose tent was open to all.

The Torah (the Pentateuch) seeks to inculcate the virtue of hospitality in the children of Israel, particularly through the plethora of precepts relating to the vulnerable, and especially the one who is not from our own community (the "stranger"). We are also enjoined to share our blessings with them as an integral part of our thanksgiving to God for God's material blessings: "and you shall rejoice with all the goodness which the Lord your God has given you and your household—you, the Levite, and the stranger in your midst" (Deuteronomy 26:11 and see also Deuteronomy, 16:14).

In other words, without hospitality and sharing our blessings with others, especially those in need, we do not truly honor the Provider of All.

These biblical references continually recall the fact that the Children of Israel had suffered persecution as aliens in the land of Egypt, as inspiration to be caring and hospitable toward vulnerable persons, and towards those different from us in particular. In fact, not only are we instructed to avoid hurting them, we are enjoined to show such persons special love: "You shall not oppress the stranger, for you know the soul of the stranger, as you were strangers in the land of Egypt" (Exodus, 23:9), "and you shall love the stranger as yourself" (Leviticus, 19:34).

Indeed, the sages of the Talmud point out that the reference to the past experience of being aliens is repeated in the Torah at least 36 times, in order to remind us to always be sensitive toward the vulnerable.

But beyond the material aspects of hospitality, of food and lodging, are the psychological benefits of hospitality which Howard's book highlights. Genuinely welcoming the other is much more than simply a matter of good manners. It even determines people's individual and collective approach towards the wider society and vice versa.

Human identities are made up of circles of associations, such as families, congregations, communities, nations, etc. When the smaller circles of identity feel comfortable within wider circles of identity, they are inclined to contribute constructively to them. So, for example, when families feel secure in a neighborhood, they will be inclined to engage that wider circle and contribute to its well-being. However, if a family feels unwelcome in the neighborhood, it is likely to further isolate itself and its negative feelings towards the wider circle will intensify.

This is the case in each expanding context, and we see how all too often entire communities, especially where they are of different ethnic or religious origin, are often made unwelcome, intensifying their alienation even further.

Alienation, more often than not, leads to disparagement of others, even to demonization and violence. As a result, a vicious cycle of increasing mutual alienation can threaten the fabric of a society as a whole.

Both individual hospitality and inter-communal hospitality countervail such alienation; give vulnerable communities a sense of their worth and value for the wider context; develop their sense of security and self-esteem; and enable them to become constructively engaged in the society at large.

Interreligious relations have a special role to play in this process, not only because religious attachments can be the most passionate, but because they very often define the core identity of the communities to which people belong.

Thus, interfaith hospitality, in the sense of positive interreligious encounters, learning and collaboration for the common good, have the power to overcome alienation and integrate communities of different cultures and origins, enabling them to contribute to the peaceful flourishing of society at large. Such activities are, in fact, the authentic expression of the heritage and spirit of Abraham and testify to our most noble spiritual and ethical origins and purpose.

It is clear from Howard's story that already at a very young age, the virtues of gratitude, appreciation, caring and sharing with others, were instilled in him.

However, his remarkable life experiences and inspiring triumphs over adversity, have deepened these virtues and enabled him to become the teacher, the "life coach" that he has become as a result.

This is not something that can be taken for granted as an inevitable result of such experiences.

Just as material blessings can make us either more generous or more egocentric and miserly; so life's tribulations can make us more insular and self-preoccupied, or they can make us into better human beings with greater sensitivity and compassion for others.

Howard is a wonderful example of the latter. The challenges he has faced and overcome, together with the values that nurtured him, have enabled him to become a bridge-builder between communities and faiths, to be a blessing, as Abraham and his descendants are called to be (Genesis 12:2,3).

The Talmud (Betzah, 32b) adds that those who show compassion to others, show that they are truly of the seed of Abraham (and those who do not show compassion show that they are not truly of the seed of Abraham).

Howard is a wonderful example of a most worthy descendant of Abraham, showing genuine care and hospitality, serving the well-being of his community and other communities, connecting these to one another in mutual respect, and bringing blessing to humanity at large.

Rabbi David Rosen KSG CBE, former Chief Rabbi of Ireland, is the Jerusalem-based International Director of Interreligious Affairs of the American Jewish Committee. Awards for his interfaith work have included decorations from Queen Elizabeth II, the Archbishop of Canterbury and a Papal knighthood.

Acknowledgements

Life is a team sport. That's a central theme of this book and it certainly was true during the more than two years of conversations, research and writing that produced *Shining Brightly*.

In that sense, this book was crowdsourced. I did not have a manuscript when I began working with my publishing house team. What I had was a global network of friends and colleagues who shared in my story of resiliency and hope. So, my Editor David Crumm and I began, even before the COVID-19 pandemic hit, organizing what became nearly 200 Zoom sessions. In many of them, I told my own stories. In most of them, we welcomed friends, family, coworkers, physicians, fellow peacemakers and cancer advocates. We even reached back and connected with two influential counselors from my childhood summer camp. The support I felt in collectively writing this book continues, now, beyond the final publication as so many men and women are helping to spread the good news.

Friendship is such an important truth in my life, and this book, that I already have named many people in the pages of these chapters. That style may seem unusual to readers, but it was a deliberate choice to show readers how important it is to remember those who have contributed to our lives—then, to express our gratitude by naming them individually. And, even though I already have named many people in these pages, there are a few more who need further acknowledgment here.

My team of Shining Stars:

Family first: To my parents Nancy and Marshall Brown and my in-laws Robert and Anita Naftaly—your kindness, generosity, support and care in our times of need knew no bounds and we are thankful for all that you have done and continue to do for us. To my loving wife Lisa Brown, I am deeply grateful to you for staying by my side on this rollercoaster ride through so many ups and downs. Thank you for inspiring me toward community service and for your excellent contributions and edits of Shining Brightly. Lisa and my mother are angels on Earth for their selfless and tireless caregiving. I am forever indebted to my "Wonder Twin" sister Cheryl Brown Gingras for saving my life with the gift of her bone marrow. More than a sister, she will always be my best friend. For Our Miracle Girl, Emily Brown, Lisa and I know the best is yet to come for you. Yes, Emily: "Get bizzy living!" Uncle Leslie and Aunt Roberta Sufrin, your Mishebarach prayers for me every day were a shining light of dedication to me and our family. Uncle Mark Burnham and Tanta Carole Burnham have been role models for caring and fun always. Huge thank you to Michelle and Richard Solomon for providing archival materials about Bubby Bertha.

David Crumm: You have been a friend since I moved to Michigan from Silicon Valley in 2005. We took our friendship to new heights as we committed to spending at least every Wednesday morning together on Zoom working on the book. Then, beyond those sessions, we spent many other mornings and afternoons as well. We walked back into my life in a way that even close friends rarely experience with each other. David, you've been my editor, publisher and dear friend—and now I also consider you a big brother I never had. This journey to write my memoir with you has been one of the best experiences I never thought I would do—become a published author. For your compassion, caring and exceptional diligence to "never bury the lede," I thank you and I am so proud of our time and work together.

The team at Front Edge Publishing: John Hile, as founder and publisher of Front Edge, we share a career in technical innovation and I appreciate your strong support for this major project. Susan Stitt you are a book marketing maven and your attention to publishing strategy is amazing. Dmitri Barvinok you worked the technical "magic" behind state-of-the-art book production that produced Shining Brightly simultaneously in hardcover, paperback and several eBook editions. Rick Nease, thank you for your creative work on the cover that, even before final publication, is being praised as "stunning," "thought-provoking" and "inspiring."

My unsung heroes: I will always be grateful to my infusion room nurses at Dana Farber Cancer Institute and Beaumont Hospital (Royal Oak, Farmington, and Botsford infusion centers). It takes a special person to administer intravenous chemotherapy day in and day out to cancer patients. You welcomed me in such a good-spirited manner as "HoBro" for endless hours that I was able to endure because of your compassionate care. Serving men and women as you do each day is such a difficult calling, especially since you inevitably get to know many cancer patients who die. May their memories be a blessing for those who knew and loved them.

Cancer patients and survivors: #KFG. Let's call for everyone 45 and over to get screened.

Greg Tufankjian of Toyota of Braintree Massachusetts: Who would have thought that being 15 minutes late for a Babson College class would evolve into a lifelong friendship? Your support and care for me and my family is a daily reminder of the life-giving power of friendship.

Priscilla Christie of Priscilla Christie Design: I transferred into Babson College and met you taping ankles in the training room before basketball practice. Your creative web and digital design help my story shine.

Patti Love of The Identity Source, Inc. and Ryan Findling (2022 Babson graduate): Thank you for helping me build our brand of *Shining Brightly* sunglasses, T-shirts, candles, mirrors, hats, water bottles and more.

Martin Davis, author of *Thirty Days with America's High School Coaches*: Thank you for including the story of my high school coach Phil "Smokey" Moresi and my player response in your book. It is such an honor. Coaching is a noble profession that builds important life lessons into our formative years. I am proud to call you a friend and coach.

Alan Bakst: Your loyal friendship and ability to push me back into shape at the gym and on the basketball court cannot be understated. You knew I needed to get back on the court to feel whole again at my happy place. For that I thank you.

Jeff Pulver: Your passion and kindness know no bounds.

Mary Jordan Abouljoud, U.S. Department of Justice, FBI Detroit, Community Outreach Specialist from the Office of Public Affairs: Very few people even know that I have been privileged to be a Jewish community liaison to the Detroit FBI for many years. I want to thank you and the bureau for your service to our communities in Michigan and everywhere! As we work toward improving interfaith community relations and understanding, we make long term friendships.

Steve Kaufman: You are a mench among menches. Your friendship, mentorship and support have meant the world to me.

HBstrong! Nation: Your prayers, cheerleading, unwavering support, cards, gifts and social media posts kept me going. Go Fund Me supporters: #inspired and #grateful.

Finally, I want to especially thank these groups that have been an important part of my life:

- Interfaith Leadership Council of Metropolitan Detroit
- Michigan Roundtable for Diversity and Inclusion
- Michigan Muslim Community Council
- Muslim Jewish Advisory Counsel
- Chaldean Federation International
- Chaldean Community Foundation
- Hindu Community Relations Council
- Imerman Angels (cancer support and mentorship)
- National Young Leadership Cabinet of the Jewish Federations of North America
- Wexner Heritage Foundation Fellowship
- American Jewish Committee—Comay Fellowship
- Framingham South High School, Class of 1984—Flyers!
- Babson College, Class of 1988—Beavers!
- Babson College Worldwide Alumni Association (BAA)—with pride and spirit!

About the Author

Howard Brown is an author, speaker, podcaster, Silicon Valley entrepreneur, interfaith peacemaker, two-time stage IV cancer survivor and healthcare advocate. For more than three decades, Howard's business innovations, leadership principles, mentoring and his resilience in beating cancer against long odds have made him a sought-after speaker and consultant for businesses, nonprofits, congregations and community groups. In his business career, Howard was a pioneer in helping to launch a series of technology startups before he co-founded two social networks that were the first to connect religious communities around the world. He served his alma mater—Babson College, ranked by *US News* as the nation's top college for entrepreneurship—as a trustee and president of Babson's worldwide alumni network. His hard-earned wisdom about resilience after beating cancer twice has led him to become a nationally known patient advocate and "cancer whisperer" to many families. Visit Howard at ShiningBrightly.com to learn more about his ongoing work and contact him. Through that website, you also will find resources to help you shine brightly in your own corner of the world. Howard, his wife Lisa and daughter Emily currently reside in Michigan.

To learn more about this book and Howard Brown,
and to get a free discussion guide for this book, please visit:

ShiningBrightly.com

CPSIA information can be obtained
at www.ICGtesting.com
Printed in the USA
BVHW071311190922
647393BV00004B/172